From Oral To Literate Culture

From Oral To Literate Culture
Colonial Experience in the English West Indies

PETER A. ROBERTS

THE PRESS UNIVERSITY OF THE WEST INDIES
Barbados • Jamaica • Trinidad and Tobago

The Press University of the West Indies
1A Aqueduct Flats Mona
Kingston 7 Jamaica

© 1997 by Peter Roberts
All rights reserved. Published 1997
Printed in Canada
ISBN 976-640-037-7

01 00 99 98 97 5 4 3 2 1

CATALOGUING IN PUBLICATION DATA

Roberts, Peter A.
From oral to literate culture : colonial
experience in the English West Indies /
Peter A. Roberts.

p. cm.
Includes bibliographical references and index.
ISBN 976-640-037-7

1. English language – Caribbean,
English-speaking – History. 2. Creole dialects,
English – Caribbean, English-speaking.
3. Literacy – Caribbean, English-speaking.
4. Education – Caribbean, English-speaking –
History. I. Title.
PE3310.R63 1997   427.9729

Set in Atlantix 10/14 x 27
Cover and book design by Robert Harris

Cover illustration: Oil on cotton, *The Book Lesson*, 1996.
Reproduced courtesy of Stafford Schliefer

Contents

List of Illustrations / vi

Preface / vii

Acknowledgements / xi

1 An Introduction to the Language of West Indians / 1

2 Nonlinguistic Methods of Communication and Transmission of Information in the Plantation Slave Society / 16

3 Aspects of Oral Culture in the Slave Population / 34

4 Political and Social Influences on the Development of Vernacular English / 69

5 Literate Communication in the Plantation Slave Society / 110

6 The Rise of Printing and Publishing in the West Indies and its Effects / 132

7 Intellectual and Literary Activity and its Effect on Literate English / 160

8 The Rise of Schools and their Effect on English / 192

9 English Language and Literacy in the Early Schools / 236

10 The Legacy of Colonial Literacy in the West Indies / 268

Bibliography / 279

Index / 297

List of Illustrations

Figures

1.1	Forms and structures of West Indian English	/ 15
3.1	A Negro Festival drawn from nature in the island of St Vincent	/ 36
3.2	Negro funeral in the time of slavery	/ 64
6.1	A letter written in 1687 by a Quaker in Barbados to a friend in Pennsylvania	/ 134
6.2	A modern printed version of the same letter	/ 135
6.3	The start of printing	/ 137
6.4	Page 4 of the *Weekly Jamaica Courant*, 15 April 1719	/ 144
7.1	Catalogue of Books remaining at the General Depot, Kingston	/ 167
8.1	Rules and Regulations for the government of the National schools of Port of Spain	/ 209
9.1	Plan of a School-Room	/ 255
9.2	Present State and Proficiency of the Boys' and Girls' School, 29 March 1831	/ 259

Preface

The period 1624-1850 saw the emergence of English in Britain from disparate dialects to a standardized, authoritative language as a result of the expansion of British dominance over a vast area of the world, a dominance which started with English colonial spread into the New World and specifically into the West Indies. The years 1625 to 1834 were also the formative phase of West Indian society during which English colonialism established itself upon a base of African slavery. The relationship between the colonies in the Caribbean and Britain was a two-way relationship in that the existence of the West Indies and the produce therefrom indirectly spurred on the standardization of the English language, which in turn dominated the path of development of language in the West Indies. There was no history of literature in the West Indies before 1625 as there was in England; the West Indian colonies started out as oral societies in which neither colonist nor slave had any use for and little competence in writing. By the first decades of the nineteenth century, however, education was being seen as necessary not only for the whites but also for the slaves.

The historical growth in literacy in West Indian society is reflected currently in the varieties of British regional dialects which have been preserved up to now, in the structure of education, and in the philosophy and language of the Church of England, for these imprinted themselves in West Indian life from the earliest times. On the other hand, West Indian language and literacy represent a variety which developed out of a multilingual and multicultural situation through a process of acculturation. West Indian English, like other geographical dialects of English, has its own particular characteristics, not only those which reflect the language and culture of the West Africans who were brought to the region but also those which emerged through interaction in the West Indian situation itself. Literacy in the West Indies has always been an economically and politically functional force and therefore differs significantly in range from literacy in Britain.

In the British colonies, English was regarded as the language of communication and known to be the language of control. West Indian English, as a distinct dialect of English, was one of the earliest varieties of English outside the British Isles. What distinguishes it from all other varieties of English outside Britain is that it developed in a context where the British and their descendants were not demographically the majority, but where at the same time the non-British part of the population did not have a general language of communication. In addition, there was no homogeneity in the British varieties that were used in the West Indies at the time – varieties of Scottish, Irish and English were probably further apart then than they are now, not only in terms of their geographical distinctiveness but also in terms of the different social levels of each one. Africans confronted with Scottish, Irish and English dialects of the time did not have an easy task making sense out of them and assimilating them into a homogeneous variety. The characteristic conservationist tendencies of the frontier colonist also meant that the English of the colonists did not evolve apace with that of the metropolis. West Indian English is therefore a special variety of English which incorporates historical and transitional features of English, regional varieties of British English, language learning and language acquisition strategies, independent language developments, fossilized features, and West African re-interpretations of English.

English, as the language of literacy in the West Indies, developed in a number of small islands which were linked geographically and politically under British rule. Like any other variety, West Indian English is made up of regional and social dialects which reflect the specific history of each island. The differences between the various islands, which seem very great to the inhabitants themselves, are generally imperceptible to English speakers outside the West Indies. As part of their history the islands also had well-known associations which extended beyond Britain. For example, Antigua and Barbados had a direct connection with New England not only in terms of migration and commerce but more specifically in the development of printing and newspapers. St Lucia and Dominica had a long and turbulent association with France, French culture, the Roman Catholic Church and the French language. All the islands had a direct connection with India, not because of the post-Emancipation importation of population from this subcontinent, but because the education system which was introduced in the West Indies had been developed in India.

West Indian English is an outstanding example of the development of the English language in a multicultural context, and is a testimony to the resilience and flexibility of the English language itself as well as to the people who speak it. From a geopolitical point of view, in its contemporaneous development with standard

English, one can see the link between economic power and high language status on the one hand, and dependence and low language status on the other.

This examination of the development of English, as the language of literacy in the West Indies, looks at the evolving methods and contexts of communication as well as the political, social and intellectual background as the matrix within which both the formal and vernacular varieties of the language developed. It relies on contemporary works to build a picture of language in society during the period starting from the time of the earliest English settlement in the West Indies up to a decade or so after Emancipation. This period was distinct in the development of communication in the West Indies because it was in effect the period during which West Indian society moved from a purely oral toward a literate culture.

This examination shows the way in which literacy, as a major feature of British colonialism, promoted and maintained the English language as an instrument of control and an index of prestige. It does this by starting with a picture of communication and its limitations in the early years of the colonies. It then presents a view of some aspects of the oral culture of the slaves and the acculturation process which it exemplified. It then shows how a common medium of oral communication developed and the influences which shaped it. The examination then proceeds to the needs for literacy in the plantation slave society and the corresponding growth of writing and printing. With the gradual disappearance of Africans with their varying, and sometimes conflicting, cultures and languages and the increase in the number of Creoles speaking the same language, a change in the methods of societal control became necessary – a change from rule by division to rule by mass indoctrination. The next few chapters therefore show how literacy was used to control the mass of the population through a system of bookkeeping as well as through a school system in which the teaching of obedience and discipline was the main objective of church doctrine, which was the principal content subject in the curriculum.

Chapter 1 is used to orient the reader by providing information on West Indian English as a variety of the English language today, as well as on its role as a literary medium and its status as a subject of academic study. Chapter 1 represents a historical point of contrast with chapters 2 and 3, which take the reader back to the early years of the colonies. After the examination of the development from oral to literature culture which is the substance of chapters 4 to 9, the book ends with an assessment of the influences of literacy and the English language on West Indian societies.

Although this is meant to be a scholarly text, it is not beyond the apprecation of educated persons interested in the development of the West Indies. In addition, because it touches on history, sociology, printing, mass communications, education, creole languages, the English language, and literacy, it should be of interest to a wide cross section of readers. As a scholarly text, it is meant to provide an interdisciplinary perspective, which in itself means that it is not presented in the technical vocabulary of any one subject, even though it respects the importance of precision. I hope this book brings the reader, whether scholar, student or general, closer to an appreciation of the West Indian past as a necessary basis for self-determination now and in the future.

Acknowledgements

I acknowledge with gratitude the assistance given by specific persons and the staff at a number of libraries: Norman Fiering and staff at the John Carter Brown Library at Brown University for their help during my several stints at the library; the staff of the American Antiquarian Society in Worcester, Mass; Phil Weimerskirch, research librarian at the Providence Public Library; the staff at the Boston Public Library; David Buisseret at the Newberry Library in Chicago; the library staff at the Cave Hill and Mona Libraries of the University of the West Indies; the staff at the National Library of Jamaica and the Barbados Public Library; the library staff in the Caribbean Section and the Sala Josefina del Toro of the University of Puerto Rico Library at Rio Piedras.

I wish to acknowledge the help given to me by the US Government through a Fulbright Fellowship as well as that from the Rockefeller Foundation through a Fellowship at the University of Puerto Rico.

1

An Introduction to the Language of West Indians

THE NAME 'WEST INDIAN'

Individuals acquire names before they have control over themselves, and given names show the preferences of parents. Individuals, on reaching maturity, may change their names to reflect their own preferences, but comparatively few actually do. In the case of the New World, the same was true for the colonies, which were named after the person who 'discovered' them, or according to how they looked to these persons, or after some other great person or thing in the culture of the 'discoverer' *eg* saints. In the minds of the European 'discoverers' the places in the New World had no names before they came upon them, so that in a sense they were like newborn babes, seeing the light for the first time and having to be given an identity. In addition to naming the islands, as the colonists spread out, they gave names to all the places they settled. Thus, names of European places were replicated across town and district as people tried to surround themselves with the familiar and comforting. Naming was therefore a parental act and a perpetuation of the identity and culture of those who gave the names.

While the naming of an individual island or a district within an island could be regarded as concrete and straightforward, the naming of a group of islands, especially when they were not geographically separate from others, involved some level of abstraction, that is, the identification of a common factor linking the islands. The obvious one from the European point of view was territorial, but even without specific names territorial concepts emerged within a specific language. Names, like other words, belong to a specific language and, when left unqualified, they acquire a primary reference. For example, the name *les Antilles*, is French and, unless qualified is interpreted by the French primarily to mean the French West Indies. The name *West Indies*, without a qualifier such as *French* or *Dutch* means those islands associated historically with Britain.

In the New World place names changed as a result of accretion in knowledge and according to political realities. In addition, variations in the spelling and pronunciation of names disappeared as printing and other agents of uniformity increased in power. As knowledge of the distinction between the mainland and the islands emerged, the distinction between *America* and *the West Indian islands* appeared. As the rift between Britain and the mainland colonies of the north deepened, the distinction between the faithful and the unfaithful became even more necessary. As the British, the French, the Dutch, the Danish fought among themselves for the islands, each of these nations had to identify its combined territory, no matter how far removed from each other the islands were, with names. This rivalry led to names for groups of islands over and above the geographical groupings. It led to a choice between the two names, Antilles, which had always been used to refer to the islands, and West Indies which, by default or desertion, had come to refer to the islands.

The British, proud of their expanding empire, preferred the name *West Indies* and their authors reinforced this by using the name in relating the deeds and misdeeds of the people in their possessions. The West Indies, like India, became a single entity in the minds of the British people because it was not necessary for them to separate town from parish or parish from island or one island from another. British authors, whether they were writing of one island or several, oriented their readers by using the name *West Indies* (or the adjective form) in the titles of their books in most cases, rather than by using the names of individual islands. This contrasted with the spirit of difference and physical distance between the islands, for though the islands were all plantation and slave islands, they were not a cohesive economic force. The name *West Indies* might have given them a feeling of belonging to a higher, metropolitan force, but the social divisions (master, servant, slave) and the plantation as the dominant unit did not make for unity within islands or between islands.

The only term which emerged out of the West Indies embodying any concept of oneness and West Indian was *Creole*. Although this term varied in meaning over the centuries, it always retained in its reference the notion 'native born West Indian'. The word *Creolian* was used by Oldmixon [1708, 2:214] to refer to the native born slaves as opposed to those brought from Africa because the numbers of the former had by then grown enough to make them recognizable. In fact, a distinction in language and behaviour between the two types of slave was apparent and had become significant to the planters as well as to the slaves themselves. As the language, culture and interests of the West Indian whites and the European whites diverged, the term *Creole* was increasingly used by West Indians (*eg* Mathews [1793]) and others (Thompson [1770]) to refer to whites born and bred in the West Indies, who presumably also were marked by their language and behaviour. The term *Creole* did not emerge as a general name as an alternative to *West Indian* and it did not generate any geographical derivation because it was used principally to identify internal social contrasts within the West Indies. Moreover, it was not specific to the English islands – it was a New World term which had spread from the Spanish to the French to the English colonies.

The name *West Indies* was maintained externally by the British in keeping with their world vision and economic interests. It had been mistakenly conferred in the first place by Europeans and had negatively reflected development in its decline from being an all-encompassing name for the New World to a term preferred by the British to identify its island possessions. It is not sufficient to analyse the evolution of the name and the entity which it represented by contrasting cultural transmission from Europe and economic forces in the colonies. In the first place, the absence of any regional or inter-island unity and the exchanging of islands between the British and the French up until the early nineteenth century did not allow for the growth of the concept of an entity and a specific name to identify that entity. Secondly, at the beginning of the nineteenth century the difference in outlook and development between the old British colonies and the newer ones was considerable – at this time Kittitians were proud of themselves as Creoles, whereas Trinidadians had no distinguishing identity. In other words, unlike America (*ie* the USA), the name *West Indies* did not represent the triumph and unity of an economic force in the colonies and the identification of that economic force. In addition, as far as cultural transmission is concerned, it was not a name which specifically related the colony back to the mother country, as did names like *New England* and *Nova Scotia*. The name *West Indies* was one of convenience—survival by default, not survival of the fittest. From the British point of view, the maintenance of the concept of an entity allowed them to discuss and formulate common policy for all and to implement without paying much attention to differences between islands. The use of the name *West Indies* was therefore a matter of cultural, conceptual and economic factors coming together in the exercise of colonial government.

The name has survived, even though most of the islands included historically under its designation have become independent political entities and even though various kinds of alliances of territories cutting across language have been formed within the last few decades. There is still a solidarity of history and culture which links the West Indies and causes the people to regard each other as the same; there is also a solidarity in sports and education which has reinforced the British legacy and made the connection even stronger. It is above all the English language fashioned by the experiences of the people and more recently by the writers in the region which has been the common thread linking them together.

THE REALITY OF WEST INDIAN ENGLISH FROM AN EXTERNAL PERCEPTION

West Indian English is now known worldwide through the mouths and pens of its users, although, in comparison with other varieties of English, its speakers number only a few million and belong to several small countries which have little or no political clout. West Indian English is featured outside the English-speaking world, at least in one of its varieties, through reggae music, for people of many different cultures and languages have become familiar with the lyrics of Bob Marley's songs, whether or not they actually understand what he is saying. In addition, influential music awards ceremonies have featured for some time now categories which include music coming out of the West Indies, as a recognition of the widespread influence of this kind of music in today's global village. Even though the language in this music as well as the actual speech of the singers may pass undigested through the ears of listeners, its rhythm and other features of its phonology make it recognizable to many more people than it was up to the end of the third quarter of the twentieth century. This is really a current phenomenon which is still evolving and its impact is still increasing.

In addition to being part of the music programming of radio and television in big cities, West Indian voices are also heard occasionally in music programmes, such as Reggae Sunsplash, which originate from the West Indies. Interest in such programmes has increased at the same time that West Indian carnivals in New York, Toronto and other big cities have increased in size and impact. In England, though the Notting Hill Carnival, one of the oldest West Indian carnivals, has declined as the one of central focus, it has spawned others in other British cities. Yet, it is difficult to tell how distinctive or recognizable West Indian language really is or will become as a variety of the English language as a result of music and music based festivals. The same doubt can be raised about the effect of West Indian English produced by famous athletes, sportsmen, sports personalities and teams coming out of the West Indies.

Historically and traditionally, people, especially in the English-speaking world outside the West Indies, became familiar with another variety of West Indian English through calypsos, which have always been part of the tourist's exotic vision of the Caribbean and which, together with the limbo dance, coconut trees and sandy beaches, conjure up in the minds of many people a carefree native whose language is very simple to match the simple island life. The songs of Harry Belafonte took the calypso outside the West Indies and made its language more intelligible to North Americans especially. The variety of calypso of the Belafonte type, which was associated with the entertainment of visitors, has always had to be tailored in its language to achieve its objective, because unlike much of modern music, including reggae music, the words of the calypsonian were intended to be meaningful and to make some specific point. As a result of its higher level of intelligibility (compared with the language of reggae music) to persons outside the West Indies, the calypso variety of West Indian English has been used in commercials, films and other promotional contexts in such a way that listeners are expected to understand the words, which almost always contain features of simplicity.

The non West Indian's experience of West Indian English through music is not one which features the language as a variety with any level of sophistication or subtlety, even though reggae music itself is in most cases very serious in its message. Perhaps the major reason for this negative view is that the singers are identified as black, Third World people, which, within the general picture of culture and development, is not associated with high intellectual achievement. Added to this is the experience of those who have come into contact with West Indian immigrants in various parts of the world. Englishmen and Americans, for example, would have found the speech of West Indian immigrants difficult to follow in many cases, and because for the most part West Indians did menial jobs, their speech was interpreted as substandard, to match their social status. In addition, part of the negative view was of course a legacy of racism and slavery, which automatically led many to conclude that anything different and not easily understood coming out of the mouths of black people resulted from lack of intelligence and lack of education. This was no more tragically seen than in Britain where a great number of West Indian children who went to Britain with their parents were placed in educationally subnormal classes in the British school system principally because their language and culture were unfamiliar to British teachers.

The linguistic response of West Indian migrants to natives in the large English-speaking cities of the world, such as London, New York and Toronto, did little to help their own case or to enhance the status of their language. West Indians tried to modify their speech in the direction of that of the host country in order to be more easily understood and to save themselves from having to repeat everything they said. This was also done out of a feeling of linguistic inferiority because in the majority of cases West Indians who migrated from their homes were poor and not well educated. Whereas they may have succeeded in their immediate intention to be more easily understood, such a reaction provided no challenge to the already established view of the inferiority of West Indian English and in fact only served to strengthen it.

In addition, the West Indian's imitation of the Englishman's or American's speech has not been limited to contexts of communication with non West Indians. It also occurs in interaction between West Indians where one speaker feels a need to impress others with 'sophisticated' speech. Louise Bennett's poem "Noh Lickle Twang" [Bennett 1966: 209-10] is a poignant example of this. In this poem a mother is totally disappointed and feels let down because her son returns from overseas and speaks with no trace of a foreign accent. She even goes further and points to the 'admirable' example of a sister who only went to work for an American family (in Jamaica) and was now speaking with a foreign accent and in such a way that she could not be understood. With this kind of negative attitude by West Indians themselves, there was little possibility of others adopting a more positive one.

It is not only in the production of speech that there has been a history of negativity, but also in comprehension. From the beginning of the contact between Europeans, the indigenous people, Africans, and later Asians, some kind of psychological adjustment had to be made by hearers, either singly or as a group, to noncomprehension or partial comprehension of a powerful non-native language (*eg* English) used in the society. Such adjustments which have evolved from then up to now have become endemic in the society and a part of every West Indian. In the same way that illiterates can often manage to conceal their illiteracy, so too many adults and schoolchildren in the West Indies have developed strategies to cope with low comprehension of standard English without revealing their level of ignorance. In fact, noncomprehension has been noted as a strategy among the lowest classes in society in the West Indies from the days of slavery. It has been used as a strategy in the sense that as a habit lower social class persons may show no visible reaction of comprehension to utterances addressed to them by persons in authority. When the lower social class person refuses to comply with orders given or questions asked, the lack of visible reaction of comprehension can be used to claim noncomprehension. As a consequence, the person in authority may regard such lower social class persons as dull and not able to understand 'plain English'; the lower social class person may regard the person in authority as gullible and easy to deceive. On the other hand, both parties may know, in spite of lack of visible reaction, when there is understanding and when there is not. In such cases, attempts to deceive suffer the consequences and genuine noncomprehension leads to further explanation.

Since the behaviour of speakers as well as that of hearers brings the intelligibility and status of West Indian English into question, West Indian English has had a difficult task asserting itself as equal to other varieties of English in the English-speaking world. Even in genuine second language situations West Indian English has not prospered or conferred any advantage on its users. For instance, the thousands of West Indians who went to Panama to build the Canal and those who went on to Costa Rica were gradually absorbed into the majority Spanish culture and even where their original West Indian dialects survived, competence in some form of English did not bestow any major advantage, even in a country controlled by English-speaking Americans. Again it was the colour of the people and their status as workers performing hard and dangerous work which removed them from any consideration of intellectual sophistication.

To suggest therefore that West Indian English is worthy of study is for some an excursion into exotic academia or an exercise of no appreciable value or for some an insult to 'proper' English. This is so even today when ethnic and cultural differences are being promoted worldwide. In order to counter such negative reactions, it is necessary to trace the development of varieties of English in the West Indies as, first and foremost, human responses to extreme and inhuman situations. Secondly, West Indian language varieties reflect the consequences of contact between peoples whose languages and cultures were significantly different. Thirdly, West Indian English retains many features of the dialects of persons coming from all over Britain and this is quite evident in the features adopted by the slaves. In other words, what are often thought to be corruptions by black slaves are identical to what is documented as features of regional British English of the seventeenth, eighteenth and nineteenth centuries. A study of the development of West Indian English therefore sheds light on British English itself it leads into an examination of the human faculty, language, and it clearly demonstrates the relationship between social and economic power and standards which are established for language.

WEST INDIAN ENGLISH WITHIN ITS OWN
SOCIAL MATRIX

A close examination of the development of West Indian English is also justifiable within the context of social and cultural changes going on in the West Indies. For where once West Indian views of the status of the different varieties of West Indian English coincided by and large with external views, this is no longer so. The coming of political independence to most of the West Indian territories has been followed by a gradual cultural emancipation of the people, especially young people. Greater tolerance and appreciation of the vernacular at all levels of West Indian society is related to appropriateness of use, even as the more divergent forms of West Indian English have been slowly declining in use.

The very music which has spread across the world is a postindependence phenomenon and the calypso, the traditional characteristic of the West Indies, has enjoyed a surge in production and popularity across the West Indies as a part of annual cultural activities in the various islands. It is true that calypsos have not had the same extraregional appeal as reggae music has had, but this might be in part because the language and references in calypsos are more localized and topical. For the West Indian, in any case, the calypso is seldom as simple as it appears to the non West Indian. It is a cultural feature which epitomizes double meaning whether in reference to sex or to topical political and economic matters.

The West Indian is always ready to interpret the apparently innocent references and images, which are the stock-in-trade of the calypsonian. The general intention of this kind of ambiguity is either to amuse at someone's expense or to attack without direct and clear confrontation, and it is related to the other practice of 'dropping remarks', which is essentially negative criticism of someone phrased in such a way that it seems to be an innocent remark not addressed to anyone in particular. In 'dropping remarks', both the speaker and the intended receiver understand the full import of the remark. In the case of the calypsonian, in addition to the pride of being able to manipulate words, there is the necessity to be able to talk about the details of sex without being branded indecent or to talk about the politician without being victimized. In such cases therefore West Indian English moves far beyond the simple language that the foreigner imagines it to be. This practice of double meaning or nondirect communication arises out of a social situation in which class conflict (today) and the master/slave relationship (previously) have prevented the powerless from speaking frankly and directly to the powerful.

Class conflict and culture conflict have also brought about changes in attitude to West Indian English outside the West Indies, in Britain specifically. For the children of many West Indians in Britain, (one variety of) West Indian English became the ingroup language of choice and it is by the deliberate cultivation of West Indian English that many black Britishers establish their identity and challenge the attitudes and beliefs of their elders. So strong and influential has been this tendency in Britain that it encouraged the British education system to move away from a philosophy in which English monoculturalism was the perceived target for all to a philosophy of multiculturalism and multilingualism within a dominant British culture.

Moving from the oral sphere to the written, within recent time West Indian English has become respectable in literature because of the accumulation of a solid body of written material coming out of the West Indies and because of the recognition given to some of those, for example, Derek Walcott and V.S. Naipaul, who brought it to this level. As is the case with West Indian music, the element of language cannot easily be separated from themes and styles and assessed by itself. While some of the written works try to reflect normal conversation and actual varieties of West Indian English, other works either remain fairly close to standard English or, like works of art generally, try to be creative in the use of language. Almost all West Indian literature, however, either directly or indirectly, tries to reflect the spirit of West Indians, as a result of which language becomes a central preoccupation. The rise to respectability of West Indian literature automatically has meant that the language element of the literature is regarded as a viable medium for the expression of literature.

West Indian literature cannot compete with the major literatures of the world in volume or impact and in a comparative sense may be of negligible influence on the world at large. Even within the West Indies itself, where there is no long and community-wide tradition of reading, written literature and the artistic language it contains are unknown to the majority of the populations in the region. Moreover, there is little likelihood of positive change in this state of affairs because of the overpowering influence of radio and television, and even though West Indian literature is compulsory to some extent for all West Indian schoolchildren. Yet, the written word is long lasting and good literature is usually durable and influential over generations. In addition, the written word in the context of literature usually rises in status as the literature rises in status. Therefore, in spite of its lack of volume, West Indian literature may be the most important avenue through which the richness and complexity of West Indian English can prove itself and overcome the stigma of being considered simple and corrupt.

WEST INDIAN ENGLISH AS AN AREA OF ACADEMIC STUDY

West Indian English has also been brought into written literature by academics through its connection with Black English in the USA. This connection has been justified by similarities in historical experience as well as by linguistic similarities in the two. In the history of the Americas, the West Indian islands were for many of the early years more important than the main land masses. In fact, early colonization of the Americas saw a movement from the islands to the mainland colonies, as a result of which there were direct linguistic links between certain islands and certain mainland colonies. This was so in the case of South Carolina, which was colonized from Barbados in the 1670s. In addition to the direct links, the parallels in the social situations across the colonies led to similarities in language. One of the clearest parallels was African slavery within the context of the plantation. In contrast, one of the clearest differences between the mainland colonies and the island colonies was that in the former the African slaves were a minority dominated by a majority whereas in the latter they were a majority dominated by a minority. The linguistic consequences of this difference are as prominent in discussion as are the linguistic consequences of the social parallels.

As a consequence or as an offshoot of the preoccupation with Black English in the 1960s, the area of creole linguistics developed and blossomed with language in the Caribbean being one of the central areas of study. West Indian English, although not so identified, has been an integral part of creole studies and therefore provides some of the evidence for theories which have tried to account for similarities in the speech of black slaves and their descendants in the New World. One of the older theories proposed was that the speech came from a single source and was taken to the various countries of the New World by sailors. This theory, graphically illustrated by Dillard [1972: 14-15], has declined over the last twenty years. It is not simply that it had little linguistic evidence to support it, for few of these theories did, but that its Eurocentric bias was so strong that it made it a constant and easy target. It did not seem probable that sailors had developed a specific language which they used to facilitate communication and trade wherever they went and that the African slaves learnt this language and that their children subsequently acquired it and developed it as their first language.

West Indian English has also been brought into world focus indirectly as a part of the Language Bioprogram Hypothesis proposed by Derek Bickerton. Bickerton's views were featured popularly in *Newsweek* (15 March 1982) and in academic circles in the journal *The Behavioral and Brain Sciences* (vol. 7, no. 2, 1984) in which experts from different fields commented on his claims. The appeal of the Language Bioprogram Hypothesis is that creole languages, to which West Indian English is integrally related, contain features which are biologically encoded on man's brain and which surface automatically when children are deprived of an adequate language model in first language acquisition. Features of West Indian English therefore have been viewed by Bickerton and others as biologically determined.

While it was in relation to first language acquisition that creoles were used to develop the *Language Bioprogram Hypothesis*, it was in relation to second language acquisition that the Pidginization theory [Schumann 1978] was developed to account for the way in which foreigners or migrants learn second languages in the contexts in which they are spoken naturally. Creole languages and specifically language situations in the West Indies were used to show the effect of social and psychological factors on attainment in a second language. Factors in the development of West Indian English have therefore been used as evidence in the development of a general theory of second language acquisition.

In contrast to its lowly status in the oral, popular, everyday sphere, West Indian English has thus attracted attention in the written, academic sphere. In literature it is accepted as a medium flexible enough to allow for world class literary pieces. In linguistics it is a subject of study which is of interest to all human beings as well as to a more select group investigating the products of the contact between Europeans and Africans in the New World. However, whether in its lowly state or with its more acceptable status, peculiarities of West Indian English vis-à-vis other varieties of

English provoke questions about what can justifiably be called English and what should not be. Even though English itself is an amalgam from different sources and even though it is recognized that natural languages are forever changing, borrowing and being influenced by other languages, the powerful normative tradition of English has established boundaries for written standard English which weigh heavily in judgements about the definition of English and the exclusion of certain language features found in the West Indies from what could be considered English.

The image of a quilt can be applied to language in the West Indies to convey the picture of something practical made up of colourful pieces of material drawn from various parts. It is of course an image which allows one to wax eloquent about the colour of the pieces as well as their source and previous status, and the practicality, blending and wholeness of the finished product. It is an image which suits almost all of the territories in the West Indies except Barbados, for which such an image is a little too colourful. The cultural and linguistic diversity which characterizes almost all of the other territories contrasts with a tendency towards uniformity in Barbados which has for a long time manifested itself in conservatism in expression as well as in cultural and linguistic assimilation.

In its political history Barbados was a colony of Britain only, and this for almost three and a half centuries. In comparison, Jamaica, which was also a colony of Britain for practically the same length of time, did not manifest the same degree of attraction to assimilation. The reason for this is that basically as a result of topographical factors Jamaica depended up until the last years of the slave trade upon constant importation of Africans to replenish the labour force, whereas increasingly from early the Barbadian population was bolstered by natural increase. The constant injection of African speakers into Jamaican slave society slowed evolution towards English and conversely preserved African linguistic influence in Jamaican speech more strongly for a longer time.

Another sociocultural difference between Jamaica and Barbados is that whereas in Jamaica postemancipation Asian immigration was added to the cultural and linguistic quilt, Barbados had no such Asian input into its population. In other West Indian territories such as Trinidad and Guyana, East Indian migration was even more significant culturally and today the literature in these territories shows such influence in the language. In the areas of dress, food and religion Trinidad and Guyana have a rich variety of words or names which are familiar to the population as a whole and which surface in the literature naturally.

In addition to East Indian influence there is also in Trinidad a strong heritage of French Creole culture, and the French Creole language specifically is prominent in the area of culture (superstitions, storytelling, carnival, flora). This is also true of St Lucia and Dominica, where French Creole is the first language of the majority of the people. In St Lucia and Dominica as well as in Trinidad the English dialect of the people has been directly influenced by French Creole. For example, structures such as

it have a man	=	There is a man
it making hot, wi	=	It is hot

are salient in their speech and literature, making them identifiable nationally and socially. There are no such identifying French Creole features in the speech or literature of Barbados, Antigua or Jamaica.

Intraregional migration has always been a linguistically unifying factor in the West Indies, especially since migration has invariably been accompanied by return traffic. Each territory therefore has and has had natives from all other territories. By and large, migrants have interacted with the local population in such a way that within two generations they have become indistinguishable from it. Over and above the normal intraregional interaction, another more recent influence has been the modern Rasta, reggae and dub culture out of Jamaica which has affected the behaviour and penetrated the artistic expression of all other West Indians territories, even though Jamaica is fairly far away from all the others. This came in the wake of the civil rights movement and the hippie culture in the 1960s and 1970s respectively in the USA. The 'black is beautiful' philosophy led to an adoption of characteristics which were visibly black and a promotion of self. As a result, the characteristic Jamaican variety of speech, being the most divergent from standard English in the West Indies, was cultivated by many throughout the West Indies.

At the same time, but in contrast, West Indian English has been subject to consistent levelling and homogenization because of education historically, but latterly also, under pressure from extensive tourism. Education has created in most territories a bigger middle class with middle class values, not the least of which is competence in standard English. Tourism, dominated by English-speaking North Americans, has encouraged a culture of service in which communication in the English language has been a powerful factor. The promotion of West Indian ethnic and cultural values has therefore been counterbalanced by the need to communicate and survive in a world dominated by English speakers whose variety of English has to be conformed to.

The racial contrast between black and white in the West Indies is not manifested significantly in language except as a factor of social class. The white section of the population does not have a dialect or a historical view of their culture which is in any way special, except in Trinidad to some extent where there is a social designation 'French' or 'Creole', which is applied to some people. Even in Barbados where the proportion of whites was higher than in most of the other territories, except for normal social class differences and a few phonological features, there is no great difference in language between blacks and whites. It is true, however, that the wide spectrum of varieties which typifies Jamaica, Guyana and Antigua and which can be related to African influence does not have many white speakers at the lower social end. The cultural diversity of Trinidad, with its Asian, French Creole and Spanish influence is dominated more by differences between its Black and Indian components than between white and nonwhite components. In Dominica and St Lucia the contrast is between the first language dominance of French Creole in private and informal society and the compulsory use of English in the official and educational systems.

The term 'continuum' has been applied to the language spectrum ranging from the speech of the social elite and educated at one end to the speech of the rural, uneducated poor at the other, which is characteristic of every West Indian territory. The paradox that the continuum between the two extremes has presented to linguist and layman alike is that it highlights the differences while at the same time it establishes the unity in the social varieties of language in each territory. Sociolinguistic variation is normal in all human societies, but in the case of the West Indies the historical source of the variety of language at the top is not identical to that of the variety of language at the bottom. If, for purposes of comparison, one were to use British English, it is clear that although Cockney differs from Standard English, the historical sources of the two cannot be said to be different. In the case of the West Indies, slavery and the plantation system brought together speakers from an Indo-European language family at the top with speakers from a Niger-Congo language family at the bottom.

Although the African languages were under pressure from the beginning, features of these languages still remain in West Indian English up to today. Moreover, evolution in the language situation in the West Indies cannot be interpreted to be one in which the 'pure' English of those at the top is slowly replacing the 'corrupted' English of those at the bottom. The contact situations in the Caribbean in some cases (*eg* in Suriname) produced a 'mixed' variety of language which crystallized quickly into a national language (a creole), one which, because of its use in intimate and essential domains in the society, changed very slowly thereafter. This phenomenon is to some degree present in all the West Indian territories, which means that the 'continuum' is really made up, not of isolatable variants of equal value stretching from one end to the other, but of interlocking systems of variants, which because they relate to social class and distinctions within social class, change very slowly in their linguistic structure.

The slow rate of change is in keeping with the gradual evolution of West Indian English, in all its varieties, as a social system of communication. In a sense, West

Indian English, as a social system of communication, evolved over four eras: the century and a quarter after Columbus' voyages, the two hundred years after the English came to the islands, the almost century and a half after Emancipation, and the short period after independence in the various territories. The distinguishing creole characteristics of West Indian English, in contrast, probably developed quickly during the last half of the seventeenth century.

During the first hundred years after Columbus' arrival in the New World, the encounters between Europeans, native Americans and Africans provided the Europeans with strategies and methods of communication that were transmitted to other European nations who later joined in the exploitation of the new lands. More generally, the exploits of the Portuguese as sailors and traders had given them some measure of competence or knowledge of procedure to effect communication with people who spoke other languages, and, no doubt, the English benefited from this knowledge. Consequently, by the time that the English established their first colony in the West Indian islands in the 1620s, there was already a body of knowledge which they used to facilitate communication in that colony. However, there is little evidence that any specific language or form of language developed in the first hundred years after the advent of Columbus and was used generally as a language of 'international' trade. There is little to suggest, therefore, that the varieties of language which developed in the English colonies after the 1620s were significantly influenced by any prior, generally used language over and above the knowledge gained about methods of communicating with speakers of other languages.

It was really in the two hundred years after the establishment of the first colony in St Kitts that the major creole varieties of West Indian English emerged. This period was dominated by the rivalry between the French and the English, the rise and fall of sugar, and the decimation and replacement of the populations in the islands of the Caribbean. This was a period of violence, disruption and expansion; it was also the period of the Industrial Revolution, which changed social organization in Europe and undermined slavery as an economic system in the New World. It was a great period for European culture and institutions. For African societies it was a low period and for Africans transported across the Atlantic it was a period of rebellion, adaptation and creativity. The varieties of language which developed in the West Indies reflected the times and the experiences of the various groups. With regard to West Indian English specifically, the figure below identifies some of the major factors which determined its forms and structures.

The Emancipation to independence era saw important demographic changes in the West Indies, but few linguistic additions to the vernaculars. The Asian element which was added to West Indian populations retained their languages among themselves, as a result of which these languages did not modify the already estab-

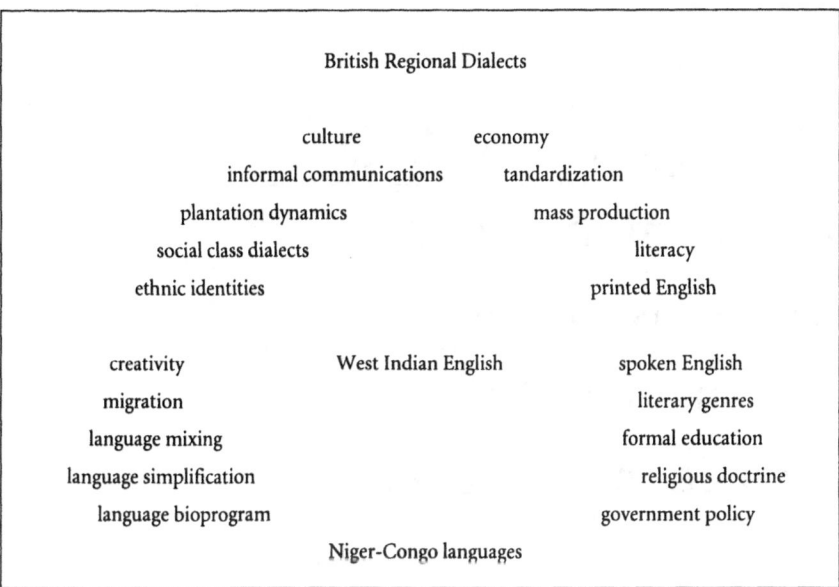

FIGURE 1.1: Major factors determining forms and structures of West Indian English

lished vernaculars to any great extent. In fact, in Guyana, the East Indians, who replaced the slaves in the rural plantations, acquired the most divergent form of the creole which had been the characteristic speech of the plantation slaves. Generally, the weakening of the rigid social stratification, which had been a feature of slavery, did not produce new linguistic structures but a gradual decrease in the number of speakers of the most creolized forms of the vernaculars. This trend continued on into the postindependence era, although paradoxically it was accompanied by a more positive attitude to the vernaculars.

The foundations of West Indian English were laid during the second era. It is the determining factors identified in Figure 1.1 which will be explored in the following chapters and it is through this exploration that the structures and forms which are collectively being called 'West Indian English' will be revealed. It is also in the exploration of the determining factors that one will see the development of the different varieties of West Indian English as a system of communication appropriate to the social structure of a colonial slave society in which norms and standards were determined by internal, regional and metropolitan forces. While social and economic factors provided a context and limitations to language development, the human brain, the human language faculty and human will were central in shaping the specific peculiarities of West Indian English. Unfortunately, assessment of the effect of these remains in the area of speculation and will not therefore be addressed in any systematic way.

2

Nonlinguistic Methods of Communication and Transmission of Information in the Plantation Slave Society

The development of a culture based on literacy and the English language were a catalyst for change in the management of West Indian society. The West African societies from which the West Indian slaves came were made up of various nations and their main method of communication was almost exclusively oral in nature. In addition, this organization into nations was paralleled by variation in language from nation to nation. The same is true of feudal England, from which the English colonists had not fully emerged at the start of their migration to the New World. The West Indian territories were therefore peopled by persons on the one hand from societies which were in the process of moving from an oral culture to a literate one and whose organization was therefore determined by this process, and on the other hand by persons whose culture was almost exclusively oral in nature and whose organization was determined by this. These two groups joined the native group whose culture was also almost exclusively oral in nature and whose organization reflected this.

The variety of languages, the presence of various nations of peoples from three different parts of the world, and their almost exclusively oral cultures initially provoked a dependence on and a greater observation of nonlinguistic methods of communication. In other words, the background elements in the framework of communication which even in cases of normal communication contribute substantially to the comprehension of information became more important because people were unfamiliar with each other's behaviour and could not communicate by speaking to each other directly. Early European accounts of the New World are dominated by descriptions of the customs of the natives. Later when the Africans were introduced in numbers in the islands, European writers, who could not understand the languages of the slaves, commented on their 'strange' customs. No doubt the natives of the Americas and the African slaves also noted the 'strange' customs of the Europeans. Observing and becoming familiar with 'external' signs in behaviour was the first step in the development of a common system of communication in the West Indies. Beyond face-to-face communication, methods also had to be selected by those in control of these new societies to effect long distance communication in a situation of linguistic and cultural diversity. A discussion of the nonlinguistic methods of communication in the plantation slave society is therefore a starting point in the examination of the framework within which English developed.

The channels of communication used in the early society in the West Indies are clear indicators of level of development in the society and level of freedom and flexibility in the individual. Before the colonization of the West Indies, channels of communication among the different peoples had been transmitted from one generation to another in a normal way. When disruption occurred and when peoples of different cultures came into contact in the West Indies, systems of communication had to evolve to suit the new situations. In the evolution of the new systems, ad hoc and temporary methods were used for some time before they gave way to more permanent systems later which were better adapted to the ecology of the situation. Systems with more generality which have survived and which are more dominant now may in retrospect be given more prominence than they actually enjoyed at a specific time and within a certain segment of the society. So, it is important to try to recover systems or elements of systems which were more typical of the oral culture of the peoples and which for individuals were meaningful because they gave identity and purpose to communication.

In the situations of conflict which existed in the early years of colonization in West Indies, communication and disruption of communication were equally important – there was a need to communicate with allies as well as a need to obstruct the communication of enemies. The Europeans, who held power, had to establish effective communication among themselves as well as to prevent the slaves, whom they saw as a threat, from being able to communicate among themselves. However, even though the white rulers saw the slaves as a threat, the two were not warring factions on different sides; they were just different groups in the same country. There had then to be some measure of communication right throughout the society so that the rulers could have their objectives met. Yet, the situation was a contradictory one in which on the one hand all members of the society had to work in concert for the survival of the society, while on the other hand measures were taken by one sector of the society to disrupt another sector of the society to prevent them from acting en masse.

In the oral plantation slave society, as is the case in all oral societies, it was necessary for people to come together face-to-face and in groups to communicate. This posed a problem because each plantation was an isolated unit and some plantations covered a wide area. On the plantation the daily execution of work was based on a system of giving orders to carry out tasks which involved the direct supervision of a large workforce by a small number of persons. The 'supervisor' at every level had to be mobile and vigilant as well as able to interact with persons of varying language competence. There had to be methods of communication in place to supplement this direct, face-to-face giving of orders and conveying of information on the plantation itself as well as methods for the business of the whole society. From the point of view of whites, methods were required for the post- and pre-work periods and for emergencies. Methods had to be in place for relaying of information from one plantation to another, from plantation to town and from town to plantation. In addition, the decisions made by and for the government of the colony had to be disseminated to all citizens. All of this communication had to be done in a context where the vast majority of persons, white and black, were preliterate.

Message carrying, which required travelling over short and long distances, was characteristic of the plantation slave society. Where written information was involved, those few who could read, whether priest or bookkeeper, had to read aloud or relay written information to the many who were illiterate. However, message carrying was a slow way of relaying information and certainly was not appropriate for emergencies or for some regular social events. For instance, in the early years of European colonization in the West Indies when fear and the threat of rebellion were constant companions of the white masters, the whites devised an easy and apparently clear method of contacting each other across plantations. This system is described by Ligon [1657: 29]: "If any tumult or disorder be in the island, the next neighbour to it, discharges a musquet, which gives the alarum to the whole island; for upon the report of that, the next shoots, and so the next, till it go through the island: upon which warning, they make ready." What started out as a simple and informal method of communication later became varied and formal, for in 1693 a law in Montserrat was passed requiring

that an alarm shall be caused or made by firing two great guns from either the Fort of Kingsale, Plymouth, Bransbee's Bay, or the Old Road, and within land, by blowing in a trunkshell, which every plantation or householder in this island is hereby obliged to have in each respective plantation or house, and cause it to be blown in on any notice of an alarm, or hearing it sounded from other plantations... [Montserrat Code of Laws, No. 38 XXI, p.25].

There is no evidence to show how often this system was used and how effective it was. Obviously it could only work where plantation houses were within earshot of each other, which means that they would have had to be close. In Barbados where the island was quickly covered with plantations and where there were not many natural barriers, as well as in Montserrat, which was small, this system might have been effective. In an island like St Lucia, where there were natural barriers and a small population, it is unlikely that the sound of a shot or a shell would have been heard or been so distinct that it could have been relied on in a matter of life and death. It is true that the law in Montserrat, and presumably elsewhere, stipulated that individuals were not to fire guns after eight o'clock at night except in the case of an alarm, but this stipulation in itself only serves to highlight the fact that such a system had to have the cooperation of all in the society. However, the use of big guns to raise an alarm became a normal part of these societies and the use of conch shells became a part of plantation business.

For some regular social events the use of specific noise-making instruments for communication by the Europeans was a matter of normal cultural transmission from Europe. The use of drums and bells had been for a long time quite common among them for attracting attention, signalling the approach of someone or something and for giving warnings. The use of bells for telling the faithful that it is time for church and the use of drums for military purposes were normal and everyday uses of noise-making instruments for communication. Much of the military parade which has become ceremonial today was once more functional. Some of these methods, however, were modified within the West Indies. For example, in earlier years in the plantation slave colonies when governors went to church, their progress towards the church was marked so that the militia and the congregation knew when the party was approaching and stood in readiness for them. This is described by Poole [1753: 260] in the following way:

Those days the Governor goes to church, the drum is beat about the town pretty soon, thereby to give timely notice to the militia to attend their duty, which is the constant custom here. The militia being under arms, present themselves in the church-yard, and there wait the coming of the Governor, of whose approach notice is given by beat of drum. As soon as the drum beats, which is the signal of his being near, they prepare in readiness, and make a lane for his passing thro' them: When he enters the church the organ is performed on for some time; after which it ceases, and the morning duty begins.

It is obvious from this that in those days messages were relayed among the whites in the society by the beating of drums and that at the time this was accepted as an effective method of communication over distance.

Another similar use of the drum among whites was for business purposes, for just as the auction sale of today is announced by a flag and/or bell, the sale of slaves was "proclaimed by beat of drum".[1] The beating of the drum in this and other cases was the signal that an event was about to begin. As a method of communication it contrasted with the gun in that its noise did not carry as far as the gun and it did not provoke a reaction of urgency or fear, but rather one of expectancy.

The bell, as a method of communication, was used not only for church purposes but also for the daily routine of the white servants in the early years. This is pointed out by Ligon [1657: 44]:

> The next day they are rung out with a bell to work, at six a clock in the morning, with a severe overseer to command them, till the bell ring again, which is at eleven a clock; and then they return, and are set to dinner, either with a mess of lob-lolly, bonavist, or potatoes. At one a clock, they are rung out again to the field, there to work till six, and then home again, to a supper of the same.[2]

While Ligon speaks of a bell for the servants in those early years, other works identify the conch-shell as the instrument used for the same purpose on some plantations for the slaves. For example, Cuffy [1823: 4] says the following:

> Early in the morn a shell de driver blow-ee,
>
> Negro he get up, – out to work he go-ee . . .

This does not mean to suggest that the use of the conch-shell was a creation or discovery by the African slaves. Although the use of the conch-shell is limited by its availability (in that the animal grows only in tropical seas), as a noise-making instrument it is said to have a history of thousands of years, a history therefore that long preceded the arrival of African slaves in the West Indies. The bell or conch-shell was not simply a time marker, but was intended to control the routine of persons on the plantation. As Dickson [1789: 8] explains, the plantation bell which rang about four o'clock in the morning "may be considered as a warning-bell to rouse the negroes from their slumbers, and to prepare them for turning out". The later bells indicated when work was to begin and when it was to stop. The bell as an instrument of control was therefore not limited to specific hours, but could be used according to circumstances. For example the bell was used in the case of bad weather, as is pointed out by Carmichael [1833, 2:24]: "The moment a heavy shower of rain is seen approaching, the estates' great bell is rung to call them in from the field . . ."

However, it is not evident in the literature that this use of the bell was general even in St Vincent and Trinidad where Mrs Carmichael lived at different times, and there is no indication elsewhere whether it had been a practice from the earliest days of slavery. In fact, this practice does seem somewhat strange, seeing that threatening heavy showers would have been apparent to those in the fields at the same time as or before they were to those in the plantation yard and it would have done nobody any good, as a matter of policy, to have the slaves stay in the fields during heavy downpours.

Of course, the bell was also used for well-known domestic purposes – to alert servants that those in authority needed some item or service: "I rang the bell for one of the boys to bring glasses and some cool water..." [Carmichael 1833, 2:154].

An obvious difference between the domestic bell on the one hand and the church bell and the plantation bell on the other was one of size and volume; another deeper difference was that the larger bells in most cases announced a routine and were time markers, whereas the smaller bell was used at the whims and fancies of individuals. While the larger bells were intended to be time markers primarily for the slaves, they were also used by the whites for the same purpose. Note, for instance, the following from Dickson [1789: 8]:

I lodged for some years, within hearing both of a church and a plantation-bell. The former rang at five o'clock, the latter a considerable time before it. I always rose early, often at five o'clock, for the benefit of air, exercise and sea-bathing; and, when I wished to be up earlier than usual, I desired to be called when the plantation-bell rang.

However, while Dickson identified the plantation bell as a time marker in the morning, Barrell [1843: 28, 29], referring to Guyana in the 1790s, identifies the gun as a time marker at night: "... the night-gun at the fort had announced bed-time ... he had not yet adopted the habit of retiring at Gun-fire". The context makes it clear that the effect of the night-gun extended beyond the fort and was a signal for the civilian population as well.

The general regimentation caused by the larger bells and guns had an effect on the whole of the plantation society and made it into an ordered society. The humanless loudness of these bells and guns in distance communication were a sharp contrast to the intimacy of the voice in face-to-face communication. Order and subordination, which were important to the masters in these societies, were therefore buttressed by nonlinguistic methods of communication. Conversely, freedom from order and regimentation, which was equally important to those who were at the bottom of these societies, was antithetical to these methods of communication.

There was obviously a limit to the appropriateness and effectiveness of noise-making methods for wide communication – noises made by guns were limited in their range and could not be repeated for ever. Visual means were therefore also developed for communication and in the area of shipping it became indispensable. Because shipping was extremely important, not only for economic and communicative purposes but also in the waging of war, a system of signalling was worked out to inform those on land about approaching vessels. This kind of signalling was not meant to be technical or restricted. In addition, the fact that it was pointed out and explained by more than one contemporary British writer travelling in the region suggests that it was not a simple adoption of a European practice. For example, Poole [1753: 279] explained the system for his readers as follows:

> The method of giving notice of a vessel's coming into the harbour . . . is by hoisting a flag at Needham's Fort. If it be a topsail vessel, either ship or snow, the Union flag is hoisted; if a brig or schooner, the red Jack; but if it be a sloop, then the penent is hoisted: And thus, by different signals, vessels of different denominations are known.

Yet, McKinnen [1804: 7], half a century after Poole, seemed to feel the need to point the system out to his readers: "Two packets are regularly sent out in every month from England, and their arrival is announced by a flag hoisted at the castle." The importance of this visual system of communication to the colonial society of that time is evidenced by the fact that changes in the system were announced in detail in the newspaper. An elaborate example of this is found in the *Barbados Mercury* of 22 September 1770:

> Charles Fort, Sept. 22, 1770
>
> Notice is hereby given, that for the Future the public signals at this fort will be as follows:
>
> The signals for vessels to Windward will be on the staff newly erected.
>
> The signals for vessels to Leeward will be on the former windward staff.
>
> The old Leeward staff is removed
>
> On the Compliment staff.
>
> For an alarm. — A large Union flag, with a red flag under it, and three guns.
>
> A Flag Ship, or broad Pendant. — A large Union flag and one gun.
>
> A man of War. — A large Union flag.
>
> A Packet. — A Union Jack.
>
> On the Windward Staff
>
> An enemy. — A red flag, and one gun with a shot to the nearest point she appears in.
>
> A ship. — A Union flag.
>
> A snow. — A large St. George's Jack with a red border.
>
> A brigt. — A large St. George's Jack.
>
> A schooner. — A small Jack, red St. George's Cross in a blue field.
>
> A Sloop. — A pendant.
>
> A red flag under the usual signal for a vessel, with one gun, gives notice that such vessel is in distress; if in much distress, the gun will be repeated.
>
> Night signals, on the Leeward staff.
>
> A ship, or square rigged vessel. — Three lights, with or without rockets and false fires.
>
> A schooner or sloop — Two lights

This visual system of communication depended on a person or persons being able to identify the sighted vessel. As can be seen from Pinckard [1806, 1:420], this was done in two stages: "Early in the morning a signal appeared at the fort, implying that a vessel was in sight. Soon afterwards, this was lowered, and the packet signal hoisted in place."

These signals were of great interest to the general public, because in the case of commercial vessels, the news of the type of vessel gave time for the news to spread and this resulted in a crowd of people waiting expectantly for the docking of the boat to see whom and what it brought. In the case of hostile vessels, the signals gave the local force time to make ready, as is explained by Pinckard [1806, 2: 51-52]: "I have before observed to you, that the alarm signal being hoisted at the fort, indicates a strange fleet in sight. When it appears every one is on the alert, and ready to take his post, and thus the signal serves to prevent surprize."

The system of signalling evolved to become more and more elaborate, and although members of the public may not have been aware of the significance of all the details of flags, they certainly understood the meaning of red flags and guns, and the distinction between commercial vessels and hostile ones.

Although the systems of communication described were widespread and functional, they of course had their inherent limitations. The aural methods of communication at that time were limited by distance, and visual systems were limited by time of day. In relation to the latter specifically, whereas the approach of a ship was indicated by a flag during the day, it had to be indicated by a light at night. Attempts were made to overcome some of the limitations by combining aural and visual symbols. Examples of the use of both guns and flags are given above and also in the following taken from Resident [1828: 82-83]: "The establishment of martial law is notified by the firing of two guns, and hoisting a red flag at the batteries; and it is annulled by the same ceremony, substituting the British colours for the red flag."

In contrast to the impending events which were signalled in the ways identified above, martial law would have lasted for some time. It is obvious therefore that the aural symbol (the firing of guns) marked the beginning and the end of martial law while the visual symbol (the flag) marked the duration of the period. Thus, visual and aural symbols were not necessarily simultaneous and redundant.

METHODS OF COMMUNICATION USED BY THE SLAVES

While the slave owners needed methods of communication to manage and control the society, slaves needed methods of communication to liberate themselves and to preserve their humanity and sanity. From the number of runaways and frequency of insurrections throughout the entire slave period it is clear that many slaves in the two hundred year period tried all kinds of methods to liberate themselves from enslavement. The two basic ways of achieving this were either to evade enslavement or to remove it. The first, which was simpler, could be done singly or in collusion with others. The second, by its very nature, required a plot. So, whether in relation to the first or the second, means of communication were devised to deceive the enslavers who were on the lookout for such deception. However, no longstanding secret method could survive in a situation where there was constant suspicion among the various factions and groups that made up the slave society. Means of plotting therefore did not go beyond the normal means of ingroup communication in use among the slaves.

Even in cases where slaves did not resort to drastic methods to liberate themselves physically, they had to find methods constantly and everyday to outwit their enslavers so that they could feel some sense of achievement psychologically. They could deceive their enslavers directly with words in order to avoid work or to avoid punishment for taking their property, but they also had to be able to use the different genres of language to confuse their masters about their real intentions. In order to do this, contexts of communication had to be manipulated so that information could be circulated.

Since the evidence that is available now came from one side only (*ie* the Europeans), there is little direct evidence which shows how the slaves themselves communicated with each other in their attempts to remove their yoke. Recovery of such methods is partly a matter of examining measures introduced to obstruct slave communication and analysing comments made about such measures. Recovery of methods of communication among the slaves is also accomplished by examining traditional West African methods of communication, with an assumption that these would have been transmitted to the West Indies and could have had some influence on the methods used there. Such analyses, however, have to be based on twentieth century accounts of traditional West African culture.

In his account of traditional methods of communication in Africa, Nketia [1971], within a framework of what he calls "surrogate" languages and in relation specifically to noise-making instruments, makes the following observations:

... forms of communication based on sounds produced by instrumental means ... may be used

  (a) as signals which elicit specific behavior when interpreted as call signals, warning or alarm signals etc.,

  (b) and as sounds which give the aural impression of speech when ordered in specific ways and which can, therefore, be used for conveying messages.

In principle any sound producing instrument can be used for this purpose. In practice, however, only a few instruments are used, some more often than others, according to their effectiveness or the clarity of their forms of communication. The media generally used include

  (a) aerophones such as flutes, trumpets and whistles (to which one may add whistling with the lips)

(b) membranophones or drums with parchment heads,

and

(c) idiophones such as the slit gong (sometimes referred to in the literature as the slit drum) and double bells (p. 700).

In spite of these observations, we must not lose sight of the fact that slit gongs and drums are the most widely used 'talking' instruments in Africa (p. 700).

Nketia's observations suggest a great deal of creativity and adaptability in the creation and use of instruments on the part of Africans. This creativity would have been even more required in the West Indies where the Africans were removed from their familiar contexts and deprived of opportunity and milieu for a full use of traditional instruments.

It is in relation to slave revolts specifically that there is some measure of speculation about the extent of communication, the methods used in plotting and executing plots, and the relevance of traditional methods. It is enticing to imagine all kinds of secret methods of transmitting information, but in reality whereas it is possible that the hour of action could have been signalled by some secret code, it is highly unlikely that a detailed plot could have been worked out without a common language. Indeed, much of the actual evidence suggests that revolts were planned by persons sharing a common language, whether they were African slaves or creoles. The possibility of far-reaching, nonverbal, secret methods is not only a contradiction in terms, but also has little concrete evidence to support it.

Many of the laws which were passed very early were aimed at what the white rulers perceived as methods used by the slaves to plot against them. This is evident, for instance, in Robertson [1730: 46]: "Severe laws were made (particularly in Barbados, where the danger from them has always been greatest) against the slaves going armed with mischievous weapons, their beating of drums, blowing of horns or conch-shells . . ." Such a comment suggests that the slaves used drums, horns and conch-shells to communicate among themselves. Actual reported evidence of this is provided by the author of *Great Newes from the Barbados*, who, in his details of the conspiracy against the whites of Barbados in 1676, says:

Trumpets to be made of elephants teeth and gourdes to be sounded on several hills, to give notice of their general rising, with a full intention to fire the sugar-canes, and so run in and cut their masters throats in their respective plantations whereunto they did belong.

From this kind of report and from the general reaction by the whites (*ie* prohibition of their use), one assumes that in reality the use of such instruments to signal rebellion was quite common and that the belief that the instruments were calls to rebellion was not an ignorant conclusion based on fear. However, on reading Sloane [1707: lii] one gets the impression that there was no real evidence for this and that the prohibition was based on reports about the use of trumpets and drums among Africans in Africa:

> They formerly on their festivals were allowed the use of trumpets after their fashion, and drums ... But making use of these in their wars at home in Africa, it was thought too much inciting them to rebellion, and so they were prohibited by the customs of the island.

Furthermore, the wording of the law in 1736 in Montserrat against the use of instruments does not indicate that its intention was to lessen the possibilities of subversive communication between the slaves:

> [Owners who] shall suffer any slave to beat any drum or drums, or empty casks, or great gourds, or to blow horns, shells, or loud instruments, for the diversion or entertainment of slaves in his, her, their plantation, he she, or they shall forfeit twenty pounds ...

The intention of the law apparently was to control noise-making for the peace and quiet of the Whites. Even in the Southern states of America where the use of the drum declined because of whites' move to ban it there is no overwhelming evidence of the drum being used as a systematic form of subversive communication. [Sharp 1989: 149] makes the point that

> The beat of the drum, an integral part of black dance, largely died out in the South after the so-called Stono insurrection in South Carolina in 1739, when escaping slaves beat drums to rally participants. Fearing a secret drum communication system among blacks, slaveowners pressed for prohibition of slave assemblies and the use of drums.

In this case, as elsewhere, it was a matter of the belief of the slaveowners rather than an observed pattern of use among the slaves which led to prohibition. With reference to practice within Africa itself, there is no overwhelming support for the view that drums and horns were instruments of communication of information for hostile purposes. On the whole, the greater body of evidence indicates that the instruments were used for pleasure or to raise an alarm or to announce that something was about to start. The concept of 'talking' drums, conjuring up visions of hostile natives communicating with distant allies in preparation for war, may be somewhat of an illusion, for 'talking' drums are really related to the expression of music. The following comments from Herzog [1964: 312, 313, 314] should be noted:

> ... in Africa this signaling, usually on drums, is based on a direct transfer into a musical medium of spoken language-elements: pitch or tone, which is of fundamental importance in most African languages, and some other phonetic features.
>
> The language of signaling is, to some extent, a technical language.
>
> ... the bulk of signaling is apt to be practised and fully understood only by specialists.
>
> ... Signal-drumming is considered difficult by the natives.

What these observations show quite clearly is that detailed communication by drum could not have been general and widespread among the African slaves because most of them would not have been able to play or understand drums. In addition, even those who could would only have been able to understand drumming in their own language. What is a more likely reaction, by both slave and master in the West Indies, is identical to the one given by Herzog as characteristic of neighbouring villagers in West Africa: "Naturally, when a village hears these drums from the next village or tribe, it is at once clear that something is 'going on', either a meeting, or a warlike celebration, including a war dance, or actual preparations for war."

It is the familiar kind of reaction of the 'cowboys' in the 'cowboy and Indians' movies made about the nineteenth century USA. It is this kind of reaction which led the white masters in the West Indies and elsewhere to ban the use of the drum by African slaves.

In fact, it is ironic that it was probably the purpose for which trumpets and drums were used among white masters themselves, as military instruments, which caused them to ban their use among the slaves. Indeed, the ignorance and fear which fuelled the reactions of the white masters were at times taken to such extremes that many slaves suffered in the West Indies because the whites were suspicious of everything they did, said and wore. This point is made by M'Callum [1805: 131]:

Now, Sir, so timid, or otherwise so diabolically ignorant and depraved are the French and Spanish inhabitants of Trinidad, and so easy is Picton's mind influenced to sacrifice the life of a fellow-creature, which he seems to consider of no value, that he immediately believes all the trifles the Africans carry about them, are to assist some supernatural talent or other; this is sufficient to put them to death.

It was not necessarily the whites' fear of 'obeah' paraphernalia that brought obeah men and women into danger, but the perception that they had too much influence over the slaves and could even cause their death. It is true, moreover, that among the slaves themselves, within their belief system, certain objects took on supernatural significance. Edwards [1794, 2:92] reported that a 1760 Jamaican law specified that obeah objects were "blood, feathers, parrot's beaks, dog's teeth, alligator's teeth, broken bottles, grave-dirt, rum, and eggshells". Such objects were used not simply for 'spiritual' purposes, but for more practical ones. Edwards [1794, 2:93] speaks of "... other and more common tricks of *Obi*, such as hanging up feathers, bottles, eggshells, &c. &c. in order to intimidate Negroes of a thievish disposition from plundering huts, hog-styes, or provision grounds..." He says further [1794, 2:90]: "... the stoutest among them tremble at the very sight of the ragged bundle, the bottle or the eggshells, which are stuck in the thatch or hung over the door of a hut, or upon the branch of a plantain tree, to deter marauders".

The warding off of evil, in both spiritual and physical form, while it remained essentially a part of a nonlinguistic system of communication within the slave community, came into direct conflict with the overall power structure of the slave society and was progressively driven underground.

One visual method of communication among the slaves which was said to be used in cases of rebellion was fire, that is, setting fire to the sugar canes. Obviously the fire was more than a method of communication in that in itself it provoked fear and panic. However, it was said to be a signal for other slaves to follow suit and to do whatever had been planned, with the fire acting as a diversion. The start of the insurrection in Barbados in 1816 is described by Thome and Kimball [1838: 78] as follows: "A signal was given by a man setting fire to a pile of trash on an elevated spot, when instantly the fires broke out, in every direction, and in less than a half hour, more than one hundred estates were in flames." Fire, as a signal, was one isolatable happening in a chain of events. Although over time it might have acquired a meaning as a signal, it still had to be preceded by secret communication. Even so, it was not a flexible, reusable signal in the same sequence of events. It was therefore of limited usefulness, was only partly within the control of its users and gave them only a temporary sense of power.

Fire did not always signal collective, mass action over a number of plantations. The words of a song cited by Carmichael [1833, 2:301] indicate that fire was used as a diversionary tactic, even though Carmichael herself called the song "an insurrectionary song". In another reference to fire, in Easel [1840: 217], it seems as if it is not only a visual symbol but takes on a more symbolic character: ". . . nigger must be free, and fire shall light him to freedom dat night . . ."

There is no indication in the immediate context of fire being a signal for any kind of action. The impression given is that fire or more specifically the deliberate burning of canes had become a symbol of freedom for the slaves.

Beside the general, threatening methods of wider communication used by the slaves, Carmichael [1833, 2:29] mentions a minor symbolic one:

When a stranger goes into a boiling-house for the first time, the head boiler-man [a negro] comes up, and after making a bow, he takes a bit of chalk and makes a cross upon your shoe; intimating by this sign, that he is aware you never were in a boiling-house before, and that therefore a douceur is expected; you generally give him a dollar, and this he shares with the other two who are his assistants.

Mention of this symbolic method of communication means that the author thought it to be quaint and not used by the white population. There is no supporting evidence to suggest that it was general or long lasting or that it could have been part of a more elaborate system. Although it comes closer to writing (the use of chalk to make a mark) than other methods, since its purpose was to make a request of a person present, it was really a feature of face-to-face rather than distance communication.

In relation to features of cultural communication preserved by the slaves, writers have varied in their presentation of these. These were not features of direct interaction, but features which gave social and ethnic information. Some European writers were moved to comment on and illustrate the dress, hair styles, and facial and other body markings of the Africans. They pointed out that in the case of some of the Africans marks on the body, especially the face, indicated tribal relationships. This information, which for the African slaves themselves was a matter of preserving their identity, was for prospective slaveowners of economic importance, since slaves from different tribes were differently valued. For the creole slaves, who were acculturated into accepting European views of beauty, such marks were most likely regarded as disfigurations and the indelible badge of 'saltwater' negroes.

The fact that the literature of the day, especially newspaper advertisements for runaway slaves, referred to different tribes by their marks indicates that the tribal markings were quite distinctive. Note, for instance, that Sloane [1707: liv] could point out from his experience in Jamaica that "the Negros called Papas have most of these scarifications".

In Jamaica also, at the end of the century, an observation about and an interpretation of the function of the tribal marks was made by Edwards [1794, 2:124-25]:

The climate requires not the aid of dress, nor are the Negroes, though naked, destitute of decorations, on which, at their first arrival, they seem to set a much higher estimation than on raiment; most of the nations of Africa having their skin, particularly on the forehead, the breast, and round the waist, punctured or impressed with figures and representations of different kinds (squares, circles, triangles, and crescents) similar to the practice which prevails in *Otaheite*, and the other islands of the South Sea, called *tatowing*, as described in the voyages of Captain Cook. Like those islanders too, some of the newly-imported Negroes display these marks with a mixture of ostentation and pleasure, either considering them as highly ornamental, or appealing to them as testimonies of distinction in Africa; where, in some cases, they are said to indicate free birth and honourable parentage.

Carmichael [1833, 2:298] in her work on St Vincent and Trinidad identified both tatoos and tribal marks, but seemed to be distinguishing between the two by claiming that some African slaves voluntarily, for decorative purposes, put marks on themselves, marks which were tattoos rather than tribal marks:

Some few like to have their initials marked on their arms, and other figures pricked: but this is a fancy of their own. This is done by themselves for each other often, and sometimes they get white sailors to do it for them, with a needle and gunpowder, and a little indigo. The native African mark is admired by them: it is generally on the centre of the chest; and I think I have seen one or two such marks on the arm, and on the cheek. They told me that this tattooing was done in Africa, when they were young, that the marks might grow as they grew up. Creole negroes are never tattooed.

Bridgens' [1837] representations of Trinidad slaves carried illustrations of contrasting facial markings and in his explanation of how tattooing was done, he claimed that the tatoos were tribal marks: "The different tribes have each their peculiar pattern, which serves to identify the subjects of the different petty chiefs."

Although such marks cannot in any way be regarded as writing, it does show, however, that the idea that a deliberate mark can have an arbitrary meaning was within the culture of Africans brought to the West Indies and that indeed arbitrary marks were used to convey information.

In contrast to the facial markings used for ethnic distinction by the Africans, marks were used among Europeans from the earliest times for the purpose of identification of property. In fact, there seemed to have developed in the European mind a great need for personal emblems to mark swords, houses, shields, coins, medallions and all sorts of property. This also extended to live property like cows and sheep and horses. In the case of live property the method of marking employed was usually branding – the burning of initials or some familiar mark into the skin of the animal. This was also used by those Europeans who came to the New World for marking slaves. The justification for branding in the case of the slaves was that it allowed Whites, who could not tell the difference between great numbers of unfamiliar people who all looked alike to them, to keep a permanent and easily recognizable label on their property. According to this recognition theory, branding was practised more in the bigger islands because the numbers of (indistinguishable) African slaves were greater there. M'Queen [1825: 255] went as far as to say that branding was done for the protection of the African slave, who, if left unmarked, not being familiar with the surroundings and not being able to speak the language of the country, might get lost and even die. The mark would therefore allow a finder to return the slave to the safety and protection of his master. According to this reasoning, there was no need to brand creole slaves because they would have been familiar from birth to the master.

Some African slaves in the West Indies therefore were doubly marked, as is shown in an advertisement for two found slaves in the *St Christopher's Gazette* of Wednesday, 4 September 1765:

Taken up upon the honourable Gilbert Fame Fleming's Grange estate, two negroes, viz. one Mandingo negro man very black, about 5 feet 4 inches; and one ditto which calls himself John Constantine, marked with the bambara mark on his face and on his breast C/HE ... (p.1)

It would seem then that since the African's tribal marks were not culturally significant to the Europeans and were not for them clear indicators of personal possession, the owner's initials branded on the chest of slaves could more easily facilitate permanent identification and easy recovery of property by the white masters.

The method of branding used in Jamaica as well as the decline in the practice is mentioned by Edwards [1794, 2:126]:

It is the custom among some of the planters in Jamaica, to mark the initials of their name on the shoulder or breast of each newly-purchased Negro, by means of a small silver brand heated in the flame of spirits . . . but it is growing into disuse, and I believe in the Windward Islands thought altogether unnecessary.

Dickson [1789: 122], reacting to the practice of branding slaves in Jamaica, claimed that ". . . the practice of branding slaves does not disgrace the island of Barbados". Carmichael [1833, 2:300] also claimed that by the beginning of the nineteenth century branding was rare: "Mr. C. [the author's husband], who has been more or less in many of the islands of the West Indies, has never, during thirty years, seen but one branded negro; and he was the property of a Frenchman in St Lucia."

Whether or not branding decreased because it was not thought to be humane or because the Whites became more capable of recognizing their own slaves by sight or simply because the number of African slaves decreased, there is no doubt that while it lasted it was a demeaning and permanent symbol of enslavement. Yet, such initials would have become familiar to the slaves themselves and in a sense would have been their earliest introduction to reading.

Mode of dress is given a similar interpretation to tattooing by Joyner [1989: 148], who argues that: "The clothing worn by the earliest generations of Afro-Americans, the slaves, served as an outward symbol of group identity and of the individual's place within the group."

Such an interpretation could only relate to weekend clothes, however, seeing that the slaves had little control over their everyday work clothes. Joyner's assessment is that the slaves were making a statement by the way they dressed on weekends: "A significant function of costume is that of differentiating between the workaday world and the festive world . . . During the week they might belong to the master, but on Sundays they emerged as self-respecting men and women" [Joyner 1989: 148]. Even so, distinctions in style would have been constrained by materials available. In time, however, the creolization process fostered the desire to display individual style and flair more so than group characteristics.

CONCLUSION

Tribal marks and obeah paraphernalia were the most significant features of nonlinguistic communication among the slaves because they identified them as African. However, they had no chance of becoming a part of the symbolic culture of West Indian society or becoming associated with intellectual sophistication because they were in conflict with European values. Europeans preferred to convey information on profession and status through variation in clothing (*ie* colours, hats, epaulettes, belts) because clothing was a prerequisite for their climates. The African preference for marks on the body to indicate status and disposition could not survive the process of acculturation towards the wearing of clothing and make-up in the West Indies. Neither could branding, which was in a sense a combination of the European and the African elements. Obeah paraphernalia remained powerful symbolically among the slaves while the African element was dominant, but as the creole and Christian element grew, the teeth, bones and other objects gradually lost their symbolic power to be replaced by the Christian cross, incense, rosaries and other symbolic objects of the European churches. It is these that acquired sophistication because they were a part of the culture of those, that is, the Christian scribes, who had developed writing and literacy.

The use of guns and flags for communication by the rulers of the colonies was in no sense linguistic. The gravity and importance of such methods of communication were self-evident, but they had little or no effect on language. Guns and flags themselves were important in the society, but it was their other main uses for military and nationalistic purposes which assured this. There was no straight line of influence between the people making decisions, the decisions themselves, the medium through which the decisions were disseminated, and the language of the people for whom the decisions were intended, when the medium was not linguistic. Even when the medium was oral and the method of communication was by messenger, the line of influence was not unbroken because the language of the messenger was not exactly the language of the sender.

In the early West Indian plantation society, therefore, when the methods of general communication were principally oral and those of distance communication nonlinguistic, the variety of language produced by the powerful (London society English) did not dominate, because there was no linguistic medium through which it could radiate its influence throughout the society. Nonlinguistic and oral methods of wider communication left the various dialects in the society relatively untouched. The nonlanguage-based methods persisted for a long time because they satisfied the requirements of the people who used them and a society which changed little. While they were refined to make them more flexible, such refinements cannot be said to have advanced the society dramatically.

On the other hand, it cannot be said that the refinements constituted no advance whatsoever, as is made clear in an argument by Birdwhistell [1970: 88-91], who modifies an example of a simple colonial signalling system to highlight the problems of communication in real-life situations. Birdwhistell's example is the use of no light, one light and two lights in a church tower to signal no enemy approaching, enemy approaching by land, and enemy approaching by sea respectively. After pointing out a number of ways in which the signals can be tampered with or rendered ineffective in real-life situations, he concludes "Our alerting alarm system is simply too simple to meet the needs of the group" (p. 89). Birdwhistell then goes on to show how features may be added to make the system more reliable to compensate for deficiencies in participants and other shortcomings of the situation of communication. Birdwhistell shows that as more and more features are added "how much of a communicational system depends upon the proper internalization of the system" (p. 90).

What this means is that when signalling systems are simple, they can be quickly interpreted and there is no cognitive demand on the interpreter. In the case of more complex systems, the system takes longer to learn and interpretation is a relatively more taxing process. In this sense, then, the refinements can be said to have constituted intellectual advance.

In the plantation slave societies, therefore, even though the signalling systems (the use of guns, drums, flags) were nonlinguistic and very unsophisticated in comparison with language, the very evolution of the systems (different types of flags, combinations of different flags, combinations of flags and guns) represented the development of cognitive complexity in distance communication and, more importantly, communal interpretation of the meaning of signals. Yet, dependence on such methods of communication points to a society of isolated entities, little different in a sense from a feudal system. This essentially meant a fostering of isolated dialects through more direct face-to-face communication and less distance communication. Varieties of English therefore developed with the plantation as the first and fundamental unit of interaction in which shared experience and self-dependence obviated the need for more explicit and detailed systems of distance communication.

NOTES

1   Poyer [1808: xvi]. Quoted from *Williamson's Campaign in the West Indies*, p. 12. Said to be the "testimony of the Reverend Mr. Williams, vicar of Exning, in Suffolk").
2   This routine and the use of a bell to control it is later restated by Blome [1672: 86]. However, the closeness of the text to Ligon's suggests that Blome copied Ligon. Blome's reference to Ligon's book (p. 96) only serves to confirm this.

3

Aspects of Oral Culture in the Slave Population

The African slaves brought their culture with them in their heads when they crossed the Atlantic, but they had little time or opportunity to express it fully when they were inserted into the routine of plantation life in the islands. The only time they got to indulge in cultural pursuits was after they had done the master's work and after they had done their own work. During the week, it was after sunset and before sleeping time that social gatherings were possible. These took place in the open air and therefore were controlled by weather conditions and the cycle of the moon, seeing that the light of the full moon was the most favourable time for such gatherings. It was on Sundays, the traditional market day of the slaves, that daytime gatherings were possible and it was only at Christmas that they were allowed more than one day at a time to amuse and enjoy themselves, even though Christmas had become associated in the minds of Whites with slave revolts.[1] Besides Christmas, the only other annual festival which the slaves had, according to Stewart [1808: 262], was '*harvest-home*'. Whatever the slaves did had to be approved as safe or, more precisely, anything that was perceived as inimical to the well-being of whites or to the slaves' own capacity for work came under immediate threat. Under such strict limits, there was not a great extent and variety of cultural practices that they could develop with the means that were available to them as slaves.

In the plantation slave society collective participation in social and cultural events by slaves was for the most part discouraged, especially if it involved speaking as the main activity. The slaves could not gather in large groups for religious or other 'educational' purposes, although Smith [1745: 229], while dealing with Montserrat, makes reference to big, all-African gatherings in Jamaica:

I am told, that at Jamaica, the Negroes have, what they call, a hearing, in some Guinea tongue, *ie* one of the most knowing of them, teaches all the rest in a long speech. This assembly, may consist of four or five hundred blacks.

Such gatherings are not reported anywhere else in the West Indies and could not have been common, seeing that the whites feared that any time the black slaves came together they would plan some kind of revolt. Transmission of knowledge and regeneration of culture had to be done in small groups and plantation by plantation. The plantation, then, for the slave, became a small society within a society and it is within this small society that slave culture and language had to evolve. In spite of the limitations, it was a culture that was of necessity live as well as social – it was moulded and defined by direct participation and interaction, while its evolution was basically determined by the two types of slaves, Africans and Creoles.

Community cultural expression was dependent on and facilitated by a common language, which meant that the features of culture which African slaves brought which were language specific disappeared or were altered significantly because no specific African language became a community language in the islands, except in the case of maroon communities, and even in such communities the African language eventually gave way to a creole language. In addition, as the number of creole slaves increased, the incorporation of European cultural items into the culture of the slaves increased correspondingly. From the very restricted early society in which nonlinguistic methods were austere and almost inflexible and in which day to day communication must have been taxing, there developed a culture among the slaves which manifested a reduction of differences among them and the forging of a common medium of communication which was flexible enough to allow for both African and Creole input. A description of aspects of the oral culture of the slaves therefore affords a view of the vitality of the medium of communication which developed and the major contexts which it had to serve. For the plantation slaves, these contexts of communication were the fields, the plantation house, the plantation yard, and the negro yard. For all slaves, major contexts of communication were markets, dances, burials and annual festivals, activities which cut across plantations and which were also a part of urban life.

THE INTRODUCTION INTO SLAVE WORK CULTURE

During the first hundred years of the island colonies, European writers repeatedly identified differences between the African slaves and reflected the white colonists' preference for and possibly encouragement of the maintenance of hostility between slaves of different nations. This is evident in the remarks of Robertson [1730: 94]:

36 / *From Oral to Literate Culture*

FIGURE 3.1: A Negro Festival drawn from nature in the island of St Vincent

Our safety, as I take it, lies not a little in this, that as our slaves are brought from different countries, so they perfectly hate one another, and are ever clashing and jarring; and tho' for good reasons we do not encourage or foment their dissensions, yet it would be ridiculous, as the case is, to pretend to put a force on their temper, and to make them love one another whether we can or no.

On the other hand, writers noted that there was a general practice of orienting new Africans into the slave community on each plantation. This was identified by Edwards [1794, 2:126-27] as a practice in Jamaica and in the smaller islands a little later by Resident [1828: 71], who said: "The newly-imported negroes . . . were put under the charge of the *old negroes*, to be taught the requisite duties."

This period of orientation or seasoning would, over time, have reduced the differences and tensions between the Africans to some degree. This kind of 'apprenticeship' – the young or new African under the tutelage of the old, seasoned and retired – must have been seen as necessary by the masters, even though it worked against their notion of 'divide and rule'. As a force for the transmission of culture, this 'apprenticeship' facilitated the maintenance of some old elements and the acquisition of new ones. It was a system of training that was also used for the creole slave.

In the case of the creole slaves, that is, those born into the system of plantation slavery, the first major pre-adult context was the estate nursery. This was a creature of the plantation system because the rearing of children on a sugar plantation had to fit in with the workings and purpose of the plantation structure. The children of slaves could not reduce the output of their mothers unduly, which meant that mothers had to be back at work four weeks after giving birth. As a result, some mothers carried their infants with them strapped to their backs or put them in the furrows in the field in which they were working. It was only when the children could walk and move about on their own that they could be put in the care of others. In some cases the mothers left their children with old relatives when they went back out to work. Few of these old relatives were fluent or competent English speakers, although they understood and communicated with English speakers from time to time. Wentworth [1834, 2:16] gives an example of an 'African negress' who cared for her grandchildren while their mother was away at work. This specific individual carried on a conversation with Wentworth in her own creolized speech, which she no doubt used in interacting with her charges.

In most cases children were left in the estate nursery, which was the place where, in the words of Resident [1828: 72], "the children are taken care of, during their mother's absence in the field, by the old women no longer equal to field-labour". It was here, then, that the creole culture of the community was regenerated and it was here that the language of the community developed. The two important elements for language acquisition in the estate nursery were the old woman as linguistic model and the peer group as the controlling social force. It is quite likely that, even in cases where there was not a change in colonial power and therefore of official language, the language of the older slaves differed from the peer group language of the younger ones. The children were therefore being directly exposed to a model of language which contained older features. In the French-influenced islands of Grenada, Dominica, Trinidad and St Lucia these older women were most likely not fluent speakers of any form of English, which meant that the movement towards English would have been delayed even further. It was the fact of the 'missing' middle generation in the estate nursery which decreased both the rate of culture change and the speed of language evolution in the community in the acculturation process.

Beside its bringing together of the old and the young, the estate nursery as a peer group context for the young allowed for more creativity in culture and language, and was more influential than the children's interaction with adults in and around the negro yard. During their period in the estate nursery the children spent more of their waking hours away from their relatives than they did with them. It was also during this period that they provided amusement for and otherwise interacted with the white children of the plantation, as a result of which it was possible to get the kind of liaison expressed in the words of a slave in Ramsay [1784: 252]: "Master, I was bred up with you from a child; I was your play-mate when a boy; I have loved you as myself..."

The period in the nursery lasted only until the children could begin to do light work, that is, until they reached around six years old, but this period was precisely when the children acquired the basic shape of their native language. The estate nursery was therefore the most important context for language acquisition in the life of a creole plantation slave.

After the nursery the children moved into a system of gangs based in the first stages on age and at the final stage on ability. Supervision by an old lady continued on into the first working gang for children, after which they had to begin to fend for themselves, as [Dickson 1789: 12] explains:

After the children on estates are weaned, and are able to run about, they are often put under the management of a careful old woman, and are employed in the picking of vines, insects, &c. for the small feathered flock. Hence they are called the hog-meat-gang, or the pot-gang, from their being fed with dressed victuals ... From the hog-meat gang, they are translated into what is called the little gang, which is employed in weeding, collecting grass, and other light work, till the individuals who compose it are able to take their station in the great gang, a transition which compleats the hardship and misery of a field negro.

The transition from *hog-meat gang* to *little gang* to *great gang* given by Dickson is only slightly different from another version of gang structure and hierarchy in the last quarter of the eighteenth century which is given by Tobin [1785: 77-79]:

... secondly, the small gang, in which are included negroes in more advanced life, young ones growing up, and women who have sucking children; and lastly, the grass gang, consisting of hardy young children, who are employed, under the care of an old woman, in gathering grass for horses and other stock, chiefly to keep them out of mischief, and to use them to an early regularity ... and there is also an elderly woman constantly in the field, to do nothing else than attend the sucking children, when their mothers are employed.

This kind of age grading and division into gangs could not but promote the development of different registers and varieties to correspond to the interests and activities of the individuals concerned. This was so especially in the gangs intermediate between the nursery and the adult stage when the slaves maturationally were most active and creative. Introduction of children into the work rhythm of the plantation by their elders was intended to ensure a benign start to slave work, but it also ensured the perpetuation of the culture of the community. It effected an integration of children into slave culture – regimen by bells or horns, recognition and verbal acknowledgement of superiors, working in concert with peers, participation and cooperation in the singing of work songs and other activities in the fields.

The graduation of the creole slave from under the tutelage of the old to a place in the great gang was complemented by the graduation of the new African from under his elderly tutor to a place in the great gang. Here again, differences between Creoles and Africans were reduced by daily communication. Although the fields would seem to have been a contrast to the privileged positions in the yard and house and the worst place to be, it did not mean that working in the fields was a totally negative experience. The fields were the place where the field slaves spent most of their life and they learnt to make the most of it; they learnt to lighten their unending drudgery. One of the well-known ways that they did this is explained by [Smith 1745: 230-31] in the following way:

The Negroes, when at work, in howing canes, or digging round holes to plant them in, (perhaps forty persons in a row) sing very merrily, *ie* two or three men with large voices, and a sort of base tone, sing three or four short lines, and then the rest join at once, in a sort of chorus, which I have often heard, and seemed to be, La, Alla, La, La, well enough, and indeed harmoniously turned, especially when I was a little distance from them.

There is an interesting resemblance between the cited words of this song and those in an observation made by Edwards [1794, 2:61]:

... and he [a Mandingo slave] has not forgot the morning and evening prayer which his father taught him; in proof of this assertion, he chaunts, in an audible and shrill tone, a sentence that I conceive to be part of the Alcoran, *La illa, ill illa!* [There is no God, but God] which he says they sing aloud at the first appearance of the new moon.

There is some evidence here to suggest that the work song, with its call-and-response technique, had some Muslim and literary influence from the Koran, seeing that the response, that is, what Smith called *a sort of chorus*, could actually have been the Muslim response, which Edwards suggested. No doubt the religious element in the songs, acted out with call and response in a situation of oppression, bonded the slaves into a working unit and a social group. Atwood [1791: 258] almost fifty years later underlined the positive elements of creativity, competitiveness, and gender distinction in this singing: "... the women singing some ludicrous songs of their own composing, which are answered in the same manner by the men, and each striving to outdo the other".

This kind of mass participation and feeling of society made the fields more attractive than at first can be imagined, so much so that the fields could actually appear to be a preferred place. In fact, Carmichael [1833, 2:200-201] put forward the following argument: "The fact is, that negro women like the gossip and the fun of the field; and to stay at home and nurse their child is too monotonous and dull a life for them."

A more objective explanation of the reasons for the women's return to the field is that they were required to by their owners for whom their production was more important than their nurturing of babies. It is conceivable, however, that in the argument about the attractiveness of the fields there could have been a germ of truth.

In any case, in spite of their differences, a spirit of comradeship and empathy developed between the field slaves as they experienced their brutalization together. They may have occasionally turned their frustrations and resentments inward on themselves, but over the period of slavery they moved from being displaced Africans of different nations hostile to each other to being communities of slaves, so much so that Stedman [1806, 2:293] could observe the camaraderie between them beyond the fields in their moments of leisure and could say, with some slight exaggeration of reality:

No people can more esteem or have a greater friendship for one another than the negro slaves, they appear to have unbounded enjoyment in each other's company, and are not destitute of social amusements, such as soesa, which consists in footing opposite to each other, and clapping with their hands upon their sides to keep in time.

This was a view of slaves in Suriname but it was little different from that in the islands.

INDICATORS OF STATUS AND ATTITUDE IN THE SLAVE COMMUNITY

Clearly, the use of the veteran to instruct the novice and the old to control and teach the young had some positive effects in the building of plantation 'village' community. It is not surprising, then, that respect for age and experience was a basic feature of the expression of social manners among the slaves. The expression of social manners, in the form of terms of address and greetings, is explained by Wentworth [1834, 2:201]:

One negro will seldom meet another on the road, even if he have no immediate knowledge of him, without stopping to speak, or in passing, exchanging a salutation, and they invariably pay respect to old age . . .

The relative family names among them are, *old granta*, grand-mother; *old daddy*, grandfather; *daddy*, father; *mammy*, mother; *sissy*, sister; *buddy*, brother; *unco*, uncle; *ante*, aunt. All of these names, excepting the last two, are frequently applied to each other, as a mark of respect, according to their relative ages, without regard to consanguinity.

Whether or not such features were typical of the West African societies from which the slaves came, the state of slavery made the mere recognition of status through age and service even more important for the self-respect of all concerned because there were few other privileges and rewards available for slaves to give to those whom they held in high esteem.

Beside the respect accorded to the elderly, respect was also paid to persons according to their position. Jobs in the plantation house and in the plantation yard were more specialized than those in the fields and socially superior because they brought the slaves into daily contact with their masters. It was usually creole slaves who worked as carpenters, coopers, blacksmiths and masons. Such jobs were important on the plantation because they required expertise and those who performed such tasks were therefore superior socially to others whose tasks were less specialized. Carmichael [1833, 1:282] points out one way in which superior position was recognized in social manners:

Drivers (that is, black overseers), head boilermen, head coopers, carpenters or masons, head servants, these are all Mr. so and so: a field negro, if asked to go and tell a boilerman to come to his master, returns and says – Massa, Mr. ___ will be here directly. They say, 'Ma'am' to a domestic servant . . .

Jobs such as nannies, cooks, attendants, washers and drivers which involved personal contact with the masters and mistresses were the most privileged positions and such persons usually insisted on recognition of their status, which, unlike the respect paid to the elderly, was not always willingly accorded.

Even less spontaneous and less genuine in many cases was the oral expression of respect paid by the slave to the master, for the power relationship between slave and master forced the slave into a substantial amount of dissembling. Since slaves were in a situation where any perceived act of subordination brought swift and violent punishment, they had to put a brave face on everything. The smiling face of the Negro was the one which provided Whites with evidence to say that the slaves were happy, especially since it was accompanied by overheard jokes and laughter when the slaves gathered together among themselves. This notion of the happy, carefree slave is expressed by Pinckard [1806, 1:289]: "This happy negro-yard forms, as it were, a little village of sixteen families, all of whom may assemble, each evening, after the labour of the day, to join in the merry dance, or smoke and sing together, free from every care."

Yet, whites also constantly said that the slaves were lying and deceitful, which meant that they realized that the smiling face was just a smiling face which hid anger, pain and suffering. They knew that the words coming out of the face did not reflect true feelings when they were addressed to any superior. As Edwards [1794, 2:77] said:

If a Negro is asked even an indifferent question by his master, he seldom gives an immediate reply; but, affecting not to understand what is said, compels a repetition of the question, that he may have time to consider, not what is the true answer, but what is the most politic one for him to give.

Whites suspected that in their gatherings the slaves mocked the white man and they knew that news from the big house, personal or general, was transmitted to the mass of the field slaves. This bred a spirit of uneasiness among the white masters, who felt compelled to continue to implement more and more measures of control and punishment.

The slave's distrust of the master concealed from the Whites a considerable amount of knowledge which the slaves had either brought with them from Africa, and passed on from generation to generation or had acquired in the Caribbean. Fermin, a doctor in Suriname, noted [1769, 1:212], for example, the great difficulty of getting medical information from slaves:

Je me suis, maintefois, adressé à plusieurs Esclaves noirs, qui sont experts dans la connoissance de nombre de ces plantes; mais ce peuple est si jaloux de son scavoir, que tout ce que j'ai pu faire, soit par argent, ou par caresses, m'a été inutile; & que je n'en ai jamais pu persuader un de m'instruire, à quelque condition que ce fut.[2]

It is only rarely through direct questioning that this knowledge was revealed, an instance of which is given by Edwards [1794, 2:67]:

She informed me also, in answer to some other inquiries, of a remarkable fact (i.e.), that the Natives of the Gold Coast give their children the *yaws*, (a frightful disorder) *by inoculation*; and she described the manner of performing the operation to be making an incision in the thigh, and putting in some of the infectious matter. I asked her what benefit they expected from this practice? She answered, that by this means their infants had the disorder slightly, and recovered speedily, whereas by catching it at a later time of life, the disease, she said, 'got into the bone', that was her expression.

It is probably because medical knowledge was not distinct from religious practice among the slaves and 'obeah', which Whites were so hostile towards, that its details were kept secret to a few and in fact virtually disappeared as the acculturation process proceeded.

CULTURAL ACTIVITIES

(a) Storytelling

The bond between the slaves as well as the slaves' duplicity towards their superiors and masters manifested themselves in the oral cultural arts of the slaves. On the plantation, gatherings of slaves outside their houses after work involved persons of all ages. During this period of the day, while they were eating the slaves would talk, tell stories and sing. It was during this period that slaves of all types communicated with each other – the young and the old, those who worked in the fields, the yard and the house. In addition, those who went to town on errands or with their masters relayed the news of the happenings in the town to those on the plantation. A description of such an after-work gathering is given by Lanigan [1844: 171]:

Sounds of every description fill the air, as soon as 'evening grey' sets in. Parties of negroes, men, women, and children, gather together in groups, worthy the illustrative pencil of Cruikshank, to gabble away their *nancy stories*, relate their quarrels, or discuss the other business of the day.

In contrast to the harshness of the daily news from town or plantation, storytelling was an occasion of respite from immediate problems and a time to create a different, fictitious world. Storytelling was for the slaves one of the main ways of educating the young and of passing on their culture, beliefs and values. It involved play-acting, audience participation, formulas, proverbs, expressions and words for special items of culture, flora and fauna. The subject matter in the cultural expression of the slaves was characterized by battles between the strong and the weak, in which very often the weak managed to outwit the strong. This was of course in part a fantasized reversal of reality. In this oral literature there was a dominance of animal characters, real in the context of the Caribbean as well as imagined, that is, foreign to the Caribbean and Africa. The characters were also given anthropomorphic qualities to go along with their stereotypical animal qualities. This attested to a lively imagination among the composers. A diversity of animals was used to reflect the diversity of the people in the plantation society. Storytelling provided lessons of achievement of success through guile rather than through power or brute strength. It also provided lessons about the avoidance of direct physical confrontation with those of superior strength, the ability to use and manipulate words to win battles, and more generally the need to employ 'guerrilla' tactics to circumvent and survive danger. On the other hand, it also, in its supernatural aspect, provided lessons of fatalism and resignation.

(b) Proverbs

One of the elements occurring naturally in storytelling was proverbs, but the kind of terse and practical philosophy embodied in proverbs was not restricted to storytelling contexts; proverbs were also a normal part of everyday exchanges between slaves. The slaves' facility with language and their ability to encapsulate general truths in short sentences seemed to surprise Europeans. For the Europeans, the proverbs of the slaves were new not only in their conceptualization but also in their form. For the slaves, the proverbs were most likely, in most cases, not new in their conceptualization, but certainly so in their form. In other words, the encapsulated wisdom of the Africans, which had been transmitted to the islands, acquired a new creolized English form. For the Europeans, then, they were like a new stock of proverbs in English, which not even the most prejudiced among them could claim to have come from Europe. The English reaction to the proverbs of the slaves is best illustrated in the words of Stewart [1808: 247-48]:

> ... yet they will often express, in their own way, a wonderfully acute conception of things. These conceptions they sometimes compress into short and pithy sentences, something like the sententious proverbs of the Europeans, to which many of them bear an exact analogy. These sayings often convey an astonishing force and meaning; and would, if clothed in a more courtly dress, make no despicable figure even among those precepts of wisdom which are ascribed to the wisest of men. When they wish to imply, that a peaceable man is often wise and provident in his conduct, they say, 'Softly water run deep': when they would express the oblivion and disregard which follows us after death, they say, 'When man dead grass grow in him door'; and when they would express the humility which is the usual accompaniment of poverty, they say, 'Poor man never vex'.

By the time of Emancipation, the prevalence of proverbs was noted by Wentworth who remarked on one occasion that "this is one of the numerous proverbs of the negroes..." [1834, 2:14]; and again later referred to "their semi-civilized proverbs and quaint sententious remarks..." [1834, 2:199].

Language which contains such folk wisdom gives weight to utterances among all peoples and, according to Wentworth's condescending second comment above, makes them seem civilized, but the frequent use of proverbs in normal conversation among the slaves in the West Indies was both evidence of the survival of a strong cultural characteristic from West Africa and, as well, a case where proverbs fitted in perfectly with the succinctness of the developing creole language, the variable language situation and the sharply stratified society in which the slaves found themselves. This was not a cultural feature that was restricted to plantation slaves, it was one which stretched beyond the plantation to link all slaves together in their characteristic language use.

(c) Speech Making

Contrasting with the short and fixed form of proverbs as well as the seriousness of the advice they normally encapsulated was the creative and lighthearted use of words which began to develop among the slaves in the eighteenth century and which was later to become an integral part of the performance culture of the descendants of the slaves in various islands. Long [1774, 2:426-27] gave what was probably the earliest evidence of this:

> The better sort are very fond of improving their language, by catching at any hard word that the Whites happen to let fall in their hearing; and they alter and misapply in a strange manner; but a tolerable collection of them gives an air of knowledge and importance in the eyes of their brethren, which tickles their vanity, and makes them more assiduous in stocking themselves with this unintelligible jargon.

For Long to have noticed this kind of usage and regarded it as common among *the better sort* meant that it must have been for some time a characteristic of slave behaviour. Edwards twenty years later [1794, 2:83] was more expansive and positive in his comments on this kind of usage:

> Among other propensities and qualities of the Negroes must not be omitted their loquaciousness. They are fond of exhibiting set speeches, as orators by profession; but it requires a considerable share of patience to hear them throughout; for they commonly make a long preface before they come to the point; beginning with a tedious enumeration of their past services and hardships. They dwell with peculiar energy (if the fact admits it) on the number of children they have presented to *Massa (Master)*, after which they recapitulate some of the instances of particular kindness shewn them by their owner or employer, adducing these also as proofs of their own merit; it being evident, they think, that no such kindness can be gratuitous. This is their usual exordium, as well when they bring complaints against others, as when they are called upon to defend themselves; and it is in vain to interrupt either plaintiff or defendant. Yet I have sometimes heard them convey much strong meaning in a narrow compass: I have been surprised by such figurative expressions, and (notwithstanding their ignorance of abstract terms) such pointed sentences, as would have reflected no disgrace on poets and philosophers. One instance recurs to my memory, of so significant a turn of expression in a common labouring Negro, who could have had no opportunity of improvement from the conversation of White people, as is alone, I think, sufficient to demonstrate that Negroes have minds very capable of observation.

It is interesting to note firstly that these comments about the loquaciousness of the slaves are similar in some respects to comments made by Antonio de Ulloa [1792: 282-83] about the native inhabitants of North and South America. It is also interesting to note that Edwards was familiar with Ulloa's writings, having quoted him earlier in the volume (pp. 13, 16, 24). Although this casts some doubt on the total authenticity of the comments about the speeches of the slaves, there is enough detail to suggest that what Edwards described was not concocted.

Edwards here partly discounts the suggestion made earlier by Long that the expressions used by the slaves were imitations of Whites and, by identification of structure and purpose in the speeches, Edwards also discounts the idea of Long that they were *unintelligible jargon*. The observation that they were *set speeches* and the slaves as if *orators by profession* clearly moved these performances beyond the extemporaneous and revealed a purposeful facility with language among the slaves. As Edwards explains, the slave on occasion chose to impress or wear down the master with words but he could also be witty and pointed. The pointedness of the slave's comment (*Sleep hab no Massa*), given in the illustration which followed the citation above, has the brevity of proverbs but a freshness which comes from the slave himself. Obviously not all slaves had a facility with words and those who did no doubt employed it to the fullest, thereby gaining the admiration of those who appreciated it or also benefitted from it.

Stewart [1808: 248-49] repeats much of what Edwards said about the length and structure of the slaves' speeches addressed to whites, but he also repeats Long's view that the slaves copied their masters, even though in a different context. The context was the parties which some of the slaves could afford and it was specifically creole slaves that Stewart [1808: 266] identified as those who imitated the whites:

The Creole negroes affect much to copy the manners, language, &c. of the whites; those who have it in their power, have, at times, their convivial parties; when they will endeavour to mimic their masters in their drinking, their songs, and their toasts; and it is curious to see with what an awkward minuteness they aim at such imitations. The author recollects having given an entertainment to a party of negroes, who had resided together, and had been in habits of intimacy for twenty years or more. After a variety of curious toasts, and some attempts to entertain each other with European songs, one, who conceived himself more knowing and accomplished than the rest, stood up and very gravely drank, 'Here's to our *better acquaintance*, gentlemen!'

The oral behaviour described here is very close to those of the late nineteenth and early twentieth centuries' 'tea meetings' which are regarded as the typical contexts for performance English. This kind of party, referred to as *an entertainment*, as well as what Beckford [1790, 1:388] called "a public assembly, at which every person pays a stipulated sum at admittance" took place on Christmas day.

(d) Christmas and New Year's Festivities

Besides such parties, aping of the manners and customs of whites was even more generally done at Christmas, which was the major holiday period for the slaves. It is again Stewart [1808: 262] in Jamaica who provides a view of this behaviour:

On this occasion [Christmas], these poor people appear as it were quite another race. They shew themselves off to the greatest advantage, by fine clothes, and a profusion of trinkets; they affect a genteeler behaviour, and more select and correct mode of speech; they address the whites with greater familiarity; they come into their master's houses, and drink with them – the distance between them appears to be annihilated for the moment, like the familiarity footing on which the Roman slaves were with their masters at the feast of the Saturnalia; to which a West India Christmas may be compared . . .

Williams [1827: 22] also relates similar Christmas activities twenty years later in Jamaica. Imitation of whites also seemed to be the main preoccupation at an event which was restricted to women, which Beckford [1790, 1:389-90] first identified as a Christmas event which took place on the plantations: "At Christmas the negroes upon neighbouring estates are divided, like other communities, into different parties: some call themselves the blue girls, and some the red: and their clothes are generally characteristic of their attachment."

However, according to Stewart [1808: 263-64], it took place on New Year's day and it was essentially an urban event:

On new year's day it was customary for the negro girls of the towns (who conceive themselves far superior to those on the estates, in point of *taste, manners, and fashion*) to exhibit themselves in all pride of gaudy splendor, under the denomination of *blues* and *reds* parties in rivalship and opposition to each other, and distinguished by these colours ... The most comely young negresses were selected, and such as had a fine and tutored voice; they paraded through the streets ... They were accompanied by instrumental music; but they generally sung together different songs which they had learned for the occasion, or those which they had caught up from the whites, in a style far superior to the negresses on the plantations.

Williams [1827: 63-64] also identified it as taking place on New Year's day and ending in town, but not necessarily restricted to town women:

Each party wears an appropriate colour, one red, the other blue, of the most expensive materials they can afford. They select two queens, the prettiest and best shaped girls they can find, who are obliged to personate the royal characters, and support them to the best of their power and ideas. .. Each party has a procession (but not so as to encounter each other) with silk flags and streamers, in which the queen is drawn in a phaeton, if such a carriage can be procured, or any four-wheeled vehicle which can pass for a triumphal car, that her person may be seen to the best advantage. Thus they parade the towns, priding themselves on the number of their followers, until the evening, when each party gives a splendid entertainment, at which every luxury and delicacy that money can procure are lavished in profusion ... and the evening is concluded with a ball ... There were many free people of colour. The men were very well dressed, and conducted themselves with the greatest propriety.

These performances were essentially two-voice events – in appearance they were imitations of white upper class behaviour and in effect they were realizations of the slaves at their grandest, at their most beautiful and using the most cultured language.

This event, though it seemed to have declined for some time in Jamaica, had parallels in Barbados and in St Lucia. In the case of St Lucia, the competition between the Roses (reds) and the Marguerites (blues), which is described by Breen [1844: 191-200], had already become a national festival by the middle of the nineteenth century and remained so there, in contrast to Jamaica. In the case of Barbados, the element of competition between two rival camps seemed to have declined into a general competition and fashion parade which survived in the form of a display of clothes and finery on Christmas morning in the urban centre of Queen's Park in Bridgetown. Elements of the event also give a foretaste of the display and competition between bands on parade in Carnival.

The activities among the slaves in Jamaica at Christmas and on New Year's day, which Beckford, Stewart and Williams described, seemed to be far removed from and not deserving of the comments made by Poole in Barbados about fifty years earlier:

Dec. 26 ... It now being Holiday-Time here with the Negroes, it makes them very noisy, reprobate, and disagreeable ... [1753: 217].

Dec 27 There is such a continual Cabal now here with the Negroes, that it makes it very disagreeable; and, what much adds thereto, is that they are so very reprobate, Cursing and Swearing so horribly, as even nearly to equal the **Gibraltar** Soldiers [1753: 218].

There is no mention here of finery or splendour or competitive imitation of Europeans. It is true that the attitudes of Europeans to the behaviour and practices of the slaves coloured the presentation of aspects of their culture and that those who frowned on the slaves' 'misuse' of Sundays and the church holidays of Christmas and Easter usually found the slaves' activities distasteful. Such was the case with the religious-minded Englishman, Poole. It must be assumed, moreover, that Poole's repeated mentioning of slaves cursing and swearing, here and elsewhere, was based on a correct understanding of what the slaves were actually saying. Yet, in order to give Poole's remarks some significance, one could surmise that in the middle of the eighteenth century cultural activities among the slaves had not developed into the more elaborate festivities which they were when Williams described them in 1827. In other words, the number of creole slaves and their penchant for imitation had not yet become dominant in the creolization and acculturation process.

(e) *The 'Cullunjee'*

An aspect of slave culture which was common to all slaves, which was fascinating to Europeans and extensively commented on was the slaves' love of music, dancing and singing. Beside work songs, which attracted the attention of English writers from the middle of the eighteenth century, there was also the singing during the freetime of the slaves which was an accompaniment to music and dancing. Ligon [1657: 48] had an appreciative reaction in the early years of colonization in Barbados to the skill of the slaves on the drums:

In the afternoons on *Sundayes*, they have their Musick, which is of kettle drums, and those of several sizes; upon the smallest the best Musitian playes, and the other come in as Chorasses: the drum all men know, has but one tone; and therefore variety of tunes have little to do in this musick; and yet so strangely they varie their time, as 'tis a pleasure to the most curious ears, and it was to me one of the strangest noises that ever I heard made of one tone; and if they had the variety of tune, which gives the greater scope in Musick, as they have of time, they would do wonders in that Art.

Leslie [1740: 310], almost a century later, presented a different kind of 'combo' in Jamaica:

They have other musical instruments, as a *Bangil*, not much unlike our Lute in any thing but the Musick; and the *Rookaw*, which is Two Sticks jagged; and a *Jenkgoving*, which is a way of clapping their hands on the Mouth of Two Jars: These are all played together, accompanied with Voices . .

Stedman [1806, 2:296], speaking of the slaves in Suriname at the end of the eighteenth century, not only gave a little more musical detail but also provided a probable etymology for what is called a *tuk band* in Barbados:

. . . they always use full or half measure, but never triple time, in their dancing music, which is not unlike that of a baker's bunt, when he separates the flour from the bran, sounding tuckety-tuck and tuckety-tuck ad perpetuum. To this noise they dance with uncommon pleasure, and most times foot it away with great art and dexterity . . .

The details given by Ligon, Leslie and Stedman only begin to show how the slaves managed to reconstruct their musical culture with the materials available and within the limits placed on them.

An urban setting for the cultural event of the slaves which combined music, dancing and singing is given by Pinckard [1806, 1:264]:

They assemble, in crowds, upon the open green, or in any square or corner of the town, and forming a ring in the centre of the throng, dance to the sound of their beloved music, and the singing of their favorite African yell . . . Together with these noisy sounds, numbers of the party of both sexes bawl forth their dear delighting song with all possible force of lungs; and from the combination, and *tout ensemble* of the scene, a spectator would require only a slight aid from fancy to transport him to the savage wilds of Africa.

While Pinckard's last comment was clearly meant to be uncomplimentary, the similarity between the cultural expression of the slaves in the West Indies and that of their relations in West Africa can be seen in the following description of activities on the coast of West Africa by Matthews [1966: 99-100]:

. . . both sexes are passionately fond of dancing, which they never fail to enjoy when they have a light moon and fair weather, from an hour after sun-set, til midnight. Besides this, the birth of a child, or the arrival of a friend or relation, furnishes them with an opportunity of enjoying their favourite amusement of singing and dancing, which they term a *cullunjee*.

Matthews' term *cullunjee* apparently did not survive in the West Indies, but the activity and its centrality in the slaves' culture certainly did.

There seemed to be little else beside the 'cullunjee' that slaves had as adult social events for enjoyment. There was mention of *private theatricals* by Resident [1828: 37] in his comments about entertainment among the slaves in 1796:

At the time to which these remarks chiefly apply, reels were the favourites; to these, have succeeded the country-dance, and even the quadrille; and, in some of the colonies, so *refined* has the taste of the slave-population become, that their amusements are varied by the introduction of *private theatricals*.

Unfortunately, there is no evidence of such *private theatricals* and what they involved, although what he most likely meant was the bands of the 'reds' and 'blues'.

There is mention of *plays* by Beckford [1790, 1:392] and an explanation given by Stewart [1808: 261]:

> Plays, as they call them, is their principal and favourite one [amusement]. This is an assemblage of both sexes, who form a ring round a male and female dancer, who perform to the music of their drums, and the songs of the other females of the party, one alternately going over the song, while her companions repeat in chorus. Both the singers and dancers shew the exactest precision as to time and measure . . . When two dancers have fatigued themselves pretty well, a second couple enter the ring, and thus the amusement continues.

However, these *plays* do not seem to have been substantially different from the 'cullunjee'.

(f) Serious Songs

In addition to singing which accompanied dancing (in the 'cullunjee'), there was also a more 'serious' type in which the words of the songs were much more meaningful. Renny [1807: 169] in almost the same words as Edwards [1794, 2:85] identified this kind of singing in the following way: "At their merry meetings, they have songs and ballads, adapted to such occasions, in which they give a full scope to a talent for ridicule, of which they are possessed in an uncommon degree..."

A little earlier, Edwards had described the songs, saying: "Their songs are commonly *impromptu*, and there are among them individuals who resemble the *improvisatori*, or extempore bards, of Italy . . . most of their songs at these places are fraught with obscene ribaldry..." [1794, 2:85].

It was not only at *their merry meetings* that such songs were sung, for Williams [1827: 23] mentions such songs as part of the Christmas celebrations when the slaves went into the big house and 'fraternized' with their masters and mistresses: "The merriment became rather boisterous as the punch operated, and the slaves sang satirical philippics against their master, communicating a little free advice now and then; but they never lost sight of decorum . . ."

As a result, whites were quite familiar with the derisive songs of the slaves and in fact showed a keen interest in them.

One of the earliest illustrations of this aspect of the oral culture of the slaves in the eighteenth century was produced by a white Kittitian, Samuel Mathews, who prided himself on being able to speak the 'negro dialect', play their instruments as well as compose and sing their songs. One of the songs cited in Mathews [1793: 138-39] and said to be "in great vogue among the Negroes" is repeated by Wentworth [1834, 2:67] and presented in more recent collections like Abrahams and Szwed [1983: 308-309] and Burnett [1986: 5]. Another of the songs is adapted in Day [1852, 2:121-22]. The following song, in which one slave is teasing another who is the 'cuckold' in a triangle relationship with the white overseer, is one which

Mathews said that he composed himself in 1786 and sang for His Royal Highness Prince William Henry in February 1787:

Vos motter Buddy Quow?
Aw bree Obeshay bong you.
You tan no sauby how
Daw bocra mon go wrong you, buddy Quow.

Chaw, tan way, lem me lone,
No so trouble begin now
Aw goo mine tik von tone,
So knock you rotten shin now, bruk you bone.

No haut burn, morrogoo,
Es granny ungry do you;
Aw hab sung bobrocoo,
Aw bring dem aw, kum foo you, morrogoo.

Dat time Quasheba tell,
Ee go bring von pickney fi me,
Aw nawngaw so aw sell
Daw hog me momy gim me, berry well.

Von kote aw buy um new,
Von rapper aw bin bring kum,
Von new honkisser too,
Aw neber bin go tink um nawsy, true.

Ven Unco Quaco say
De pickney he bin kum, mon,
Aw nawngaw morer tay
Me haut bin nock pum, pum, mon, true Gran Jay.

Gor Mighty day law bup,
See how Quasheba do me,
Daw Bockra mon ee lub,
Ee bring mulatto foo me, Gor na bubb.

Ee ye ee nose, ee mouth,
Me bin goo mine foo bit um,
Tan ebry mossel bout,
Like Obeshay bin pit him out he mout.

[Mathews 1793: 135-38]

The songs of the slaves must have been very appealing to whites and regarded as an appropriate reflection of the colony for a white Creole to imitate them, and to be permitted to and actually sing them on a formal occasion. The presentation by Mathews before the prince was in a sense a precursor of the Al Jolson type of 'black face' presentation in the United States, for Mathews himself said:

I have, upon my first arrival at Antigua, Dominica and Barbadoes, disguised myself like a field negro, my bonglaw in one hand, my bonger in tother, a junkey pipe in my mouth, and thus equipped, I have sallied out after dark, gone to the market place and drawn all the negroes around me, and I have entertained them by singing the most favorite negro songs, accompanied with the instrument, for hours together, and they have been ignorant that a white man was present . . . [1793: 143].

The Mathews' imitation, at that time, would have to be regarded as the best form of compliment paid to the slaves for the quality of their songs and music. At the same time, it can be thought of as a reverse of the festivities in which the slaves imitated their masters and mistresses.

There was a variety of songs sung by slaves in Jamaica in the first quarter of the nineteenth century. One of these is a song [Williams 1827: 297] showing the slave's observation of the duplicity of the white foreigner:

> Hi! De Buckra, hi!
> You sabby wha for he da cross de sea
> Wid him long white face and him twinkling yeye;
> He lub, make lub, as he preach to we,
> He fall on his knees, but he pray for me,
> Hi! de Buckra, hi!
>
> Hi! de Buckra, hi!
> Massa W-f-e da come ober de sea,
> Wid him roguish heart and him tender look;
> And while he palaver and preach him book,
> At the negro girl he'll winkie him yeye.
> Hi! de Buckra, hi!

Others, on other topics, are to be found in Monk Lewis' *Journal*:

The favourite song of the night was,

> Since massa come, we very well off;

Another of their popular songs this evening was –

> 'All the stories them telling you are lies, oh!' [Lewis 1834: 193]

. . . a copy of the following song was found upon the King Song of the Eboes

> Oh me good friend, Mr Wilberforce, make we free!
> God Almighty thank ye! God Almighty thank ye!
> God Almighty, make we free!
> Buckra in this country no make we free:
> What Negro for to do? What Negro for to do?
> Take force by force! Take force by force!
>
> Chorus
>
> To be sure! to be sure! to be sure! (p. 228)

Negro Song at Cornwall

> Hey-ho-day! me no care a dammee! (i.e. a damn,)
> Me acquire a house, (i.e. I have a solid foundation to build on)
> Since massa come see we - oh!
>
> Hey-ho-day! neger now quite eerie, (i.e., hearty,)
> For once me see massa - hey-ho-day!
> When massa go, me no care a dammee,
> For how them usy we - hey-ho-day! (p. 233)

A negro song. –

> Me take my cutacoo, (i.e. a basket made of matting,) and follow him to Lucea, and all for love of my bonny man - O - My bonny man come home, come home! Doctor no do you good. When neger fall into neger hands, buckra doctor no do him good more. Come home, my gold ring, come home! (p. 253)

These songs, which refer to different situations, show that the slaves used their songs to comment on a variety of topics perceived deception by the masters and proposed action, the happy consequences of having a good master and the power of Negro 'medicine' over white medicine. It was no doubt songs like the *Song of the Eboes* which roused the passions of both those on top and those on the bottom in the slave society and caused the songs of the slaves to be focal features across the whole society.

Another instance of a 'serious' song is given by Carmichael [1833, 2:301]. In this case, the hesitancy displayed by the slave who recited the song to Mrs Carmichael, the wife of the master, was an obvious reflection of his unwillingness to reveal the ill-will which slaves bore towards their masters: "Misses, it no good song . . . Cause misses, it a funny song, and me no mean bad by it."

Carmichael [1833, 2:301] said that the song, which she called "an insurrectionary song", was being sung by "some of the young negroes" not long after "the meditated insurrection in Trinidad":

> Fire in da mountain,
> Nobody for out him,
> Take me daddy's bo tick (dandy stick),
> And make a monkey out him.
>
> Chorus.
> Poor John! nobody for out him, &c.
>
> Go to de king's goal,
> You'll find a doubloon dey:
> Go to de king's goal,
> You'll find a doubloon dey.
>
> Chorus.
> Poor John! nobody for out him, &c.

The song seems to be really celebrating a case where a fire was used, not as a signal to insurrection, but as a diversionary tactic, that is, the masters had to go to put out the fire, accompanied by some slaves who pretended to help, while others stole the masters' money.

A popular song in Barbados around the same time arising out of a personal incident reflected some of the tensions of colour and class in the free coloured population. This song is cited by St Clair [1834: 373], who demonstrates some interest in local gossip in his explanation of the circumstances of the song:

I put up at an inn kept by Nancy Clark, a black woman of considerable celebrity, on whom the Negroes of this island made the following song:

> If you go to Nancy Clark,
> She will take you in the dark;
> When she get you in the dark
> She will give you aquafortis.
>
> If you go to Susy Austin,
> She will take you in the parlour;
> When she take you in the parlour,
> She will give you wine and water.

These verses, on my landing, were howled about by every Negro in the place, and, on inquiry, I found them to have originated in the conduct of Nancy Clark towards a young girl of colour; she having, in a fit of jealousy, taken an opportunity of throwing in her face some aquafortis to destroy her beauty, which she succeeded in doing most completely. Susy Austin, another woman of colour, kept the other inn, and perhaps, might have bribed the poet for the second stanza.

Here again, it is clear that the songs of the slaves were able to capture the attention of all types of people and to put into focus as well as to record incidents, attitudes and practices which were of considerable importance in the society of the time. The songs arose out of incidents either on the plantation or in the town but they managed to spread their message across the island in a quick and effective manner.

THE MARKET

The composition of songs as well as singing were cultural features common to all types of slaves, even if the topics of interest varied according to situation. It is quite clear, for instance, that the burning of canes and the acts of overseers – topics of some songs – were not directly relevant to urban slaves. The contexts of communication which shaped the culture of the plantation 'village' or community were not an integral part of the experience of urban and other slaves, even though these latter could not escape the influence of the plantation slaves, who were by far the vast majority of the population. The urban slaves, whose tasks related to small businesses, did not really constitute closely-bound communities among themselves, as was the case among the plantation slaves. Atwood [1791] introduced his comments on non-plantation slaves by saying: "The slaves belonging to people in the towns of the English islands, are composed of house servants, tradesmen and porters" (p. 263).

He went on (p. 264) to list the *domestic negros* as *cooks, washers, attendants* and the *tradesmen* as *carpenters, coopers, blacksmiths, masons*. All these categories of workers were also part of the plantation complement, but in the town their context of operation was different. Because of more direct and constant contact with speakers of English, the language competence of these slaves extended further than that of the plantation field slaves. In addition, being urban, they were more sophisticated than plantation slaves. In this respect Resident [1828: 81] says: "In this display, the town's negroes and people of colour take the lead; the estate negroes being generally a little behind in the *fashions*, and in *fashionable deportment*." The urban slaves were therefore models to be copied in fashion and language because of their apparent sophistication.

In addition to such urban slaves there were slaves who were fishermen and others who were boatmen, directly involved in buying and selling for their owners or in moving goods from one part of the island to another. The use of boats to move goods was advantageous in those islands with difficult terrain and small internal populations. Boatmen, although as a percentage of the total population they were insignificant, linked the various areas of the country not only commercially, but also communicatively. The plantation as an isolated unit was kept linked to the main port and to other areas of the country by the constant movement of boatmen. Black boatmen had a role then, no matter how minor, in the diffusion of culture and language across the different areas in each island and therefore in the evolution of the national culture and national varieties of language.

While there were differences between slaves who worked on the plantation, those who worked in town and those who worked at sea, the one activity which involved all types of slaves was the market. Market day for the West Indian plantation slave particularly was a major happening and for the development of language in every territory the market was a major context of communication which affected the mass of the population. The magnitude of the event in Kingston in Jamaica is related by Edwards [1794, 2:33]:

Sunday is their market day, and it is wonderful what numbers are then seen, hastening from all parts of the country, towards the towns and shipping-places, laden with fruits and vegetables, pigs, goats and poultry, their own property. In Jamaica it is supposed that upwards of 10,000 assemble every Sunday morning in the market of Kingston, where they barter their provisions, &c. for salted beef and pork, or fine linen and ornaments for their wives and children.

In the early years of the development of marketing among the slaves, the emphasis was on the economics of it, as opposed to later years when the emphasis was much more on the social activity. In the last years of slavery when the slave market was already more than a hundred years old, Wentworth [1834, 2:198] commented on this latter aspect of the market in Antigua as follows:

> The principal, or weekly market, which was held at this time on Sundays, is near the southern entrance to Saint John's, where the slaves of every description assembled, and where the gratification of their vanity in the display of their finery was no inconsiderable incentive to their congregating, as well as the more ostensible motive of traffic ...

Marketing among the slaves probably started with isolated, itinerant vendors who could peddle their wares in understandable language. In the early years of slavery a market could not function in a situation where easy communication between people was impossible. In other words, for there to have been a market, language had to evolve to a stage to allow for group interaction in a meaningful way. It is, therefore, significant in the retracing of linguistic development to note that slave markets had already developed in St Kitts by the 1720s, for Robertson [1730: 21] was at that time already criticizing the slaves for their non-Christian practices of *markettings and merry-makings on the Lord's Day*. It would seem then that by this time the slaves' language in St Kitts was a flexible medium through which they could carry on their business in an effective way. The time of development of the slave market in the other territories varied according to local circumstances.

The actual slave market, as a context of communication, started even before the vendors reached the market, for on the way there the lines of walkers got longer and the hustle and bustle and chatter increased as they neared their destination. There were also well known resting spots along the way where persons exchanged news. The road to and from market therefore might have been long, but it was certainly not silent. The market itself was a context in which many different people came into contact – buyers and sellers, urban dwellers and rural, natives and non-natives. This was a context in which the ability to use language appropriately, in a competitive situation, made the difference between gain and loss. Whether it was the buyer or the seller, the urban 'trickster' or the rural unsophisticated, the native or non-native, each one was trying to gain advantage over the other and had to do it by talking. Such a competitive situation led to endearments to entice the unwilling or undecided to buy or sell; it also led to cursing and swearing, by which rivals tried to get the better of each other; it also led to colourful language, with which goods for sale were presented in their best light.

The market was not only a place of buying and selling, but also of gossip and fashion. Here the mores of the people determined the ways in which they interacted and the networks they established. Loud, demonstrative, verbal behaviour as well as secretive whisperings between close friends were all part of the market place. The fashionable language of the urban would have become familiar to the rural person; the terms of the plantation and its crops would have become familiar to the urban person. Each in turn would have broadcast new acquisitions further. The element of sophistication and fashion in the market in Port of Spain at the end of the first quarter of the nineteenth century is presented by Coleridge [1970: 63]: "The Spanish and French females, their gay costume, their foreign language, and their unusual vivacity give this market the appearance of a merry fair in France." Clearly, the market here had become a central activity for most levels of society and had moved beyond the early days when it was principally dominated by agricultural slaves.

The central role of the human voice in the market place is captured by Poole [1753: 279] in the comment: "They make it not only a market-day, but also a day of rendezvous and riot; singing, whistling, ranting, cursing, swearing, &c. from morning even until night." Such vibrant and sustained intercourse could not have been maintained unless the common language was flexible and colourful enough to express the varying sentiments of all those involved. If indeed there was one context that forged a common, flexible medium of communication, it was the market place. Here, all were temporarily unrestrained and so could vent their feelings in words among themselves. Here developed also the verbal duelling which is said to be characteristic of African American communities. The difference between violent confrontation and verbal duelling was apparent even to passing observers like Mathison [1811: 2]:

Great bustle and activity prevail in this market. The groups are full of spirit, but by no means pleasing. Loud laughter and noisy bargains assail the ears at every corner of the market. Quarrels, productive of violent gestures and apparent agitation of mind, but rarely leading to bloodshed, give an alarming and a false appearance of the prevalence of the most angry passions in the Negro character.

The same was clear to Day [1852, 2:111-12] who, commenting on a negro market, made the following remark:

When negroes quarrel, they seldom look each other in the face. Nay, generally they turn back to back and seem to appeal to the bystanders, who usually answer each speech made by the belligerents at each other with a shout of laughter, until it comes to: 'I mash you up', 'I cut your t'roat', when some friends, male or female, judiciously interfere, and lead the infuriated demons off.

This was a typical situation in which the protagonists, seemingly bent on physical violence, really expected to be restrained at the last moment and so used up their energies in outdoing their rival in words.

The market, dominated as it was by the rural plantation seller, was the domain of the creole language, the basilectal form of it. However, this form was in turn affected by more urban patterns, not only because markets were usually situated in or near urban areas, but also because the buyers were more urban themselves in their speech. The general interaction between rural and urban slaves is pointed out by Wentworth [1834, 2:202] when he speaks of "their ungovernable love of hearing themselves talk, of bartering the gossip of the country for that of the town". The market was therefore a dynamic situation in which language was central and in which language had to change to reflect the vibrancy and dynamism of the situation.

The market was dominated by females, as is attested by Thome and Kimball [1838: 66]: ". . . the majority were females, as usual with the marketers in these islands . . ." It is for this reason that the market woman's language has become the stereotype of 'common, ordinary' language. The market was the bastion of the powerful, independent female, who was intent on defending the fruits of her hard-earned labour in no uncertain terms or, on the other hand, using her feminine charms to 'sweet talk' the undecided or unwilling. In some cases, also, she had to ward off the amorous without losing their interest. She had to establish her own position among her peers in order to safeguard herself in her absence or for help in times of illness or need. The complex network which she therefore established with peers, rivals, suitors, relatives and customers depended on a wide ranging competence in language, which in itself belies the very stereotype of the market woman's language.

RELIGIOUS PRACTICES

The market woman's language and the vulgar culture of the market place may seem to be diametrically opposed to the 'holiness' of religious rites, but it is not only in their scholastic opposition that these two have been tied together but also in the reality of their evolution. The market place is a feature of all societies, one traditionally dominated by oral culture and direct communication. Its particular manifestation in each society is determined by local conditions, the status of the participants and the goods for sale. The goods for sale are basically agricultural products, which are seasonal in their growth and availability. In many societies the agricultural seasons of planting and harvest are associated with religious rites as, for example, in Europe where there was a direct relationship between the agricultural re-emergence of leaves (spring) and the time of the spiritual re-emergence or resurrection of the Christian God (Easter). This religious practice was translated from Europe where it naturally coincided in its evolution with the change of seasons (winter to spring) to the West Indies where there was no natural event to heighten its import. It was not natural to the West Africans either, whose seasons resembled those of the West Indies. In the West Indies the imposition of European religious traditions and a dominant monocrop culture of sugar for export hardly allowed for the spontaneous development of a relationship between planting and harvest on the one hand and religious rites on the other among the slaves in the English islands. In addition, in the West Indies the Africans did not own the crops, so there was no necessity and no natural context for the continuity of their ancestral practices which were tied to the cycle of planting and harvesting of crops. They were in fact in control of very little and so the kind of belief system as outlined by Edwards [1794, 2:70-71] had no foundations and no role in the West Indies:

They believe that *Accompong*, the God of the heavens, is the creator of all things; a Deity of infinite goodness; to whom however they never offer sacrifices, thinking it sufficient to adore him with praises and thanksgiving.

Assarci is the god of the earth; to him they offer the first fruits of the ground, and pour out libations of the liquors they drink to his honour.

Ipboa is the god of the sea: if the arrival of ships which trade upon their coast is delayed, they sacrifice a hog to deprecate the wrath of Ipboa.

Obboney is a malicious deity, who pervades heaven, earth, and sea; he is the author of all evil, and when his displeasure is signified by the infliction of pestilential disorders, or otherwise, nothing will divert his anger but human sacrifices; which are selected from captives taken in war, or, if there be none present, then from their slaves.

It was not therefore the cycle of birth and death of crops that was celebrated with religious rites by the slaves but the life and death of human beings.

For the slaves it was the *professors of Obi*, that is, obeah men and women who were able to intercede on their behalf to overcome the problems of life, and Europeans became quickly aware that the slaves had a deep belief in their power. Edwards [1794, 2:90] explained that

The Negroes in general, whether Africans or Creoles, revere, consult, and fear them [professors of Obi]; to these oracles they resort, and with the most implicit faith, upon all occasions, whether for the cure of disorders, the obtaining revenge for injuries or insults, the conciliating of favour, the discovery and punishment of the thief or the adulterer, and the prediction of future events.

The religious practices of the slaves, because they were always under threat from the Whites, were kept hidden, as Edwards [1794, 2:90] went on to explain: "A veil of mystery is studiously thrown over their incantations, to which the midnight hours are allotted, and every precaution is taken to conceal them from the knowledge and discovery of the White people." As a result of this secrecy, European writers were only able to make general comments about obeah practice, and since they were deliberately excluded the comments made were negative.

It was the celebration of death more so than birth that was recorded by European writers. The slaves' celebration of death was part of a belief system in which ancestors were transformed into deities. Edwards' account of the Coromantyn system [Edwards 1794, 2:71] gives some idea of this:

Besides the above deities [Accompong, Assarci, Ipboa, Obboney], every family has a peculiar tutelar saint, who is supposed to have been originally a human being like one of themselves, and the first founder of their family; upon the anniversary of whose burial, the whole number of his descendants assemble round the grave, and the oldest man, after offering up praises to Accompong, Assarci, Ipboa, and their tutelar deity, sacrifices a cock or goat, by cutting its throat, and shedding the blood upon the grave. Every head of a household of the family next sacrifices a cock, or other animal, in like manner, and as soon as all those who are able to bring sacrifices have made their oblations, the animals which have been killed are dressed, and a great festival follows.

In sharp contrast, the religious practice of the Whites was controlled by the doctrines of the Protestant churches which were tied to the Bible as well as by rituals, prayers and songs which were all written down in books. In contrast, except for a small number of Muslim Africans, the supernatural beliefs and practices of the slaves were all within an oral culture. One of the fundamental beliefs among the slaves, repeatedly identified by European writers, was transmigration of souls. It was a belief that allowed the slaves to bear their burden more steadfastly, since it gave them an assurance of being reunited with their own in Africa after death. Death therefore was interpreted by them as a release from earthly bondage, as a happy occasion, and as one for celebration. Death rites were characterized by several features, some of which involved oral expression. For the Africans, death did not represent a complete and sudden break between the physical world and the spiritual or hereafter. Even though it was marked by a ritual of burial of the body in the ground, death was a transition, a journey, a passing or passage to which certain physical links still applied, *eg* food and communication. Preceding the burial itself was, in most cases, a wake, and nine days or some set period after there was another stage in the marking of the passing. The slave burial itself was therefore a strange experience for English Protestants in the middle and last half of the eighteenth century. Smith [1745: 231] regarded the slaves as having no religious practices because what the slaves did did not correspond to his conception of religion: "They sing too at burials, but get drunk, and have no sign of devotion, calling out to the dead person, and asking him, Why he died, when he wanted nothing the world could afford, to support nature?"

In addition, Smith's version of the remarks addressed to the dead (*ie* Why die?), though repeated by at least one other writer, Atwood [1791], were not the most typical remarks made. What other later writers recorded was that when the body was committed to the ground, those standing around the grave would shout messages to the dead to be taken back to others on the other side and would also ask for help from the other side. Such requests as well as the offering of food to the dead are a little more fully illustrated by Atwood [1791: 261-63]:

a man or woman accustomed to the ceremony, takes of each meat laid in dishes round the grave, and pulling some of it in pieces, throws the same on the grave, calling out the name of the dead person as if alive, saying, 'Here is a piece of such a thing for you to eat; why did you leave your father, mother, wife, children and friends? Did you go away angry with us? When shall we see you again? Make our provisions to grow, and stock to breed, don't let any body do us harm, and we will give you the same next year'; with the like expressions to every thing they throw on the grave. After which, taking a little of the rum or other liquors, they sprinkle it thereon, crying out in the same manner, 'Here is a little rum to comfort your heart, good bye to you, God bless you;' and drinking some of it themselves to the welfare of the deceased, they set up a dismal cry and howling, but immediately after begin to dance and sing round the grave.

Pinckard [1806, 1:273], for his part, makes no mention of food being offered to the dead but he does give his own version of the remarks addressed to the dead after the burial:

When the whole of the earth was replaced several of the women, who had staid to chant, in a merry song, over poor Jenny's clay, took up a handful of the mould, and threw it down again upon the grave of their departed friend, as the finishing of the ceremony, crying aloud 'God bless you, Jenny! good-by! remember me to all friends t'other side of the sea, Jenny! Tell 'em me come soon! Good-by, Jenny, good-by! See for send me good ... tonight, Jenny! Good-by, good night, Jenny, good-by!' All this was uttered in mirth and laughter, and accompanied with attitudes and gesticulations expressive of any thing but sorrow or sadness.

Stedman [1806, 2:293], writing about the years 1772-77 in Suriname, notes that remarks were made to the dead but takes issue with the idea that the slaves believed in return to Africa after death:

This done every one takes his last farewell, speaking to him as if alive, and testifying their sorrow at his departure; adding, that they hope to see him, not in Guinea, as some have written, but in that better place, where he enjoys the pleasant company of his parents, friends, and ancestors; when another dismal yell ends the ceremony, and all return home.

In spite of the variations in the accounts of these writers, the addressing of the dead after burial seemed to have been a fairly universal feature among the slaves in the eighteenth century. As a reaction to the status of bondage and as a expression of a desire for continued links with the homeland, it was a peculiarly New World response.

Contrasting with speech addressed to the dead after burial was the practice of the 'dead' addressing comments to the living before the burial, during the procession to the burial ground. This is described by Stewart [1808: 251-52]:

Previous to the interment of the corpse, it is pretended that it is endowed with the gift of speech, and the friends and relatives alternately place their ears to the lid of the coffin to hear what the deceased has to say. This generally consists of complaints and upbraidings for various injuries, treachery, ingratitude, injustice, slander, and, in particular, the non-payment of debts due to the deceased: this latter complaint is sometimes shewn by the deceased in a more *cogent* way than by mere words; for on coming opposite to the door of the negro debtor, the coffin makes a full stop, and no persuasion nor *strength* can induce the deceased to go forward to his grave, till the money is paid; so that the unhappy debtor has no alternative but to comply with this demand, or have his creditor palmed on him as a lodger for some time.

As a social practice, it is clear that it was seen as the responsibility of the friends and relatives of the dead to settle his/her affairs so that the dead could leave the living world in peace. In this specific case, Stewart does not record any comments addressed to the dead after burial, which means that this practice could have been a variation of the former or an evolution from the former. In other words, rather than words of atonement after the burial, action arising from the words and apparent intransigence of the 'dead' seemed to have been adopted as a better strategy of atonement.

What seemed to be universal in burials was the singing and dancing during the procession to the burial ground as well as during the interment itself. In this case, cultural transmission from West Africa combined with the notion of return home could have been responsible for this. A fairly full description of an urban funeral in Barbados in the middle of the eighteenth century is given by Poole, who, though disapproving of what went on, was somewhat more perceptive in his analysis of religious beliefs of the slaves:

Yesterday Evening, after returning to my Lodgings, a Negro Funeral passing by inclined me to attend the same at a Distance, and observe the whole of the Ceremony on this Occasion, as being what I have for some Time been wishing for. I receiv'd a Notice of this, by hearing the Singing of Negroes in the Street, which I at first supposed was a Rejoycing on Account of its being *Saturday* Night, the Eve of their Rest, when it is no uncommon Thing for them to be merry and joyful; but on casting my Eyes into the Street, I perceived I was mistaken, and that it was on Account of the Death of an Infant one of the Negroes then had in a Coffin, carrying it to *Fonte Belle* for its Funeral, attended by a Number of others, rejoycing over the Dead with Tokens of exceeding great Joy. The Mother of the Child was there also. The Musick they made in the Procession, was by gingling of Shells and Stones, or Nickars, in little Bags, shaking them up and down; beating of Sticks together; and thumping upon a Sort of Drum, prepared for the Occasion. They jump'd, skip'd, danc'd, and sung as they went, seeming almost to be frantick with Joy.

Being come to the place, the Coffin was measured, and the Length of the Grave dug accordingly. The Place being all Sand, requires no great Labour or Time herein; during which there was continual Dancing and Singing among the Negroes, whose Number at the Grave considerably increased, many running to them from other parts, and join'd in their Mirth. Such gestures, such Distortion of Limbs, such different Positions of Body were shewn, that they seemed as tho' they were acted upon by a Spirit of Frenzy; a Madness that stung them into strong convulsive Motions, rather than the natural Act of the Will. But tho' there was so much Agitation of Body shewn, which they call Dancing, yet they scarcely moved out of their Place. Such odd Behaviour, such strange, ridiculous Motions, however they might have a Tendency to excite Mirth in some, yet, I confess, I was thereby moved with Concern; a Sort of Veil of Sadness and Pity over-spread my Soul, that such Pains were taken in Shewing so much ridiculous Mirth by these poor Creatures, from a false Notion of the buried Object being now made free, and returning to its own Country; which is a common, prevailing Notion among them, upon the Decease of any of their Friends [Poole 1753: 295-96].

There is evidence in Poole's words of spirit possession (*ie* "acted upon by a Spirit of Frenzy; a Madness that stung them into strong convulsive Motions"), but there is no mention of a corresponding speaking in tongues. In another urban funeral (for a washerwoman) described by Pinckard some fifty years later, there is no indication of spirit possession, although there is a certain similarity to Poole's account of the funeral for the child. There is mention in Pinckard's account of what he interpreted to be an African song sung by an old lady:

Seeing a crowd in one of the streets, and observing a kind of procession, we followed the multitude, and soon found ourselves in the train of a negro funeral. Wishing to witness the ceremony of interment we proceeded to the burial ground, with the throng. The corpse was conveyed in a neat small hearse, drawn by one horse. Six boys, twelve men, and forty-eight women walked behind, in pairs, as followers, but I cannot say as deeply afflicted mourners. The females were neatly clad, for the occasion, and mostly in white. Grief and lamentations were not among them: nor was even the semblance thereof assumed. No solemn dirge was heard – no deep-sounding bell was tolled – no fearful silence held. It seemed a period of mirth and joy. Instead of weeping and bewailing, the followers jumped and sported, as they passed along, and talked and laughed, with each other, in high festivity. The procession was closed by five robust negro fisherman, who followed behind playing antic gambols, and dancing all the way to the grave . . .

During this process [the burial] an old negro woman chanted an African air, and the multitude joined her in the chorus. It was not in the strain of a hymn, or a solemn requiem, but was loud and lively, in unison with the other gaieties of the occasion . . . [Pinckard 1806, 1:270-73].

From this and the previous accounts, it is evident that the slaves' celebration of death and the notion of death as a happy release was troubling to whites.

Their anxiety might have been because it seemed to make suicide appealing to the slaves, which for masters meant a loss of property and the further expense of replacement. Jumping overboard slave ships, dirt eating, the suppression of pregnancies and child killing had furnished whites with enough evidence to show that some slaves regarded death as a better alternative than life. Yet, Edwards [1794, 2:86-87] was apparently trying to allay the fears of whites in this respect when he argued that suicide among the slaves was less frequent than it was in Britain. In any case, the slaves' celebration of death also helped them to convince themselves that the negro's life had little value. So, even in spite of the fact that in the European Christian theology heaven was supposed to be the wondrous place where God was, the idea of death as a happy entrance to this place was unacceptable. For the whites, there was an equally strong link in the practice of Christianity to the material world. The live, authentic, vibrant expression of a theological belief among the slaves, though it coincided with the one in Christianity, was shocking to Europeans, whose theology had been committed to books and had to be reinterpreted for the faithful by priests working within a social class system and a church institutional system which required live workers and a large mass of converts respectively. There was therefore a sharp difference between the direct acting out of a belief by the slaves in the context of their oral culture and the European order of service reified in writing and re-enacted in each case by the Christian faithful.

64 / *From Oral to Literate Culture*

FIGURE 3.2: Negro Funeral in the time of slavery

That the slaves' celebration of death was a cultural continuity from West Africa was most likely known at the time, for a similar practice of rejoicing on the occasion of a death in West Africa is described by Matthews [1966: 100-101]:

> The death of a child, friend, or relation, adds no less to the enjoyment of this pastime, by performing the wha', or cry: but, from the manner in which it is performed, a stranger to their ceremonies would rather term it a rejoicing.
>
> On the evening of the day appointed the friends and relations of the deceased assemble together, and proceed, by a slow and solemn movement, to an open space before their houses. Here they begin singing the praises of the deceased, and dancing to the music of a drum. In the dance they frequently vary the figure; sometimes forming one great circle round the music, and clapping hands at every period or repetition of their song. Sometimes one person performs the dance, the rest sitting or standing round in a circle, joining chorus and clapping hands as before: at other times two, three, or four, will dance together till they are weary, and then are relieved by others; the rest singing and clapping hands. This, with firing of guns, continues from evening till near daylight, without intermission . . .

Here the activity described is more in the form of a cultural event and much closer to the activities of a wake or to the kind of ceremony which followed some days after the burial. However, Edwards' comments [1794, 2:85] in relation to Jamaica that "their funeral songs too are all of the heroic or martial cast" maintains the idea of *singing the praises of the deceased* in the African version described above.

Associated with the grave as a part of supernatural beliefs but not as a part of a burial was the practice of using grave dirt together with some spoken formula for uncovering and punishing crimes. The method of application of this practice in a case of stealing is explained by Poole [1753: 246] in the following way:

> Moreover, if any one has lost any Thing, and after some Time it cannot be found, nor suspected who it is that has stole it, they retire to *Fonte-Bell*, and there place themselves by the Grave of their Relations; or, in Case of Failure herein, then they go to the Grave of one of their Countrymen, and taking some of the Mould of the Grave in their Hands and Mouth, pronounce a Curse and with Destruction to that Person, whosoever it is, that has robbed them; then, kissing the Grave, return Home: And this, by repeated Examples, I am inform'd, has been found to prove destructive to the Person that was the Thief.

Another case – a test to see whether a wife was unfaithful or not – is explained by Edwards [1794, 2:71-72]:

> Human blood, and earth taken from the grave of some near relation, are mixed with water, and given to the party to be sworn, who is compelled to drink the mixture, with an imprecation, that it may cause the belly to burst, and the bones to rot, if the truth be not spoken.

It was the belief that ancestors could intercede in the physical world which provided the basis for this practice, but it was a kind of practice that was of course frowned on by slaveowners, whose major interest was preserving the sanity and strength of their slaves for as long as possible. They did not want their estate to be undermined by such practices or by obeah men, who could exert influence over their slaves.

CONCLUSION

The cultivation of the intellect, the spirit and the soul is spontaneous in all human society, and is naturally done through oral means. In the case of the slaves in the West Indies, who had been uprooted from their respective native cultures, transported to foreign lands, mixed with others and kept in a state of imprisonment, the cultivation of human qualities was subordinated to the survival of the physical being. Yet, in time, the slaves managed to forge a creole culture and language out of both the disparate and the common elements among themselves. Having been cut off, most of them at an early age, from their relatives and society, the Africans had no way of preserving the continuity of their ancestral past in oral literature. In the plantation society in which literacy was beginning to emerge as a cultural force, they therefore had no recorded history to transfer from the oral sphere to the written, even if they had had materials and social contexts in which to do so. The folktales and folklore which they preserved and developed were essentially a part of live, oral culture, didactic and entertaining in nature, but part of the informal education that is characteristic of all societies, literate or not.

Intellectual skills were not required of slaves and were seldom credited to them in the planting, cultivation or harvesting of crops, in the production of sugar, rum or other by products of sugar cane, or in the preservation of health and life. Even in the area of domestic self-government (home economics), slaves were thought to prefer the 'carefree' status of prisoners for whom everything is provided rather than freedom which entailed having to think about provision of food and clothing for themselves. The only activity that was permitted to slaves to use their intellect was marketing, and this in itself soon allowed for the slave agricultural plot and the market place. Even though the entire procedure – from planting to sale – required intellectual and verbal skills, because it was grossly subordinate to the sugar plantation, was local and not powerful enough, in general, to be an avenue to freedom and wealth, there was little or no perception of it as cultivation of the intellect and there was no possibility of it being aided by literacy. In the world of work, therefore, the slaves did not develop any extensive tradition of passing on knowledge and information from generation to generation, seeing that they could not, as a right, bequeath their plots and business to their offspring. For them the world of work was essentially a world of the temporary rather than one which was preserving and improving a way of life for succeeding generations.

At first, the cultivation of the souls of the slaves was deemed to be a nonexistent problem, since, as Christians, the Whites could not acknowledge the enslavement of beings with souls. The slaves were accordingly left to their own practices. However, because of the diversity of origin of the slaves, no uniform belief system and practice emerged as dominant across any slave community in the West Indies. In addition, the only root contexts for religious practice which did not conflict with the restrictions of the slave structure were celebrations of deaths. As the religious element in Europe gained ascendancy in the debate about the salvation of the souls of the slaves, the religious practices of the slaves came increasingly into conflict with the powerful literary traditions of the European churches and therefore had no avenue for transfer and validation of their own rituals in a literate medium. Moreover, it was in the formal educational system, the cradle of western literacy, that the churches had a powerful ally and the oral culture of the slaves had its most formidable enemy, in this respect and generally.

In the African world from which the slaves originated there was a system of belief which conceived of the world as being made up of the living or material sphere and the dead or spiritual sphere, in which the former at death transferred to the latter, which in itself had a hierarchy and variety of spirits with good and bad qualities. The dominant idea in this system was that ancestral spirits which were aware of the material world should be propitiated, that homage should be paid to them and that they could be asked to intercede in the material world to solve problems. The location of the spiritual world for the African slaves, who had been moved from their homeland, at first would naturally have had to be where the rest of the ancestors were, and it is this that led European writers to highlight the notion of transmigration of souls to Africa. It is significant, however, that by the third quarter of the eighteenth century Stedman could say that the location of the spiritual world was "not in Guinea, as some have written, but in that better place, where he enjoys the pleasant company of his parents, friends, and ancestors". It would seem, then, that by this time there was a big enough generation of 'creole' ancestors from the Caribbean to make the African world of ancestors recede in significance, except for the recently arrived Africans. The variety of questions and statements cited by European writers as remarks addressed to the dead after burial of the body conforms to the idea that the spirit of the dead had to be addressed candidly, either because the spirit was now a part of an omniscient spiritual world and could not be lied to or to make that spirit leave the material world and go to its appropriate place in the spiritual world. Questions about the reason the person died testify to some uneasiness among surviving relatives and friends about some unresolved problem and the need for atonement; promises such as *we will give you the same next year* and requests such as *Make our provisions to grow* confirm the slaves' belief in the power of communication with their ancestors.

Ancestor veneration and the belief in their powers of intercession were in a sense an extension of the respect for the old in the material world and the belief in their greater wisdom and better guidance. The terms of address that were used as marks of respect for the elderly were parallelled by terms for the hierarchy of ancestor gods. These latter were largely unknown to European writers and were recorded only in brief by Edwards [1794, 2:70-71]. While the orientation for newly arrived Africans and the experience of the estate nursery fitted the African system of respect for the wisdom of and veneration of the old, unfortunately the harshness of slavery did not allow the majority of slaves, especially males, to grow old, and therefore did not allow for the regeneration of a fully developed culture of ancestry in the West Indies. In addition, the movement of slaves from one master to another militated against continuity in relationships. As a result, the overall benefit of old age and wisdom to the young through direct communication was not uniform and was not extensive. For both the young and the old, the peer group was more influential and the immediacy of the realities of life were much more apparent. The expression of oral culture was a reflection of immediacy – the enjoyment of life through singing, through storytelling, through ridicule and jokes, verbal sparring and ostentation in the market place, all attested to the dominance of the present in the life of the slaves. This was essentially a culture removed from the solitary, reflective nature of the literary. The only major feature of the oral culture of the slaves which may have retained some influence from literary sources out of Africa was the work song.

NOTES

1 Wentworth [1834, 2:39]: "It is worthy of remark that most insurrectionary movements on the part of the negroes in these islands have taken place, or been mediated to take place, about Christmas."
2 "Many times I have spoken to several black slaves, who are expert in the knowledge of many of these plants; but these people are so jealous of their knowledge, that however I tried, either by money or by flattery, it was useless; and I was completely unable to persuade even one of them to tell me."

4

Political and Social Influences on the Development of Vernacular English

Nonlinguistic methods of communication in the early plantation slave society were complemented by and to some extent supplanted by the vernacular based on English which quickly developed there. It was this vernacular which embodied and expressed the culture of the people and it was this vernacular which stood in contrast to literate English, coming principally out of British sources. It was a vernacular with a high degree of variation, which resulted from the various dialects of languages that were brought to the West Indies, the constant flux that has always been a part of these societies, and the conditions under which the majority of the populations came into contact with and moved towards English, the language of the rulers. Since anglo-West Indian societies did not all start at the same date and evolve at the same pace, it is necessary to give some idea of starting points for local varieties, radiation of linguistic influence from one territory to others, independent developments, critical periods in development of specific dialects, emergence of characteristic dialects and dominant factors in their development. Determining priority and importance in these specific areas and in fact in language in general is subject to contention and disagreement in the best of circumstances, and is even more so in a case where there are inconsistent data and writings which were not subject to a high degree of critical objectivity and whose authors were writing in a milieu which did not require such objectivity.

The date of settlement by the English varied from territory to territory with a span of almost two hundred years between the establishment of the first colony in

St Kitts in 1624 and the final acquisition of St Lucia in 1815, but citations of dialectal peculiarities do not appear in the literature accordingly as they emerged in individual islands. It is not until the last few years of the eighteenth century that actual examples of West Indian speech begin to appear frequently and with substance in the literature. Before that comments about language tended to be odd remarks which were general and not substantial. In other words, there are no early eighteenth century illustrations of Kittitian dialect, although by the early years of the eighteenth century a characteristic dialect must have emerged in St Kitts. The reason for this kind of absence is that in the seventeenth and early eighteenth centuries writers were merely reflecting their own (European) responses to emergent colonies. However, as the debate on slavery heated up and as 'first-hand' accounts were presented to support arguments, writers increasingly began to describe a general British West Indian identity which had become very apparent, an identity which was an integral part of the general political development in the West Indies from rich slave colonies with absentee (in England) owners toward postslavery, dependent colonies with greater local dominance.

Differences in the nature of the literature substantially determine the kind of analysis that is possible. For the seventeenth and eighteenth centuries one is restricted to speculations about language development using principally historical data on ethnic groups, population ratios and other relationships, together with known linguistic facts about source (*ie* English and African) languages. For the nineteenth century the increase in language samples allows for a more detailed linguistic analysis. Fortuitous and ironic though it may be, it is from the most bigoted and disagreeable authors in the nineteenth century that one gets some important examples of language features. This is so because such authors were at pains to illustrate how different the inhabitants in the colonies were from 'civilized' Englishmen, which they did by identifying specific features of language that they regarded as annoying or symbolic of lack of sophistication. Such a desire to illustrate social and cultural superiority was merely an extension of such rivalries from Europe. Ethnic distinction therefore remained for a long time a significant factor in language development in the West Indies.

The most distinct example of social conflict from the very early years is of course evident in the belief in racial superiority. However, analysis of the linguistic consequences of the conflict between black and white and other races is dealt with within a more general discussion of social stratification and its effect on language learning. Rivalry among ethnic groups is in some ways distinct from racial conflict in that the latter is always vertical social class conflict whereas the former is often a horizontal struggle within racial strata. Rivalry between the European nations is an area of interest that has dominated histories of the Caribbean. Although such rivalry is extensively documented, it tends to be political and economic in nature. However, it is the social, cultural and specifically linguistic consequences of such rivalry that are the focus of attention here.

In addition to conflicts between European powers, what is also influential in the development of specific vernaculars of English in the West Indies are the relationships first between those speaking different dialects of English, that is, the English, the Scottish, the Welsh and the Irish (and the subdialects among them), and secondly between the Africans, who spoke different languages and dialects of languages. Ethnic conflict within each of the two major races of course did not start in the West Indies, but because it affected the socialization process here it determined the way in which English developed.

LANGUAGE IN COMMUNICATION AND SOCIETY IN THE EARLY COLONIES

Before looking at intra-European and intra-African relationships more closely, it is necessary to get an understanding of the dynamics at work in the start of a colony and to consider the role played by language in these undertakings. Official history, garnered from documents in Europe and elsewhere, might differ somewhat from accounts of the day, but these latter, being more impressionistic, occasionally give better clues to human relationships and social tensions. For example, John Smith [1630] gives an account of "The first planting of the Barbados" which he gets from "the relations of Captain John White, and Captain Wolverstone", two persons who were right there at the time: "The first planters brought thither by Captain Henry Powell, were forty English, with seven or eight negros; then he went to Disacuba in the maine, where he got thirty Indians, men, women, and children, of the Arawacos..." (p. 55). From this short extract one can go on to picture the start of a project in an uninhabited island far from the home of any of the participants – a project in which people from at least three language groups had to live together and communicate in order to survive. A language researcher could hardly have thought up a better experiment to examine communication and survival.

Yet, the fact that this kind of project was repeated several times over suggests that communication was not really a problem. That there was friction is clear, but in the case of Barbados it seemed to be more among the English than between the ethnic groups as a result of language differences:

Master John Powell came thither the fourth of August 1627, with forty-five men, where he stayed three weeks, and then returning left behind us about an hundred people, and his sonne John Powell for his deputy, as Governour; but there have beene so many factions amongst them, I cannot from so many variable relations give you any certainty for their orderly government ... [Smith 1630: 55].

Of course, the disposition of power ensured cooperation, but in such a fragile situation there had to be in the earliest stages accommodation on all sides as well as willingness to communicate. At the same time as a result of language differences there must have been a low level of understanding among the groups and misunderstandings which would have led to suspicion and hostility, which in turn would have led to 'hardening' of positions within ethnic groupings.

With the addition of more English speakers and with power in the hands of the English, the English language became the sole basis for general communication in Barbados. The extent to which the other two ethnic groups tried to understand and speak English was a matter of the dependency relationship in this early society. The Africans, according to Harlow [1926: 4], were taken from a captured ship and because of their number and dependence on English speakers would have had no choice but to learn some English. On the other hand, the native Americans, who were more familiar with the region, who seemed to have travelled from Guiana as families and who held some key to the success of the project in Barbados, were not wholly dependent on the English and were not compelled to learn English because they already had a community language to use among themselves.

In fact, as the years passed and the black segment of the population grew, the native Americans learnt the language of the blacks in islands like Dominica and St Vincent, where native Americans remained in numbers for a long time and intermixed with the blacks. The fact that native American speech was not dominant and is said to have had little effect on the varieties of English that developed in the West Indies is normally explained by the disappearance of these natives from the islands. Even Douglas Taylor [1977], who carefully studied the languages of those in Dominica principally, made no claims for a Carib or Arawak or Taino or other kind of English. The reason for this, vis-à-vis what happened to the Africans, must be the difference between a colonized community, which could exist without being drawn headlong into the dominant culture, and imported workers, who had no traditional community roots in the new place to withstand the pull to the dominant culture. When the native Americans finally learnt the creolized languages of the blacks, this was more a matter of peer group learning.

From the very early beginnings right through the colonial period the English, who were in the position of power, made little attempt to learn the languages of the Africans whom they kept on bringing to do their work. Each individual African had to go through the same language acquisition process which all who preceded had gone through. There was little possibility of preparing the slaves for what was ahead of them because, as Dickson [1789: 112] points out specifically in relation to the slave auction in Jamaica, nobody had a comprehensive knowledge of the languages of the slaves:

We are told that they are 'generally preinformed of what is to happen'; but who is the interpreter? A sailor who has made more than one voyage to Guinea may understand some words he hears on the coast; a captain may know many such words; but is it possible that any man, white or black, should be skilled in the endless variety of dialects, spoken at the distance of many hundred miles up the country?

In the early period of slavery, therefore, West Indian societies were dominated by a mass of language learners in a way that no normal society is. In these early colonies it was a matter of a large segment of the population, undergoing a traumatic experience but not being able to give vent to their feelings and emotions through language communication.

THE HISTORICAL SPREADING OF ENGLISH COLONIES ACROSS THE REGION

The growth of the English language in the West Indies is directly correlated with the movement of English speakers across the region as they established colonies. However, the speed with which the language grew in individual colonies and the specific varieties that evolved are determined by the specifics of each contact situation. Up until the nineteenth century the countries of Europe treated the New World as property to be kept or bartered in trying to increase the national purse. The resultant changes in ownership affected cultural and linguistic development in that on the one hand where a country (*eg* St Lucia) changed hands about fourteen times there was no constant single European language as a linguistic target, whereas on the other where there was no change (*eg* Barbados) there was. In an outline of settlement history, therefore, it is important to keep in mind the pattern of constancy or change in target language. The following is a picture of the spread of English colonies in the West Indies (extracted from Holm [1986: 18-19] and modified slightly):

Date settled by the English	*Territory*	*Pattern*	*English speakers coming from*
1624	St Kitts	Constant	England/Ireland
1627	Barbados	Constant	England/Scotland, Ireland
1628	Nevis	Constant	St Kitts/Ireland
1628	Barbuda	Constant	St Kitts/Ireland
1632	Antigua	Constant	St Kitts/Scotland
1633	Montserrat	Constant	St Kitts/Ireland
1650	Anguilla	Constant	English, Leewards
1655	Jamaica	Constant	Barbados/England/Leewards
1740s	Guyana	Varied	Barbados/Leewards
1763	Dominica	Varied	Barbados
1763	St Vincent	Varied	Barbados/Leewards
1763	Grenada	Varied	Barbados/Leewards
1763	Tobago	Varied	Barbados

1797	Trinidad	Varied	Barbados/Windwards
1815	St Lucia	Varied	Barbados

Generally speaking, the English spread from St Kitts to the other Leewards, and from Barbados to the Windwards. English spread to Jamaica from Barbados directly and through Suriname (when it was English) and from the Leewards; and to Trinidad from Barbados and the Windwards. The spread of English speakers through the West Indies was therefore essentially a matter of radiation from two main points. Another significant factor which the table above suggests is that the later acquisitions by the British underwent about a century less of English language influence than the earlier acquisitions. This difference was indeed noticeable for most of the later acquisitions up until the late nineteenth century.

Whereas details of times, people and places can be extracted from official colonial documents, it is from the writers of the time that one gets an understanding of prevailing impressions about dominant influences in the society and about population composition. For example, Oldmixon [1708, 2:17] tells about the kind of English speakers who settled in Barbados: ". . . so this island was not settled by Puritans, as New England, and some other colonies are. The Inhabitants were for the most part Church of England Men, and Royalists; yet some there were who were of the Party call'd Round-heads, or Parliamentarians."

The traditional view held up to today by Montserratians about Montserrat is supported by Blome [1672: 114]: "This isle is most inhabited by the Irish, who have here a church for divine worship." The same author's comment about Anguilla leaves no doubt about the social level of the settlers there: "The inhabitants are English, which are computed to amount unto two or three hundred, who are but poor, the isle being said not to be worth keeping" [Blome 1672: 116].

Thompson [1770: 107], referring to a visit to Antigua in 1756, says:

All the good living is amongst the planters in the country. Where, if you are a Scotsman you may be well entertained . . . The greatest part of the estates on the island are conducted by overseers, the most of which are Scotsmen; who perhaps have been transported to Virginia, and from thence escaped to rule here . . . These light gentlemen treat us, who are come to defend their island, by the genteel appellation of alien and foreigner . . .

It is not clear why Thompson thought that the Scotsmen came from Virginia, unless it is that they did not sound exactly like Scotsmen in Scotland and were not Creoles either. It is also significant that Thompson's perception of a dominant influence by Scotsmen is not a commonly cited view. However, the cosmopolitan view of Trinidad, which is still popular today, is supported by M'Callum [1805: 23], who says:

Perhaps there is not a local spot in the universe that can boast of such a medley of inhabitants: English, Scotch, Irish, Welch, Spaniards, Germans, Swiss, Haitians, Americans, and French; the latter are the most numerous, having been particularly encouraged and regarded as favourites, you know by whom [Governor Picton]. Indeed he has encouraged all denominations to settle in preference to the British, *numbers of whom have been oppressed and banished . . .*

These are only some of the impressionistic comments made by contemporary writers about people in the islands. They show not only the intense prejudices that existed at the time but also the prominence of ethnic differences in the minds of people, a feature which would have had to be evident in dialects.

RIVAL COLONIAL PROPAGANDA IN THE EARLY YEARS

The main European rivalry in the Eastern Caribbean was between the French and the English. This political and economic rivalry was sustained not only by naval forces but also by information flow backward and forward between Europe and the colonies. Almost without exception reports, commentaries and histories were nationalistic and geared to promote the policy and intentions of the respective European powers. Such prejudice is seen from the earliest years when the native population was still a subject of fascination and interest for Europeans. For instance, de Rochefort in his *Histoire naturelle et morale des iles antilles de l'Amerique* (first published in 1658) says:

Nos Francois ont remarque, qu'ils ont grande aversion pour la langue angloise, jusqu'a ne pouvoir souffrir qu'on la parle devant eus, par ce qu'ils leur sont ennemis. Que s'il se voit dans leur langue corrompu plusieurs mots tirez de l'Espagnol, qui est aussi leur ennemy, c'est qu'ils les ont a pris, durant le tems qu'ils avoient communication avec cette nation-la, & quelle ne les avoit pas encore maltraitez.[1]

Whether the native populations actually were attracted to or disliked any specific European language is doubtful, for there is also contrary evidence from an English source which suggests that they had nothing against English:

For some of them, pointing to the limbs of their body one after the other, told us the names in their language and desired to know what they were called in English. This they then kept repeating till they were able to pronounce it well, or what to them seemed well enough and was fairly well indeed.[2]

It is interesting that the comment of de Rochefort, which is clearly not an unbiased one, is repeated fifty years later by Oldmixon [1708: 2:230]: "Some French Men have observed that they have a kind of Aversion for the English Tongue, and carry their Aversion so far, that they cannot endure to hear it spoken."

This repetition is but one example of a kind of historiography which was responsible for the perpetuation of many myths and half-truths – 'historians' quoting almost word for word accounts of earlier 'historians'. More interestingly, however, it illustrates the belief in some higher intrinsic beauty of the French language, a belief that was fostered in seventeenth century France as part of the magnificence of Louis XIV, and a belief which seemed to have been accepted by Englishmen. This belief coming out of the great century of French literature, together with the revolutionary philosophy of late eighteenth century France differentiated between the French and the English in the kind of cultural face and policy they presented to their overseas possessions.

COLONIAL LANGUAGE POLICY AND THE SPREAD OF ENGLISH

Policy is usually conceived of as explicit statements, but in the history of the West Indies language policy has to be seen as attitudes inherent in and consistent with an economic endeavour, as understandings evident in actual practice and only in a few cases expressed by explicit statements or laws. In this case language policy may also be seen as actions (not necessarily premeditated) which were integrally a part of protecting property and business. In other words, though in most cases there was no need to spell out what language should be used and when, there was sharp reaction to practices or intended practices which threatened the success of business. Explicit policy was therefore preventive and in a sense negative in that its sole motive was to forestall or prevent rather than to stimulate or improve. So, for example, explicitly stated policy was required when a language in the community, whether African or European or other, was seen as a threat to the control of the rulers of the colony. Since policy is synonymous with power, consideration of language policy in the pre-Emancipation West Indies is a matter of analysing the views and attitudes of the owners and managers of the plantations and those who constituted the legislative body at the time. In the case of the postemancipation West Indies, language policy was more properly a matter of language education policy.

It is said that France in dealing with its overseas territories, at least in the nineteenth and twentieth centuries, pursued a policy of assimilation, a policy based squarely on two planks – first, that by learning French the colonial gained access to the highest form of human culture and civilization, and secondly, that the learning of French by all was a way of removing the divisiveness occasioned by many different local languages and cultures. The policy of France also had another plank, which though not explicitly stated, was a known factor in economics. This plank, the essence of which is explained in the term 'cordon sanitaire' [Spencer 1971: 544], was in fact a characteristic of all the European colonizers. It is that by linking each colony in language, trade and finance to one specific European power, this not only cut it off from its very neighbours (unless its neighbours had the same mother country) but also set up a dependency relationship with the European country which was vigorously protected. This dependency relationship in turn caused the colony, except for those in the Spanish world, to be outward looking and to see as its ultimate goal the attainment of the features, linguistic and cultural, of the mother country. Language was a key factor in the maintenance of this 'cordon sanitaire'.

The English, in contrast to the French, did not pursue any specific cultural and linguistic policy, but from the very start focused almost exclusively on economic matters, while treating with disdain or at best paternalistic indulgence anything from the colonies. The British actually 'fostered' a sense of inferiority and separateness in the colonies. In any case, there were no attractive ideals or models in the British world to match those that the French revolution presented to the French world. The royal blood-nobleman-commoner distinctions bred into the mentality of the British extended into the colonies and served to justify acceptance of social stratification. Such stratification of course created tension and rivalry between groups, it created sharply differentiated social dialects and it made differences in dialect and language as important as shades of colour.

Policy is to a large extent determined by the persons for whom it is intended and the status of the worker becomes a major determining factor. There is an essential difference between the treatment of migrant workers and the treatment of a colonized people. In the case of migrant workers, persons are workers and no more, as far as the business owners are concerned; in the case of a colonized population, the business owner is initially an intruder who cannot totally disregard the fact that persons already form a society and have customs and languages which must be dealt with in some way. The slave in the West Indies was a special kind of migrant worker who ceased to exist socially when his official work was done. In this sense the West Indian slave contrasts with the colonized African in Africa and with the native American, and the policy of the Europeans was correspondingly different in each of these cases.

As far as the slave in the West Indies was concerned, the greatest need for a language policy, if it could be called such, was to ensure that the slave could understand enough of the European language to carry out his tasks. This was achieved through the apprenticeship system, as is explained by Willyams [1796: 13]: "... the new comer ... is placed with one of the old negroes, by whom he is instructed in his business".

This statement was made about Barbados, but the fact that this was a widespread practice meant the comment made for Suriname by Stedman [1806: 2:281] is relevant: "I have also observed, that under the care of some old negroes, appointed for that purpose, they [the newcomers] soon become fat and sleek, and learn the language of the colony." In this way the linguistic dependency and subordination of African slaves was ensured.

In contrast to this kind of implicit language policy, the language policy which is highlighted in the literature is that of mixing slaves in order to make sure that they did not conspire to overthrow their rulers. In accounts of Barbados there is repetition of the statement that mixing of slaves of different language groups prevented insurrection. This idea of mixing, first arising out of a statement made by Ligon [1657] and then repeated by Oldmixon [1708], is of course counterbalanced in the literature by statements claiming that slaveowners favoured certain tribes. For example, Henry Drax, one of the biggest planters in Barbados in the seventeenth century, in giving instructions to his manager, said: "I have observ'd the Caramantines, and Gold-Coast Slaves, have always stood and proved best on my Plantations, therefore you'l do well rather to buy those than of any other Sorts" [Belgrove 1755: 51].

Both of these positions are discounted by those who claim that the overriding factor in the acquisition of slaves was availability and price, which means that slaveowners could seldom exercise preference one way or the other. Even so, in the statement by Ligon, which is repeated in essence by Oldmixon, it is not clear that mixing was being identified as a conscious policy. For Ligon [1657: 46] says: "They are fetch'd from several parts of Africa, who speak several languages, and by that means, one of them understands not another . . ." This appears to be the reporting of a fact (mixture) and its consequences (lack of communication) rather than a policy adopted by slaveowners. Conversion of fact about Barbados to a general policy may well have been the work of historians.

The diversity of slave origin is also reported for St Kitts/ Nevis as late as 1730 in a letter addressed to the Lord Bishop of London by Rev. Robertson: ". . . there are so many different languages among them, that very probably not above one in ten or fifteen of themselves understands one another". One does not get the impression from this writer either that the diversity resulted from a deliberate policy, although here, as elsewhere, it is clear that this diversity was regarded as an advantage to the white masters.

As far as other language policies are concerned, laws which had the effect of placing restrictions on certain persons could be interpreted as having the effect of a language policy. For instance, the 1699 Laws of Barbados forbade anyone from bringing Indians (native Americans) into the island, and Jews could not without permission have more than one slave. However, although such laws effectively removed or reduced the possible influence of those people identified, these kinds of restrictions cannot be regarded as a significant factor in the development of English in Barbados specifically or in the West Indies.

BARBADOS AS THE LEADING EXAMPLE OF THE GROWTH OF ENGLISH

The specific variety of English which evolved in each society was determined in part by the dialects that were present and the relative strength of each. In this respect, social function and numbers of speakers of specific dialects were crucial. An earlier section referred to the pattern of influence and the places from which the settlers in individual territories came. This section now shows how demographic factors and social positions affected the evolution of individual dialects and the case of Barbados will be used as an example.

The specific case of Barbados will be examined because not only was it the main point of dispersal of English influence in the early West Indies but also there is more consistent information on Barbados than there is on St Kitts, the other dispersal point. In the early years the two ends of St Kitts were owned by the French and the middle by the English, which makes it difficult for one to factor out the influence of the French in the development of Kittitian English. Barbados, on the other hand, was never partitioned, did not change hands and because it was so quickly and completely settled, overcrowding caused people to leave to seek their fortune elsewhere. That Barbados is unique in this respect may suggest that it is qualitatively different from the rest and therefore should not be used as the guiding example of the development of English in the older British islands in the West Indies. However, the early demographic history of St Kitts is little different from that of Barbados. In both islands the early dominance and later decline of the white population under the influence of the plantation system had a significant effect on language development. In addition, in contrast to St Kitts, Barbados' geographical position and its economic prominence in the seventeenth century caused it to be regarded as a key island in the development of the British West Indies. So, it seems reasonable to use Barbados as the guiding example of the development of English in the West Indies and to follow the language dispersal argument – that patterns of language were taken along with migrants as they moved to other territories to settle.

There was no single dialect of British English that dominated in Barbados at any time while the English controlled Barbados. There were a number of dialects, both social and geographical, in evidence from the beginning of the settlement by the English and this variety did not diminish in the pre-emancipation period. Early writers pointed out not only the variety of Europeans but more precisely that the residents of Barbados were from different parts of the British Isles. This is seen, for example, in Blome [1672: 83] who used information garnered from Ligon: "The inhabitants of this isle may be ranged under 3 heads or sorts, to witt, Masters (which are English, Scotch, and Irish, with some few Dutch, French, and Jews), Christian servants, and negro-slaves."

Historical sources providing data on persons leaving for Barbados in the 1640s show that emigrants came from all parts of the British Isles. They started coming in 1627 and kept on coming in droves, so much so that in a very short time the whole island was covered with large and small holdings and in sixty years its population was about one third of its present size. In less than thirty years, that is by 1655, the white population reached 23,000, the highest that it ever reached, which is about three times its current size. The major demographic difference in Barbados, besides the presence of African slaves and a few Amerindians, was that in Barbados, there was no geographical separation of English speakers (*ie* English, Scottish, Irish) to correspond to that in Britain.

There is no evidence showing that during this period when the island was dominated by British natives specific regions of the island were settled by specific groups – not even the Scotland district can be shown to have been dominated by Scottish immigrants. There was a mixture of people and dialects across the island, a mixture which was only superseded by the native born population when it later became numerically dominant. Of course, as the power structure of the society took shape and reflected dialectal prejudices in Britain, dialects acquired their social values and relative prestige in the Barbadian society.

Social distinctions and therefore social dialects among the English speakers were present from the very start of the Barbadian society in 1627. For instance, although there is no general agreement on the exact number of settlers who came in the first batch, it is clear that among them there were both masters and servants, the latter brought to do the hard work. In the period up to the mid 1640s when small-crop farming was the norm, white servants were seen as the normal workforce in the same way that they were in Britain. The speech of the whites in Barbados in 1650 therefore was little different from that in Britain. The major linguistic curiosity in Barbados at this time was the language of the Africans, who by 1645 are estimated to have numbered between 5,680 and 6,400 [Handler and Lange 1978: 15].

In the literature of the time there are few direct comments on the language produced by the Africans, who were brought from a wide geographical area containing many languages and dialects. These Africans had to live in Barbados without being in contact with a sufficient number of people who spoke the specific dialect of their own language in each case. Not being socially or linguistically a coherent group, they had to learn English for functional purposes. The functions varied from extensive to limited according to the degree of social and psychological support available from peers speaking the same language. In other words, if an African did not have nearby a speaker of his own dialect, then he would have to learn English in order to communicate, no matter with whom. On the other hand, if he had several of his countrymen nearby, his need for English would have been limited.

From Ligon we get some indication of the slaves' restricted knowledge of English. Ligon tells of a case of some slaves who revealed a plot to their master and then explained why they refused to be rewarded for it. The language difficulty which these slaves had is seen in the comment by Ligon [1657: 54]: "The substance of this, in such language as they had, they delivered, and poor Sambo was the orator . . ." Ligon also makes a more general comment on the slaves' lack of English when he says [1657: 54]: "And this is all I can remember concerning the Negroes, except of their games, which I could never learn, because they wanted language to teach me."

The extent of variation among the Africans in their knowledge of English is hard to determine, but that there was variation is without question. In this period when small farms were more numerous, the more direct and constant contact between the English speaker and the African resulted in acquisition of English by some Africans. The safest conclusion one can come to about the competence in English of the black population in the period up to 1650 is that it varied. However, the implication of Ligon's comment about African language mixture obstructing communication is that the Africans generally did not speak much English, at least publicly and openly, and furthermore that there was no community language (*eg* creole) among them at the time. In other words, their non-African language competence was idiolectal (individual) interlanguage (system between the native and the target).

The most important development in the history of the West Indies to affect population and society was the change to sugar as the main crop. In Barbados the effects of this change quickly became clear. According to Handler and Lange [1978: 16], "The introduction of sugar changed Barbados from an island with 8 – 11,000 landowners in the mid 1640s to 2,639 in 1679." This increase in the number of large plantations was brought about by the dispossession of many small landowners who, as a consequence, left Barbados to try their luck elsewhere. Many indentured servants also left the island when their term finished. By 1680, "175 Barbados planters (7% of all property holders) owned at least 53% of the land and 54% of the slaves" [Handler and Lange 1978: 17].

In addition, whereas the white population and the black population were about equal in number (around 20,000) in 1660, by 1684 the white population was 19,568 and the slave population 46,602. In 1712 the white population was 12,528 and the slave population 41,970.

The change in the organization of the society, the decrease in the white population, and the sharp increase in the black population had a significant, if delayed, effect on language in Barbados. The society changed from one in which the blacks were a minority to one in which they were the majority; it changed from one in which the blacks were in close and direct contact with the English language to one in which the degree they came into contact with it varied according to their job on the plantation – if they worked in the plantation house or in the yard, they came into direct and constant contact with it, but if they worked in the fields, as the majority did, their exposure to it was much more restricted. The degree of contact that they had with English and the extent to which they had for practical purposes to communicate in it determined the extent of their competence in it.

The changes in population ratio and social organization did not have an instant effect however. In fact, it was the effects of the pre 1650 social situation which manifested themselves linguistically in the last half of the seventeenth century. Some of the clearest remarks about the slaves' competence in English are made by Godwyn [1680]. Godwyn's remarks (in his book called *The Negro's and Indian's Advocate*) have to be tempered by the knowledge that he was on one side of the long and continuous debate between those who wanted to convert the slaves to Christianity and those who opposed it. However, there is no doubt that even if there was some exaggeration, there was at the same time a great deal of truth in what he said. His remarks about the language of the slaves are as follows:

'Tis true, the Negro's ignorance of our language was for some time a real impediment thereto [conversion], and so long a tolerable plea for the omission; but none afterward, when they had arrived to an ability of understanding, and discoursing in English equal with most of our people; which many thousands of them long since have . . . (p. 2)

. . . upon my baptizing a male Negro of hers, of about thirty years old, speaking English plainly . . . (p. 38)

But as to the second [their want of English], there are, 1. Many who have lived a considerable time in the island 2. Others that were born in it. A 3d sort that have been brought up and baptized in England; who can all of them speak English, no worse than the natural born subjects of that kingdom. These I presume will make more than one moity of the whole.

What Godwyn was saying was quite clear – more than half of the black population spoke English just like Englishmen. Remarks that more than half the black population spoke English are also made by Oldmixon [1708, vol. 2], who is less detailed than Godwyn in that he only divides the slaves into Creoles and Africans. Oldmixon's position is that "the Creolian Negroes . . . all speak English" (p. 124) and that more than half the slaves in Barbados were Creoles by this time. The actual numbers for slaves given by Oldmixon may be inaccurate, but he makes his point quite clearly: ". . . whereas now of 60 or 70,000 Negroes, which are suppos'd to be in Barbados, 40,000 of them are Natives of the Island, as much Barbadians as Descendants of the first Planters" (p. 14). Oldmixon was of course not a first-hand observer, unlike Godwyn.

The ethnic subgroupings given by Godwyn above and the general one given by Oldmixon (Creoles and Africans) affected language acquisition because relations between all the members of the black population were not smooth and cordial. That these subgroupings were real is quite clear from events of the day reported by contemporary writers. For instance, with regard to the revolt of 1676, *Great Newes from the Barbados* reported that "this conspiracy first broke out and was hatched by the Coromantee or Gold-Cost Negro's"; and with regard to that of 1692 a broadsheet report of a person who arrived in Barbados the very day of the discovery of the plot says: "The Plot was formed by the Negro's that were born in the Island, and no imported Negro was to have been Admitted to partake of the freedom they intended to gain."

These are merely two references, but they certainly point to a conclusion that ethnic grouping was a significant restrictive factor in language spread among the black sector of the population in the early years. These references to actual plots are supported by writers' comments, the strongest of which is made by Oldmixon [1708, 2:124]: ". . . they hate one another so mortally, that some of them would rather dye by the Hands of the English, than join with other Africans, in an attempt to shake off their Yoke . . ." Such perceptions on the part of whites in the society might have led them to try to foster divisions.

The plotting of a revolt in 1692 by creole slaves in Barbados is interesting in that it contradicts the generally held belief that the world and vision of life were different for persons born into slavery as opposed to those who were enslaved as adults. It seems even more contradictory that Oldmixon writing in 1708 on the one hand sings the praises of creole slaves who are said to fit into society well:

There's a great deal of Difference between the Negroes; those that are born in Barbadoes are much more useful Men, than those that are brought from Guinea. Mr. Ligon could not make this Observation, the colony was too young; but the Creolian Negroes are every way preferable to the new Comers, (which they call Salt-Water Negroes) whom they despise, and value themselves much on being born in Barbados. The children that come over young from Africa are also better Servants, when they are grown up, than those that come thence Men or Women (p. 121).

and on the other is amazed at them: "When we consider that above half of the Blacks are Creolians, or Natives of the isle, their Folly and Madness appear the more unaccountable; that they should be willing to change their natural Lords for foreign" (p. 61).

This latter comment is made in view of the fact that not much more than ten years earlier than the time he was writing about, the creole slaves in Barbados had plotted to kill the governor and the planters and set up their own government. What is even more interesting about this plot is that the plotters *design'd to have taken up the Sirnames and Offices of the Principal Planters and men in the Island* (Broadsheet) – which must be construed as a plan to dupe people in England for some time. This in itself could only have been possible if the plotters believed that their English was good enough for external and internal communication, which gives some credibility to Oldmixon's statement that the Creole negroes all spoke English.

The ethnic differences and rivalry within the black population which the early literature demonstrates are supported and made more specific for the African population by Warner-Lewis, who in describing the behaviour of nineteenth century Africans in Trinidad underlines the effect of ethnic differences. Warner-Lewis analyses the speech of Yoruba speakers in Trinidad who most likely were direct descendants of African indentured labourers who went to Trinidad between 1840 and 1860. Although the language of these Yoruba speakers had little effect on the formation of Trinidad English Creole, one can extrapolate backwards and speculate about the development of African languages and dialects of these languages during the early slavery period. In this way one can appreciate the effect of African languages as a retarding force in the spread of English.

Warner-Lewis [1971: 46, 48] says:

Although there is much oral evidence of tribal prejudice* between certain African 'nations' in Trinidad, there does not appear to have been subtribal discrimination. In other words, one does not hear of Ijebu/Ekiti confrontation, for instance, and whereas informants claim to be "Yaraba", they do not know the subtribe of Yoruba to which they belong, or supply this information only after questioning on the specific issue. Probably exile brought solidarity on a more nationalistic level and these overseas Yorubas could not discriminate against each other's dialect peculiarities when Ijesa dialect speakers, for example, had more in common with an Ekiti speaker than with a Congolese. Under these circumstances of dialect contact, therefore, Yoruba standard/s probably emerged, among those communities that intermingled, if even one does not want to be bold enough to suggest that all Yoruba-speaking communities in the island shared the same standard.

[*Yorubas looked down on Congos, tolerated Coromantees, disagreed with Hausas, and fraternized with the Dahomeans.]

Warner-Lewis [1979: 103] also says:

The [19th century] African community was itself fragmented along linguistic and cultural lines . . .

Language was therefore a powerful tool of ingroup identification. And since it was not understood by the society at large, it became a secret code. They abused the police in it, they warned each other against police raids . . .

Using Warner-Lewis' analysis of the ethnic rivalries among the Africans in the nineteenth century to look backwards at the situation in the preceding centuries, one could argue, in reference to developments in Barbados specifically in the seventeenth century, that because of ethnic subgroupings the development of English across the black sector would not have been in nature that of a continuum but rather in strata which corresponded first of all to the social distinction between Creole negroes and saltwater negroes, to tribal distinctions between Africans, as well as to ownership and occupational distinctions. However, overall it is quite arguable that a significant proportion of the black population, probably mostly the Creoles, spoke a recognizable dialect of English.

Yet, there is still no mention in the literature up to this time of a 'bad' or 'degenerate' kind of English spoken by the slaves, even though the African born slaves could not have spoken English like Englishmen. Even in the case of the 1676 plot, which "was hatched by the Coromantee or Gold-Cost Negro's", the speech of one of the ringleaders (who was about to be burnt at the stake) is not represented directly or by comment as deviant in any way:

... which the spectators observing, cryed out to Tony, Sirrah, we shall see you fry bravely by and by. Who answered undauntedly, If you roast me to day, you cannot roast me to morrow: (all those Negro's having an opinion that after their death they go into their own countrey).

It is quite possible that this particular slave, who was not a plantation slave and who was in direct and constant contact with his master, had learnt English reasonably well and was therefore unlike most African born plantation slaves at the time. For the argument that was used by the planters during Ligon's days in Barbados was still being used in 1680 by 'the Gentlemen Planters in London' who, according to Harlow [1926: 325], are reported to have said: "... the disproportion of blacks and whites, being great, the whites have no greater security than the diversity of the negroes' languages which would be destroyed by conversion, in that it would be necessary to teach them English".

It is also quite possible that the 'Gentlemen Planters' in London were either out of touch with reality or merely using a tried and tested argument which served to stir up fear for the safety and survival of the whites. In any case, it is clear that up to the end of the seventeenth century there were sharp ethnic differences between slaves in Barbados which were reflected in typological language differences.

In summarizing the language situation in Barbados in the last half of the seventeenth century, it can be said that there were various dialects of English spoken by the white population and the creole black population. The African born slaves for the most part operated in African languages and it must be assumed they also produced varying learners' versions of the dialect of English with which they came into contact.

RADIATION OF LINGUISTIC INFLUENCE FROM BARBADOS IN THE SEVENTEENTH CENTURY

Emigration from Barbados to other English possessions in the West Indies was caused by the introduction of sugar as the main crop. The small farmers who were forced to leave Barbados took with them in many cases the slaves that they had. The indentured servants, who had no slaves in most cases, left alone. The language spoken by those who emigrated from Barbados varied according to the period, the length of time the persons were in Barbados, and their place of birth. Indentured servants who served their time and left would hardly have changed their normal dialects. The same is true of the small farmers who had come from various regions of Britain and spent only a short time in Barbados. It is only the creoles, black and white, who could have spread Barbadian varieties across the region. Unfortunately, the precise number of creoles who migrated from Barbados is not known.

Speculation about the role of Barbados in the radiation of linguistic influence has produced opposing views in the literature. In Cassidy [1980] the claim is made that Barbados acted as a dispersal point for creole to Suriname and Jamaica. In making this claim, which essentially matches language with settlement history, Cassidy argues that when early planters moved from Barbados with slaves to Suriname around 1651 and to Jamaica after 1655, the slaves took with them a creole language which had developed in Barbados, and that the creole of Barbados was the model for that in Suriname and Jamaica. A contrary argument about the early vernacular in Barbados is presented by Ian Hancock [1980] who, following comments by Cruickshank [1916], argues that the early demographic dominance of white English speakers in Barbados caused there to be right from the start onward among the slaves a dialect of English in Barbados, without any true creole. Hancock's point is therefore that there was no direct connection between the vernaculars of the three territories. These arguments by Cassidy and Hancock were not presented in a vacuum. In previous arguments about creoles generally Cassidy is known for his support of the notion of a single origin for creoles and maritime transmission of these creoles. Hancock's refutation of Cassidy's argument is consistent with his previous proposal for a point in West Africa (and not Barbados) as the dispersal point for English based creoles.

From our earlier conclusion about the language competence of the black population of Barbados around 1650 it is clear that neither Cassidy nor Hancock is correct in their contentions, for there seemed to be no community language among the slaves in Barbados at this time and their knowledge of English appeared to be insignificant and at best would have varied from individual to individual. As far as the latter part of the seventeenth century is concerned, it is very difficult to come to a conclusion about the nature of the language the slaves took to Jamaica and other islands from Barbados. There is no mention of, and there probably was not, any generally functioning, common, slave language; it seems more likely that there was a great deal of variety in the slaves' language and the more so among the African born slaves. Not even Hans Sloane, who himself travelled on a boat from Barbados to Jamaica in 1687 and who was very detailed in his descriptions, makes any comment about transmission of language, except to put forward an argument in support of the influence of sailor language. He says:

When a plantation has many men or women, 'tis said to be well handed, or in case of a few, it is said to be bad handed, or to want hands. This expression comes, as some others, from the planters of Jamaica, coming a long voyage at sea, whereby they get some of the sea phrases. At sea a man is call'd a hand, because his hands are chiefly useful there [Sloane 1707: lii].

It is interesting to note that nearly a century later Edwards repeated the same notion, with an additional comment about its source and with no indication of any other variety being transmitted from anywhere:

Another peculiarity in the manners of the English in the West Indies (in Jamaica especially) is the number of nautical expressions in their conversation. Thus they say, *hand such a thing*, instead of bring or give it. A plantation well stocked with Negroes, is said to be *well handed*; an office or employment is called *a birth*; the kitchen is denominated the *cook-room*; a warehouse is called a *store*, or *store-room*; a sopha is called *a cot*; a waistcoat is termed *a jacket*; and in speaking of the East and West, they say to *windward* and *leeward*. This language has probably prevailed since the days of the buccaniers [Edwards 1794, 2:9].

Except for these comments about 'nautical' language in Jamaica, and this is really a more general argument, there is nothing to support the Cassidy argument that a creole language was transported from Barbados to Jamaica in the seventeenth century or to any of the other Windward or Leeward islands.

BRITISH ETHNIC RIVALRY AND THE LINGUISTIC ROLE OF THE SCOTTISH
IN THE EIGHTEENTH AND NINETEENTH CENTURIES

Although no one dialect of British English was dominant in the West Indies up to the end of the seventeenth century, the arrival of more Scottish immigrants around the beginning of the eighteenth century, when the white population there was declining through migration, raises the question whether Scottish dialects of English could have had more than a minor effect on the language in those territories they went to, with a radiating effect in neighbouring ones.

In his claims about the increasing mistreatment of Scotsmen at the end of the seventeenth century Ridpath [1703] makes a case for the invaluable contribution of the Scottish in the development of the English colonies. He says:

They have been very instrumental in Peopling, preserving and improving these colonies, which are now become such a mighty addition to the Grandeur, Strength and Riches of England. Those of Barbadoes were so sensible of this, that they prefer'd them according to Merit and without distinction, to all Offices Civil and Military; so that of the Eight Militia Regiments in that island, commonly one half of the Field Officers were Scots-Men, or their Sons, and 'tis very well known there, that the Natives of Scotland have ever been as forward as any to venture their Lives and Fortunes in defence of the Country, and that they sustain'd a great part of the Fatigue, Charge and Danger of several Expeditions against the French at Martinico, and other Islands. Upon this Consideration, when Barbadoes was in danger of being invaded by the French Squadron under M. Pointi; and when it came to be debated what people they ought to encourage by particular Laws, to come and reside among them; it was unanimously resolv'd for the Scots, because they look'd upon them as good Men, firm Protestants and brave Soldiers; and worded it to that effect in the Act of their General Assembly.

Ridpath then goes on to make the following statements about the numbers of Scotsmen in the colonies:

> Several Ingenious Writers have computed the Number of the Inhabitants in the English Plantations to be 300,000; and it's believed that a third or fourth of those are Scots, or their Off-spring. But supposing, which is less than any man alledges, that the 6th part only of 300,000 are Scots, or their issue, that makes 50,000. If we allow 20,000 to be Women and Children, and others uncapable of earning their Livelyhood, there will remain 30,000 Men. If this be thought too great a Proportion of Men, it must be considered that the Number of Men imported does infinitely exceed that of Women (pp. 10-11).

In his account of the rise of the gentry in Antigua, Richard Sheridan [1961: 349] makes the point that: "From the standpoint of national origin the Scots were prominent after 1706. By 1775 some thirteen Scotsmen had established family dynasties of some importance. Numbered among these families were at least ten doctors and nine merchants." What is important about these Scots is that, according to Sheridan, "they moved with ease from one vocation to another". They were not therefore a class apart and out of reach of the mass of the population.

With regard to migration of Scotsmen into Barbados shortly before 1703, Ridpath makes the following comment: "As has been said already, above 2,000 Scots Servants were Imported Into Barbadoes alone in one Year, about 3 Years ago" (p. 14). There is no way of knowing how many of the Scotsmen who came to Barbados at the beginning of the century actually remained in Barbados. However, the earlier claim made by Ridpath about the proportion of Scotsmen in the colonies is worthy of note, if one bears in mind that it was the servants who were closer socially to the black population and who provided them more directly with their model of the English language. Yet, if these servants were dispersed all over the island, their influence would not have been great unless they were adding to an already significant number and unless in the levelling of British dialects Scottish suffered less than the others.

Contemporary literature provides no answer to this question. In spite of Ridpath's claim that there was clear discrimination against Scotsmen, the impression is created that, although there were differences within the colonies themselves, there was no dominance of one group over the others. For example, Oldmixon [1708, 2:17], influenced by an early comment by Ligon [1657: 57], refers to the political rivals, the Cavaliers and Roundheads, who "for many Years, liv'd peaceably and amicably; and by an Agreement made among themselves, every Man who call'd another Cavalier, or Round-head, was to forfeit a small sum to the Person offended".

This reference to the settling of political disputes in Barbados is extended to ethnic disputes in the Montserrat Code of Laws from 1668 to 1788:

And whereas also there are several persons of his Majesty's Subjects of his Three Nations, that is to say, England, Scotland, and Ireland, residing in this island, and oftentimes, as well in Drink as sober, certain words of Distinction do arise between his Majesty's Subjects of the said Three Nations, as English Dog, Scott's Dog, Tory, Irish Dog, Cavalier, and Round-head, and many often opprobrious, scandalous, and disgraceful Terms, to the Breach of his Majesty's Peace, &c and by certain Quarrels that may arise by Reason of such ill Language by the several Natives of the said Three Nations, to the endangering the Loss of the Lives of many of his Majesty's good subjects of the three Nations, which now are or hereafter shall be remaining, inhabiting, or abiding on this his Majesty's Island of Montserrat... if... shall presume to use, utter, or declare any of the Terms of Distinction afore mentioned, or any other scandalous or opprobrious Terms... he, she, or they so offending shall be proceeded against as Violators and Breakers of his Majesty's Peace... (p. 7, no.xi).

The similarity in the two extracts suggests that ethnic as well as political rivalry was general throughout the colonies, but there is no indication in either reference of dominance of one group over the others at the beginning of the eighteenth century.

A clear case of resentment of the Scottish and the idea that the Scottish were pervasive in Antigua and Barbados is given later in the century by Thompson 1770. Thompson was a naval officer in the West Indies in 1756-57 and he did not like the treatment he received. He claimed that he was regarded as a foreigner and that the locals had little respect for the mother country. In a poem entitled "The Creole" (in Thompson [1770]) he vents his rage on creole whites and quite unmistakably identifies them as 'Scots', thereby clearly indicating Scottish dominance in both Antigua and Barbados.

The writer who called himself 'a Resident' and actually lived in Dominica from 1796 claimed that: "Numbers of young men, some of them well educated, particularly those from Scotland and Ireland, engage as book-keepers, or overseers on estates" [Resident 1828: 225]. Although again the Scottish are mentioned, they are described as 'well educated', which is consistent with the characteristics of the gentry described by Sheridan [1961] for Antigua, but different from the kinds of comments coming from most other authors.

A few decades later the influence of the Scottish is again pointed out, in this case in relation to St Vincent, by Mrs Carmichael [1833] who, commenting on an expression used by the black population, says: "... they have probably learnt this and other decided Scotticisms from the number of Scotch managers and overseers". Although Mrs Carmichael, like most others, was not always objective in assessing general features, the fact that she herself had come from Edinburgh gave her an advantage in identifying what was Scottish in St Vincent. Furthermore, her comment shows that the social positions of the Scots as managers and overseers made them more direct models of the English language for the black population.

About thirty years after Mrs Carmichael's stay in St Vincent, Charles Day [1852] was putting forward an even stronger argument about the Scottish there:

There are a great many Scotch in St Vincent, and Scotch, too, of an inferior class ... Most of the Scotch come to the West Indies as indentured servants, and their countrymen being proverbially clannish, they get preferment as soon as qualified [vol. 1: 81].

Not only was it St Vincent that Day identified as having major Scottish influence but also Trinidad:

French and Spanish mulattoes abound here, and almost every white native of Great Britain will turn out to be a Scotchman, vulgar, coarse, ignorant and dogmatical. The horrible twang of 'Glaskie' and Ayr, and of Dumfrieshire predominates, and the refuse of all Scotland seems to have found its way to the West Indies, cottars in rank, and shopmen in mind [vol. 1: 174].

Even though Day's characteristic virulence and prejudices require temperance, it seems as if he actually did hear a significant amount of lower class Scottish dialects of English and that these were common enough to have some effect on both the Vincentian and Trinidadian dialects.

So, if the views, especially of Thompson, Carmichael and Day, which cover the period from the middle of the eighteenth century to the middle of the nineteenth, are to be accepted, there is a sustainable argument for the influence of Scottish dialects of English on the varieties of English which developed in the West Indies. There is no claim anywhere in the literature, however, that the amount of influence from the Scottish in any territory was as great as that claimed for the Irish in Montserrat. In the case of St Vincent and Trinidad whatever Scottish influence there may have been in the first half of the nineteenth century, it may not have survived because there was competing influence from French creole and also from dialects of neighbouring islands, especially Barbados.

COLONIAL RIVALRY AND THE PROGRESS OF ENGLISH IN GRENADA

In contrast to the older colonies, typified by Barbados, the newer colonies were different in their linguistic development. As a result, their individual cases have to be looked at more closely. In 1763 Grenada and Dominica were both predominantly French creole and French-speaking islands. In 1974, after two hundred years of English influence, Grenada was predominantly English creole and English speaking while Dominica was still predominantly French creole speaking. The most important factor in language change in Grenada was the bitter antagonism that developed in Grenada itself between the French and the English in the years between 1763 and 1795. Up until 1763 the French alone had controlled Grenada. From 1763 to 1779 it was a British possession. In 1779 the French recaptured the island and held it until 1783. The British regained it in 1783 and held it until 1795, a year which saw the culmination of the antagonism when an attempt was made in the name of the French Republic to recapture the island. The attempt did not succeed and the British held on to Grenada for the next 180 years.

The antagonism between the two colonial powers in Grenada was not normal and characteristic. It sprang up initially in great measure as a result of the behaviour of the slaves and 'gens de couleur'. When the British took over in 1763 many of the French proprietors sold their lands to the English, but the new masters instituted a new policy of rule that seemed to have been even harsher than that of the French. This was reflected in the following comment from l'Abbé Raynal:

> The new proprietors, misled, no doubt, by national pride, have substituted new methods to those of their predecessors. They have attempted to alter the mode of living among them. The negroes, who from their very ignorance are more attached to their customs than other men, have revolted (Quoted in Devas [1964: 66]).

As a result, relations between slave and master became difficult and on the whole production dropped. The fact is that the slaves hated the English because of their different treatment and the masters distrusted the slaves because they tended to be more French in manners, religion and language. This hostility drove the slaves together and to follow in rebellion the 'gens de couleur', whose numbers, according to Cox [1984: 20], had grown from 210 in 1777 to 1,125 in 1783 and whose treatment by the British did not differ from that described for Trinidad by Wood 1968 (see below). The attitude of the British and their need to secure their position also led them to discriminate against the French colonists and the Roman Catholic Church by passing unfair laws. The priests of the Roman Catholic Church, which was the Church of the majority of the population, resented the strictures that the British put on them and did not encourage support among their flock for the English.

The changing back and forth of the island from British to French only served to aggravate circumstances and to create an atmosphere of reprisal and recrimination. The French took advantage of their rule when they returned to power in 1779 to make the English pay for all they had done during the years 1763 to 1779. But since the second period of French control was so short, there was no time to forget the reprisals and the English were even more severe in their turn when they returned to power in 1783.

General civil unrest increased, but it was the doctrine of the French Revolution which seeped into the island from other French colonies, especially Haiti, that accentuated the problem. The connection between the French (creole) language, the ideas of the French Revolution and possible revolt was very high in the minds of the English. This is evident in the literature of the day. For example, Eyewitness Turnbull [1795] says:

... and the French language being the prevailing one with them [the slaves], contributed greatly to the seduction and ruin of by far the greatest part (p. 10).

But this ungrateful dereliction of the highest order of the negroes must be attributed, in a great measure, to the connexion which subsisted between them and the free coloured people. The field negroes, or those employed in the culture of the ground, and particularly the African negroes who had not been long in the island, and whose minds had not yet imbibed the baleful principles of the system already mentioned, were the last to associate with the insurgents (pp. 11-12).

With respect to the more remote causes of the revolt, it may be sufficient to remark, that its principal source was most indubitably in the great number of French inhabitants of every description, who were admitted, first as capitulants or afterwards on various pretences to settle in Grenada (p. 13).

After the revolt the antagonism diminished principally because of the drastic reduction of French colonists, 'gens de couleur', and French creole-speaking slaves.

Grenada, then, is an example of a colony in which the 'cordon sanitaire' policy of the French was so strong that it worked to their own detriment in that it led to rebellion and decimation of the population. It should be clear then that when slaves spoke African languages this posed no particular threat to their English masters, but when they were part of a rival European culture and resisted change from their language this was an ever-present irritant that had to be dealt with. However, for the English it was not a matter of dominance over slaves and 'gens de couleur', but rather a matter of rivalry with another European power because for them the slaves and 'gens de couleur' were mere foot soldiers in the army of their rival.

In Grenada the English language was given an opportunity to develop as a result of the decimation of the French and their language. According to Cox [1984: 20], the white population dropped from 1,661 in 1771 to 633 in 1810. However, this did not result in the immediate dominance of English because the majority of slaves and 'gens de couleur' were still French creole speaking and Roman Catholic and the traffic between the French creole-speaking islands, including Trinidad and Grenada, continued for the whole of the nineteenth century. With the receding of the French threat, the English no longer considered the language and culture of the slaves as dangerous and left them to their own devices. It was not until attempts were later made to educate the slaves in English that their language was again seen as an impediment.

LACK OF RIVALRY AND THE SLOW GROWTH OF ENGLISH IN DOMINICA

Dominica presents a different picture from Grenada. It was one of the last islands to come under European domination because it could not be easily taken from the native inhabitants, who defended it stoutly and did not welcome the Europeans with open arms, as Blome [1672: 111] comments: "the natives which are cannibals, and very barbarous, doth much hinder the comming of the English to settle here".

In 1687 when Sloane passed the island on his way from Barbados to Jamaica, it was still regarded as a Carib island. Sloane makes no mention of French settlers or of hostility of the native inhabitants to the English. He says: "We came the seventh [1687] in sight of Dominica, which is an island belonging to the Caribe Indians, who are at present inhabitants of it ... It has two hot baths in it, and used to afford refreshment to the English sailing that way [Sloane 1707: 41].

It seems clear then that the French and French creole that came to dominate Dominica within the next sixty years were substantially brought from neighbouring islands and did not develop there. In the same sense English and English creole did not develop in Dominica.

When the English claimed the island from the French in 1763, they tried, as they did in Grenada, to stamp their authority on the island officially. For example, they passed a law stating that all legal documents except wills and testaments were to be written in English. In spite of this and other laws with similar intent, the English language made little headway in Dominica. An explanation for this is given by Christie [1983: 42]:

Demographic and economic factors played an important part in the resistance to English in the early days and even for some time afterwards. For at least a hundred years after the arrival of the English, the French planters remained numerically and economically superior.

There was also a significant difference between Grenada and Dominica. Geographically Grenada was important in that from before 1763 it was used as a stopping point for ships trading between the islands and the South American mainland. Dominica did not have such strategic importance, seeing that it was in the middle of a chain of islands.

The English did not consider Dominica to be of great economic value because the terrain did not allow for extensive sugar plantations. It was not an island that the French were intensely interested in regaining either, although they did periodically try to claim it. In fact, the French really regarded Dominica for a long time as a Carib island. There was therefore no spur to rivalry in Dominica, and the residents, who happened to be mostly French and French creole speaking, were allowed to carry on with little interference or cause for concern. Atwood [1791: 208-209], in giving population figures at the time, claims that "the British inhabitants consist of English, Scotch, Irish, and the said American refugees, who altogether, including men, women, and children, do not exceed the number of six hundred, exclusive of the regular troops stationed there." This small number of English speakers had little effect on the rest of the population. French and French creole therefore served as a strong retarding force in the spread of English as a functional language in Dominica. There was very little necessity for English in Dominican society of the eighteenth and nineteenth centuries and especially so among the Caribs, none of whom according to Atwood [1791: 222] could speak English.

However, the text here referred to as Resident [1828] gives a picture of Dominica which is very English. It was written by a person who went to Dominica in 1796 as a young man 18 years old and spent a number of years there. The book was published in 1828 but refers to the early experiences of the author. The author makes the comment that "[Twenty years ago] . . . there were more French than English negroes; now the case is different, and hand-in-hand, education, and moral and religious instruction, are rapidly extending their beneficial effects" (p. 241), and also that "The African customs are fast wearing out; the creole negroes speak English much better than they did . . ." (p. 238).

These two comments do not give an accurate picture of the whole of Dominica at the beginning of the nineteenth century, for Dominica with its rugged terrain and Carib history was not brought under the effective cultural influence of the British until well into the nineteenth century. However, the topography of the island, the small size of the population and the self-contained nature of the plantation meant that both French and English plantations could exist in isolation from each other and that one area of the island could exist relatively unaffected by the rest. This was also true for the Caribs, who also were restricted to specific areas of the island.

THE BLACK CARIBS' OBSTRUCTION OF ENGLISH
IN ST VINCENT

English was first introduced into St Vincent as the official language in 1763 when the British acquired sovereignty over the island, but it made little progress in the next thirty years because of the constant struggle between the British and the French, and the refusal of the Black Caribs to accept British rule. The Black Caribs, who were a major force in St Vincent, aligned themselves with the French to resist the British. Their alliance with and preference for the French was so strong that it caused Young [1795: 122] to remark: "Sad and fatal experience has shown that the combination of barbarous and of national enmity is not to be broken, and that the Charaib will ever be French."

So persistent and unyielding were the Black Caribs that the only solution the British could see was to expel them from St Vincent. This expulsion therefore made it easier for British influence to dominate and for the English language to develop.

However, the historical influence of the French did not disappear overnight because at the end of the eighteenth century French creole was still being spoken by a significant number of slaves in St Vincent. Yet, by the time of Mrs Carmichael's stay in St Vincent in the 1820s French creole seemed to have declined and English creole to have grown, for there is almost no mention of French creole in her account.

THE RISE OF IMMIGRANT ENGLISH IN TRINIDAD[3]

Trinidad was emerging out of the shadows of Spanish neglect at the end of the eighteenth century when it became British, but paradoxically it emerged as a country of immigrants, most of whom came from the French world. Montlezun [1818, 1:318-19] claimed that: "En 1783, la population de la Trinidad n'était que de 126 blancs, de 295 de couleur libres; de 310 esclaves et de 2,032 indiens, total 2,763."[4] He goes on to say that in 1797, when the British took it over, it had 2,151 whites, 4,476 coloureds, 10,009 slaves, 1,082 Indians for a total of 17,718. Montlezun [1818, 1:319] continues: "L'émigration qui se fit de Saint-Domingue et des colonies anglaises à la Trinidad, en 1803, avait élevé sa population, en 1807, à 31,000 habitans, dont 21,000 esclaves."[5] Whether Montlezun's figures are accurate or not, what they do show is that immigration caused the native population to be greatly outnumbered, that there was a consciousness of this, and that 1803 was like another starting point for language in Trinidad.

The mixture of peoples and the emergent nature of the situation no doubt led Bridgens [1837] to characterize the language in Trinidad as "a mongrel lingo, locally termed, 'talki-tak', a jumble (unintelligible to a novice) of corrupt French, Spanish, English, and native African".

In the early years of the nineteenth century English-speaking persons in Trinidad were in no sense a uniform group and were, in addition, a minority up to the late years of the century. Not only were the English-speaking persons divided according to the usual social and racial distinctions of plantation societies but they had also come to Trinidad from several different places and were of different nationalities – varieties of British, varieties of West Indian and some Americans. The most dominant group in this mixture, however, was those who came from Barbados; this group included both slaves and masters. Even though the claim of the 1831 census taker, cited by LePage and Tabouret-Keller [1985: 52-54], that in 1831 approximately half of the population was Barbadian born seems exaggerated, it clearly points to a significant influence of Barbadians on language in Trinidad. The major influence in this case was the language of the slaves and not that of the masters.

As far as the noncreole English-speaking whites are concerned, official statistics do not show a clear dominance of any one group, but impressionistic contemporary comments do. As was pointed out before, Day [1852] lamented the fact that the majority of British were from Scotland. Even if this claim is exaggerated, what Day's comment highlights is that Scottish dialects were being used widely and were being heard because the Scottish were interacting with all classes in the society. Some of these Scottish migrants who came to Trinidad had left other islands to try to improve their fortunes in Trinidad.

As far as the creoles are concerned, traffic from Barbados and other British islands to Trinidad continued for a century and a half after Trinidad became British. So, in contrast to the older British islands where varieties of English, including creole English, emerged through language contact between Europeans and Africans and then developed independently, in Trinidad the varieties of English were brought to Trinidad by masters, slaves and others and continued to be reinforced from their sources even at the same time as the very varieties in Trinidad were developing their own peculiarities. It seems quite unlikely, then, that by Emancipation there could have been characteristically Trinidadian varieties of English produced by whites, blacks or coloureds. In other words, while Pinckard in 1806 could identify a Barbadian by his language, it would not have been possible for him to identify an anglophone Trinidadian in the same way at that time.

While the English, in the person of authors like M'Callum [1805: 23] and Day [1852, 1:174], resented their subordinate position in Trinidad, from Coleridge [1826: 126-27] one gets the impression that the various nationalities were cooperating with each other and had accepted British rule. It is difficult to assess these conflicting impressions of contemporary authors, who were reacting directly to personal experience. A recent commentator, Wood [1968: 40-41], points out that the 'gens de couleur', who had come from the French world, resented the treatment of the British, and presumably opposed them:

Mulattoes had come to expect equality in legal matters with whites and to be granted subtle graduations of respect in social life depending on their degree of whiteness. The British took little notice of this hierarchy of prestige; animated partly by insensitivity, partly by fear of the way the 'gens de couleur' in San Domingo, Martinique, and Guadeloupe had acted staunchly as a class against the whites, and partly by the continuing devotion of many of them to the first principles of the Revolution, they passed discriminatory legislation against the people of colour in the early years of their rule.

This suggests that the picture of general cooperation with the English was not a true one. So, if the divisions of ethnicity and language are taken as the reality of early nineteenth century society in Trinidad, then the growth of English would have been slow and difficult and the anglophone part of Trinidad would have taken some time to overcome the general society's view of them as a minority voice and a voice of immigrants, like almost everybody else.

THE EFFECT OF RETURNING MIGRANTS WITH BRITISH EXPERIENCE ON WEST INDIAN VARIETIES GENERALLY

From the middle of the seventeenth century onwards English involvement in slavery in the Caribbean and in the slave trade resulted in an influx into England of an increasing number of black Africans and black West Indians, who soon swamped the small number of black residents already in England. By the 1770s, the number of black residents in England was estimated by various persons[6] to range between 10,000 and 20,000 persons, a number that caused great concern to those who wanted to keep England white. By the middle of the eighteenth century the vast majority of Blacks in Britain were domestic servants, living and working in the households of the wealthy and those who pretended to be. These domestics, for the most part, had been brought back by British planters on their return from the West Indies and were kept in the same status of slaves as they had been in the West Indies. Not unexpectedly, there are few comments on the language of West Indian domestics in Britain to be found in the literature, but it is reasonable to assume that their position as domestic slaves, which in the West Indies had allowed them some facility in English, would have provided them with the kind of experience in Britain for them to achieve a high level of competence in English.

Even though, in general, attempts to get Blacks to leave England were largely unsuccessful, some actually returned or were sent back to the West Indies. The 'dangerous' effect of the English experience of returning Blacks was commented on by Fielding [1768]:

> and indeed, it is the less of the two to let them go about their business, for there is a great reason to fear that blacks who have been sent back to the plantations, after they have lived some time in a country of liberty, where they have learnt to read and write, been acquainted with use, and entrusted with the care of arms, have been the occasion of those insurrections that have lately caused and threatened such mischiefs and dangers to the inhabitants of, and planters in the Islands in West Indies ... (Quoted in Shyllon [1977: 97]).

A slave being able to read and write as well as speak like an Englishman would obviously have been more than the many illiterate plantation owners in the eighteenth century could tolerate. They would have thought twice before allowing such slaves to 'infect' others. Yet, it is quite likely that such slaves, who were domestic slaves in any case, may have felt themselves removed from the mass of slaves and would not have fitted back into the plantation system very well. On the other hand, such slaves, especially in small islands and small populations, could have been shining examples to slaves who had never even been far outside their own plantation. The problem, however, is that the incidence of such returning slaves is virtually beyond recovery from the historical data and their overall effect indeterminable.

THE ROLE OF BLACK SEAMEN IN THE SPREAD OF ENGLISH

Another substantial group of black persons whose base was in Britain was those who worked on English ships. As Shyllon [1992: 203] says:

> At the same time, significant numbers of Black crewmen began to appear aboard both merchant and Royal Naval shipping... Although it is as hard to quantify the Black seamen as it is the Black servants, it is very clear that by the eighteenth century they were a feature of virtually every major British port.

The reason for the use of black slaves in a previously white domain, was, as was the case also in semiskilled jobs on the plantation, a matter of economics. Bolster [1991: 53] explains its development as follows:

> Eighteenth century maritime slavery grew primarily out of the voracious demand for seafaring labor brought on by the expansion of colonial shipping. Between a rapid succession of wars draining merchant vessels of their manpower, and the availability of slave-labor to Anglo-American merchants and ship captains, slaves were sent to work aboard ship.

Although the role of maritime transmission in the spread of creole languages was at one time a leading theory put forward to account for similarities in these languages and, in fact, to link pidgins and creoles across the world,[7] it was assumed, probably through ignorance, that all sailors were white and European, and so the theory of maritime transmission positing a Portuguese origin arose and died because of its European bias. The presence of black seamen on English and other ships puts a different perspective on the role of sailors in the spread of creole languages generally, but more specifically, as is relevant here, on the spread of varieties of English.

The language competence of black seamen resident in Britain was shaped by their experience both during and between voyages. Between voyages they had to find work wherever they could, which meant that they did all kinds of jobs in and around the ports where the ships docked. This kind of urban, lower class experience provided them with a language variety typical of persons of this class in England. During voyages their close and constant association with white seamen affected them linguistically even more. The effect of the association is claimed by Bolster [1991: 54] to have moved those resident in the New World closer to Europeans than all other slaves:

> Seafaring slaves, numerous as they were, remained something of an anomaly, and were undoubtedly among the most acculturated to Euro-American norms of all slaves. In fact, maritime work blurred the social boundaries and status definitions of New World workers, scooping up in its net white sailors, free black sailors, and slaves, who often worked aboard the same ships, sharing similar duties and conditions.

No doubt, those who were resident in Britain were even more English, as a result of their experience between and during voyages.

Black seamen working on English slavers were influential from the time the boats docked to collect slaves in Africa until they reached the West Indies. In fact, a strong case can be made that these black seamen served as the initial models of 'English' for African slaves brought to the English colonies. Whatever the effect of such temporary models was, there is little doubt that black seamen would have bridged the gap between white English speakers speaking their own varieties of English and Africans speaking many different languages. Black seamen would have acquired competence over a range of varieties from their experience in Britain, the West Indies, North America and Africa. In addition, their varying social status on and off ship would have taught them to use varieties to their advantage.

Evidence shows[8] that in West Indian ports when local black pilots addressed black ship hands, they did so in a very authoritative manner and their language took on a fairly formal tone, as if to impress those on board. While this formal tone could well have been used to impress the white passengers, it is quite likely also that the language of black seamen was nearer to British English and that this provoked a change of register among those slaves in West Indian ports who had to deal with these seamen. Overall, the influence of black seamen on the development of English in the West Indies may have been minor, but at least they provided a symbolic link between the West Indian colonies, British North America and Britain which is not negligible.

NATIONALITY, SOCIAL CLASS, FAMILY AND RACE RELATIONSHIPS

National feelings began to increase in the West Indies not only because of perceived inequities of British policy towards the colonies but also because of the numerical increase of the native population, especially in Barbados. In this island the general picture of historical development shows that the last half of the seventeenth century witnessed the overall demographic dominance of the creole slave and the first half of the eighteenth century saw the emergence of creole white dominance in the white population. However, this was not so for the white population in the other islands, for as Resident [1828: 224] says: "In most of the islands, therefore, the proportion of Europeans is equal to, or exceeds, that of the creoles, Barbados excepted." This comment relates to the end of the eighteenth century and shows that foreign influence was still strong in most of the islands.

As early as 1722 the constitution of Barbados, in identifying those eligible to vote or to be representatives, spoke first of all of "natural born subjects of the age of twenty-one years . . ." *ie* Creoles. This alone indicates the growing power of the native population. In fact, if slaves and whites are taken together, by the first half of the eighteenth century Barbados was predominantly native Barbadian. Such a change affected attitudes not only in Barbados, but also in neighbouring islands which were influenced by Barbados. In the seventeenth century the white populations in the New World had been for the most part migrants who were still attached by family ties to their native countries; by the end of the eighteenth century this was no longer so. The 'no taxation without representation' position, which led to US independence in 1776, had become a common sentiment in most, if not all, the British New World colonies. The colonists reached a stage where they no longer felt themselves to be Europeans and were unwilling to surrender the fruits of their labour to the European mother country.

Detachment from England and attachment to Barbados are pointed out by Pinckard [1806, 2:132]:

Some have not been able to trace back their pedigree to the period when their ancestors first arrived, and therefore have no immediate thought or regard, concerning the mother country; but abstractedly consider themselves only in the detached sense of Barbadians . . .

According to Pinckard, the Barbadian pronunciation was even acquired by some of those who came to live in Barbados and stayed there for some time. It could be suggested then that since the European colonists were not necessarily aristocratic, since Barbados had acquired an importance of its own, since nonwhite persons were at the time socially unimportant in matters of language, a 'European' accent in itself had no perceived social value, did not carry significant advantage and there was therefore no conscious effort made to maintain it. This suggestion however has to be tempered by the fact that the whites throughout the West Indies continued to send their children to England for their education and so for them England and Europe generally were still seen as superior. Yet, even in this respect Barbados seemed to be different, according to the comment from Resident [1828: 221-22]: ". . . there being, in that colony alone, a very large portion of the white population who have never been out of it, and who are truly *Barbadian born* and *bred*". The effect of this was that the Barbadian 'accent' and Barbadian speech generally were more perceptible in the mouths of white creoles than were the corresponding 'accents' and *speech in the other islands*.

Even though national identities were developing as a result of the increasing influence of creole whites and creole domestic slaves, the massive influx of Africans throughout the first three quarters of the eighteenth century had a considerable influence on language development, especially in a context where the white population was declining and particularly the indentured servants, who provided the black population with models of English. The increase in the ratio of black to white coupled with the constant replacement of a sizeable proportion of the field slave population by adults speaking African languages meant that there was 'regression' or at least fossilization in the general drift towards English among the black population. This 'regression' in turn influenced the white population, which was moving closer to the black population as characteristic linguistic identity crystallized.

From the way that Pinckard presents his comments about the speech of the whites in Barbados, it can be deduced that he viewed their pronunciation as originating from the black sector of the population, for he says that it was not "confined to the people of colour only". This influence of the slaves' speech on the whites resulted from the way in which the plantation was organized and run. Since slaves were used to relieve whites of all kinds of work, including childrearing, this led to a system of nannies and house servants in which the children of the white masters from their earliest days as well as the masters and mistresses themselves were cared for by slaves.[9] The effect of the relationship between nanny, child and mother on language acquisition is explained in the following way by Wentworth [1834, 2:183]:

But of the married ladies: one crying evil is their disdaining to suckle their offspring, resigning them almost entirely to the care of a negro or mulatta wet-nurse, from which they may not only engender some latent malady, but as soon as they can lisp, they insensibly acquire that drawling dissonant gibberish, that awkward carriage, and vulgar manner, which a few years at an English boarding-school often fail totally to overcome. The consequence is, that mothers too often adopt the same abominable elongated sentences, to suit the comprehension of their children, until they as insensibly interweave it, in their ordinary manner of speaking.

In addition, slave children were used to provide company and amusement for the white children and such age group interaction was even more influential than the nanny-child interaction. The effect of this was pointed out in the case of Jamaica by Leslie as early as 1740: "... for a boy, till the age of seven or eight, diverts himself with the negroes, acquires their broken way of talking, their manner of behaviour ..." The language that was acquired as first language by the children of those in the highest class in the society was therefore also the language of those in the lowest class of the society.

After a hundred years of this kind of interaction, the language of each territory became more homogeneous for native born inhabitants and included features which were generalized across all classes in the society. So, for instance, with reference to Barbados, Pinckard, while attributing the syntax and colour of cursing, which had already developed by the beginning of the nineteenth century, to 'the lower orders of Barbadians', was also saying that it was common across the society. The national language variety which developed in each West Indian territory followed this pattern and was therefore the result of movements in opposite directions – black towards white and white towards black.

The movement of the races towards each other in language was also strengthened by the realities of the physical world. The Christian religion and the philosophy of the day set up monogamy and the separation of the races as ideals. Reality, however, was different. The easy availability of black women, who had little or no control over their own bodies, and subsequently the preference of coloured women for white men, led to a situation where there was scant respect for the vows of Christian marriage and less for maintenance of racial purity. Indeed, it became normal and excusable for white men to get their pleasures from the female slaves, as Dickson [1789: 92] points out: "... many white men are not ashamed to live in such habits of intimacy with the female domestic slaves, that it is next to impossible a revolt could be hatched and come to any dangerous crisis, without being discovered".

By the end of the eighteenth century the evidence of the relationships was plain to see. Throughout the Caribbean there developed a group born of these encounters, which became so numerous that it was specifically identified and named – in the French world people in this group were called 'gens de couleur', and in the English world they were called 'people of colour' or simply 'coloured'.

The relationship between race and language, which had been from the beginning a distinguishing feature in the New World, was made a little more complex with the addition of colour distinctions. This resulted from the fact that the white fathers, who felt that they had some responsibility for their coloured offspring, set them up in the society above their black brothers and sisters but below their white ones. In some territories it seemed to have become a normal practice for coloured children to be given their freedom, as is reflected in the comment in Carmichael [1833, 1:91]:

Those coloured children, who are the illegitimate offspring of white men, are, with few exceptions, free: when they are not so, the father is most justly detested, and held up as a character anything but respectable: I never could hear but of two instances of this.

As far as their position in society was concerned, they were seldom field workers and were in fact given relatively easy jobs, as Day [1852, 1:90] points out: "For a creole lady also to talk to you of 'a coloured sister or brother of mine', is a matter of course. These illegitimate female relations generally act as servants to the more fortunate brothers and sisters." Although this comment was made in reference to St Vincent, it was equally applicable to all the territories.

There is also evidence which shows that white women had liaisons with black men which produced children (Barbados Census 1715 – mentioned by Beckles [1992]). Such women were poor whites and such liaisons and coloured children born from them were not significant in number as far as influence on the whole community is concerned. Children born of such liaisons and raised by their mothers would naturally have acquired more features of white speech than coloured children whose mothers were black. There is little doubt, however, that the latter set were far more numerous, had a greater chance of moving into favoured positions of service (because of their fathers' influence), and as such had more influence linguistically than the former set.

The coloured people became a group intermediate socially and linguistically between the whites and the blacks. The favoured ones among this group, having been given some advantages, increasingly sought more through education or other means – language being one of them – through which they could distinguish themselves from the black population and also preserve an advantage for themselves. In relation to Barbados, Dickson [1789: 92] points out that: "The very negroes and mulattoes, who are generally sober and industrious, are well attached to the whites, on their relation to whom the mulattoes very much value themselves."

Commenting on coloured creole slaves, Carmichael [1833, 1:84-85] makes the point that:

They always address each other with much ceremony, never using the Christian name without putting Miss, or Sir, before it. This is universal among coloured slaves; and even the white population, in speaking of a coloured female slave, always calls her Miss. To omit these forms, would appear to them a downright insult, and few things would displease them so much as to forget addressing them in this way.

Wentworth remarks that: "The coloured women, in maintaining a grade of superiority over the negroes, are extremely tenacious of the distinctive prenomen of *Miss*, as well as a mark of respect among themselves" [1834, 1:186n]. In these slave societies where social stratification was very rigid, forms of address in everyday conversation were of the utmost importance and a conscious indicator of social station. In this specific case it meant that white and coloured women were addressed similarly, in contrast to blacks, who were given no 'prenomen', except, in a sense by their own children, for as Carmichael [1833, 1:270] explains: "I have frequently seen mothers flog their children severely for forgetting to say yes or no ma'am, to them; for a negro child is early drilled by them to call their mothers 'ma'am', or a reputed father 'sir'." Slave children were then the ones at the bottom of the social ladder.

The reality of race and colour in everyday West Indian plantation society was kept constantly in the psyche of the population by accepted terms and descriptions. In addition to general terms such as *white*, *coloured* and *negro*, there were other well-known and familiar adjectives used especially to identify the nonwhite population. In the early years euphemistic or poetic colour adjectives such as *tawney* and *sable* were used to refer to the native American and the black portions of the population respectively. As the native American part of the population declined in importance in the West Indies, the term *tawney* became less common. In North America generally *tawney* gave way in favour of the less precise (in terms of colour) *yellow*, which in turn was superseded by the more dramatic *red* (Indian). In the

West Indies *sable* continued to be used for some time before it eventually disappeared.

In the West Indies the term *coloured* was used to refer to those persons who were a mixture, direct or indirect, of black Africans and white Europeans. This category of persons was important in real terms because of their middle position. They were a constant reminder of miscegenation and illegitimacy in a previously sharply divided social structure in which the legitimate and white were free and the black were without rights and slaves. It was only in this section of the society, in the case of a child born of a direct relationship between a European and an African, that a decision could be made by a parent about a child's status. Since such decisions were often made according to the sex and colour of the child, shades of colour became very important for coloured persons and eventually for the whole society.

A system of terms therefore developed which indicated differences in parentage but which also gave some idea of differences in colour. It was a system of terms which was 'negatively' based in that it identified the proportion of *negro* in those who were classified as coloured. The following diagram from Stedman [1806: 103] shows terms used to identify offspring from different combinations:

```
                    white      black

            white        mulatto          black

       white      quaderoon      sambo       black

              mestice(octoroon)       mongroo
```

Although these terms were not commonly used by European authors, they were very important to the coloured people at the time, who automatically divided themselves into higher and lower classes according to this system of relationships, legal status and occupation.

For the coloured, therefore, the English language developed a set of terms to identify them and they themselves saw in the use of the English language a means of distinguishing themselves from those whom they regarded as inferior and a way of matching those who were considered superior. Language was both a marker and a tool. In addition, the white to black colour spectrum which developed in all West Indian societies generally correlated with a movement from greater to lesser competence in the English language. However, as is the case for all other groups in the plantation society, any suggestion of a uniform or homogeneous classification of coloured people throughout the West Indies would be misleading, for in many cases there was little distinction in habits or speech between coloured and black.

PERSONALITY FACTORS IN THE LEARNING OF ENGLISH AMONG THE SLAVES

In the plantation society of the West Indies where English was the perceived language of communication, in order for a person to succeed in his/her intentions, manipulation of some form of the English language was essential. One of the determining factors in second language acquisition especially and language use generally is said to be the characteristics of the learner. These characteristics – personality, attitudes, motivation – vary according to the individual and are regarded as features which assist or obstruct the individual in the manipulation of a language and in the achievement of different levels of proficiency in a target language. Success in the manipulation of the English language, whether in the case of the creole slave or the African slave, was therefore dependent to some extent on personality, attitudes and motivation.

What is significant in the case of the slaves in the West Indies is that they were generalized by authors into a single personality, having the same attitudes and motivation. An example of this European perception of uniformity occurs in Coleridge [1970: 81]:

> The negros cannot be silent; they talk in spite of themselves. Every passion acts upon them with strange intensity; their anger is sudden and furious, their mirth clamorous and excessive, their curiosity audacious, and their love the sheer demand for gratification of an ardent animal desire. Yet by their nature they are good-humoured in the highest degree . . .

Although such a perception was based on the conception of the negro as an animal controlled solely by instinct, the comments themselves point to vibrant social relations among the slaves and a normal situation for language acquisition in the first quarter of the nineteenth century. In other words, such a situation would not have made language acquisition difficult for any specific personality type.

It is obvious that in spite of the harshness of the experience, which did indeed mould the behaviour of all the slaves, the uniformity of personality which was portrayed was merely a comforting fiction. However, such fictions have a measure of reality if the persons so portrayed feel it necessary to satisfy the expectations of those who have such notions, especially when they are superiors, and also if they have no other outlet for their abilities, as Ramsay [1784: 245] points out: "The truth is, a depth of cunning that enables them to overreach, conceal, deceive, is the only province of the mind left for them, as slaves, to occupy." This to some extent was the reality of the situation for most of the slaves in the West Indies. They were in large measure forced to play roles, and language was an integral part of those roles.

The character of the slave which was built up in the literature is that of an incorrigible liar who was deceitful, evasive and ambiguous as well as a person given to exaggeration and flattery. On the other hand, this person who was so able with words could be extremely obtuse and could exhibit persistently high levels of noncomprehension. From the circumstances in the literature it can be seen that this characterization applied to men more so than women because the latter were on the whole less problematical for the white masters. No specific uniform characterization of female slaves emerges from the literature.

The kind of generalized character that is given for the slave of course arose out of the relationships between the slave and his white superiors. It is a characterization which has language as the main point of focus, as is natural in a social situation in which the subordinate had always to be accounting for behaviour or trying to avoid work or trying to manipulate his superior. From one point of view, it would seem that a slave characterized in this way would have had to be reasonably competent in some form of English. From the other point of view, however, such a characterization could have resulted from a great amount of nonverbal behaviour on the part of the slave and even limited competence in English. The reality of the situation was that slaves had varying levels of competence in English because of social and other reasons more powerful than character. This being so, the influence which character had on proficiency could not by itself have led to a significant increase in proficiency in English.

The way in which the slave spoke to his white superior had to conform to the social position of a suppliant – the slave's speech had to be characteristic of a person of a lower class, otherwise it could be interpreted as insubordination and result in punishment. It was therefore not in the slave's interest in talking to the white superior to demonstrate a high level of proficiency in English – articulate speech is not consistent with acts which are apologies, pleas for clemency, feigned stupidity and ignorance, simpleminded happiness, or deliberate flattery of a superior. Such speech had to be deferential and constantly punctuated by appropriate terms of address. It had to give leads for the white superior to display knowledge and understanding and even where it imitated the white superior's example, it had to do it a little imperfectly. Therefore, paradoxically, the slave's linguistic behaviour towards a white superior would not have demonstrated the slave's best English.

CONCLUDING STATEMENT

What this account of the social and political influences on West Indian English highlights is a great number of registers to suit interaction between all social levels of persons, between persons performing different jobs, as well as a variety of geographical dialects across and within the various islands. As far as language 'teaching' and learning are concerned, one of the most significant factors was the role of old, 'retired' persons, for these were the persons who were put to instruct not only the newly arriving Africans but also almost all of the children born in the creole society. What this meant was that the speech of the old continued to serve as the model for language acquisition over a long period of time, thereby providing for maintenance of older varieties. In addition to this, the whites in the society slept with, were nursed by, and played with the blacks in the society – a fact which led directly to the movement of the language of the whites in the direction of that of the blacks. In general, then, there was an entwining of the languages of these two racial groups and their miscegenated offspring. As a result of all these factors, the competence of persons in West Indian societies of the time was highly variable.

During the formative period of West Indian vernaculars, West Indian societies were predominantly oral, but within these predominantly oral societies there was a phenomenon which can only be described as pre-oral. Oral societies are characterized by features which facilitate their intellectual development. For example, according to Ong [1982: 34]: "Sustained thought in an oral culture is tied to communication." In such societies communication (*ie* interaction with an interlocutor) is a fundamental method of stimulating and moving forward thoughts and ideas. In addition, Ong continues, protracted, intelligent and tested ideas are preserved in rhythmic or formulaic language (*eg* proverbs) and intertwined with memory systems. This means that the repository for such ideas, especially philosophical ones, is the heads of old people and 'poets', as for example the griots of West Africa. In such societies, therefore, old people and performers have a special respect, and gatherings and communities of people are essential for the cultural and intellectual health and progress of the societies.

When, therefore, West Africans were brought to the West Indies to work on sugar plantations but were effectively isolated by the restrictiveness of their languages, they were de facto in a pre-oral society state, deprived of communication and social interaction and unable to enjoy intellectual stimulation. Even though the newly arrived Africans were often put under the care of old seasoned slaves, they could not benefit normally from such tutelage because of language difficulties. Bearing in mind that a considerable number of slaves brought over were in their teenage years and that this was an intellectually critical period of maturation, the damage done by linguistic isolation was considerable not only for the individual but for the intellectual health of the black section of West Indian society. With the development of West Indian vernaculars and with the vernaculars acting as a closer target than the European language for the Africans who were being continuously brought from Africa, the intellectual level of the black communities in the West Indies could then move back nearer to that of normal oral societies. However, the constant addition of new Africans meant that the society still was not able to benefit fully from all of those who were in it because such Africans were to some extent still isolated both linguistically and socially, thereby being unable to participate fully in social interaction.

As the creolization and acculturation of the slaves advanced, the slaves drew closer to the literate methods of communication which characterized European societies and as their language grew closer to the language of literacy, they were able to benefit from as well as to be indoctrinated by written information. There were many who remained far removed in their native vernacular from the language of literacy but even these persons were affected by growing literacy in the society. It is only in the case of isolated communities like the Black Caribs that it was possible to be outside the influence of literacy in such small islands.

In the white society, paradoxically, the native vernaculars of the white creoles moved further and further away from the language of literacy as they increasingly moved nearer to the language of the blacks. The colour codes in the system, which preserved privilege for the ruling whites, provided little incentive for most of them to pursue any further advantages through literacy. The whites were content therefore to live in an oral society which seemed to them ideal, but one in which there was no vibrant climate or tradition of literacy on the part of either the British or creole colonists. It is only with the increasing challenge to the system of slavery that, as a community, they were forced to indulge in literacy to defend their position. In having to do this, they were forced to respond in the language of those who were opposing them in Britain. The white society in the West Indies generally therefore had to move closer to literacy to understand their foes and to respond adequately to them.

As was pointed out earlier, this move to defend positions also led, ironically, to the appearance of the language of slaves in literate communication, as 'first-hand' accounts were needed to substantiate arguments. In actual fact, those who opposed the abolition of slavery, in their attempts to show the distance of the slaves from 'normal' English, highlighted the vernaculars, whereas those on the other side in many cases presented or published 'first-hand' accounts in English little different from the standard variety.

NOTES

1   "Our French people have noticed that they have such a great aversion for the English language that they cannot tolerate any one speaking it in their presence because the English are their enemy, and that if there are in their corrupt language several words taken from the Spanish, who are also their enemy, it is because they were taken during the time they were in communication with that nation, and they had not yet mistreated them."

2   Quoted in Taylor [1977: 25-26] from Hakluyt [1903-5, vol. 3]. These are the comments of Dr Layfield, chaplain to the Duke of Cumberland talking about the Caribs of Dominica in 1597.

3   Winer [1984] gives a detailed account of English and English creole speakers in Trinidad in the first half of the nineteenth century.
4   "In 1783 the population of Trinidad was only 126 whites, 295 free coloured, 310 slaves and 2,032 Indians, making a total of 2,763."
5   "Emigration from St Domingue and the English colonies to Trinidad in 1803 had raised the population, in 1807, to 31,000 inhabitants, of whom 21,000 were slaves."
6   E.g. Edwards & Walvin [1983: 18]; Fryer [1984: 68].
7   See Dillard [1972: 14-15].
8   In both Bayley [1833] and Lanigan [1844].
9   The effect of the slaves' speech on women is noted from as early as 1732 in the *Barbados Gazette*.

5

Literate Communication in the Plantation Slave Society

Dependence on nonlinguistic channels of communication for transmitting messages was an integral part of early plantation societies in the West Indies. The noise of gunshots and drums and the sight of flags provided for an unsophisticated way of communication, but one which was immediate and intelligible to all. While such communication was suitable for conveying limited, preformulated, nondetailed information over distance, it was not suitable for complex, variable information. For this latter kind of communication literacy was necessary, but literacy was effective only to the extent that it was within the competence of persons in the society. As frontier societies made up of people of different classes and cultures, the West Indian islands mirrored the stages of development in the societies from which the people came. In other words, there were elements of preliterate, transitional and literate communication in these societies.

In the historical development of human societies, in order to move beyond the restrictions of natural, spontaneous, face-to-face communication and clearly nonlinguistic means of relaying information, man devised several types of paralinguistic systems which gradually became more and more closely related to language. These systems eventually overcame the major restrictions of speech by giving permanence and greater reach to language; they supplemented the human voice, which has two inherent weaknesses – it produces sounds that quickly fade away and while the sounds are audible the distance they can reach is very limited. The movement beyond speech involved one necessary requirement and one inescapable consequence. The requirement was that, in order to move beyond the voice alone, an instrument of some type (*eg* a pen) had to be used to produce a supplement or replacement. The inescapable consequence was that moving beyond the oral involved an additional stage of processing for the brain, that is, the oral had to be translated by the brain into another arbitrary set of representative symbols.

It is this requirement and this consequence which are thought to have moved man forward intellectually. It is specifically writing, both through its technology and its expression, which is thought to have moved man forward by giving him greater freedom and flexibility. The technology of writing was gradually refined, thereby leading not only to better 'pens', but also to ink, paper and eventually books. The practice of writing, which was initially the function of specific persons, became less individualistic as persons developed and taught styles of writing thereby permitting greater access to different human experiences. Written language itself gradually diverged from the spoken principally because it was divorced from the immediacy of oral face-to-face communication. Writing involved a sole individual turning in upon himself, with ample time for reflection as writing proceeded. Through this increased time for reflection and with the availability of an increased volume of records of the past, it allowed for a greater movement away from the immediacy of the present and for greater projection into the future.

Yet, writing was not a natural group activity – it required silence, private space and time. It was in a sense, therefore, an antisocial activity. The integration of this antisocial activity into the society as a system of communication was not automatic. In fact, in the European world and subsequently the New World writing and written material spread throughout and across societies only because of religious proselytizing and the need by religious organizations to manage and control people and property. The relationship between writing and religion is enshrined in English vocabulary. In the English world, the word 'scribe', the basic meaning of which is simply 'writer', is associated in the minds of most people with historical religious persons; the word 'scripture' has long moved away from its original meaning 'anything written' to represent what is in the Old and New Testaments. It was the unity of Church and State which facilitated the spread of writing into all areas of social interaction.

Literacy as a competence in a language medium actually involves two skills – reading and writing. The first may be regarded as a passive skill (comprehension) and the second as an active one (production). Closely related to literacy and the two skills is the cover-all term, *book*, which has two meanings directly related to these two skills: a book is either already filled with writing or it is to be filled with writing. In the academic study of *the book*, an area including all shapes and sizes of written and printed material, handwritten material usually comprises letters, journals/diaries, log books and account books. All of these were important in the use of literate communication in the West Indies because they were an integral part of exploration, trade, plantation business and religion. However, the way in which literacy developed in West Indian society can be conceived of in relation to the two types of book and the two skills in literacy. These were used as two complementary forces in the plantation society – the Bible and other church material (filled books) together with the record book (the book to be filled) were used to control the minds and the actions of the population through religion, and the record book for management and control in business.

LITERACY AND THE CHURCH

The beginnings of European exploration of the New World coincided with the split in the Christian Church between Catholics and Protestants. During these times God and religion were constantly cited by various European nations as giving their exploits right and validity. Accordingly, the legal requirement for conformity with and belief in the doctrine of the Church of England was part of the divine mission of the English in their colonization efforts. As a result of this, a close relationship between the church and the state was established by law from very early in the West Indies. Harlow [1926: 27] notes, for example, that

> By another enactment ... regular church services and catechizing of the youth by the parochial clergy was insisted on. Family prayers every morning and evening, and attendance twice every Sunday at church for all within a radius of two miles, and twice a month for those beyond, was ordered under heavy fines. The absence of a white servant from service was punished according as the fault lay with himself or with his master.

It was a relationship that lasted throughout the colonial period and fashioned the model of literacy. It was specifically a literacy for governing and management, a literacy used to control social organization, both secular and religious, for Protestantism, of which Anglicanism was an early part, involved conversion to and retention of specific beliefs and in the evangelizing effort textual use of the Bible became more and more important.

Protestantism, from its beginnings in 1517, fostered literacy because it encouraged the individual to read the Bible. Support for this relationship between Protestantism and literacy is provided by Laqueur [1983: 52], which points to research done by E.P. deBooy giving a difference in levels of literacy between Catholics and Protestants in Holland over a long period: "In Holland ... there was a systematic variation in the literacy of Protestants and Catholics, in nine rural parishes from 1580 to 1800, across all social categories."

Throughout this period literacy among Protestants was significantly higher than among Catholics, a fact which prompts Laqueur to repeat the adage that 'Protestantism is the religion of the book'. In the West Indies there was subsequently a similar pattern of difference between those countries with a heavy Protestant population and those with a Catholic population, a factor which reflected the historical difference of use of literacy on the two sides. It was also the case that printing and newspapers came to the Protestant colonies (Jamaica, Barbados, St Kitts, Antigua) before it came to the Catholic ones (Dominica, Grenada, Trinidad, St Lucia).

Protestantism spawned further protest within itself and each successive wave of 'protestant' seemed to be more and more radical and became embroiled in arguments about various versions of the Bible and textual interpretations of it. By the seventeenth century the 'older' Protestants (*eg* Anglicans) regarded the 'newer' Protestants (*eg* Quakers) as dangerous and revolutionary and tried desperately by passing laws to control their activities in the colonies. It is ironic therefore that the 'older' Protestants, whose following had grown because of the power and range of print and literacy, tried to prevent the 'newer' Protestants from extending their numbers by opposing education and literacy among the slave population. Such attempts to educate the slave population would clearly have been disruptive to order and stratification in the slave society, to the practice and philosophy of slavery, and of course to the hold which the Church of England had over the society. In order to survive the wrath of the established church in the West Indies, the 'newer' Protestants had constantly to disclaim that they intended social restructuring and to abide by the wishes of the planters.

Within the first forty years of English colonization in the West Indies, the Anglican Church took its first major step towards establishing itself in Barbados and in the West Indies generally through literacy, for according to Schomburgk [1848: 93]: "In September 1661, the ministers in their respective parishes were enjoined to keep a register of christenings, marriages and burials, for which the churchwardens had to provide a book, and certify the same into the Secretary's Office in the month of March . . ." Ten years later, George Fox, the Quaker leader, was encouraging his followers to do the same when he visited Barbados in 1671. Fox's advice to his followers was:

Likewise concerning Registring of Marriages, Births and Burials, I advised them to keep Exact Records of each in distinct Books for that only use: and also to Record in a Book for that purpose, the Condemnations of such, as went out from Truth into Disorderly Practices; and the Repentance and Restoration of such of them, as returned again [Fox 1671].

What the Anglican Church and Fox were recommending for their overseas branches was the same as what they were doing in England, and what was seen as necessary by organizations generally. It was a matter of identifying members in order to separate them from non-members in relation both to their privileges and responsibilities. The substance of the Anglican Church's recommendations in 1661 and Fox's in 1671 was virtually identical to the Laws of Barbados [1704]:

Records

Act 5. The Secretary shall draw an Exact list of the several Books of this island, that the said Records may be transcribed with all convenient Speed, and kept by some able Man for the Preservation thereof: And what Records shall hereafter be made, shall be sent by the Secretary to the said Officer (p. 251).

I The Book of Common-Prayer and Administration of the Sacraments, &c. according to the Use of the Church of England, shall be solemnly read by the Minister or Reader in every Church in this Province (p. 251).

XIII Every Vestry shall provide a fit Person for a Register, who shall keep a true Registry of the Proceedings of such Vestry. The said Register shall make true Entry of all Births, Marriages, and Burials (Negroes and Mulatoes excepted) (p. 253).

XVI The Vestry of every Parish shall, at the Parish Charge, provide a Book or Books (in case they be not already provided), within six months, wherein to Register such Proceedings as aforesaid ... (p. 253).

Record keeping relating to births, marriages and deaths was in this context religious in intent. It had clearly in view the sacraments and was meant to keep the people strong in the Church of England by making baptism, confirmation, monogamy or Christian marriage, and Christian burial compulsory. It was also used as a method of determining the size of the parish and the salary of the priest. Record keeping brought about an identity of government and church and literacy was a strengthening force for both. Of course, the nonwhite population were not directly affected by literacy because they were not Anglicans or Christian souls.

LITERACY AND PLANTATION BUSINESS

Literacy became a part of society in the West Indies not only through church and State but also for security reasons and for plantation business. A system which was used to avert rebellion was to try to isolate the slaves on self-contained plantations and to deter them from communicating across plantations. One of the ways of doing this was to institute a pass or ticket system to regulate the movement of slaves. The relevant law specified that ". . . no person whatsoever, being owners or overseers, give leave to any negro slave under their ownership or charge, to depart or leave their plantations on the Sunday without a ticket, expressing his or their business, and whither going..." [Laws of Montserrat, p. 17 No. 36, III 1693]. Such a law could only have been meaningful if there was someone on each plantation who could write and if the ability to read was fairly general among the white population.

In contrast to the warning system using gunshots described by Ligon, which was to be used to announce an emergency in progress, the pass system was preventive in nature. This latter system lasted up until the time of Emancipation. Part of its success was due to the exclusion of the slaves from literacy, which forestalled the possibility of forgery to circumvent the system. The pass system became institutionalized and far-reaching in its application; it was more permanent and less subject to misinterpretation than the 'musquet' shot method of communicating, which was immediate and very transient.

Around the same period Fox visited Barbados and about the same time the laws mentioned above were being enacted, Henry Drax, a Barbadian plantation owner who probably died in 1684, gave instructions for the management of his plantations in which the functional use of literacy is set out in detail (see Belgrove [1755]):

On your first entring upon the Estate, I would have an exact Inventory taken of all Things on the Plantation, a true Copy of which must be sent me (p. 51).

I wou'd have to eat at the table with you, the Person who keeps the general Waste-book and Account of making and dispatching of Rum: The Doctor; the chief Accomptant or Bookkeeper; and also the Head-Curer (p. 55).

Let every Sort of Sugar be weighed in Bags as it is brought from the Barbacue, which Weight must be put in a Book kept for that purpose, as also all Sugar daily knock'd out; what Number of Pots; that your knocking out may agree with your weekly Receipts of Pots (p. 60).

Let the Sugar both by ramming and shaking the Cask be as close packed as possible. Besides, comparing the Sorts in packing, the several Sorts must be expressed with Chalk on the Outsides of the Cask (p. 60).

... and the Sort of Sugar contained in each Cask must be immediately enter'd in a Book kept for that Purpose (p. 60).

As the Sugars are carted to the Bridge, let the Number be expressed in the Book, that you may at any time know what is sent down (p. 61).

These Accounts must be kept in a Book, in which must be inserted all [pots and jars] that are broken, the Day when, and by what Accident (p. 61).

Whatever is in this Store, charge one of your White-Servants that can write with, who, in some book, where a List of the same Things must be kept, must mention, what White or Black by Name, he delivers any of these Particulars to; which when return'd back, must be expressed at the End of every Line, but if not returned, then the said white Receiver, must immediately acquaint you therewith, that you may enquire into the Matter. The oftner you inspect all these Accounts, the more careful you will make the Parties concerned (p. 62).

I had commonly every Fortnight, and sometimes oftner, a List brought me where every Negro in the Plantation was employed; which custom will be for your Ease and Satisfaction to continue (p. 66).

As the Rum is daily sent up, let an exact Account be kept of it in a Tally, and every Week the Stiller must take the Rum-Keeper's Receipt in a Book, which is to be kept for that Purpose. Let the Rum be disposed of, and an Account kept thereof (p. 79).

On the first of January, I would have an Inventory taken of all Things whatsoever in the Plantation, and the same fairly entered in a Book to be kept for that Purpose called the Book of Records ... a Copy of all which I wou'd have sent me to London by the first Vessel that sails after the first Day of January (p. 85).

From these instructions by Drax there are a number of conclusions about the social significance of literacy at the time that one can come to. First, those persons who kept the records were important, even if the recognition they got was not public. Secondly, books were the most important connection between the plantation and its absentee owner. Thirdly, literacy and numeracy went hand in hand. Fourthly, record keeping was not just a matter of post facto documentation; it was deliberately used for control and checking. It therefore carried with it accountability, punishment and improvement ("the oftner you inspect all these accounts, the more careful you will make the parties concerned"). Fifthly, as was the case with the church, the nonwhite population was excluded from literacy in the early years.

This model of functional literacy for the governing and management of the plantation slave society in the West Indies was fashioned in the latter half of the seventeenth century and remained in place for a long time. About a hundred years after Drax spelled out his instructions they appeared as the last part of the book by William Belgrove published in 1755 ["Instructions for the Management of Drax-Hall and Irish-Hope Plantations: To Archibald Johnson, By Henry Drax, Esq"]. The book was advertised in the *Barbados Gazette* of 2 August 1755 in the following way:

> Just arrived, and to be had, at
> Mr. William Butcher's
> In the Rot-Buck
>
> Printed in a handsome Manner, on very good
> Paper, with a large Margin, for making Remarks.
>
> *A Treatise of Husbandry,*
>   *or Planting,*
>
> By William Belgrove.
>
> Necessary to be considered by all Persons; who on an attentive Perusal of it, will think Five Shillings cannot be better laid out, than in having this Book, which will prove very useful, on many Occasions.

There is no doubt that the preservation of Drax's instructions at this time meant that they were still regarded as a good model and guide.

By the end of the eighteenth century the plantation journal had become a standard instrument in management and was the more important in cases where the manager was not resident on the plantation. Even though daily matters could be dealt with by lower levels of management, the plantation journal assumed great importance because it was what those at the top depended on to make final decisions. Barrell [1843] relates his experiences as administrator of a number of plantations in Guyana in the 1790s and underlines the importance of the plantation journal as a way of keeping check on the different estates:

Though the Loo may be 150 miles from Bel-Air, I had once in every month to be present there, as on the other estates, to investigate whatever passed: and few flagrant délits could escape me: for even the omission of an entry on the plantation journal was considered a fault (p. 13).

In these situations literacy provided for a non-immediate, detached form of decision making based on reporting, which even at best would have been unavoidably biased. Some measure of objectivity was probably aimed at, for Barrell points out that "the writing up of this journal is usually the overseer's province, under the manager's direction: therefore in Barbados the overseers are all called Book-Keepers..." (p. 13). However, his following comment: "... though many of them [book-keepers] never turned over the leaf of a book" not only calls into question the literate competence of overseers but also leaves one to wonder who actually made the entries in the journal in such cases. In Jamaica, although overseers and bookkeepers were not the same, the same comment was made about bookkeepers there:

Book-keepers are in subordinate command to the Overseers, they attend the still-houses in crop, and out of crop, the field. There are many so little deserving the name they bear, that so far from being able to calculate accounts they cannot many of them even read: and yet from this situation, from being frequently indented servants they become overseers, and have the conduct of a plantation [Beckford 1788: 89].

Evidently, the need to protect certain jobs for whites led to the disparity between the title of the post and the actual tasks performed. So, since the bookkeeper was not necessarily the person who actually wrote up the books, the task of making the entries in the journal fell to someone else whose role was not distinguished by appropriate title. The fact that bookkeepers were known to be illiterate and to be responsible for tasks which had nothing to do with books meant that the post did not in itself raise the status of literacy in the plantation society.

In a sense, then, although the functional role of literacy led to a need for literate competence, it restricted the need to specific contexts and the persons in question did not acquire status through their competence. The 1699 Barbados laws specified that books be provided, that specific persons be provided to write in those books, and also that the priest or some other person in the church be able to read; the instructions of Drax precisely identified who should write, where, and for what purpose in the management of a plantation. The privilege that the bookkeeper was accorded was that he would sit at the dinner table with the master or plantation owner. By the beginning of the eighteenth century, reading and writing were becoming a formal, legal and practical method of communication in the colonial society, but literacy was not treated as a spectacular skill and it was not increasing in any dramatic way among the general population. On the other hand, literacy, because of its functional intent, had a widespread and long lasting effect. Later literature suggests that this functional literacy, which stressed accountability, punishment and improvement, seemed to be eternal in the British mind, for when a school system was proposed at the beginning of the nineteenth century, this was one of the features that was highlighted:

> The simple contrivance of daily reports is admirably fitted to correct idleness and detect negligence in their origin, and to bear testimony to merit and demerit, even if overlooked in passing.
>
> The Black Book too is a simple and effectual instrument in maintaining order, diligence, good conduct, and the most rigid discipline, at the least expence of punishment ... [Porteus 1808: 41].

This was part of a model of literacy which seemed to focus on the controlling power of literacy rather than its liberating power. In the plantation system itself, over the years it mushroomed through a number of books: estate day books, field journals, cash books, crop records, receipt books, loan books, and others.

Besides record keeping, one of the major commercial changes which literacy effected in the plantation slave society was the adoption of a money system in place of a barter system. Payments for goods and services in an oral society are usually in kind, a practice which was evident in the early laws of the colonies in that they stipulated how much sugar (or other commodity) had to be paid as penalty, tax or in exchange for goods or service. A coin system and moreso a note system are based on literacy and can only be workable if literacy is a norm in the society. Coins and later notes were transferred from Europe to the colonies, but there is no exact historical account of the growth in the general use of coins in the West Indies. However, Schomburgk [1848: 92] points out that in the middle of the seventeenth century "all dealings were conducted by barter" in Barbados. Up until about the middle of the eighteenth century the laws of Montserrat were still specifying fines in terms of quantities of sugar. By the time of Emancipation, however, even the slaves were using coins in their private business dealings. Overall, the slow progress from barter to money in the West Indies is a good indication of the time it took for literacy to become a norm in these societies.

LITERACY AMONG THE WHITES

The bookkeeping and commercial type of literacy required in plantation, church and government business did not involve writing in extended prose and so did not bring into focus either local or foreign varieties of English. It was only in letter-writing that such considerations surfaced. When persons in the West Indies wrote letters, it was to family, friends and business connections in the North American colonies, in England, Scotland and elsewhere in Europe mainly with the intention of transacting business of some kind. Such letters differed from printed material in that they were more idiosyncratic, nearer to the dialects spoken by the individual writers and a better reflection of their competences and preferences. For instance, it is not difficult to identify George Gray as a Quaker from his use of the second person forms *thee* and *thy* in his 1687 letter. In this and similar letters, writers spelled words and used punctuation marks without uniformity. Such letters were not an everyday occurrence, even if they constituted a system of literate communication, and it is unlikely that any normal planter would have written a considerable number of letters in his lifetime so that the written variety of the language would have changed his way of thinking or affected his language competence. Yet, the fact that a monthly mail service was said [Paton 1896: 76] to have started in 1703 between Antigua, Barbados, St Kitts, Nevis, Montserrat, Jamaica and England indicates that there was an appreciable volume of mail and therefore of writing across the islands.

At the beginning of the eighteenth century there was as yet no stigma of ignorance or disability attached to illiteracy, for reading for pleasure was not a normal practice in the society of the time, reading for business reasons was not absolutely necessary, and reading of the Scriptures was not attractive to many. One can sense that letter writing was still a relatively new medium for individual expression from the remarks of Poole [1753: 299], made as he journeyed through the islands:

The Art of Writing is a very happy invention, inasmuch as thereby we are able freely to converse together, tho' at great distances from each other; yea, and to spread Correspondence from one End of the Globe to the other; By this Means the Hearts of Lovers are still open to each other, and tho' the Secret flies far, yet it comes surely to the Object it is design'd for. How very acceptable is such a Present from a distant Friend? what Grief assuage? what Joy excite! O happy Invention! for the Merchant, the Mariner, and the Lover . . .

In the area of politics and representation, voting throughout the eighteenth century in the American colonies and the West Indies was oral, a practice that reflected the reality of the times. There was no formal or actual requirement for literacy either for voters or for representatives. Note, for example, that William Duke, in his 1741 history of Barbados (Appendix, p. 4) comments favourably on Henry Peers after his death in 1740. This was a man "who was first elected a Member of the Assembly, the 6th of Aug. 1706, and from the 18th. of July 1727, was constantly chosen Speaker". What was significant about this man, Duke points out, is that "he wanted [=lacked] a liberal education, and had never been but once (and that a short time) off the island". It is clear that this man who would have been at best barely literate found no difficulty in serving in parliament, was admired by some of his contemporaries, and vigorously contended to become Governor of Barbados.

However, as the century progressed, literacy became more institutionalized, for on 30 May 1753 a set of laws passed in Montserrat made writing compulsory in a number of legal areas and gave it precedence over the spoken word. The laws specified, inter alia, that

No leases or estates of freehold or negro or other slave shall be granted or surrendered by word (p. 148)

Devises and bequests of land to be in writing, and witnessed by 3 or more credible witnesses (p. 148)

All declarations or creations of trust shall be in writing (p. 149)

Assignment of trust shall be in writing (p. 149)

No will in writing to be set aside by will by word of mouth (p. 151)

... all and every memorial of deeds, conveyances, and wills, so to be entered and registered, shall be in writing ... (p. 154)

What the passage of such laws meant was that the society had moved to such a position that the written word could be used to regulate the wishes of the majority of those who had property. Such citizens, even if they could not write themselves, had access to the services of those who could and accepted that what was expressed on paper was binding, would remain unchanged and could be retrieved on request. If Montserrat is used as an example of the region generally, there is no doubt that by this time the written word had assumed a high level of importance in West Indian society.

To try to determine what percentage of the adult population in the West Indies made use of literate communication at this or any other point in the eighteenth century would be mere conjecture. There are no detailed figures about literacy and the general statements of commentators, then and now, are contradictory. For example, Lewis [1983: 91] argues that: "Frontier colonists rarely take a metropolitan literary culture with them, at any time; and the Caribbean was no exception." In fact, Lewis goes on to make a case that the Caribbean islands were even worse in this respect than the mainland of the Americas. On the other hand, the publisher of *Caribbeana* (a collection of copies of the *Barbados Gazette* of the 1730s) claimed that "not one family amongst them would chuse [choose] to be without a book".

This suggests that the colonists at that time in Barbados and similarly in the other territories were attracted to literature. In addition, what is significant about the eighteenth century is that it was during this period that printing and newspapers were introduced into the West Indian colonies. Even though printing in itself cannot be used as a good barometer of general literacy in the society at the time, because much of the printing done was for government business and not general reading, the newspaper required a reading public and, where it existed, it suggests that there were a fair number of people who could read and were thus affected by literate methods of communication and written language. Yet, the fact that the early newspapers were not financially successful suggests, among other things, that the volume of readership was not sufficient to sustain them.

By the beginning of the nineteenth century the importance of literacy seems to have increased in the area of political representation, because although there was still no formal literacy requirement for voters, literacy seemed to have become normal (but not formally required) for representatives in Barbados. This conclusion can be gleaned from a cynical remark made by Poyer [1808: 241], referring to the Act of 1722 which identified who could be voters and representatives: "But, in Barbadoes, every illiterate possessor of ten acres is born a legislator, or is at least eligible to a seat in the general assembly, as a representative of the parish in which his freehold lies."

Although Poyer does not go on to comment on literacy, his very mention of it in this way indicates that it had by 1800 become a societal norm among the ruling class and that he was scornful of the idea of illiterate people being able to hold office. This conclusion is supported by an even earlier comment in the *Barbados Gazette* of 2 September 1789 where "a real Colonist" asks the question:

Is the government of the slaves, when settled in the British colonies, the best possible? or, are the slaves there, usually, or often times, exposed (without remedy, or legal protection) to the inhumanity of the illiterate and unfeeling white servants.

The correspondent's characterization of the white servants as illiterate suggests that among the masters literacy had become normal. Whether it was widespread, however, is not easy to determine, although a casual comment by Mathews [1793: 42] suggests that it was in St Kitts: ". . . an Overseer will not flog a negro for this offence if he brings a simple note from a neighbour requesting the fault may be looked over".

Whether or not such requests were actually part of a common practice, the reference to a *simple note* presumes a certain competence among neighbours. However, Mathews' comment is a modification or slightly different version of a remark by Ramsay [1784: 250]: "It is usual for slaves, who expect to be punished for their own fault, or their master's caprice, to go to some friend of their master's, and beg him to carry them home, and mediate for them." In contrast to Mathews' comment, that of Ramsay suggests an oral, face-to-face intervention.

Although literacy on the part of political representatives seemed to have become normal by the end of the eighteenth century, it was not seen as a requirement for voters until some time later. According to Campbell [1891], the written ballot was not generally instituted in Britain until 1872, which is after it had become normal in Australia and the United States. Its use in the West Indies followed its introduction in Britain. Before that the law required that the eligible freeholders be convened to be polled. Although the introduction of the written ballot did not rest exclusively on literacy as a societal norm, it clearly could not have been practical until this was so.

While there is detailed documentary information on the political structure of plantation colonies in the West Indies and some about the (lack of) competence of representatives and voters, there is less on the procedures and formalities of decision making and the use of written documents in the business of governing. Of course, from early minutes were kept for each session and were read out at the beginning of the following one. By the eighteenth century bills had first and second readings, and petitions from individuals and groups were also read out. This was necessary because not only was multiple copying not possible but also members were not necessarily literate. One would have to assume that, to the extent that they were able, the decision makers copied the practices of the mother country, and where writing capability was unavailable, governing depended more on the spoken word and memory.

One gets some sense of this from Baxter [1740] who, in recounting the struggle between Governor Byng and Speaker Peers, relates the method of proceeding as follows:

The Speaker gets his Assembly-men together, and dictates to them a Message to be sent to the Governor... (p. 21)

The Act for appointing Commissioners of Fortifications was read, the Words and Meaning of which were clear enough to all, except a very few, who had an uncommon Share of Illumination. (p. 22)

But our Hero in Politicks [Peers], who was not us'd to be staggered by Trifles of Law and Right, declar'd, that the Opinion of no Lawyer on Earth should weigh down his own, for that Lawyers construed Acts by the Rules of Westminster-Hall; but he knew what the Meaning and Intention of the Legislature, tho' it could not be collected from the Words. (p. 23)

From this one gets the impression that for some of those in power at that time literacy was still of no significance, because decisions depended on their own interpretations and intentions rather than on any conventional respect for written words and records. Such a manner of proceeding demonstrates the characteristics of an oral society and traditional methods of governing, in which persons in councils, parliaments, and other such bodies came together to make decisions face to face and orally.

Originally, writing had had little to do with the decision makers and property owners themselves who made up such councils; it was the responsibility of clerks whose task was at first a matter of record keeping, principally bookkeeping, for the purpose of control of property. In time, however, writing was also used for recording facts and decisions, as well as for transmitting facts and decisions to various persons and places. The development of printing facilitated this and consequently caused an increase in reading among the ruling classes and eventually an increase in writing, which in turn led to reading and writing becoming an integral part of the procedure of decision making as well as aiding the development of parliamentary formalities, or, more properly, the transmission of these formalities from England. Forms of address for certain officials and posts, ways of beginning and ending speeches, ways of interrupting and interjecting, procedures for introducing matters for decision, all these became more formalized and prescribed as a result of writing. This eventually added another, more formal dimension to the English of the colonies.

LITERACY AMONG THE SLAVES

As far as the African slaves were concerned, literacy was new to virtually all of them. Almost all the West African societies from which the slaves came were nonliterate, a factor which is recorded, at least in one case, as causing some bother to European traders. The nonexistence of literacy conventions among the West Africans and the difficulties this engendered are illustrated in the following extract from Snelgrave [1754: 87]:[1]

> Whereas, on the contrary, these Dahome Traders would come ten times a day with their Notes; tho' they were sensible the Sea was so great on the Shore, that we could land no Goods. And when I expostulated with them, about the needless trouble they gave me and themselves, in coming so often to me to read their Notes; it not being in my Power to pay them, 'till I could get goods landed; they angrily replied, 'They did not like a bit of Paper for their Slaves, because the writing might vanish from it; or else the Notes might be lost, and then they should lose their Payment.' Upon that I used to shew them my Book, telling them their Notes were entered therein, and should they lose them by any Accident, yet I would pay them by my Book: And as to the writing it would never go off the Paper; but this did no ways satisfy them.

The only ones who were said to be different were those who were Muslims. One of the earliest references to Muslims is by Labat [1724, 2:46] who, in passing, identifies slaves from *Cap-Verd* as *Mahometans*. Less than fifty years later Oldendorp also identified the Fula on the River Senegal as Muslims. It is the account of a single Fula slave which Oldendorp [1770: 199-200] uses to present a picture of the Fula. The account presents them as educated and literate people who used a holy book for a variety of purposes:

> In the course of religious services, the priest makes use of a book, from which he reads the entire liturgy. But the book is also used for some other purposes. The priest can predict from its contents the fertility of the year and the type of weather to be expected the following day. The holy book is also used for the purpose of taking an oath, in which case the person in question is expected to lay both hands on the book. For it is believed that a person guilty of perjury will not go unpunished. The book is also used as a text, from which the young people are taught how to read and write. Thus, all students are provided with copies of the book which are supplied to them . . .

There is little doubt that the book described here is the Holy Koran.

Edwards [1794, 2:61], in Jamaica, also gives first-hand experience of Muslim Mandingoes based on conversations with two of them, one of them who could chant prayers from the Koran and the other about whom he said:

> Besides this man, I had once another Mandingo servant, who could write, with great beauty and exactness, the Arabic alphabet, and some passages from the Alcoran. Whether his learning extended any further I had no opportunity of being informed, as he died soon after he came into my possession.

In a general statement about the Mandingoes Edwards [1794, 2:62] made the following observation:

> The advantage possessed by a few of these people, of being able to read and write, is a circumstance on which the Mandingo Negroes in the West Indies pride themselves greatly among the rest of the slaves; over whom they consider that they possess a marked superiority . . .

According to Edwards, however, literacy did not seem to make them better people.

A little more than a decade later, Stewart [1808: 236] also mentioned some literate competence among the Mandingoes in Jamaica:

> The Mandingoes are a sort of Mahometans, though they are too ignorant to understand any thing of the Alcoran, or of the nature of their religion. Some of them, however, can scrawl a few Arabic characters, but without understanding, or being able to explain, much of their meaning. Probably they are scraps from the Alcoran, which they have been taught by their imans, or priests.

Whether through prejudice or not, Stewart had already begun to discount the slaves' literacy by suggesting a residual rather than a vibrant competence. Even though Stewart had clearly read what Edwards had said about the feelings of superiority of the Mandingo slaves, he did not repeat the idea. On the other hand, about another twenty years later, Williams [1827: 31] reports positively on the religious convictions of his Muslim slave, though admitting his own ignorance about the extent and nature of the slave's literacy:

> My other attendant was an African, a Papau, a true believer in the faith of Mahomet, as far as he understood it, which might have been to some extent, as he could read and write what might be Arabic for ought I knew . . . His name was Abdullah, but according to the phraseology of the negroes, pronounced Dollar; and he had as thorough a contempt for the Christian miracles and mysteries he had heard preached . . . as any of the muftis of Constantinople could have felt or expressed.

Already here one gets the impression that this literacy coming out of Africa would have been in direct confrontation with that coming out of England, not only because the writing system itself was different and unknown to the English, but also because it was tied to a rival religion to Christianity.

Around the time of Emancipation Lloyd [1837: 22-23] presented the Mandingoes in Trinidad and neighbouring islands as Muslims and as literate people:

"Negros in the Colonies are of various tribes, as Mandingoes, Coromantees, Whydaws, Eboes, Congos, and Angoloes. The Mandingoes have the most intelligence; many of them read Arabic, and are Mahomedans."

Halliday [1837], writing around the same time, goes even further in his description of Mandingoes in Trinidad. He refers to them as ". . . the best informed of all the native tribes, and all Mohometans . . ." He, however, goes on to claim that ". . . [they] formed a distinct society of themselves, strictly bound together by their Mahometan faith . . . The whole of these people confine themselves, as regards residence, to a particular portion of the city . . ." It is evident in Halliday's presentation of the Mandingoes that he believed that their relative economic and social success in Trinidad was due to their literate culture. In the case of Jamaica, M'Neill [1788/89: 26] stated that "the Mundingoes are frequently engaged as domestic slaves" – and this seems to be borne out by the fact that the slaves whom Beckford, Stewart and Williams referred to were all domestic slaves.

In spite of the fact that European identification of the origin of the slaves was not always accurate, in the case of the Muslims identified over a fairly long period of time by Labat, Oldendorp, Edwards, Stewart, Williams, Lloyd and Halliday there is a fair measure of consistency. The Fula and the Mandingoes were neighbours and although the Cape Verde islands are some distance off the African coast, they lie directly west of Senegal (the area of the Fula and the Mandingoes) and were most likely populated by the tribes from these areas. However, it is not clear whether specific comments made about a few Muslim Mandingoes in the late eighteenth century and the early years of the nineteenth century are valid for most Mandingo slaves in the early eighteenth century when the system of slavery and the slave trade were at their most intense level. There is no easy way to determine how far into sub-Sahara Africa Islam had spread by the eighteenth century and the extent of literacy among its adherents. Oldendorp's Fula slave speaks of people who "bring salt along with some books to his nation on camels in exchange for livestock". It must be assumed that it is through these North Africans that Islam was spread southward, but the extent of the trade in itself does not tell the extent to which the practice of Islam, especially literacy, had become a part of West African societies.

Most of the slaves brought to the English colonies were not from the areas associated with Islam anyhow and there is no evidence to suggest that the slaves that did come from these specific areas had any effect on the mass of slaves in the West Indies. M'Neill's claim that the Mandingoes were mostly domestic slaves and Halliday's claim that the Mandingoes were a tribe apart who banded themselves together after buying themselves out of slavery do not suggest that their literate influence was widespread even in the last decades of slavery. In any case, the early literature gives the general impression that writing was not familiar to the slaves.

The reaction of the 'Dahome Traders' (mentioned above) was a reaction of Africans in their own nonliterate society. The reaction of these Africans transported to the West Indies where literacy was already becoming a controlling force in the society was different. This is exemplified firstly in the words of Labat [1724, 2:60] in Grenada:

Cette bonne opinion qu'ils ont d'eux-mêmes n'empêche pas qu'ils ne soient extrêmement simples, sur tout quand ils arrivent de leur païs. Il y a une infinité de choses qu'ils ne peuvent comprendre, & entr'autres comment nous nous faisons entendre nos pensées par le moyen de l'écriture. Ils disent qu'il faut être sorcier pour faire parler le papier.[2]

From this it can be seen that the slaves interpreted writing according to their own experience and culture. The use of visible marks on objects or on the ground has always been a part of witchcraft and so has the use of images (*eg* dolls) to represent victims. For the African slaves confronted with a practice by the white persons who had enslaved them, writing was both the use of marks as well as the use of images to preserve speech, and the purpose of this could only have been to do some harm or undesirable thing to others. The association of witchcraft with writing and with the practices of the white masters is made clear in the testimony of a slave, said to be Barbadian, during the Salem witch trials in Massachusetts in the 1690s. The slave's argument was that she was made a witch by being forced to write by her white mistress. Her testimony is as follows:

Q. Candy! are you a witch?
A. Candy no witch in her country. Candy's mother no witch. Candy no witch, Barbados. This country, mistress give Candy witch.
Q. Did your mistress make you a witch in this country?
A. Yes, in this country mistress give Candy witch.
Q. What did your mistress do to make you a witch?
A. Mistress bring book and pen and ink, make Candy write on it.

The normal reaction of fear and amazement caused by witchcraft is exemplified in the comment of Robertson [1730: 32] in St Kitts, who said:

When the newer Negroes observe that we can read and write (or as they word it, *make paper speak*) and do many other things above their comprehension, they seem to take us for a sort of Superior Being, made as it were on purpose to rule over them ...

Notwithstanding the latter writer's attempt to rationalize dominance, it is clear that the cultural context in the West Indies changed literacy, for the Africans, more from being a practice to be feared into one to be admired. In a situation of acculturation in which the white master's characteristics were the target and where literacy was one of these characteristics, it is obvious that the Africans would have overcome their initial suspicion of literacy and would soon have seen it as a desirable thing.

By the beginning of the nineteenth century literacy was apparently already being adopted from the white society into the customs of the slaves for the *entertainments* and balls which they had, usually at Christmas and on New Year's day. Carmichael [1833, 1:285] mentions the use of written invitations among the slaves in St Vincent:

It is quite common for negro slaves to give parties, and employ some one to write invitations for them . . . These invitations are expressed in the same way as if one lady wrote to another, and I shall here faithfully copy one:- 'Mr. — requests the honour of Mr. —'s company to a dance and supper on Tuesday evening, at nine o'clock. — Three dollars.'

Wentworth [1834, 2:228-29] also says the following:

These formal invitations are by no means uncommon; some of them printed on cards, in which, probably, the orthography is amended by the compositor at the printing-office in town. Very few of the slaves can write, but there are few, if any estates, that have not coloured people who have acquired some proficiency in the art, who are applied to on such occasions by the negroes, and among this class it is that the etiquette of sending cards is principally observed.

In a situation where the majority of persons attending parties given by slaves were unable to read it seems illogical that the persons holding such parties would go to the expense of having invitations printed if they were meant to be read and understood. It is more likely that the invitation was really a ticket to enter which gave the holder some privilege. In fact, Mrs Carmichael's focus was on the price charged and not the invitation itself. From the general context of Mrs Carmichael's comments it seemed as if she was talking about the house slaves, who would have been familiar with the social graces of the whites. Wentworth's identification of coloured persons as the principal set of persons who used invitations supports the idea that it was the house slaves who announced their parties by cards, for many house slaves were coloured persons.

Another use of writing among the slaves cited by Carmichael [1833, 1:308] was for purposes of identification of personal property: "Misses, me just buyed one handkerchief for me, will ye mark me name for me?" In this case it was a field slave who was making the request. It is not clear whether this identification of personal property among the slaves was simply imitation of the practices of the whites or whether it was caused by increase in personal property among slaves which had in turn had given rise to stealing and disputes about ownership. On the other hand, it could have emerged out of the practice of branding for identification, which was used on the slaves themselves, or from the ethnic practices of facial marking and tattooing which were common among the slaves. In any case, it is clear from this kind of practice that writing was becoming functional among the slaves even before Emancipation.

Beyond the personal level, literacy increasingly afforded a few slaves the opportunity to get minor supervisory jobs, but not to such an extent as to make this a realistic avenue to progress. Literacy purely for communicative purposes among the slaves was rare. Wentworth [1834, 2:225-26] cites the contents of a letter written by a slave who ran away to England and wrote back (in 1802) to his relatives to give them information about his whereabouts. There are no other cited examples of similar occurrences, but the size of the black population in Britain in the eighteenth century and the numbers of them who had gone or been taken there from the West Indies suggest that personal letters sent back from Britain by former slaves might not have been absolutely rare.

One of the longstanding fears of the planters was that the ability to read would enable the slaves "to read newspapers and pamphlets, filled with the most pernicious doctrines" [Porteus 1808: 19]. These fears led to even more repressive and extreme behaviour on the part of slave owners, who generally opposed attempts to teach slaves to read in order to lessen their access to information coming from Britain. However, in the years before Emancipation, news of antislavery agitation in Britain did reach the slaves as well as news about imminent freedom. Some of this news came through the ability of some slaves to read, but there is little evidence showing that reading newspapers was a widespread or common activity among slaves.

CONCLUSION

The primary role of literacy as it developed in the West Indies was to permit easier management and control in church, state and private business. in relation to the church, the ability to read was intended to give citizens additional and direct access to the doctrine of the church while the ability to write was intended to make it easier for priests and others in charge to control the size and behaviour of the flock. in relation to state business, literacy facilitated the execution of laws, the compilation of accounts and deeds as well as the identification of citizens and voters. In relation to private business, the ability to read gave the ruling class access to commercial information and the ability to write allowed for distance communication, both internally and externally, for business purposes. Literacy as a vehicle for the individual's intellectual and artistic pursuits was secondary and virtually nonexistent among the majority of the population in the plantation slave society of the West Indies.

The primary purposes for which literacy was intended in plantation societies of the West Indies meant that literate language (*ie* writing) produced by West Indians did not have to be uniform or standard. Since the kind of writing needed for record keeping was not extended prose, there was little preoccupation with the language itself and there was no building up of expertise in extended writing in these societies.

The English language as literate method of communication was therefore not exploited very extensively in the plantation slave society and as a consequence did not develop any significant varieties there. Almost paradoxically, limited expertise in writing and limited access to written literature in themselves caused literate English to affect people in its oral expression. Information of varying types had to be read out aloud and the principal place where this took place was in church, which was for a time compulsory. Reading out of written English also took place in government assemblies and councils. As a result of this, the most formal type of spoken English was actually written English (which was read aloud). Written English therefore filtered downward to the illiterate in these societies to provide a model which was in a sense unnatural as a model of spoken English.

Slaves were an integral part of these societies, but literacy did not apply equally to them. The slaves were generally regarded as beings outside Christianity and so there was no need initially for them to be able to read to have access to religious doctrine and material. There was no need either for them to be identified and recorded as individuals since they could not be members of the church. The slaves had little permanent property to manage and control and so they had no need for account books and the ability to write in them. At the personal level, writing, that is, initiating or responding to distance communication, was generally unnecessary for slaves. They were deliberately isolated on self-contained plantations for security reasons and were cut off from family and friends in Africa, in neighbouring territories and in Britain. Slaves therefore lived in a small world, in an oral culture of direct and face-to-face communication. Acculturation to the practices of the whites was inevitable for most slaves, but their status as slaves meant that they continued to have no business to transact with distant peers, no great amount of property to manage, and as partly Christian souls their acquired freedom to read was actually, like all others in the society, a channel for religious indoctrination and inculcation of respect for the order of the society. Control of access to material was intended to limit or eliminate ideas such as those of the French Revolution as well as discussion of and reflection on such ideas.

Writing, as a solitary and antisocial activity, was in direct conflict with the reality of slave life in which neither the implements nor the conditions nor the time were available for writing. Even in the case of the Muslim slaves who worked as house servants and whose ability to write became evident to their masters, what they wrote about did not seem to move beyond the reproduction of learned parts of the Koran and prayers. In this respect, then, it could be argued that they were ready to be shifted from obedience and discipline in one religion to the same in another. Those slaves who were allowed to make entries in plantation journals no doubt came to understand the power of control and the effectiveness in management that literacy gave, but there was little or no transmission of this knowledge from the 'white collar' to the 'blue collar' worker. The way forward for the slave who grew or produced items for sale in the market, and who made some money doing so, was seen as producing children who would move away from the hard work of their parents and get closer to the easier occupations on the plantation. The use of writing to keep better records and to maximize profits would have been interpreted as condemning children to hard and unpleasant labour and to change them from the sharing and community minded people that their parents were into mercenary ones. The social models of success in the plantation society were fancily dressed ladies and gentlemen who used sophisticated language, danced at balls, got drunk and did no hard work. The role of literacy in this success was not immediately obvious or apparent to the slaves.

Competitive imitation of the whites by the slaves in the context of a yearly festival no doubt required more than the immediate and extemporaneous. Planning and preparation of costumes, behaviour and speeches became necessary. The involvement of house slaves, urban slaves and free people of colour in these activities brought them nearer to the facilities provided by literacy, that is, printed invitations and initialled handkerchiefs. However, these were merely the trappings of an activity rather than the basis of it. It was not the thought and the appropriateness of the *genteeler behaviour*, or of the European songs and toasts that were important, for they were not a part of everyday communication. It was their function as indicators of grandeur that was. Literacy was not needed to validate the literary or the dramatic in such 'private theatricals'; no prepared script could adequately deal with the 'mock' battles and challenges which arose in live competition. The actor in such dramas had to be both player and author at the same time. This was not a matter of acting out and vicariously experiencing the thoughts of another. There was really no sharp division between creator, actor and critic in these festivities and more generally in the culture of the slaves. The separation between these three only eventually came through schooling in a literacy in which exact memorization of the details of the medium (*eg* letters of the alphabet) as well as of the subject matter (*eg* printed religious material) was presented as a goal in itself. In like manner, the prescribed ritual of burial reified in its printed form in the Anglican's *Book of Common Prayer* did not allow the dead to speak to debtors and did not allow friends and family to address the dead. While there was some room for the spontaneous (not scripted by the church) praise of the dead in the European burial, there was no room for direct verbal communication between the dead and the living. It was only proverbs, among the slaves, which clearly represented a reflective culture. It was in these that thought had been translated into fixed form and then used in a manner which did not require a direct verbal response. However, proverbs were not a genre apart but a feature of communication in various contexts.

NOTES

1   Page 87 is actually misnumbered as page 71.
2   "This high opinion which they have of themselves does not prevent them from being extremely simple, especially when they arrive from their country. There are many things they cannot understand, among which is how we manage to express our thoughts by means of writing. They say you must be a sorcerer to make paper talk."

6

The Rise of Printing and Publishing in the West Indies and its Effects

Literate communication in the West Indies from the earliest years included the use of printed material, but the commercial production of printed material did not begin in most of the West Indian territories until well into the eighteenth century. The availability of printing facilities in the West Indies not only fostered the growth of literate communication and increased the volume of printed material but it also gave resident and local persons some say in the development of language norms in each community where there was a printing press. In addition, it provided direct and quicker avenues for persons who had influence with local printers to get their views and ideas in print.

Printing was intended as a specialized form of literate communication to be used for material of high volume or value, but it was a slower method of communication than writing, and much slower than speech. Its main advantage over speech and writing, however, was the capability to repeat without change of form, which, more than anything else, gradually removed from the minds of readers the reality of dialectal variation in language and actually created the illusion that language could have a single correct form which was the real and perfect form of the language. This illusion about the printed form of the language was also a result of the association of strong forces – the persons associated with printing were influential in the society, the material printed was the doctrine of the church and the laws of the state, and the form of the language as a consequence came to be the most important one.

In the European societies which developed printing, its consequences were fundamental and extensive, for whereas writing was individualistic and restricted, printing was almost the opposite. Printing brought greater uniformity to letter formation and gradually to spelling as well as punctuation. Printing brought about an increase in volume and quality of texts. Reading material not only became more widely available to a greater number of persons but also it was much easier to decipher when printed. It was infinitely easier to teach persons to read using printed texts than it was using written ones. As a result of printing, books, newspapers and pamphlets became practical realities. The flow and exchange of information from these affected the knowledge of people, the governing of countries, the method of controlling classes in the society, and the method of building empires.

While it is not difficult to understand the consequences of printing, it is much more so to appreciate the difficulty involved in reading a letter of the seventeenth century, for most people are unaware that, as Stryker-Rodda [1986: 9] points out: "There were as many styles of handwriting as there were authors." To illustrate the actual difficulty involved in reading written documents in the seventeenth century and to appreciate the improvements which printing brought, one can compare a letter written in 1687 by a Quaker in Barbados named George Gray to a friend in Pennsylvania with a modern, printed translation of the same letter (see over). The written letter requires careful examination in order to keep the lines apart, to isolate the words and to identify the letters in the words. In addition to these problems, at that time spellings and punctuation were not uniform and predictable enough to help the reader to follow the meaning and sentence structure respectively without actually focusing on each word. Although literate persons at that time would not have had the same difficulty deciphering a written letter as persons today, there is no doubt that reading was much slower and more tedious then. The printed version of the letter makes reading a much simpler task, and although for reasons of economics and convenience printing was at that time restricted to multiple-copy and longer documents, there is no question that the technological advancement encouraged more reading, which brought about an escalation in printed material and so had far-reaching consequences.

The production of printed material, which is usually subdivided into books, pamphlets, broadsheets, maps, reports, newspapers and magazines, requires and reflects a certain level of development in a society. An apt comment on the relationship between printing and the state of society's development is given by Hallewell [1982]:[1]

The book exists to give literary expression to cultural and ideological values. Its design is the interface of aesthetics and the available technology. Its manufacture requires the supply of particular industrial products (which may be imported, made from imported raw materials, or wholly manufactured locally). Its marketing is a commercial process conditioned by geographic, economic, educational, social, and political factors. And the whole provides an excellent measure of a country's degree of dependence or independence, both spiritual and material.

FIGURE 6.1: A letter written in 1687 by a Quaker in Barbados named George Gray to a friend in Pennsylvania

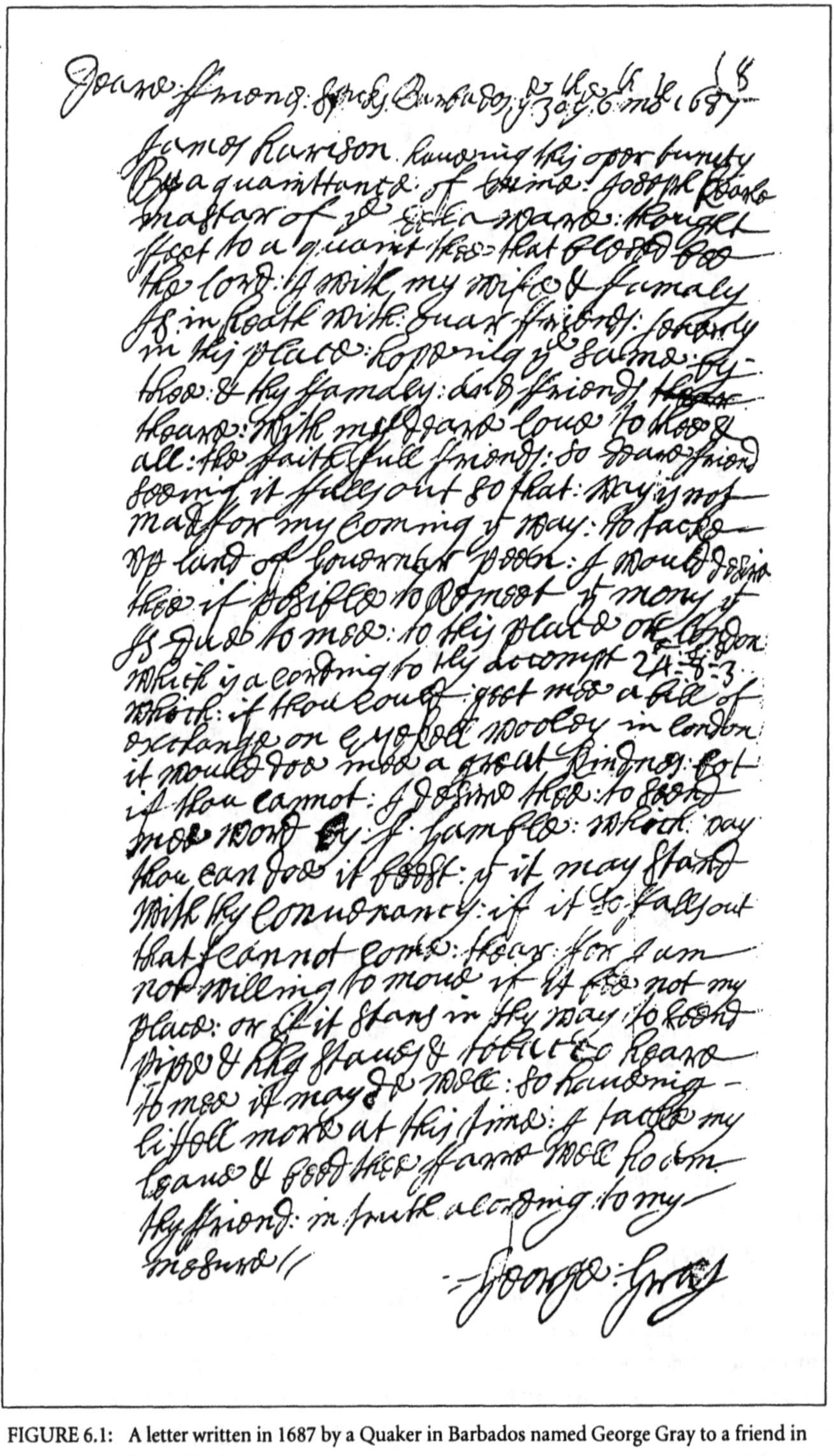

> Deare friend: Spiks. Barbados: ye 30th yeth 6th moth 1687
> James Harison: haveing this oportunity by aquainttante of mine Joseph Keare mastar of ye Delaware: thought feet to aquaint thee that blesed bee the lord: I with my wife & famaly is in heath with: ouar friends: jenerly in this place: hopeing ye same by thee & thy famaly: and friends theare: with my deare love to thee & all: way is not mad for my coming yt way: to tacke up la.nd of Governor Peer: I would desire thee if possible to remeet yt mony that is due to mee: to this place or London which is acording to thy accompt £24: 8s: 3d which: if thou could geet mee a hill of exchange on Ezekell Wooley in London it would doo mee a great kindnes: bot if thou cannot: I desire thee to send mee word by J. Gamble: which way thou can doe it beest: thyt it may stand with thy convenancy: if it so falls out that I cannot come: thear: for I am not willing to move if it bee not my place: or if it stans in thy way to seend pipe & h*g staves & tobacco heare to mee it may de well: so haveing littoll more at this time: I tacke my leave & beed thee farre well ho am thy friend: in truth acording to my mesure
>
> George Gray

FIGURE 6.2: A modern printed version of the same letter

It is with this idea of printing as a measure of dependence/ independence that one can look at West Indian society. More specifically, one can look at printing as an index of levels of literacy, literature and intellectual activity. Most importantly, however, printing is intimately linked to the standardization of a language and to the general diffusion of this standard version of the language. In the West Indies, therefore, printing can be looked at as the most important method through which standard English was spread into different sectors of the society.

In the history of Western Europe printing proved to be a major catalyst for change since it was fed by the Renaissance in the fifteenth century and blossomed in the sixteenth century with the Reformation and with European expansion in the New World. This blossoming in Europe affected the colonies in the New World indirectly in that the visions and prospects of a new world generated a need for information, oral, printed and written. Ships' logs, accounts of trade, accounts of property, descriptions of men, beasts and plants, accounts of adventures all increasingly involved more and more people in the practice of reading and writing. European countries were transformed by the riches of the New World and these countries rivalled each other for these riches. Colonial accounts and colonial government were therefore of paramount importance. By the middle of the nineteenth century the volume of books and printed material had increased substantially and the level of scholarship therein had helped to bring about an industrial revolution.

Printing, of course, was not solely a European invention, seeing that it had varying manifestations among the Chinese and native Americans long before Gutenberg and his use of moveable type in Germany. In the case of the West Indies, however, there is no known direct influence other than European on the introduction or establishment of printing. There is no record of influence from Chinese, native American or African sources, even though persons of all types were employed in the operation of printing presses in the West Indies. Both the skill and the machinery of printing came from Europe. This was a clear case of transfer of technology both directly and indirectly from the mother country to the colonies – the printing presses were in many cases used ones brought from England and the earliest printers were British or had learnt their craft from the British.

THE GROWTH OF PRINTING IN THE ENGLISH COLONIES

In the Americas in general printing was introduced first in Mexico City in the 1530s, which is not long after the advent of Columbus. The reasons given for its introduction into Latin America were related to religion, language and literacy. The following explanation is given by Johnson [1988: 5]:

Juan de Zumarraga, the Franciscan friar who went to Mexico City as its first bishop in 1528, was instrumental in the introduction of the printing press into the Spanish American colonies. Religious materials were urgently needed for the conversion of the natives, and European printers were ill-equipped to handle manuscripts in Indian languages. At the bishop's insistence, Juan Cromberger established a branch of his Sevillian publishing house in Mexico City and shipped to the New World all the equipment and supplies vital to its operation.

Printing was introduced into British North America a hundred years after, and into the West Indian islands about ninety years after that. Printing actually drifted downward from northeast British North America to the British West Indies (see Figure 6.3). In British North America itself it moved downward from Cambridge/Boston to New York to Philadelphia to Virginia; and it moved directly from Philadelphia to Barbados and Antigua. It is only in the case of Jamaica that printing was introduced directly from England.

Frank Cundall, librarian at the Institute of Jamaica in the early twentieth century, was the earliest authority on early printing in the West Indies and Jamaica specifically. Much of his data is invaluable, although his date for the start of printing in Jamaica is challenged by McMurtrie [1942], who also provides dates for the start of printing in Trinidad, Antigua and Tobago. As to the people who started printing in Barbados and Antigua, the most intimate knowledge of them comes from the autobiography and letters of Benjamin Franklin [1793] who in his young days was a printer and had direct printing connections with both of these islands.

City	Name of Printer	Date of 1st printing
Cambridge, Mass.	Stephen Daye	1639
Boston	John Foster	1674
Philadelphia	William Bradford	1687
New York	William Bradford	1693
Newport, R.I.	James Franklin	1732
Williamsburg, Va.	William Parks	1729
Charleston, S.C.	Eleazar Phillips	1762
Savannah, Georgia	James Johnson	1762
Kingston, Jamaica	Robert Baldwin	1718
Bridgetown, Barbados	D.Harry/S.Keimer	1730
Basseterre, St Kitts	Thomas Howe	1747
St Johns, Antigua	Thomas Smith	1748
Roseau, Dominica	William Smith	1748
St Georges, Grenada	William Weyland	1765
Kingstown, St Vincent	Joseph Berrow*	1784 or 1788
Port-of-Spain, T'dad	Don Juan Cassan (Span)	1786
	(Engl)	1799
Scarborough, Tobago	John Smith	1783? 1798
Essequebo & Demerara	J.C. de la Coste	1796
Castries, St Lucia	Joseph Berrow*	1780
Charlestown, Nevis		1871
Plymouth, Montserrat	William Humphrey*	1875

[*Data taken from Cave 1987]

FIGURE 6.3: The start of printing in British colonial America and the West Indies

What in a sense seems fortuitous, *ie* this downward geographical drift in printing, may be more truly a reflection of the mentality and intent of the various European nations, for printing was tied to religious conversion and education. In contrast to Latin America and northeast British North America, the major reasons for printing and the majority of publications in the West Indies were not to convert the native or other non-European peoples. In fact, there were no large native American communities to evangelize. The islands quickly became established slave societies in which the populations were stratified and controlled to service a clear economic policy.

In addition, the European-Catholic response to the peoples (natives and others) of the New World in certain ways allowed for greater cultural diversity than the English-Protestant response. For example, in addition to the respect shown to the native American languages from early, there were in later years translations of the Bible into Negerhollands (Virgin Islands) and the use of French Creole by European priests in Haiti and other islands. There is even the case in Grenada in 1698 where the Catholic priest, Labat, took the trouble to learn one of the languages of the Africans "pour comprendre tout ce qu'ils disaient, & pour leur expliquer mes pensées".[2] These have few parallels in the history of English-Episcopalian conversion in the West Indies. It is only in Quaker-influenced printing in Barbados and Antigua that some difference may be detected. This difference may be seen in the printing of pieces which expressed support for the idea of regarding slaves as people, a view which was not in keeping with the status quo which the established church in the West Indies supported.

PRINTING FOR BUSINESS

Printing, when it was introduced into the West Indies, was first and foremost a business and the people who started such businesses either got their work from the government, institutions and individuals, or had to become involved in publishing, or both. The most profitable business for printers undoubtedly came from governments, which had all sorts of notices, proclamations, laws, records and other documents to publish. According to the records some printers in Jamaica were able to make a substantial sum of money from printing.

Government work accounted for a great share of the printer's work in some cases, because it was to do government work that printing was ostensibly introduced into many territories. Note, for example, McMurtrie [1942] who points out that in Jamaica, as early as 1715, a message from the Council to the Assembly said: "... heartily wish that their house will join them in establishing a printing press for publishing the minutes of both bodies". In the case of Tobago late in the eighteenth century Governor Delancey, writing to the Duke of Portland, said:

I beg to inform Your Grace that a printing office is now established at Scarborough and that I hope soon to have it in my power to obey your Grace's directions contained in your circular of 23rd of April last respecting a printed collection of the Laws of the island of Tobago [McMurtrie 1943b].

There is no record of how promptly printers were paid and whether in all cases the local governments were satisfied with the work of the local printers.

The changes occasioned in the society as a result of printing of government forms and documents were very real and concrete. Where previously there were limited copies of documents, in some cases handwritten, the method of disseminating information to the public was slow as well as tedious. For instance, when some laws were passed, the law itself stipulated how it should be made known to the public. For example, one of a number of laws relating to slaves in 1699 in Barbados says: "This Act shall be read in all Parish-Churches the first Sunday in February, and first Sunday in August, yearly" [No. XXXI, An abridgement of the Laws of Barbados 1699, p. 243]. Bear in mind that the Act in question had thirty-one clauses, some of which were five or more lines long. If the stipulation was adhered to, then it means that the church was much more than a religious forum and that the alliance of church and state exercised a rigid control over the people, for judging from 'Drax's instructions' attendance at Sunday church at this time was virtually compulsory for all whites. Local printing of laws meant that the laws were more easily available in multiple copies and would have relieved the Church of this kind of disseminating function.

An example from Guyana before the introduction of printing also shows the harsh reality in the method of disseminating information. Rodway [1918] provides the following:

> ... all government notices were written and circulated by means of colony slaves in corials, who passed up and down the rivers, exhibiting the document at each plantation. The Manager wrote Vertooned, Vise or Seen and signed his name, after which the same document was carried from one to another, only one copy being available for a district.

Local printing, which made several copies of documents available reduced and removed the need for such methods and brought about structural differences in the society. It became the foundation of the civil service, which increasingly requested multiple copies of blank forms for shipping, registration and tax collection.

SCHOLARLY PUBLICATION

However, much of the printing that took place in the West Indies was given to belles-lettres. In fact, probably the very first job given to a printer in the British West Indies (Robert Baldwin in Jamaica) was to print "a Pindarique Ode of anonymous authorship, designed to greet and acclaim the island's new executive" [McMurtrie 1942: 6]. The earliest newspaper in Barbados, the *Barbados Gazette*, consistently published a fair number of literary pieces from its very beginnings in 1731. In Antigua one of the surviving works from the first printer there (Thomas Smith) from his first year of printing was *The Ladies Advocate: A Poem* written by William Shervington in 1748. This production of belles-lettres draws the following comment from Swan [1970: 44]: "Considering the surviving printed matter from the Caribbean, the one thing the scholar notes is the comparative scarcity of sermons and religious tracts, and the relatively high ratio of belles-lettres ..."

This contrast given by Swan indicates a difference in preoccupation between persons in northeastern North America and the West Indies. The explanation given by Swan is in keeping with the obvious difference between the two regions, for Swan accounts for this high ratio of belles-lettres in the West Indies by claiming that [1970: 45]: "It is not surprising that in a slave society there should have been leisure for those interested in composing poems or writing history, and both these forms of belles-lettres are fairly prevalent in West Indian printing of an early date."

Whether or not it was true that leisure time caused by slavery afforded the masters the time to produce creative works, there is little doubt that printers were given an amount of creative work to produce that was striking in a context of slavery.

The literary works which appeared in the eighteenth century came from various islands. From Antigua the following can be identified:

1749	*Occasional Poems* William Shervington	
1757	"A Poem, addressed to a Young lady" (pamphlet)	
1760	"An Ode to the King of Prussia" (pamphlet)	
1763	*Miscellanies* William Shervington	
1774	*A Short Treatise on the Slavery of Negroes in the British Colonies* Samuel Martin	
1785	"The Duties of Masonry. An Oration Delivered in the Lodge"	

From Barbados the following works are notable:

1767	*A general description of the West-Indian Islands . . . attempted in Blank verse* in four books John Singleton. Printed by George Esmand and William Walker
1796	*The rules of whist.* Published by Mathew Carbery

From St Kitts came the following:

1790	"The Source of Virtue; A Poem" Richard Nisbet
	Where Am I? How Came I Here? . . . Rev. Temple Henry Croker

From Dominica the following is identified:

1767	"The Shipwreck" (a poem in three parts)

As is generally the case with surviving works, it is difficult to determine what percentage of total printing in the West Indies the surviving works cited above actually represent. In any case, it is clear that when these are taken with other creative work published in newspapers, the total amount was significant enough to have an effect on the literate segment of the societies in the West Indies.

In British colonial America and in Latin America printing was intimately related to institutions of learning and formal education. In the case of the West Indies, however, this was not so. Unlike the start of printing in British colonial America, which was centred at an institution of learning (Harvard), both in Barbados and Antigua the earliest printing presses were commercial ventures started by individuals in the town area. However, some educational material was produced from the presses in the West Indies. This comprised, principally, a few treatises on the prevalent diseases and their causes and also on the management of plantations and on farming. For example, in Barbados in 1744 William Beeby published a medical thesis on dysentery (61 pp.) by Dale Ingram, 'a professor at Codrington College' and in Antigua in 1750 *Medulla Medicinae Universae: Or, a New Compendious Dispensatory.* Also from Antigua in 1750 came *An Essay upon Plantership* by Samuel Martin, a book which saw several editions; and in 1752/1756 *An English Grammar, wrote in a plain familiar manner, adapted to the youth of both sexes. To which are added, some general rules in orthography, – stops or points, – emphasis, – and composition.* From St Kitts late in the century came the following:

1780   "An Essay on the Reduction of Interest"
1790   "A Treatise on Planting from the origin of semen to ebullition . . ." The Second Edition J. Peterkin.

In addition to these works there were a number of historical accounts of various islands. The first book published in Barbados (1741) was historical in nature; it was titled *Some Memoirs of the first Settlement of the island of Barbados and other CARRIBBEE Islands with the Succession of the Governours and Commanders in Chief of Barbados to Year 1741*. It was written by William Duke and printed by William Beeby. It was 'quoted' extensively and influenced many subsequent histories of Barbados, as Ligon's history had done earlier. The appendix gave significant later events in the history of Barbados (*ie* during the author's time); it quoted Codrington's will; and set out the structure of parliamentary and overall government in Barbados, which provided Poyer, for example, with his information on this subject. In addition, a list of names of persons eligible to vote in Barbados (1638) was reproduced from this book and published in the Naragansett Register of 1888 – it was justified as being of interest to those New Englanders who wanted to trace their early family history.

Three other historical accounts appearing at the very end of the century were:
(Grenada)
1795   *A Review of the Events which have happened in Grenada from the commencement of the insurrection to the 1st of May: by a sincere well-wisher to the Colony*   T.T. Wise
(Dominica)
1795   A Diary of the Defence of the Island of Dominica, against the Invasion of the French Republicans, & the Revolt of the Dominicans of the Quarter of Colyhaut, in June 1795
(Barbados)
1798   *A Narrative of the insurrection and rebellion in the island of Grenada*   Henry Thornhill

As can be seen from the titles of these works, they were really eyewitness accounts of events which had taken place shortly before they were published.

There was not a great amount of religious material published, but one work which appeared in the early years was a religious pamphlet by Thomas Chalkley [1735]. Thomas Chalkley, a Quaker and merchant-seaman who plied the route between Philadelphia and Barbados, said in his memoirs:

It was this Voyage [1735] that my Friends in Barbadoes published a little Piece I wrote at sea, which I called, Free Thoughts communicated to Free Thinkers; done in order to promote Thinking on the Name and Works of God; which had, as far as I understand, a good acceptance among the People . . .

This piece is included in Chalkley's autobiography, which was printed in London in 1766.

NEWSPAPERS

Even though scholarly publication in the West Indies was in evidence throughout the eighteenth century, it certainly did not match the flood of journalistic publication which dominated printing for some time in the West Indies. From the earliest years of printing in the West Indies the publishing of newspapers was the most attractive venture. This resulted in a proliferation of newspapers, most of which survived only a short time. A sample of the names appearing in the eighteenth century is as follows:

1718	*The Weekly Jamaica Courant*
1731	*The Barbados Gazette*
1747	*St Christopher Gazette*
1748	*The Antigua Gazette*
1781	*The Antigua Chronicle*
1788	*The Antigua Journal*
1765	*The Royal Grenada Gazette*
1789	*St George's Chronicle* and *New Grenada Gazette*
1794	*Weekly Courant,* and *Charibbee Advertiser*
1765	*The Dominica Gazette*

Although, as in the case of the Antiguan newspapers, the name suggests a restriction to that island, in reality the printers took in business from neighbouring islands and the newspaper was also meant to service those islands.

From the point of view of literacy and the dissemination of knowledge, the newspaper was more important than any other kind of printed material. The rise of the newspaper in the West Indies coincided, with a slight delay, with the rise of the newspaper in the British North American colonies and with Britain itself. This rise of the newspaper started at the beginning of the eighteenth century and one of the reasons for it was, as Armytage [1965: 48] points out, that after the Printing Act lapsed in 1695 in England, the provincial press "was able to emerge without fear of prosecution". So, newspapers began to appear all over England in great numbers: there were "24 by 1723 and 130 by 1760". Another reason for the rise of the newspaper in England then was that the literate public had grown big enough to support newspapers and make them a viable economic concern. This growth in the literate public had come about as a result of the fact that the schools for the poor which had begun to be established in a more concerted way from 1699 onwards were producing a greater number of people who could read.

The first newspaper appeared in the West Indies in 1718 in Jamaica; this was followed by one in Barbados in 1731 and one in Antigua a few years later. As far as format is concerned, it is important to appreciate what a newspaper was in the early years in the West Indies and how it changed subsequently. The first newspaper in the West Indies (*The Weekly Jamaica Courant*) was at first a single sheet of paper slightly smaller than a quarto sheet printed on both sides. This paper, as the name suggests, came out once a week, as did most of the newspapers which were later published in the other islands. By 1750 some of the newspapers were bigger, but there was no uniformity in size of sheet. Most of them soon had four pages, that is, one big sheet of paper folded into two. The *Antigua Gazette*, in the last half of the eighteenth century, had a predictable format – advertisements (including arrival and departure of ships and cargo) on the first page, international news (reprints) on the second and third pages, local news on the third page, and further advertisements on the last page. The printer did of course make changes to this format and insert other materials according to his wishes.

In its appearance the newspaper was very dense in comparison with newspapers of today. It had solid print without illustrations or drawings, except for stylized pictures of male and female slaves, houses, horses, cows, mules and pigs, which accompanied advertisements announcing the sale or loss of these. In addition, the earliest newspapers were not set out in columns and so the look of the page was not very different from that in a book.

Some newspapers reflected the language situation in the territory concerned in that they tried to cater to various readers. For example, in Grenada and Dominica (and probably other islands which have no surviving issues), there were bilingual newspapers. The *Royal Grenada Gazette*, which appeared in the 1760s, carried some items in English alone, some in French alone, and some in one of these languages followed by a translation in the other. The *Freeport Gazette* or the *Dominica Advertiser*, which also appeared in the 1760s, was mostly in English with some advertisements given in a French version. It is interesting that in an issue of this newspaper (Saturday, 18 July 1767) there are two advertisements by persons asking the freeholders in the town of Roseau and the parish of St Peter to vote for them in the House of Assembly; the request for the former is in both French and English whereas that for the latter is in English only. When a newspaper was first proposed in British Guiana at the end of the eighteenth century, the 'prospectus' said that it would be published in both Dutch and English and that the advertisements and public notices would appear in the language in which they were submitted. What is clear is that the printers of these newspapers took whatever was offered to them and were capable of handling more than one language. It is also clear that readers had varying capabilities and read whatever they could.

In its early years in the West Indies the newspaper was not a welcome introduction. The following remark, which is said to have been made in 1671 by Governor Berkley of Virginia, accurately reflects the attitude of British colonial administrators and colonists in slave societies:

Times, and that the said Fair, do hold Three Days; and another to hold the same Time on the
First Day of November next, and so every Year.
N. B. That the Mayor of LITTLEWORTH will be chosen on the said First Day of May,
as usual, with all the Solemnity on that Occasion.

TO be run for on Saturday the 2d of May next, at Littleworth Fair in Kingston, a very fine
repeating Gold Watch, with a Gold Hook and Chain, value 100 Pistoles, by 5 Horses,
Mares or Geldings that never run for above 10 l. each, the Race one quarter of a Mile, Weight
&c. to be adjusted by 2 indifferent Persons chose by the Owners of the Horses the Morning they
run, the Horses to be Enter'd at R. Baldwin's in Kingston, by Monday the 28th of April.
N. B. If this meets with Encouragement, a Plate of 50 l. value will be run for Annually.

ADVERTISEMENTS.

Kingston, April 8. 1719.

THIS is to inform the Publick, That the Printer has Workmen just arriv'd from England,
who binds Books neatly in Vellom and Parchment, and in all Sorts of Leather, likewise
Guild and Letter them on the Backs; Those Gentlemen who have Books to Repair or New
bind, may have them Done by him with all Expedition at such reasonable Rates, that Shop-
keepers may be furnished with Books for Accounts of all kinds as Cheap as they can have
them from England, likewise Painted Paper for Hangings, Pocket-Books, Letter-Cases and
Super-fine Cards; with all other Stationary-Ware, sold at his Shops in Church-street, Kingston;
and likewise by Mr. Taylor on the Parade Spanish-Town, and Mr. Fisher's at Port-Royal;
who will then be supplied by him constantly, as may likewise other Shop-keepers in any other
Parts of the Country; where those who have Books to Repair or New-bind may leave them
with Directions how they'd have them done.
N. B. School-Masters may be furnish'd with all sorts of Copy-Books for Children.

LATELY Publish'd, TOBACCO: A Poem, in Two Books, Translated from the
Latin of RAPHAEL THORIUS. JAMAICA: Re-printed by R. Baldwin in Church-
street, Kingston, Price 2 s. 6 d. stitch'd in Blew Paper, and 6 Ryals bound in Marble Paper.

THIS is to Advertise one James Williams (who liv'd some Time since in Kingston) That
if he will Repair to R. Baldwin, Printer, in Kingston, he may hear of something to his
Advantage, by the Death of a Friend in England.

STray'd from Thomas Harris of Clarendon, a young White Horse, about Three Years Old,
Marked with Three O's, with an S. a-cross. Whoever gives Notice to Mr. Edward Hancock at the Cross in Clarendon, shall have 30 s. Reward, or whoever shall detain him be it at
their Peril.

Kingston, April 10. 1719.

RUN away from John Price, of Port-Royal, Mariner, a Caromontine Negroe Woman,
Named Venus, she is low of Stature and speaks good English; by Intelligence, she has
Hired her self in Kingston. Any Person that shall bring the aforesaid Negroe, or give
Intelligence of her to her aforesaid Master, so that she may be taken in Custody, shall have
Twenty Shillings Reward; but whomsoever Detains or Hires her, be it at their Peril.
John Price.

RUN away on Saturday last the 11th Instant, from Charles Green, Joiner, in Kingston, a Mulotto Man, named Joseph Kebern, aged about 19, an Apprentice. Whoever gives Notice of him to his Master aforesaid, so as he be had again, shall have
20 s. Reward and Mile Money; and those that entertain him shall incur the Penalty of the
Act in force for that Purpose.

To be Sold,

A Negroe Man-Boy, Named Monmouth, who has been brought up under a Surgeon
for Three Years past, aged about 20. Whoever has a Mind to Buy him, may apply to his Master, Mr. Michael Diore, Surgeon at the Plantation of Daniel Gotier Esq;
in Liguanea, he intending to go off the Island.

AT the Fair, held in the Precincts of Littleworth, in the Parish of Kingston, the 3 First
Days in May next, Persons may be furnished with all sorts of Glass Sconces, fine Dressing-
Glasses, of the best and newest fashion, made in England. Note all sorts of Looking-Glasses,
old or new, may be new Silver'd, Polish'd or Cleaned, to as good a Perfection as at first,
By Mr. John Johnson, at his Shop fronting the King's Store-houses there.

ON the 21st Instant April, will be expos'd to Sale, the Houshould Goods of James Teber,
Deceased, at his House at Halfway-Tree, in Liguanea; and on Thursday the 23d of this
Instant, will also be expos'd to Sale, the Negroes formerly belonging to the said James Teber,
at the House of Mrs. Rachael Sheperd's in Kingston.

JAMAICA: Printed by R. BALDWIN in *Kingston,* MDCCXIX.
[Price One Bit, or Three Half-Crowns a Quarter.]

FIGURE 6.4: Page 4 of the *Weekly Jamaica Courant*, 15 April 1719

I thank God that there are no free schools, nor printing, and I hope we shall not have, these hundred years; for learning has brought disobedience and heresy and sects into the world, and printing had divulged them, and libels against the best of government. God keep us from both [Swan 1970: 11].

This wish on the part of administrators to govern without criticism was clearly disturbed by the introduction of printing and newspapers, whose editors had a commitment to promote probity and accountability. The effect of the start of a newspaper in the West Indies as well as the reaction of administrators is exemplified by incidents in Barbados, as related by Poyer [1808]:

The inhabitants of Barbadoes had not long enjoyed this advantage, when an attempt was made to restrain the exercise of it. Mr. Adams, one of the council, had published some remarks on the sugar trade of the colonies, which produced an answer, in which the honourable author's literary talents were treated with less ceremony and respect than some of his friends thought due to his rank. At the instigation of some persons, smarting under the censorial rod, the grand jury presented Keimer for publishing a malicious, scandalous and seditious paper, and particularly for printing a false and defamatory libel on Mr. Adams. When the presentment was brought before the court, the attorney-general declared that there was nothing in the publication complained of which could possibly warrant a criminal prosecution; but the printer was nevertheless bound to keep the peace for six months.

The effect of the start of the newspaper in Barbados can also be seen in the words of a "waggish correspondent", who wrote the following letter to the editor:

Mr. Samuel Keimer,
Sir,

I am one of those many persons who look upon you to be a very dangerous fellow; and I will offer some reasons to support my opinion, which I shall be glad if you can answer.

It is well known to the good people of Barbados, that we, and our ancestors, time out of mind, have had and enjoyed a privilege of venting falshoods, scandals, absurdities, scurrilities, and contradictions, whenever the good of our country demanded the exercise of this our privilege. We could heretofore, without fear, or shame, send home addresses and representations in favour of an *Ex--y's wife and mild administration, and by the same conveyance transmit charges of extortion, plunder, and oppression against the same Ex--y.

In those good days, one half of this island could represent the other as French traders and disaffected persons, while the accused party retorted the imputation upon their accusers, with equal grace and truth. You might then have heard one body of men bewailing the decayed condition of our trade, and another rejoicing at its prosperity. This was done in such a style and manner as the passion of the writer or speaker dictated, without ever expecting that any proof of the premises be required on either side, or that our remonstrances would be communicated to any more than a few persons in authority at home, who, by reason of their high stations and weighty affairs, were not likely to receive deep impressions from such foreign occurrences.

This with many other valuable privileges of the same kind, we enjoyed, to the admiration and envy of our neighbouring colonies, who had nothing like it, until your printing-shop, for our sins, was opened in our metropolis.

But now, so it is, that no sooner is a seasonable untruth uttered for the benefit of an honest party among ourselves, but you, Mr. Samuel Keimer, instantly divulge it to all his majesty's subjects, without distinction. If a learned patriot happens, by the torrent of his zeal for his country's service, to be hurried into that vehement species of oratory, which the English call Billingsgate, your officious press is at hand to record it for the inspection of Lloyd's coffee house politicians, and the critics of the Sword-Blade.

Thus are we brought, by the accursed machine of yours, unknown to our forefathers, under the miserable dilemma of either dropping our ancient and undoubted privilege, or becoming the ridicule of phlegmatick Londoners, who are strangers to the sallies of a warm imagination in this climate, and think we ought to treat publick business with decency and temper, as they do. To you alone are owing those frequent impertinencies we meet with in our English letters, Lord! cries one, How can gentlemen treat one another in such a manner? – Where did your great men learn their language, says another? Are these extraordinary personages of your own growth; or, like other rare productions, brought from foreign parts? This is not to be endured by any true lover of his country, to have the genius, and talents of its brightest members scoffed at, by a parcel of cool-headed-thinking fellows.

I therefore take this opportunity of assuring you, Mr. Samuel Keimer, if you do not speedily change your pernicious trade of printing, for one more innocent, I will move the House, of which I have the honour to be an unworthy member, for leave to bring in a bill for the utter demolition of all printers and printing-shops, which are, or may hereafter be in this island: Or if it should be thought too severe to prohibit the exercise of a lawful calling, absolutely and without reserve, there should be grievous penalties enacted against printing any thing but sense accompanied with good manners, which will amount to a total prohibition. I am, in proportion as you deserve well of my dear country,

Yours, &c.

P.S. It is possible you may have the assurance to print this letter, which my passion for the publick good has extorted from me. But do, if you dare

Thickets, Aug. 10, 1732

Two decades later the press was still a major topic of discussion, for the lead article in the *Antigua Gazette* of 12 April 1755 was 'Of the Use, Abuse, and Liberty of the Press, with a little Salutary Advice'. The article, which took up the entire first page, started: "Whether the *Art of Printing* has been of greater Service or Detriment in the World, has frequently been made the Subject of fruitless Controversy." The writer then went on to point out the positive changes that the press had brought about and ends by giving advice to printers about what they should and should not accept for publication. It is clear from the article that the editor of the paper still felt the need to defend the relatively new and challenging role of the press in the society of the time.

Whereas some of the opinions expressed in newspapers were justified criticisms, no doubt others were malicious and intended to belittle or destroy opponents. In this connection Dickson [1789: 46n] makes the following comment:

All small communities are, more or less, infested with slanderers. In Barbadoes, such persons do not always content themselves with whispering defamation; but I have known the two presses teem, for months together, not with political, only, but with indecent and virulent, personal invective. This assertion and several others I have advanced, I could support, if necessary, by extracts from a collection of Barbadoes papers, now in my hands. I have no personal cause to complain of the anonymous writers of Barbadoes, having never been once so much as alluded to by them. But I always detected the practice of scribbling in newspapers, on any other, at least, than general subjects. In no newspaper, did I ever make even the remotest personal allusion, except, in a piece signed Octavius, in the Barbados Mercury, of November 13th 1784. That piece was intended to place in the proper point of view the character of a respectable gentleman of the Island who possesses good qualities, which he in vain endeavours to conceal, and who had been rather lightly indeed, than injuriously treated, by one of those scribblers. – Octavius never was answered.

What is also significant in Dickson's comments is that correspondents could write anonymously and that the newspaper seemed to be the acceptable forum for carrying on disputes, personal or otherwise.

Where for one reason or another a correspondent could not gain access to the newspaper to express his opinion or if his opinion was lengthy, he had the option of having his view printed as a pamphlet. This could either be done locally or in England, if the author thought the matter needed wider ventilation. So, for instance, Thomas Baxter had his view of the dispute between Governor Byng of Barbados and the Speaker of the House, Henry Peers, published in a pamphlet in London in 1740 in order to counteract the local support for Peers, even though both men had died earlier.

Whereas most of the disputes which were dealt with in print had to do with the intrigues among the ruling whites, from one of Dickson's comments [1789: 58] it can be seen that the nonwhite population did not completely escape from abuse in the newspapers: "Several free negroes and some slaves regularly attend divine service. I could mention a family of the former, whose devotion is sometimes the object of what, in the present cant, is called *skit*, in the Barbadoes newspapers" (p. 58). No doubt the language of these persons was the main feature in these 'skits'.

In the British colonies the newspapers seemed to have a fair amount of freedom, but in the Spanish empire governments exercised direct control over the press. Note the following, for example, which took place in Trinidad during the rule of the Spanish:

The governor of Trinidad, José María Chacón, wrote to the King on January 27, 1790, that he had ordered Juan [Jean?] Viloux, editor of the *Gazeta*, or weekly newspaper, which was printed on the island, to depart from there 'for having reprinted in it, without my approval, various articles from the foreign newspapers about the present revolution in France, in which were published items calculated to spread discussion, corrupt the true faith, and disturb the good order of our rule;' a decision which was approved by the royal order of May 25, 1790 [McMurtrie 1943c: 3].

In the British territories censorship of content was less direct and authoritarian, but it was there nonetheless. For instance, Luffman [1789: 143] reported that in Antigua:

... certain persons, thirty-three in number, some of whom having weight in the island, and others of no weight at all, put their names to a paper which they sent by a messenger (one of those who had signed it) to the printer's office, the purport of which was that they, the undersigned, would withdraw their subscriptions, if such letters were not discontinued. This dreadful intimidation had the desired effect; notwithstanding several public spirited men offered to make up the deficiency to the printer, by additional payments...

A less formal version of the same is noted by Manross [1965: 241]:

Abel Clinkett to Bishop Coleridge, High St, Bridgetown, Dec 22, 1827. He will have to tone down his championship of the education of Negroes and have fewer religious articles in his paper because he is losing readers and he is heavily in debt and unable to be as independent as he would like.

These episodes in Antigua and Barbados are not censorship from a government source but from those in the society who had money and power and intended to have their wishes respected whether they were justified or not.

The precarious situation of printers, in the face of the need to appease offended citizens, is best illustrated by the judgement in the case brought against Samuel Keimer (referred to above). It was pointed out by Poyer that the charge was dismissed as groundless, but Keimer was nonetheless put on probation for six months. In such circumstances, therefore, printers often had to side with the government of the day and to respect the wishes of the powerful not only to get government business but also to avoid being put out of business altogether.

Even as late as 1852 there was still opposition to newspapers. For instance, the Englishman Charles Day, who spent five years in the West Indies from 1846 to 1851, in reference to what he called "two Radical newspapers" in Barbados, was in no doubt that they should be suppressed because they were "productive of much mischief". Day's real source of resentment was that one of the newspapers was edited by a coloured person, who, he thought, was inciting the coloured and black population to take over the island.

The content of the early newspapers tended to be restricted to factual information such as reports on the arrival and departure of ships and their cargo as well as news from North America and Europe. However, the purely factual information was in some cases complemented by literary information and pieces of verse. Literate persons in those days, and this obviously included printers, regarded themselves as cultured and as Poyer [1808: 278] says: "Some of the most enlightened members of the community availed themselves of the advantage of a free press, and devoted their pens to the instruction of their countrymen." It seems unlikely that the enlightened members of the society would have contributed to newspapers unless the printers themselves had some kind of literary or educational standing. In addition, the European tradition, as explained by Eisenstein [1985: 29], cannot be disregarded: "Thus some of the views that later became characteristic of the

Enlightenment were first shaped in certain sixteenth-century printing shops under the aegis of merchant publishers who plied their trade during the religious wars." Yet, the extent to which the character, mentality and philosophy of the early printers shaped West Indian societies and directed the vision of later printers is difficult to assess.

It is uncontentious in the case of British colonial America to claim that Benjamin Franklin helped to shape the emergence of the United States of America, but to attribute this substantially or even partially to his early adult life as a printer and publisher in Philadelphia would be hard to establish. There is no clear evidence that printers were seen at that time as intellectual leaders in the society. However, in a real sense they exercised control over what literature was provided to the public and they helped to shape the societies intellectually, whether people were aware of it or not. It is therefore of some interest to look at the kinds of persons printers were in the early days in the West Indies.

Of the early printers the ones we have most information on are those in Barbados and Antigua. This information comes to us principally from Benjamin Franklin, who had connections to early printers in both islands, as well as from the content and philosophy of the publications which have survived. David Harry, the first person to set up a printing press in Barbados, and Benjamin Franklin had both been employees of Samuel Keimer in Philadelphia. Keimer himself followed Harry to Barbados, worked for him for a short while and took over the press from him when he returned to Philadelphia. The picture we get of Keimer from Franklin is prejudiced, of course, because it is part of Franklin's memoirs which are looking back at a man with whom Franklin had had a major disagreement. The picture we are given of Keimer is for the most part negative, both in the profession as journalist and otherwise. Commenting on his first contact with Keimer as a printer in Philadelphia Franklin [1793] says:

I found Keimer's printing materials to consist of an old damaged press, and a small cast of worn-out English letters (p. 68).

I endeavoured to put his press in order, which he had not yet used, and of which indeed he understood nothing (p. 69).

The two Philadelphia printers appeared destitute of every qualification necessary in their profession. Bradford had not been brought up to it, and was very illiterate. Keimer, though he understood a little of the business, was merely a compositor, and wholly incapable of working at the press (p. 70).

As far as Keimer's religious beliefs are concerned, Franklin says:

At the time of our first acquaintance he professed no particular religion, but a little of all upon occasion (p. 70).

Hence he formed so high an opinion of my talents for refutation, that he seriously proposed to me to become his colleague in the establishment of a new religious sect. He was to propagate the doctrine by preaching, and I to refute every opponent (p. 92).

Keimer wore his beard long, because Moses had somewhere said, Thou shalt not mar the corners of thy beard. He likewise observed the Sabbath; and these were with him two very essential points (p. 94).

About his character and other abilities Franklin says:

He was totally ignorant of the world, and a great knave at heart, as I had afterwards an opportunity of experiencing (p. 70).

His wife and relations in London had given me a bad character of him (p. 138).

He was, in fact, a strange animal, ignorant of the common modes of life, apt to oppose with rudeness generally received opinions, an enthusiast in certain points of religion, disgustingly unclean in his person, and a little knavish withal (p. 150).

Keimer also made verses, but they were indifferent ones (p.69).

This was the man, through the eyes of Benjamin Franklin, who charted the way for the newspaper in Barbados and all other parts of the British West Indies except Jamaica. In fact, Keimer's influence was even greater, seeing that he had subscribers in the French and Dutch Caribbean. This was the man who published the first newspaper in Pennsylvania and the first in Barbados. This, however, is not the man who comes out through the pages of the *Gazette*, a man who gained the respect of his readers and continued publishing the *Gazette* for at least ten years.

In the *Barbados Gazette* of 4 May 1734 Keimer wrote a piece of verse from which the status and possible influence of printers in the British colonies can be garnered. In the poem Keimer bewails his own lot in comparing it with that of his peers in other colonies. He identifies printers in Pennsylvania, New York, Maryland and Virginia, and Jamaica, pointing out how well they are rewarded by their respective societies. Then referring to himself he says:

Tho' working like slave, with zeal and true courage
He can scarce get as yet ev'n salt to his porridge.

It is quite likely that Keimer's woes were of his own making, judging from the fact that he had a history of financial troubles even before he came to Barbados. If it is true that the governments in the North American colonies had made provision for their printers and in Barbados they had not, it was probably the result of hostility between Keimer and the local authorities. Keimer's poem might have been a way of getting back at some of those who had supported the court case against him the previous year, as well as a means of embarrassing would-be gentlemen who refused to pay their debts. Whatever the true reason for Keimer's complaint, what the poem shows is that the printer (in other parts of the West Indies) at the time had some social and economic standing.

There is therefore some measure of contradiction between the expressed view that the printer was a threat to the establishment and the fact that in some colonies the printer was being given an official stipend. Although a part of this contradiction is simply that not all printers published newspapers, in the case of those who did and also did well financially, the reason is no more than what obtains today – when the newspaperman's views are at odds with those of the rich and powerful, he is reviled, but when they are in concert with them, he is rewarded. Keimer's words about the honesty, honour, zeal, courage and justice of printers were of course not objective, and although there is little to suggest that printers and newspapermen were more than most other colonists, except that they were literate and literary persons, by the end of the eighteenth century, that is, more than fifty years after printing and newspapers were first introduced into the region, the following comment from Dickson [1789: vi] maintained the favourable image of printers:

> The spirit good sense and humanity of the printers of the Jamaica newspapers ought not to be forgotten: for they have shown themselves superior alike to the taunts of the 'profligate' and the malevolence of the 'unmerciful'; discouragements which all good men must expect to meet with in the discharge of their duty. Were I to give a similar account of the Barbadoes printers and their worthy correspondents, it would be said that I courted their applause. Let the humane enquirer into this subject compare the *Barbados Gazette* and *Mercury* with the other West Indian prints, and judge for himself.

Whether or not printers of the time enjoyed the support of their contemporaries, printing had become an integral part of eighteenth century West Indian society, which meant that printers, being literate and literary, were essentially conduits for cultural reproduction from England and a link in the triangle between Britain, the North American colonies and the West Indian colonies.

The real effects of the newspaper in the West Indies can only be assessed historically. In England and the northeastern British American colonies newspapers flourished in a situation where there was a continual increase in literacy, an increase in commerce which promoted advertising, a search for avenues for publication and knowledge of literary and scientific subjects, a thirst for gossip, scandal and news of political strife. In addition, as Armytage [1965: 75] points out: "The Napoleonic war facilitated the entry of the newspaper into the lives of the working classes, who, hungry for news and avid for sensation, would even buy them when a day or two old, often by clubbing together." The effect of all this in England was that people became more socially conscious and better educated in a general sense.

In the West Indies slavery and the plantation system put certain strictures on the possible circulation of the newspaper, which meant that the majority of the population was outside the ambit of the newspaper. In addition, in the West Indies newspapers came into being much later in the Catholic colonies (*ie* those that came under English control later) than in the Anglican ones and in the former they were under much stricter control. In the Anglican colonies the Anglican Church had a tighter control of education and government than was the case in England itself, as a result of which the broadening of education (away from only medicine, law, religion and teaching) towards science, mathematics, crafts and commerce, subjects which were vigorously pursued by the nonconformists in their 'academies' in England, was not a part of West Indian education and so not encouraged in the newspapers in these colonies.

In spite of the strictures on newspapers in the West Indies, they soon proliferated. For example, in the 1780s in a small society like Antigua there were three weekly newspapers – the *Antigua Chronicle,* the *Antigua Gazette* and the *Antigua Journal.* By the time of Emancipation each island was producing more than one. Writing in 1841, Peter Simmonds stated that

> Barbadoes has now 5 semi-weekly, and 1 tri-weekly newspaper ... in addition to an official weekly Gazette for government notices ... St Kitt's, Grenada, Tobago, Antigua, Dominica, and St Lucia, have each 2 weekly political journals, in addition to the government Gazette in some islands ... St Vincent has 3 weekly papers ... At Trinidad there are 2 semi-weekly papers, besides the Royal Gazette ...

Simmonds also noted that four papers were being published in Georgetown and one in Berbice. Yet, one should not be misled by this into thinking that there was a big and hungry reading public capable of absorbing so many papers. The reality was that papers arose and disappeared very quickly and it was only those that had government business which managed to last. One factor which aggravated the situation, judging by the constant pleas of the printers, was that many subscribers were constantly in arrears. As a result, only a few newspapers throughout the region were solid enough to last for more than a decade, publishing regularly.

Without doubt there were positive effects resulting from general enlightenment provided by the newspaper. In the case of Barbados social, political and economic results can be identified. An early historian (referred to by Poyer [1808]) claims that the success of Lord Howe as a governor in Barbados (in the 1730s) in bringing social cohesion by reducing political animosities was facilitated by the weekly circulation of the *Barbados Gazette.* Poyer himself claims that the newspaper had significant beneficial effects:

> By the publication of many spirited and ingenious letters and essays on political and commercial subjects, the mischievous designs, sinister views and corrupt motives of those incendiaries, who, under the specious garb of patriotism, had plundered the public and disturbed the peace of society, were developed, scrutinized and frustrated. Relieved from the illusion which had long imposed on their senses, the Barbadians now began to see and understand their true interests.

Newspapers also brought the colonies closer together by establishing a constant flow of information between them. Rodway [1918: 274] points out that up to 1793 "Englishmen in Demerara subscribed to the Barbados newspapers and the Dutch to the *Amsterdamsche Courant*". The editor of the *Barbados Gazette* in the 1730s had subscribers and correspondents in the neighbouring islands.

The effect of the newspaper on the enslaved population of St Vincent in the 1820s is clearly pointed out by Carmichael [1833, 1:244]:

> Although few slaves can read, yet there are many negroes and coloured people who can, and who do read the English newspapers; and the very memorable debates in parliament upon the subject of slavery soon found their way, in a most distorted and mangled form to the negroes, – and the effect was instantly visible. There was a total change of conduct . . .

What Carmichael points out for St Vincent would no doubt have been the same for all the other territories.

Increasingly the coloured population saw the newspaper as an avenue for having their voice heard. For example, in the early 1820s a coloured man was the editor of the main newspaper in Antigua (see Coleridge [1825: 253]); Samuel Prescott had a newspaper (*New Times*) in Barbados in the 1830s; and a protégé of Prescott, Charles Falconer, took over *The Dominican* from three coloured creoles who had founded it in 1839. By the middle of the nineteenth century, therefore, Charles Day [1852, 2:299] was moved to say with his usual venom: "Coloured men are very fond of being editors of newspapers, as it increases their importance in the eyes of their own race." What is more important as far as the influence of these newspapers is concerned is that, as Day goes on to point out (p. 300): ". . . it is from these papers that extracts are usually printed in England". In other words, even unlike today, news and analysis of the situation in the West Indies was seen in England through the eyes of the local press, which in some cases mirrored the views of the aspiring coloured population.

The spread of information across the world at that time, although it was slow, was very significant. There is no fundamental difference between the news interests of papers then and now; the major difference today is speed of communication. At that time news was transported backward and forward by ship, which meant that shipping itself was a source of interest and was featured in the newspapers. Printers received newspapers and other forms of printed materials from England, Europe and North America and made selections from these to make up the international section of their newspapers. Throughout the eighteenth century matters related to trade and politics, especially the growing conflict with the New England states, were reproduced from papers received from London, Philadelphia, Boston, Paris and other cities. Conflicts between the French and the English later in the century were also reproduced in the local newspapers.

The delivery of news followed the ship route, which meant that news from England and Europe went to Barbados first and was then transshipped to other islands. News from New England, Virginia and the Carolinas either went to

Jamaica, Antigua or Barbados directly or according to the route of the ship. One feature of these routes of communication is that Jamaica, being fairly distant to the north west, was not always directly linked to the islands of the eastern Caribbean, although around the time of Emancipation this was not so, for Thome and Kimball [1838: 53] point out that "there are several English steamers which ply between Barbadoes and Jamaica, touching at several of the intermediate and surrounding islands, and carrying the mails". A probable example of the lack of familiarity with Jamaica in the earlier years is that although the *Jamaica Weekly Courant* appeared in 1718, the *Barbados Gazette* of 1731 was thought to be the first newspaper printed in the West Indies. It is not that the earliest printer in Barbados was unaware of the fact that printing (of government and other documents) was going on in Jamaica, but rather that he did not receive any newspaper news directly from Jamaica or indirectly through England or Philadelphia. It is quite possible that at the time the *Barbados Gazette* started in 1731 the newspaper in Jamaica had declined, but the reason for the ignorance is more likely that since printing came to Barbados and Antigua from Philadelphia and it came to Jamaica from England, and also since Barbados was the first stop in several ways from England, it did not occur to those in Barbados and in England that newspaper publication had long before started in Jamaica.

The extent to which circulation of newspapers led to norms in language is not easy to determine. There is no doubt that lifting items and stories from a newspaper in one country and reproducing them in another, if done frequently and on a wide scale, would have provided models of language and style which in time would have had a normative influence. A case can also be made that because correspondents saw the newspaper then, in part, more like the literary journal of today, requiring standards of literacy and style for pieces submitted, the newspaper would have disseminated a certain literary style. In fact, many of the pieces submitted to newspapers were essays and pieces of verse and editors not only determined which were suitable for publication but also reserved the right to edit them. So, although the producer of the newspaper was invariably referred to as the 'printer', this person actually performed the functions of an editor.

It was not only the local newspapers which had a normative influence on the local population, but also the English newspapers. These were especially important to those who felt themselves away from home and who were intensely interested in what was going on in the real world of London and Europe. The papers were one of the items eagerly awaited when ships docked and they were eagerly read and passed from hand to hand. These English newspapers were therefore a constant point of comparison with local papers. In any case, in the early local newspapers there was little possibility for differences in written English because the editors of these were English born or not far removed from being English. Later in the eighteenth and nineteenth century when some editors were native West Indians, their language and style still could not vary significantly from what was to be found in the English newspapers, because these latter were always available as a guide.

SOME IMMEDIATE EFFECTS OF PRINTED MATERIAL

The increase in communication through the printed word made literacy a desirable competence, even in the plantation society of the West Indies. For although in fact the printed word needed to be deciphered only by a few persons in the society for oral dissemination thereafter, those persons who could read became important and consequently literacy also became important. However, there is no easy way of showing the growth in influence in what was essentially a two-way, supply-demand relationship between increase in printed material and increase in literacy.

There is no doubt that the ability to read the newspaper would have given a plantation manager some business advantage, in that from this source he would know when and where slaves and other goods were available. There is no doubt either that newspapers would not have contained this kind of information unless they were being read on the plantations. It is reasonable to assume therefore that, if only for the business content of the newspaper, literacy assumed some importance on all plantations. The level of literacy required for this was functional and rudimentary; it did not stretch to the level of being able to cope with literary books, which would have required some sophistication. Yet, the fact that several books were written about common diseases and their treatments suggests that this type of functional information could have increased the need for persons who could read such texts and save the lives or extend the usefulness of the workers on the plantation.

One fact that was quite clear was that by the end of the eighteenth century persons in the West Indies were aware of books written about them and reacted strongly to them if they were not favourable. The best example of this is probably Samuel Mathews' response to J.B. Moreton's *Manners and Customs in the West Indies*. The title of Mathews' response was *The Lying Hero* and in it he took Moreton to task in a vicious manner for almost everything that he wrote. However, Mathews was merely following the example of his countrymen (Some Gentlemen of St. Christopher [1784]), who earlier had done the same thing to the Rev James Ramsay, who had returned to London and written a book about the treatment of slaves in St Kitts.

Fifty years after Mathews, the reaction to Mrs Carmichael's book in St Vincent and Trinidad was commented on by Charles Day [1852, 2:129-30]: "Excepting perhaps Mrs. Trollope's good tempered, truthful book on America, there has not been a work more grossly and unjustly abused than Mrs. Carmichael's excellent book on the West Indies." From Day's further comments it seemed as if all sections of society, and moreso the coloured people, in both islands thought that Mrs Carmichael had lied and exaggerated in her representation of them. The obvious generality of this opinion indicates an even wider reading public by the middle of the nineteenth century.

If the people in the West Indies were aware of what authors said about them, authors and others in Britain were also sensitive to the reactions of West Indians and the challenges to the truth of what they wrote. From the days of Peter Martyr's *Decades* (1516), accounts of the New World were riddled with distortions because the writers, driven partly by their own imaginings and partly by national and personal interests, gave accounts of things which they had no first hand knowledge of. Gradually, more accurate accounts emerged as the information flow backward and forward increased and as the New World societies began to represent their own interests. In fact, it was as a result of the exchanges, the desire to be truthful and accurate, and the need for first-hand accounts that the speech of slaves and ex-slaves came to be represented in print.

On the very first page of the response of Some Gentlemen of St. Christopher to Ramsay [1784] the following point is made: "Dean Swift has an observation, which, though a glaring truth, is not sufficiently attended to – *That it is rather necessary for an author to understand something of a subject, before he presumes to write upon it.*" It was an argument that touched a sensitive nerve in those who were arguing for the abolition of slavery in England and who represented their accounts as accurate and first hand. Within five years of this publication two major works appeared in print in Britain written by former slaves from the West Indies – Cugoana [1787] and Equiano [1789].[3]

In reaction to these, in 1792 the West India lobby in Britain tried to discredit Equiano in the British newspapers by claiming that he was not an African.[4] In addition, in the West Indies in 1793 Samuel Mathews, in his response to J.B. Moreton's criticism of slavery in Jamaica, reiterated with a slight variation the point made by his countrymen nine years earlier:

Again, I never could in all my travels, discover a Creole or European that was able to discourse with me in the negro language; surely if I have any grievances to complain of, it is necessary that the person to whom I am to communicate the cause of my trouble should be able to comprehend what I say; besides, there is not one white man in a thousand that would take the trouble (to me it was a pleasure) to converse with negroes as I have done.

I have visited at least five hundred plantations, and conversed with at least one hundred thousand negroes, principally upon the subject of their treatment; . . . [Mathews 1793: 141-42].

Mathews then, in order to support his defence of slavery, proceeded to give an illustrative conversation "in the negro language" between himself and a slave. As a consequence of this, those who opposed slavery had to produce their own stories with some amount of slave language, while others with other interests [Wentworth 1834; Day 1852] simply reproduced or adapted Mathews' stories, songs and verse. After 1793 there was, therefore, a marked increase in the citations of slave language as well as the language of other groups in West Indian society.

The extensive citations of nonstandard varieties of English no doubt brought the grammar of English more into focus in the West Indies, and made those having to write books, pamphlets and even letters to the newspaper more aware of the rules of the English language. This must have been especially so for West Indians, for when Mathews (a Kittitian) wrote his book in 1793, he jokingly tried to exonerate himself from any errors in the book by conceding the poverty of his own education and suggesting that the printer should be blamed:

ADDRESS to the READER

Reader,

You know, or at least you ought to know, that all typographical errors are laid to the charge of the Printer. – Now you will oblige me much, if, while your hand is in, you will blame him for all grammatical errors and bad orthography you may meet in the following sheets; for I confess to you, as I did to him, that I know no more of grammar, than a bastard calf does of his grandfather; and as for orthography, you may judge what an adept I ought to be, when the best Tutor I ever had whipped me severely for making three syllables of the word synagogue; I'll synagogue you says he; spell it after me; and thus he went on, s y sy, n a na, sy-na, g o go, sy-na-go, g u e gey, sy-na-go-gey. Now, as I have dealt with so much candour, do deal with a little generosity, if you do not, you know the alternative – let it alone.

In spite of the light-hearted nature of the anecdote and Mathews' admission of his restricted knowledge of grammar, it is clear that correctness in English had become a concern for authors by the beginning of the nineteenth century.

CONCLUSION

In accounting for the development of printing and the effects of printing in the West Indies, it could be argued that the transfer to the West Indian colonies of the culture and technology of the Europeans was inevitable, since it was the Europeans who were in control of the situation. One could counter this general argument by claiming that the local situations would have dictated not only what elements of the culture and technology would be transferred but also the rate of transfer. However, neither one of these arguments captures fully the dependency relationship between the colonies and the mother country. The colonies were not exact replicas of the mother country; the colonies served the interests of the mother country, especially in terms of trade – the colonies were the consumers and the mother country the supplier. Eisenstein [1985: 27], in reference to Western Europe, points out that: "In addition to special Christian motives and long-lived apostolic drives, Bible printing was powered by the capitalist urge to expand markets, outdo competitors, and increase book sales." The colonies were a captive market for British printers and it was not really in their interest to foster printing in the West Indies. So, Britain controlled technology and trade in such a way that the colonies were made to be dependent on the mother country as supplier. Even when technology was supplied, it was of a hand-me-down nature with a constant need for spare parts and supplies to make it functional. The mother country remained the creator of technology and supplier of expertise. The colony was always in step and behind by a number of years. In this way the instruments of the mother country (including standard English) became the models for the colonies.

According to Eisenstein [1985: 29-30], in England in the seventeenth century "printing made it possible for craftsmen, artisan engineers, 'reckon masters', barber surgeons, painters, and potters who had not mastered Latin to contribute to public knowledge". This was so because these persons were able to use the vernacular in print. As a consequence, English, which had previously been of low status and thought unsuitable for scholarly purposes, gradually became the norm for the educated. The same kind of language development did not take place in the West Indies: there was no use of West Indian vernaculars (ie creole languages) in print either for religious or secular purposes. The variety used for belles-lettres and historical writings in the West Indies was (British) English. West Indian vernaculars therefore remained low status varieties in the face of the increasingly powerful standard coming out of the mother country.

The major sustaining force for the dependency relationship in the West Indies was not the economic structure in itself but the fostering of a powerful philosophy that Britain was the centre of the world, the quintessence of civilization and development. The creation and sustenance of this philosophy was facilitated by literacy, printing, a liberal education, and the emerging result of all these, standard English. With the control of printing and educational material in the hands of the mother country, the hold of the English language strengthened. What Eisenstein [1985: 31] says in reference to individuals is equally applicable to colonial rulers:

Presses also served to implement equally powerful drives for power and for fame. By providing rulers with their own independent propaganda machines, printing offered a way for them to extend their charisma... to transmute private interest into public good.

The printed word, whether in its form, its meaning or the view it was representing, moved beyond being the speech, interpretation and opinion of a person or class and assumed an objective authority, one which only increased with repetition.

Eventually, then, the printed variety of English coming out of British presses, a variety which initially had been a low status vernacular, came to dominate all other geographical and social varieties. Moreover, since there was never any break in British control in the West Indies definitive enough to weaken the philosophy that Britain was the centre of the world, there was no challenge to the authority of printed British English or any attempt to promote West Indian language preferences, as was the case in the USA after 1776.

NOTES

1 This is also quoted by Norman Fiering in the Foreword of Johnson [1988].
2 "To understand all they were saying and to better explain my thoughts to them."
3 See chapter 7.
4 See Fryer [1984: 111].

7

Intellectual and Literary Activity and its Effects on Literate English

Intellectual and literary flowering in a society is usually paralleled by and directly related to refinement in language and development of characteristic language for specific genres. It also fosters admiration for the language and its elevation beyond functional and practical communication to a level of artistry and beauty. Absence of significant intellectual and literary activity, on the contrary, means absence of development of literary and other varieties of learned language and absence of admiration for the language as a source of beauty in itself. Although in plantation society in the West Indies up to the middle of the nineteenth century there was a growth in literacy, the question is whether the level of academic, literary and other learned activity in the West Indies was significant enough to add positively to the varieties of English used there or to allow those varieties to achieve any level of admiration in the societies themselves. In essence, the question is whether literacy was able to sustain, perpetuate and validate itself in the areas of culture 'higher' than those of religious and political control, and so, at least, begin to project West Indians with a characteristic and positive identity.

The early colonists in the West Indies could not have lost much of their European cultural characteristics, but, as the West Indian societies evolved, context and economics became greater determining factors in the intellectual pursuits of the ruling class. Bailyn [1991] contrasts the glorified historical picture of the American frontier colonist pressing forward with a gleam in his eye with the more realistic picture of the uncertain exile at the periphery of civilization looking back to the centre for sustenance and confidence and glorifying the customs and achievements of the centre. The frontier colonist's look backward to Europe for standards might even have become stronger in the small islands, as opposed to the US which gradually began to sustain itself as a viable entity.

Children of colonists born in the West Indies were nurtured with the values of their parents and so were not for the most part drawn to intellectual pursuits because they were brought up and coddled by a system of slavery. In fact, their attitude to all exertion was negative. These children vacillated between extolling the cultural values of Europe and gratifying their own physical desires. They vacillated between going to Europe where social and intellectual life was more satisfying and living in the West Indies where physical life was much easier. For them the arts and literature were at best social trappings, and excursions into these areas were not propelled forward by competitiveness or by a necessity to excel or by a strong tradition.

The European poor and criminals who came in numbers to the West Indies were less inclined to look backward, because the colony was for them an escape from the harsh reality of Europe. These previously powerless persons who now had some measure of independence and power over those below them in the rigid social scale would have been ready to challenge the claims and values of the European nobility and to champion their own power and current values as pragmatic, valiantly gained and unpretentious. Yet, for a time, race protected them and reserved for them positions in the society. When these privileges began to be eroded, harsh necessity removed them from having time and energy to engage in artistic and literary pursuits.

The Africans, deliberately cut off from information and beaten and brainwashed into accepting their lot, at first clung to the belief in the transmigration of souls to the homeland after death and later changed it into a belief in a spiritual heaven. For them, reality of Africa was not couched in any glorious ideal, and life in the colonies was neither an escape to freedom and wealth nor a temporary exile from and a glorification of the homeland. The hope of the future was neither a continuation of the present nor a recovery of the past – it was a pragmatism of the present, a matter of survival. In such circumstances the African and creole descendants of Africans adapted the ideas, folklore and culture of the Europeans into their own intellectual and spiritual traditions if only to survive the daily cruelties inflicted on their minds and bodies. The creolized languages which they developed reflected the orality of their traditions as well as their experience in the West Indies.

Gordon Lewis in his book *Main Currents in Caribbean Thought* [1983] introduced his characterization of Caribbean society in a paradoxical way. He first says:

> The Caribbean colonial society . . . was an anti-intellectual society. In Père Labat's lament, everything was imported into the West Indies except books. The Caribbean slavocracy never learned the lesson, as did the slave-owning classes of the ancient world, of combining slavery with the arts (p. 26).

Then he also goes on to say:

> The truth is, of course, that if a wider Caribbean perspective is adopted, and if the totality of published works on the entire region is taken into account, the Caribbean is possessed of an intellectual history of no mean proportions (p. 26).

The apparent conflict between these two remarks begins to disappear when one realizes that what Lewis is actually pointing out in the first quotation above is not that there is no intellectual history, but that Caribbean colonial society cannot be regarded as significant in the history of ideas of man. However, his claims that no books were imported and that the Caribbean slavocracy did not combine slavery with the arts have to be examined carefully in the case of specific territories in the West Indies. To make a general assessment of the intellectual and literary climate of West Indian colonial society is difficult not only because of the lack of objectivity and lack of general applicability of comments, but also because of limited and scattered material from which one can draw conclusions.

Although it may not be possible to get a view of the literary and intellectual climate of the colonial West Indies in the seventeenth and eighteenth centuries which is comprehensive and objective, it is certainly possible to examine comments from varied sources in order to temper the generalized negative view. Such comments can be found in travellers' reports, books and other literature coming out of the West Indies, and above all in newspapers. Of course such comments completely exclude the slave population except to the extent that specific slaves were said to be able to speak 'good English' and to be able to read or write.

Relevant to this presentation of the literary and intellectual climate of the pre-emancipation West Indies are different explanatory theses which come out of theoretical frameworks for the development of literacy and culture, and either regard environment as the most powerful factor or claim that culture is transferred according to the people themselves. These two frameworks, although not mutually exclusive, are at times presented in that way, as, for example, in Cressy [1983] and Laqueur [1983]. The argument of the former is that "everything hinged on the demands of the environment (p. 40); and the latter's response is that"... the ability to read and write is not simply the product of economic necessity or the inevitable product of schools and formal education (p. 46). While there is no intention here to use the intellectual and literary activity in the plantation slave society to illustrate either one of these theories, they will be used as starting points for a consideration of the early period for which there is not a great amount of recorded evidence.

LITERARY ACTIVITY IN THE FIRST CENTURY AFTER 1625

As far as the white population is concerned, it is possible to project a level of illiteracy for the West Indies based on statistics for the areas from which these people came. In this case, one is using the argument that the culture which the colonists brought with them would not have changed significantly. In this regard, therefore, especially in reference to the seventeenth century for which there is a great lack of relevant information on the West Indies, one can turn to characterizations of Europeans in Europe and project these onto plantation life in the West Indies. Cressy [1983: 28] in an analysis of England of that time, says

> In East Anglia, a prosperous area which sent a significant number of emigrants to colonial America, 79 percent of the husbandmen were unable to sign [their names], and the proportion grew higher rather than lower as the seventeenth century progressed (p. 28).
>
> In his other roles also the husbandman was under no pressure to become literate. As tenant and farmer, subject and householder, the world of print and script made few inroads into his life (p. 28).

A projection from this analysis would indicate that not much more than twenty percent of the white plantation population in the West Indies could have been literate, even allowing for a higher level of literacy among officials in the town areas. Such a level of literacy may also be substantiated by referring to methods of communication among Europeans which were common in the West Indies at the time, methods of communication which of necessity had to reflect the capabilities of the people and the 'technology' available for practical communication.

Richard Ligon was one of the earliest commentators on West Indian life and his comments are respected because, unlike several other writers of his day and afterwards, he actually spent some time in the place which he later described. Ligon [1657: 107] says the following about the early Barbados colony:

> And though I found at Barbados some who had musical minds; yet, I found others, whose souls were so fixt upon, and so riveted to the earth, and the profits that arise out of it, as their souls were lifted no higher; and those men think, and have been heard to say, that three whip-sawes, going all at once in a frame or pit, is the best and sweetest musick that can enter their ears; and to hear a cow of their own low, or an assinigo bray, no sound can please them better. But these mens souls were never lifted up so high, as to hear the musick of the sphears, nor to be judges of that science, as 'tis practised here on earth; and therefore we will leave them to their own earthly delights.

Because there were few other first-hand commentators, Ligon's comments were readily repeated and generalized without the obvious note that Ligon was talking about transplanted adult Englishmen who could not have changed significantly in their ways because of the few years they had spent in Barbados. Ligon's comments, of course, support both frameworks, although from the emphasis that he gives to the economic thesis later commentators were easily led to generalize that the early colonists were interested only in 'profits'.

The former framework is used to make the claim that plantation slavery militated against refinement and resulted in a gross society. This is powerfully expounded by Patterson [1967] as a whole and specifically pointed out in the Preface (p. 9):

This was a society in which clergymen were the 'most finished debauchees' in the land; in which the institution of marriage was officially condemned among both masters and slaves; in which the family was unthinkable to the vast majority of the population and promiscuity the norm; in which education was seen as an absolute waste of time and teachers were shunned like the plague; in which the legal system was quite deliberately a travesty of anything that could be called justice; and in which all forms of refinements, of art, of folkways, were either absent or in a state of total disintegration.

It should be noted that this view contrasts somewhat with that of Swan [1970: 45] which claims that slavery afforded those masters who were interested time for the arts.

To some extent the early ruling class in the West Indian colonies is done a disservice when a picture is presented of them as no more than 24-hour-a-day slave masters and when the claim is made that the 'dung-heap' affected everyone – those in it and those on it. In fact, the impression created that the whites of the day were all obtuse Europeans and that genuinely educated Europeans would have found the society of the colonies intolerable and unacceptable is based on an erroneous vision of Europe of the seventeenth and the first half of the eighteenth centuries as a good and glorious place. This is a vision that does not take into account that it was the colonies that transformed Europe and fed the Industrial Revolution, thus creating wealth, power and sophistication.

The historical literature indicates that the New World was attractive to all sorts of persons for different reasons – for some it was money, for others it was adventure, for others curiosity about flora and fauna, for others freedom. Glimpses of educated priests and doctors occur or are referred to in the early literature. For example, Mavrile de S. Michel [1652: 95] identified among the English in St Kitts "un Gentilhomme, qui parlait fort bien latin", who simultaneously translated a sermon into English which Mavrile de S. Michel delivered in Latin. In the Preface of de Rochefort [1658], the author refutes the view that the majority of the populations in the islands were bankrupts and evil people and argues that the opposite was true. Dr. Hans Sloane commented in the Preface to his two volume work of 1707 that the medicinal herbs used in the West Indies had been taken back to England and "are used in medicines everyday, and more may, to the great advantage of physicians and patients, were people inquisitive enough to look after them". Such a comment does not give the idea of great disparity between the colonies and Britain in the level of sophistication of medicine. Christopher Codrington, in the first quarter of the eighteenth century, was said by Labat to have had a large collection of books on many different subjects. These glimpses, stretching over the first hundred years, suggest that during that time the upper social level in the West Indies was no different in mentality from their counterparts in England.

The cultural transmission thesis can be used more generally to make the claim that European social and cultural behaviour in the West Indies was a reflection of what obtained in Europe. To take Barbados as one example, the designation 'Little England' from early was a well-known characterization of that island, and such a designation as well as the following comment made in 1741 in *Caribbeana* (the *Barbados Gazette*) – "Here, indeed, they may see Great Britain in miniature" – gives further substance to the cultural transmission thesis. There were other early commentators who had a positive view of the island and compared it with England. For example, John Oldmixon, writing in 1708 essentially about the last part of the seventeenth century, says:

This island was the soonest peopled of all our Colonies; the Riches of the planters produc'd by that Soil, tempted Gentlemen of good Families and moderate Estates, to transport themselves thither to improve them. And tho it seems trivial to relate Particulars of the Honours bestow'd on private persons; yet for the Credit of Barbadoes, there have been more of that Island knighted by the kings of England, than of all the rest of the English Plantations in America, for since the Settlement of the island 13 Baronets and Knights were made, for the Incouragement of the Industry of the Inhabitants [Oldmixon 1708, 2:110].

Oldmixon maintained his vision of similarity by going on to make the following comments:

Enough of this digression, which is only design'd to shew, that the common Reflection made upon the Plantations, as to the Meanness of the Planters Origins, is groundless as to Barbadoes, where there are as many good families as are in any of the Counties of England, where Commerce and Trade flourish (2:111).

Their Dress, and that of their Ladies, is fashionable and courtly; and being generally bred at London, their Behaviour is genteel and polite; in which they have the Advantage of most of our Country Gentlemen, who living at great distance from London, frequent the World very little; and from conversing always with their Dogs, Horses, and rude Peasants, acquire an Air suitable to their Society (2:114).

The Gallant People delight most in Balls and Consorts; the good fellows, in drink and good company ... (2:127).

It is interesting to note that a vision of similarity was still uppermost in the mind of the Englishman, Anthony Trollope, one hundred and fifty years later in a characterization of Jamaica:

In Jamaica too there is scope for a country gentleman. They have their counties and their parishes; in Barbados they have nothing but their sugar estates. They [Jamaicans] have county society, local balls, and local race-meetings. They have local politics, local quarrels, and strong old-fashioned local friendships. In all these things one feels oneself to be much nearer to England in Jamaica than in any other of the West Indian Islands [Trollope 1860: 96].

However, although Oldmixon presented his view of similarity based on transmission in accounting for the ways of the whites in Barbados at the beginning of the eighteenth century, he also introduced the thesis of context, and specifically climate, as a tempering factor to explain some differences:

> The servants in Barbados follow the Sports and Exercises of the common People in England, as far as consists with the Heat of the Climate; and being all Englishmen like ourselves, the Reader is not to expect much Difference in their way of Living, Exercises, or Diversions, from our own [Oldmixon 1708, 2:127].

This idea that climate had a role to play in determining the ways of Europeans in the West Indies was taken up very strongly again at the end of the eighteenth century and in the nineteenth.

As to the provision of books and other printed material from England, as an indicator of the level and nature of cultural transmission, one of the earliest works of the eighteenth century which gives an indication of this in Barbados is a Catalogue by a Mr Zouch [1715-16]. It was described as: "A catalogue of books to be sold by Mr Zouch in the town of St. Michael Alias the Bridge-Town, in the said island [Barbados] where gentlemen and others may be supplied with great variety of books not contained in this catalogue." The catalogue contained a list of about 780 [Handler 1991: 8] published works, and to show how up-to-date it was it has a special section with "books, sermons and pamphlets published since April 1714". The catalogue had the books listed in the following fifteen categories:

Law
Miscellanies (including Blome's book on Jamaica)
Dictionaries
Ecclesiastical and Civil History
Greek and Roman History
Voyages and Travels
Geographical, Astronomical, &
Divinity
Devotional
Philosophy, Chymistry, Physick and Surgery
Poetry (including The Art of Poetry, by E. Byshe, 4 vol.
    Poems, & by E. Waller
    Prior's Poems on several Occasions
    A New Collection of Miscellany Poems for 1715
    Essay on Criticism, by Mr. Pope
Plays (including The Tragedies, Comedies, and Operas,
    by Dryden, 2 vol.
    The Works of Mr. De Molière, in 6 vol.
    The Plays and Poetry of W. Shakespear, in 9 vol.)
Letters, Novels and Romances
School Books (including Bibles, Common Prayers and
    Testaments of several Sorts and Sizes, some richly bound.
    Psalters, Primmers and Horn-books.

(13)

No. 3.

CATALOGUE OF BOOKS

REMAINING AT THE GENERAL DEPOT,
KINGSTON,
ON THE 1st OF DECEMBER, 1823.

10 Bibles, Nonpareil, 8vo.
66 Testaments, Brevier
128 Prayer Books, Nonpareil
    24mos.
111 Iremonger's Questions
62 Waldo on Sacrament
216 Psalters
83 Wilson's Family Prayer
142 Watt's Divine Songs
2 Watson's Apology
6 Young Man's Monitor
98 Woodward to Swearers
107 White's Dissuasive from Stealing
83 Woodward on Drunkenness
22 Do. on Backbiting
19 Yardley's Exposition
5 Duke's Lectures
68 Seaman's Monitor
38 Stanhope to the Sick
21 Assheton's Death Bed Repentance
90 Explanation of Holidays
10 Admonition for Sunday Schools
28 Best's Essay
195 Bishop of London on Late Earthquakes
136 Country Gentleman's Advice
2 Burkitt's Help and Guide
64 Country Clergyman's Advice
6 Christian Monitor
40 Crossman's Introduction
360 Church Catechism
18 Do Broken into Questions and Answers
140 Directions for Public Worship

80 Christian's Way to Heaven
8 Old Chaplain's Farewell Letter
7 Bowen's Companion to the Prisoner
220 History of our Saviour
280 Discourses of Do.
35 Directions for Young Students in Divinity
200 Christian's Daily Devotion
70 Exhortation to Prisoners
38 Ellesby's Caution
15 Elementary Questions
150 Serious Exhortation
3 Collects
25 Fleetwood on Swearing
18 Do, Communicant
160 Parables of our Saviour
155 Kettlewell's Tract
80 Observance of the Lord's Day
100 Child's First Book
76 Mrs. Trimmer's Charity School Book
12 Kettlewell's Trial of the Soul
100 Sin and Danger
300 Trimmer's Lessons
130 Gibson's Family Devotion
70 Gibson on Intemperance
30 Gibson on Sacrament
140 Do. on Lord's Day
12 Gastrell's Faith and Duty
17 Hort's Instructions to The Clergy
120 Newton's Pastoral Advice
250 National Society Central School Book, No. 2
18 Reilly's Evidences
21 Ostervald's Abridgment

From the Report of the Jamaica District Committee of the Society for Promoting Christian Knowledge, 1824

FIGURE 7.1: Catalogue of books remaining at the General Depot, Kingston, on the 1st December, 1823

> A Construing and Parsing Phaedrus's Fables,
> English and Latin, necessary for all who
> wou'd be Scholars, by Mr. Bayley
> Lilly's Accidence and Grammer with Construing
> The Oxford Grammer
> Leed's Greek Grammer
> Corderius's Colloquies
> Aesop's Fables
> Ray's Nominclatura, &c.
> Garretson's Exercise
> Willmot's Particles
> Spelling Books
> Catechisms)
> Maps and Prints

The range and focus of this catalogue were clearly appealing to teachers and the educated who had a British vision. There is no title in this list that moved outside the British view of the cultured and the selection does not make anything 'local' available except *Blome's book on Jamaica*. If, as Oldmixon claimed, there were a fair number of 'gentlemen of good families' and that they behaved little differently from those in England, then it is not too far-fetched to believe that books were read and even discussed among small groups interested in such matters. The catalogue shows that the areas of poetry, drama and language were of special interest, which is consistent with the vision of refinement that was typical of that day. The publication of the catalogue therefore indicates that within the first hundred years of settlement the colonists were trying to maintain a lifestyle like that in Britain and that they saw themselves as up-to-date and in contact with their contemporaries.

Besides books, more evidence of cultural transmission from England at the turn of the century is provided by Oldmixon in the following comment about a drama group:

> There was once a Company of Poppet Strowlers in this island [Barbados]; they came from England, and set up their Fairy Drama at the Bridge, where, for the Novelty of the Matter, they found a good Market; From thence they went to the Leward Islands, and thence home. We wonder their Example has not been follow'd by some of the young Fry of Poppet Players at London, who would do better to go over, and either play or work at Barbados voluntarily, than rake at home till they are sent thither by the Magistracy against their Wills [Oldmixon 1708, 2:127].

However, there is little doubt that, in comparison with England, dramatic activity in the West Indies was sporadic at the beginning of the eighteenth century and that such as they had would not have had any significant effect on the society generally.

In contrast to the general practice of importing literary material into the colonies, in Jamaica there is evidence of local production. The newspaper, *The Weekly Jamaica Courant*, of 8 April 1719 carried the following advertisement:

Lately Publish'd, TOBACCO: A Poem, In Two Books,
Translated from the Latin of RAPHAEL THORIUS. JAMAICA:
Re-printed by R. Baldwin, in Church-street, Kingston, Price 2s. 6d.

Here, the subject matter, the author and the printer all contributed to a much more 'local' product, thereby indicating that there was beginning to develop an essentially creole literature. Unfortunately, not many issues of this paper are available for an examination of the policy of the editor or the interests of the reading public in the first quarter of the eighteenth century in Jamaica.

LITERARY AND INTELLECTUAL ACTIVITY IN THE LAST THREE QUARTERS OF THE EIGHTEENTH CENTURY

A more positive picture of a society with literary material, books and literary groups emerges from the pages of a newspaper in the second quarter of the eighteenth century in Barbados. In the *Barbados Gazette*, from 1731 onwards, the impression is created that literary activity increased and became more consistent there. Publishing of newspapers, which had started with the *Jamaica Courant*, was still in its infancy when compared to the production of a newspaper today, which exists in a vast milieu of information and purveys a mass of material starkly and radically different from the beginning of the eighteenth century, but the role of the publishing house then was more lofty. In a colonial society at that time the publishing house was the sole producer of literature, which means, in fact, that by monopoly the 'newspaper' was the highest form of local literature. The role of the publishing house for a newspaper in the colonial West Indies was obviously not as glamorous as that identified by Eisenstein [1985: 24-25] for those in Western Europe:

> Thus the printing shop did more than issue products that enriched libraries and literary diets. It provided a new setting for intellectual activity. It served as a kind of institute for advanced learning . . . which rivaled the older university, court, and academy and which provided preachers and teachers with opportunities to pursue alternative careers.

However, there is no question that the early West Indian newspapers catered to the literate and sophisticated of the day.

The *Barbados Gazette* made its appearance in 1731 and came out at first once and then afterwards twice a week. The paper was maintained by subscription, was distributed to neighbouring territories and was keenly read by those who received it. Most of the original copies of the *Gazette* have not survived, but fortunately much of the text was collected together and published in London in two volumes in 1741 under the title *Caribbeana*. In itself it is not without significance that the contents of a Barbadian newspaper were republished in book form for readers in London. The newspaper carried items on politics and economics as well as what were referred to as productions "of a lighter sort". These latter were "letters and dissertations together with poetical essays on various subjects and occasions". Whereas the items on political and economic matters produced both friendly and hostile reactions, the matters of the lighter sort seemed generally to have been well received and the poetry was highly regarded by the editor himself.

The poems together with the items on social relations (including women and slavery) provide important data from which one can come to conclusions about the literary and intellectual climate of Barbados and the wider area. The poems were in the general scheme of the newspaper considered to be of lesser importance than the political and economic pieces, but on the other hand, as one contributor put it, "... they tend to improve our taste, refine our manners, and give a polite turn to the mind, while they serve to amuse also with a variety, which seems to be agreeable to the nature of man". The editor of the two volumes of *Caribbeana*, commenting on the selections that he made from the poems in the *Gazette* on local subjects, says "... they give variety to the whole, and may besides be a principal entertainment to the young of either sex, and such as are of a gay and airy turn, who do not care to be confined to serious and intense studies". The editor of the *Gazette* itself, in the words of one of his correspondents, regarded the literary pieces as "productions of our own growth, free from personal reflections and party disputes". The 'variety' in the newspaper must have reflected the interests of those who could read and it suggests that there was a large enough number of people in the society to subscribe to and sustain a newspaper of this type.

The first issue of the *Gazette* appearing in *Caribbeana* includes poems coming out of what could be considered as a small literary circle which met to savour a poetry writing contest between two gentlemen; the resultant poems were referred to thus: "two copies of verses which were lately composed at a gentleman's house in the country, where a set of friends of both sexes were met, purely to pass away a few days agreeably". In the 19 March 1731 issue of the *Gazette* the editor makes the following comment:

It is hardly necessary, I presume, to acquaint my readers, that, about three years ago, some gentlemen were pleased to act plays for the diversion of themselves and their friends, but more especially of the ladies of this place. I shall therefore only observe, that after they had given general satisfaction in tragedy, they were at length persuaded likewise to attempt a comedy; on which occasion, the following performances were composed ...

In addition to this, there is reference to and citation of epilogues and a prologue in verse composed in Barbados specifically for plays acted in Barbados.

How extensive and consistent this literary activity was in the first half of the eighteenth century is difficult to determine precisely. The fact that the editor of the *Gazette* admitted that occasionally he had to borrow pieces from colleagues in

England to fill out his paper suggests inconsistency in production. In any case, the picture of literary activity which emerges out of the *Gazette* should not be exaggerated to make the ruling class in the West Indies seem like a generally sophisticated society. External views at the time were not all positive, for Robertson [1730: 56] quotes a pamphlet published in England in 1725 as saying:

> It [Barbados] is a place of so much luxury, and such dissolute morals, that it must at first sight seem a very improper situation for a general seminary intended for the forming missionaries, and educating youth in religion and sobriety of manners. The same objections lie against the neighbouring islands.

A view of Jamaica toward the middle of the century is given by Leslie [1740: 36]:

> There are indeed several Gentlemen who are acquainted with Learning, in some of its most valuable Branches: but these are few; and the Generality seem to have a greater Affection for the modish Vice of Gaming than the *Belles Lettres*, and love a Pack of Cards better than the *Bible*. To talk of a *Homer*, or a *Virgil*, of a *Tully*, or a *Demosthenes*, is quite unpolite . . .

Also, Poole [1753: 235] (and this is a work that is generally favourable towards Barbados) says:

> This island furnishes no booksellers shops. There is a printer in this town, who prints news, advertisements, &c. but being very illy provided with good types, and other necessary materials, the work done is dear, and badly executed: Hence any thing requiring to be well done, is generally sent to Philadelphia; where it is better printed, and at a less expence. There is also a bookbinder but by that alone a subsistence cannot here be obtained.

In addition, William Hillary, in introducing his book, makes the following comment:

> As I write on this Disease, as well as on most of the other Diseases in this book, principally for the Use and Benefit of the Inhabitants and Practitioners in Barbadoes, and the other West-India Islands, who in general have too little Learning, I have been more explicit and copious in the Theory and Reasoning on those Diseases, than would have been necessary if I had only written for the Use of the Learned, which I hope the last will excuse, and pardon this and the preceding Digression [Hillary 1759: 211].

In fact, this was the general kind of impression that was had of the West Indies in England and sharply contrasted with the more urbane views that people in the West Indies had of themselves.

Yet, while those in England might have had a low opinion of what was going on in the West Indies, the local literature looked on Europe favourably. Comments in *The Barbados Gazette* indicate that literary persons in Barbados were aware of works in Europe, for there are references to 'Mr. Pope' and 'Monsieur de Voltaire' and remarks which they had made recently. There was specifically a Dr. Towne, a resident of Barbados, two of whose pieces appear in *Caribbeana* [vol. 1: 37-38], who had done a translation of Voltaire's *Henriade* and who was said to be an acquaintance of Voltaire.

The familiarity with artists in Europe presumably fed a desire for a high degree of artistry at the local level, even if the consistency was not always maintained. This is reflected in the following comment from Martinique:

As in your first Gazette you told us you expected such a supply of entertaining pieces from some of your top geniuses in Barbados, as would make your paper in request in foreign parts, as well as with your friends there; it is with pleasure I acquaint you, that your fame has already reached to distant regions

as well as in the *Gazette* editor's own comment

I have reason to rejoice that having often been obliged to my fellow-labourers in Europe, by borrowing from their weekly papers, I am like to be able to return the favour; since they will, no doubt, readily enough transcribe from me what cannot but be acceptable to the politest readers of the age.

The poetry in the *Gazette* seemed to have been alive and functional – people wrote witty verse to each other and friends met to listen to poetry. They saw themselves operating at an international level and able to move beyond the crude behaviour which was common in the colonies. For, as one correspondent to the newspaper said:

a fine copy of verses, a tender song or madrigal, has often produc'd wonders that way, especially with ladies of taste, and been no less effectual even, than a lac'd coat and hat, a fine horse and furniture, getting drunk, breaking windows, firing pistols, or the like pretty recommendations, and prevailing acts of gallantry.

Such an expression of opinion is in direct contrast to the one-sided and gross picture of these societies presented by Patterson [1967].

Even in men's dealings with women the typical views that one would expect of that day were not universal. For example, in an open letter to local women a correspondent said:

Read a little more: Read divinity, morality, history, innocent poetry, and the stories of prudent generous love... don't, as some, be mutes and statues in company; nor, as others, perpetual larums ... be as polite in your language as in your dress; and learn to write a stile ... we mean, to be able to write on all occasions, not as scholars, but as gentlewomen.

As poets, women were not thought to be intellectually incapable, and in spite of the fact that negative comments made elsewhere about their behaviour were reported, the *Gazette* featured women prominently. Not only was there repartee in verse between men and women, but also substantial pieces were written by women, including some by a specific poet who was given pride of place in the *Gazette.* In fact, one correspondent made it clear that local women were better at poetry than men.

The level of modesty or, on the other hand, grossness permissible in the society at the time can in some measure be gauged from subject matter and its treatment. There are examples of risqué verse in the *Gazette.* The following is one example:

Since, Madam, you see
The learned agree,
No words can express, what is love;
By actions let's try
How, both you, and I
May better our knowledge improve.

A riddle (a few lines of which follow), reproduced in the newspaper from the *Gentleman's Magazine*, suggests that sensibilities in Barbados were no different from those in England.

I am an implement that's common,
Much occupy'd by man and woman;
Not very thick, not very long,
Yet tolerably thick and strong...
And yet the fairest nymph will use me,
The Queen herself will not refuse me...
And none esteems a lady polish'd,
Who has not often me demolish'd...

The answer to the riddle was apparently not given in the text taken from the English magazine, but in a continuation of the riddle in the *Gazette* it is. The answer (a pen) might have been given as part of the last line of the Barbadian reprise for the sake of modesty or because some readers might not have worked it out on their own.

Modesty, or deference to the sensibilities of women, of course depended on the percentage, status and upbringing of women in the society. Towards the end of the century Dickson [1789: 107] presented an argument that there was greater refinement (specifically better treatment of slaves) in Barbados than in the newer colonies, because of "the much greater proportion of *ladies*". Whether this was actually so or not, the fact that it was put forward as an argument indicates that there was perceptible influence by the ladies in Barbadian society. As if to increase this refinement, a correspondent to the *Barbados Mercury* of 4 December 1787 advised that for the 'right' upbringing of girls over twelve, "Choice books are instructive, they teach them how to avoid the wicked arts of men. But by no means let them go to the Circulating Library, rank poison is to be found in every girl who subscribes to it." The last statement suggests that local women at the time were reading, but it might have been no more than a restatement of a sentiment in Sheridan's *The Rivals* [1775: Act 1, Scene 2].

Information on social life in the Leeward and Windward Islands in the first half of the eighteenth century is sketchy. There are some casual remarks made by visitors which might not have been representative. For instance, Charles Leslie (1740) on his way to Jamaica in the late 1730s stopped in St Kitts and commented that "The Gentlemen of Basseterre... seem to be well bred (p. 13). He then goes on to talk about a Scotsman there who had an impressive library, thus suggesting that in this the oldest British West Indian colony at least a few persons of worth existed. In the neighbouring island, Nevis, lived Rev Robertson, who wrote his letter to the Bishop of London in 1730, endeavouring to rationalize slavery and treatment of slaves.

By the end of the eighteenth century St Kitts was prominently involved in the Emancipation debates. This was as a result of the fact that James Ramsay, who had lived there for a number of years, had returned to England, joined the abolition forces and produced a treatise in 1784 critical of the treatment of slaves in St Kitts. Kittitian planters reacted violently to this, and over the next ten years there appeared works by Kittitians viciously attacking critics of West Indian planters. However, other than this kind of political writing and Croker's philosophical/religious offering of 1790, there seemed to be little other artistic activity in St Kitts at the time.

Antigua, because of its printing connections with Philadelphia and with Benjamin Franklin specifically, developed a fair level of sophistication from about the middle of the eighteenth century. In 1750 Samuel Martin, a successful planter in Antigua, had his book *An Essay upon Plantership* published, in which he set out some very lofty qualifications for a good planter (see pp. 382-84). It is interesting to note that Martin's ideals were very much in keeping with the impression of sophistication that one gets from Zouch's catalogue of books for sale. In addition to this work of Martin, which was republished several times and in addition to the appearance of three weekly newspapers at one time, a number of poetic works were printed in St Johns as well as several sermons and speeches. What seemed most impressive, however, was an advertisement printed in St Johns on 25 April 1753 for a "course of experiments on the newly discovered electric fire". This course of experiments was divided into two lectures, the first of which had twenty experiments and the second twenty-three. The lectures were to be given by Ebenezer Kennersley, a friend of Benjamin Franklin. According to McMurtrie [1943a: 6], Kennersley "had previously been giving the same lectures in cities throughout the colonies on the mainland. For example, like lectures were advertised in the *Boston Evening Post* of 23 April 1751 (see American Antiquarian Society Proceedings [1901, 14: 222-24]". The fact that such lectures associated with the most recent scientific discovery (the relationship between lightning and electricity) were taken to Antigua and were expected to attract a sizeable paying audience suggests that Antigua at that time could not have been made up exclusively of obtuse farmers.

At the end of the eighteenth century literary activity in Antigua took a leap forward with the establishment of a theatre. The beginnings of this theatre in January 1788 are described by Luffman [1789: 120]:

Our little house opened on the 17th instant, with Venice Preserved, preceded by an occasional prologue; the evening's entertainments were well received by a numerous and genteel audience, and upwards of one hundred pounds sterling was taken. On the 24th the same play was repeated, with Foote's after piece, The Mayor of Garratt, which gave as much satisfaction as the first performance had done, and brought nearly the same sum into the theatrical treasury. I shall not boast of the brilliancy of the scenery and decorations, or of the elegance of the dresses; suffice it to say, they surpass, by far, what I have seen belonging to itinerant companies in England. The orchestra is composed of the band of the 67th regiment, under the direction of a Mr. Green, organist of the church in this town, assisted by a Mr. Van Ruyven. Mr. G. is a complete master of the musical science, and very obligingly undertook this laborious task, to add to the public pleasure; I believe no other person, on this side of the atlantic, could conduct a business of the kind, with more ability and judgment. The house is divided into boxes and pit only; the price of admission into the first, is two dollars (about nine shillings sterling); and to the latter a dollar and a half.

Luffman stated that the performances were well attended and one gets the impression over all that genuine dramatic activity was going on and that it was well supported backstage and in the audience. A close look at the choice of pieces shows a selection of both contemporary and classic pieces, with a preference for the comic as opposed to the tragic: "The Orphan, King Henry the Fourth, West-Indian, Lethe, and Lying Valet, are among those already played, and King Lear. The Fair Penitent, Jane Shore, and several farces are getting in readiness..." (p. 155). However, there seemed to have been no attempt at local dramatic compositions.

It seems fairly clear that in the latter half of the eighteenth century Antigua was very much in tune with what was going on in Philadelphia and London. The publication of a grammar book, poetic works, newspapers, books on planting and medicine, the establishment of a theatre and the production of a number of plays, the advertisement of lectures on a scientific topic, all taken together, no matter how isolated they may have been in actual time, point to a measure of enlightenment and international interest on the part of at least a segment of the population.

The attitudes and aspirations of the white ruling class in the West Indies during the eighteenth century were very much like those in the plantation areas of North America. For this reason it is interesting to compare analyses of the life style of the North American ruling class. One of the best analyses is by Louis B. Wright, who made the following comments [1939: 95-96]:

The attitude toward the classics and the libraries mentioned here illustrate a prevailing and consistent taste among the Virginia ruling class throughout the eighteenth century. Gentlemen were expected to have familiarity with the literature of Greece and Rome, and they gathered in their libraries collections of the standard works of the ancient world. It would be a mistake, however, to assume that these men were scholars in the technical sense of the word, or that their knowledge was profound. The gentleman's ideal was not to be a specialist, but to have a familiar acquaintance with the good things of life, whether in the realm of the material, the spiritual, or the intellectual. Gentlemen looked upon classical literature as a great repository of practical wisdom. They read Homer, Plutarch, Livy, Cicero, or any one of a score of other ancient writers more for practical utility than for esthetic delectation. The ancients had discovered great stores of wisdom, and from these reservoirs gentlemen of the eighteenth century drew much of their own learning and philosophy... That Virginia leaders were profoundly influenced in their political thinking by their contemplation of the works of the Greek and Roman historians is indisputable. That morals and ethics were subtly affected by Aristotle, Plutarch, Seneca, Epictetus, and Epicurus cannot be denied. But no one in this day can say how great was this influence.

Wright's argument about the gentlemen of eighteenth century colonial Virginia seems equally applicable to those of the West Indies. It is not only that these communities were in contact with each other but also they were virtually made up of the same kind of people having direct relationships with English society. The plantation society of the eighteenth century, made up as it was of various cultural elements and not having a tradition of education and letters to become a courtly society, contented itself with the veneer and occasional snatches of such society. Martin's ideals for the education of a master/planter, as set out in his 1750 publication, are consistent with the comments of Wright. The well-rounded, scholar, scientist, lawyer, soldier, philosopher, manager was seen by Martin as the saviour of plantation society in the tradition of *noblesse oblige* – he was the example to follow. It is quite likely that the vision that these colonial gentlemen had of themselves was just the same as that that those in the mother country had, even if the reality of the situations was different.

At a lower level among the whites attraction to intellectual discussion seemed to be less a matter of transmission from elsewhere and more a matter of factors in the local situation leading to disputes. Edwards [1793, 2:9] noted:

... eagerness for litigation and juridical controversy, which so remarkably predominates in most of these islands. From this unfortunate passion, ruinous as it frequently proves to individuals, this advantage however results to the community at large; that the lower orders of men, from their frequent attendance at the courts of law as jurymen, acquire a degree of knowledge, and a clearness and precision of reasoning, which are not generally to be found in men of the same rank in England. Thus the petty juries in the West Indies are commonly far more intelligent and respectable than those in Great Britain. Every candid person who has attended the courts of criminal jurisdiction in both countries must confirm this observation.

Later writers, notably Dallas [1803: CXIV], attributed this penchant for litigation and juridical controversy (as they did many other things) to the warm climate. This was a special version of the 'environment' theory which was very attractive during the eighteenth and nineteenth centuries as an explanatory theory for characteristics of the New World generally. In was the theory used by Edwards [1794, 2:12] to explain the 'fact' that white creole children displayed greater mental powers earlier than European children:

Perhaps, the circumstance most distinguishable in the character of the Natives to which the climate seems to contribute, is the early display of the mental powers in young children; whose quick perception, and rapid advances in knowledge, exceed those of European infants of the same age, in a degree that is unaccountable and astonishing.

Although it was not until the middle of the nineteenth century that the scientific version of the 'environment' theory reached its peak in the era of Darwin, it had long before been used to sustain the superiority of Europe over the New World. It was rare, as is the case here, for this version of the 'environment' theory to be used to show superiority in the people in the West Indies.

LITERARY AND INTELLECTUAL LIFE IN THE EARLY NINETEENTH CENTURY

The more familiar arguments about the ill effects of context in the West Indies and specifically concentration on economic profit dominate Stewart's [1808] observations about literary activity in Jamaica at the beginning of the nineteenth century:

Literature is little cultivated in Jamaica; nor is reading a very general favourite amusement (p. 171).

The ardent thirst, and eager pursuit of gain, by which so large a proportion of the people of this country are more or less actuated, is a passion naturally hostile to literary pursuits and intellectual enjoyments (p. 173).

This was virtually the same comment made by Leslie about seventy years earlier. Of course, there was no shortage of moral and religious reading material, as is quite evident from the SPCK's Catalogue of Books remaining at the General Depot in Kingston in December 1823 (see p. 167).

A different view of scholarly life and education in the smaller islands in the first quarter of the nineteenth century is presented by Coleridge [1826]. Like several other Europeans who spent a few months or years travelling through the islands, Coleridge made observations and comments which reflected contemporary life in the West Indies. Coleridge was positive in his attitude to the West Indies and was, in addition, a man with a liberal education who had a good command of classical and modern languages. This competence allowed him to visit and make enlightened comments on not only the English islands but also on Martinique, St Lucia, Grenada and Trinidad, where more than English was required. This competence also led him to point out literary and educational features in each island he visited, if they were worthy of note. In 1825 when Coleridge visited Barbados, he noted that: "There are two literary societies in the town, which consist of all the leading persons in the colony, have good libraries, and give four times per annum very luculent dinners... (p. 44). Schomburgk [1848: 132] also noted that an agricultural society existed in Barbados at the beginning of the nineteenth century, at the meetings of which "papers on agriculture were read". Such societies clearly do not suggest totally gross inhabitants.

In fact, the whites in the West Indies obviously believed themselves to be sophisticated, and especially so in Barbados, where those in charitable organizations thought that the most natural way to raise funds was by holding concerts and plays. Thus, Orderson [1827: 54-55] mentions a fundraising proposal which gives a view of local society which is very positive:

> ... it is proposed through the medium of annual Theatrical and Musical entertainments to raise such further sums as those rational and elegant amusements are likely to produce in a community where the refinements of society and the elegances of life are so well understood and cultivated.

This was not just a casual opinion, but one by a person who was in the publishing business in addition to being a playwright. Indeed, dramatic activity, which was seen to have been popular in Antigua in the 1780s, also had some support in Barbados in the early nineteenth century, according to Schomburgk [1848: 251] who points out that a theatre was built and opened there in 1812, and after its destruction in the 1831 hurricane another building was erected a few years later at a different location.

Coleridge's positive picture of Barbados and a similar view given by Orderson contrast somewhat with the general comments on the West Indies made just a few years later by Bayley [1833: 577]: "Literature in the West Indies is at a low ebb. Booksellers are hardly known, and books little patronized. Reading is by no means a favorite amusement among the inhabitants..." It should be noted, however, that Bayley's words are very similar to and as if inspired by those of Stewart [1808: 171]. Yet, Bayley's negative view is to some extent corroborated by Schomburgk [1848: 126] who said:

> Native periodical literature (with the exception of a few newspapers) meets with no support as yet in the West Indies. Attempts have been made from time to time in Jamaica, Demerara, Antigua and Grenada, to keep up a monthly magazine devoted to literature and science, but they have all failed; and the only periodicals at present maintained, exclusive of the newspapers, are annual almanacs, in some of which literature finds a nook.

It might have been that societies and libraries were mainly for show to give the appearance of education and scholarship and furthermore that societies of this type were an excuse for hosting dinners and parties.

The negative view of the level of education in Barbados is supported by Coleridge himself in referring to the justice system:

> In Barbados the laws are administered by some twenty-seven or twenty-eight judges. They are all planters or merchants and are appointed by the Governor. Not one of them has ever been educated for the bar, nor is any previous knowledge of the law a necessary or an usual qualification for the office. They neither comprehend the extent, nor are agreed upon the validity of the laws which they are called upon to interpret; they can none of them settle the limits of British and colonial enactments; they adhere to no fixed principles; they are bound by no precedents (p. 288).

From this one gets a picture of Barbados as a society in which education was of little significance and in which class, wealth and connections were synonymous with power and rule. Barbados and the other islands were still at a stage in the last years before Emancipation when the social structure of the plantation society was almost unchanged.

The lack of change, especially intellectually, among the ruling class in the West Indies is accounted for by Coleridge in terms of their umbilical link to Britain, as opposed to a spirit of independence exhibited in the French West Indies and North America. Coleridge argued that, were it not for this clinging to Britain, systems of communication and commerce would have developed which would in turn have had a fundamental effect on the intellectual development of the West Indies. His argument went as follows:

The sight of books to sell in the West Indies is like water in the desert, for books are not yet included in the plantation stores for our islands. The cause is this (p. 138).

... every one regards the colony as a temporary lodging place, where they must sojourn in sugar and molasses till their mortgages will let them live elsewhere (p. 139).

The consequence of this feeling is that every one, that can do so, maintains some correspondence with England, and when any article is wanted, he sends to England for it. Hence, except in the case of chemical drugs, there is an inconsiderable market for an imported store of miscellaneous goods, much less for an assortment of articles of the same kind (p. 139).

Bridge Town would rapidly become a wealthy place, if another system were adopted: ... a steady, safe and abundant importation, and separate preservation of each article in common request ... [rather than] a system of parcel-sending across the Atlantic. Supply will, under particular circumstances, create demand. If a post were established in Barbados, or a steamboat started between the islands, a thousand letters would be written where there are one hundred now. I want a book and cannot borrow it; I would purchase it instantly from a bookseller in my neighbourhood, but I may not think it worth my while to send for it over the ocean, when, with every risk, I must wait at the least three months for it (pp. 140-41).

Coleridge's argument was perceptive and seems unusually modern for a writer of his day. Moreover, it is consistent with his other progressive argument for a tertiary level institution in the West Indies. Coleridge identifies practical developments with the often nebulous ideas of independence, national feeling and attachment to the colony. In fact, though Coleridge claims that the French in the West Indies, in their conception of the colony as 'home', were different from the English in the West Indies in the 1820s, he does point out that 170 years previously the reverse had been true, that is, that the English were more attached to the colonies than the French. He however gives no reason for the change.

The change among the white inhabitants in the English colonies from being independent minded settlers to loyal colonials may have been the result of greater assertiveness of Britain in the West Indies after the American declaration of independence, or the threat of the English colonies becoming black independent countries like Haiti, fed by the notions of liberty, equality and fraternity which swept the French world. In other words, the whites in the English territories may have seen their best means of security in the protection of Britain and considered intellectual development through literacy as encouraging a threat to this security. The move to literacy and general education could not be reversed, but it could be guided by strict control from Britain. Intellectual stagnation in the West Indies was therefore the result of the dynamics of context in which there were two major contending forces – with the one, self-preservation, being stronger than the other, formal education.

Education had not yet reached the stage in West Indian society of being a social force which could confer power regardless of the class origin of the individual, but one area in which it was beginning to have some effect was among the free coloured class, who saw it as an avenue to progress. Bayley [1833: 577], while making the general point about the low level of literary pursuits in the West Indies, in contrast highlights the free coloured as different:

Were I asked, I should give it as my opinion, that the colored people read more than any other class of inhabitants in the Antilles. They have an innate desire for information, and a wish to acquire knowledge, which is always most praiseworthy, and very often most successful.

As an example of the educated coloured, the case of S.J. Prescod of Barbados, presented by Lloyd [1837: 16-17], may be cited:

We have been introduced by Lieut. Ladd to J. PRESCOD, at present editor of the *New Times*, a liberal paper; he is a coloured [the word colour is applied to all African descendants, however remote] gentleman, liberally educated, and resides at the edge of town, in an elegant cottage. He gave much interesting information, dwelling forcibly on the disabilities of the free coloured inhabitants of Bridge Town. We thought we had seldom met with more refinement and intelligence; he is happily married, has no distinguishing marks of negro complexion, and in England he would be esteemed as a gentleman, whilst in Barbados he is in some degree despised as a coloured man.

In spite of the 'refinement and intelligence', the coloured section of the population did not make a significant contribution in literary and other nonpolitical spheres, even in Grenada and Trinidad where the numbers of educated coloured were greater, probably because much of their time was spent trying to better their own social situation through political and legal channels. To this end they established societies, held meetings, drafted addresses to government officials (see, for example, Philippe [1824]) and exhausted their energies proving their equality. Even so, this kind of activity increased the legalistic and formal writing in the West Indies.

The idea of scholarly life in the West Indies in the second decade of the nineteenth century is bolstered by comments from Trelawney Wentworth, who was in the West Indies in the late 1820s. Among the activities which Wentworth commented on was dramatic activity. It appears as if the playhouse which had opened in Antigua when Luffman was there at the end of the eighteenth century was closed when Wentworth was there in the 1820s, but a pantomime was put on during Wentworth's stay there and what was significant about it was that it was "admirably adapted to the taste and temperament of a tropical audience" and further, that "the audience, white, yellow, and black, freemen and slaves, were all vastly delighted, and notwithstanding the price of admission was high – namely, Boxes 18s. Pit 13s. 6d. Gallery 9s. currency – the house was crowded in every part" [Wentworth 1834, 2:177]. The presence in the audience of all sorts of people, including slaves, was not strange, because dramatic activity attracted and involved people outside the ruling class whites. This diversity is also illustrated in another case – a play written by John Orderson and performed in the 1830s, which had as one of the main characters a slave and it also had other slaves as supporting cast in the background. There is no indication that the main slave role or those in the background were played by a white persons. Besides these cases, Handler [1974: 214] in his account of the activities of freedmen in Barbados, mentioned that "in 1805, freedmen were 'forming a company to act plays' " and also that "by 1828 the amateur theatrical group, called the Lyceum, was functioning in Bridgetown and that Samuel Prescod was its manager". Dramatic activity therefore not only had a wide appeal but also required a variety of supporting characters.

Another area which, according to contemporary and later commentators, linked the ruling class in the West Indies to the slave population was that of speechmaking. Bayley [1833: 585], referring to the whites, remarked that: "In the West Indies there is a sort of rage for this table elocution, and there are some gentlemen who really speak well, but who, unfortunately, have also a propensity for speaking *long* (half an hour for instance) ..." Caldecott [1898], with a liking for the thesis that context has a major influence on the evolution of society, explained the type of social intercourse which developed in West Indian plantation society as a product of the weather. What is significant in his thesis is the development of the prominence of conversation as a climatic (*ie* contextual) consequence rather than as a part of cultural heritage:

> But life in the West Indies had, of course, its aesthetic side in some form. The chief amusements were Conversation and Dancing. The conversation which chiefly filled the hours of social intercourse of the men was, after its kind, more artistic than the conversation of a community which is largely absorbed in reading. In furtherance of it great dinners were in vogue, and every opportunity was seized for holding them ... Seated round a table loaded with the varied products of these fertile regions, with the chief native liquor, rum, supplemented by imported wines and spirits of Europe, the hearts of West Indian Planters expanded with the chief enjoyment they knew, and tale and song and practical joke, too, filled up the long evening hours (pp. 39-40).

Caldecott, in the picture he paints, a picture which is typical in the West Indies up to today, explains the love of talking, joking and artistic conversation among the white population as a product of a hot climate. Caldecott's suggested picture of Britain as a "community which is largely absorbed in reading" was clearly incorrect for that or any other time. In fact, the thesis of context may have been more a factor of the time at which he was writing (the Darwin era) than a factor of the time he was supposed to be describing and analysing.

Again it is interesting to look at Wright's analysis of colonial Virginia to see how he accounts for the rise of oratory:

Looking backward, we might surmise that Virginians who read Cornelius Nepos's *Lives of Illustrious Men* were stirred by these biographies of Greek, Carthaginian, and Persian patriots, that the germ of Patrick Henry's oratory could be found in such reading, and in the orations of Demosthenes and Cicero. That Virginia oratory owed much to the precepts and examples of Quintilian and Cicero is perfectly clear [Wright 1939: 95].

Wright's explanation for the oratory that developed in Virginia is again related to classical literary influence. In other words, he regards it as learned oratory, in keeping generally with classical ideals rather than as spontaneous, as is suggested by Caldecott. Wright's analysis in relation to the oratory of lawyers seems reasonable, for one can very well imagine that lawyers would have patterned their speeches after well known classical examples. However, the models for speechmaking in the West Indies in the 1780s were decidedly British and this is clear even from the way in which the evidence of notable speechmaking in the law courts in the West Indies is presented. Luffman [1789: 148-49], in his treatment of Antigua, says: "The solicitors are advocates also. A Mr. Burke . . . stands foremost for energetic declamation; Mr. Hicks and Mr. Wise, for ingenuous argument; the language of the latter is elegant possessing, at the same time, the luxurious flowers of rhetoric and fine oratory . . ." So impressed was Luffman with the language skills of these gentlemen that he goes on to say [1789: 149]: "It is to be deplored that such abilities should be confined to so small a circle as this island, abilities, which would possibly enable the possessor (if at the bar of the Westminster courts) to raise himself to the first eminence in his profession." References to 'energetic declamation' not only relate back to the oratory of persons such as Edmund Burke, Charles James Fox and William Pitt, but more precisely to the case of Warren Hastings and the celebrated speeches of Richard Sheridan, the reactions to which are recorded by Nettleton [1906: xxvii], as follows:

His so-called 'Begum speech', delivered on February 7, 1787, was the supreme triumph of Sheridan's oratory. For five hours and a half he held the crowded House of Commons in breathless attention . . . Sir Gilbert Elliot, member of Parliament, declared that Sheridan's speech surpassed 'all I ever imagined possible in eloquence and ability . . . he surpassed, I think, Pitt, Fox, and even Burke, in his finest and most brilliant orations'. Burke, a generous rival, declared that Sheridan's charge was 'the most astonishing effort of eloquence, argument, and wit united, of which there was any record or tradition'. Fox acknowledged that 'all that he had ever heard, all that he had ever read, when compared with it, dwindled into nothing, and vanished like vapour before the sun'. Said Pitt, his political adversary: 'It surpassed all the eloquence of ancient and modern times.'

The fact that Warren Hastings was put on trial for colonial deeds (in India) no doubt attracted the attention of persons in the West Indies to the event as well as to the speechmaking related to it.

More generally, the conversations and speeches of white society in the West Indies seemed genuine, so that even if they were influenced by British models and refined by classical literature, they could not have developed spontaneously from a remote source. Two decades before the Warren Hastings affair started, the genuine social interaction and sophistication in West Indian society of the time were captured in verse by Singleton [1767: 29]:

> Alternate round the turf, high jests prevail,
> With decent language grac'd, the artful pun,
> The repartee unstudy'd, free from gall,
> Diffuse sweet mirth and pleasantry around.

Here we can see quite clearly an attraction to refined language. The writer himself was a part of this society and so his verses may well have been influenced by written literature, but when he talks about "the repartee unstudy'd", he is suggesting a natural facility with language.

In the final analysis, the best or most reasonable explanation which can be given for the development of the attraction to oratory, speechmaking and refined language generally among the white upper class of the eighteenth and nineteenth centuries in the West Indies is that it was a product of dislocated people in a violent situation trying to reassure themselves by direct communication that they were cultured. The upper classes in the West Indian plantation societies simply tried to duplicate the courtly behaviour of European capitals without the literary talent and sophistication associated with them. Having no tradition of written literature, they enjoyed themselves with oral language. They had to dress up, drink and talk in order to escape from the dung-heap of daily living. There was no recourse to literacy to achieve this air of culture because most of the ruling class was still illiterate and remained so for a long time as a result of the fact that there was no real need for formal education in a society based on a system of slavery and distinct social stratification. In fact, the attraction to speechmaking among the white element of the society can be explained in terms of Ong's psychodynamics of orality. In a discussion of modes of expression, thought processes and recall of thought processes Ong [1982] argues that "sustained thought in an oral culture is tied to communication ... An interlocutor is virtually essential ... (p. 34). Ong then goes on to develop his thesis by saying that:

Your thought must come into being in heavily rhythmic, balanced patterns, in repetitions or antitheses, in alliterations and assonances, in epithetic and other formulary expressions, in standard thematic settings (the assembly, the meal . . .), in proverbs which are constantly heard by everyone so that they come to mind readily and which themselves are patterned for retention and ready recall, or in other mnemonic form (p. 34).

According to this thesis, speechmaking in the plantation slave society can be interpreted as a typical intellectual activity in an oral culture. It was not simply a matter of individuals distinguishing themselves as speakers or performers, but a communal harnessing of thought within a certain format.

What is interesting about the development of facility in speechmaking among the white population is its possible relationship to a similar facility among the black population. The late nineteenth and twentieth century phenomenon of performance English, which is documented throughout the anglophone Caribbean as part of the culture of the black population, is linked by Abrahams and Szwed [1983: 79] to British traditions and originally to slave-to-master communication: "This kind of speech is regarded as a borrowing from British sources rather than as an adaptation of African style to New World language, setting, and occasion. It seems clear that the early references in the literature by Long [1774, 2:426-27] and Edwards [1794, 2:83] to oratory or speeches among the slaves, even though they were not instances of the kind of performance English that became a cultural characteristic of the black population in the latter part of the nineteenth century, were a developmental phase of it. So, while there is no generally sustained argument that the oral language facility and artistry in the black communities derived from white society, there could hardly have been totally independent development of the same type of phenomenon in two sectors of the same society.

What is even more fascinating about 'oratory' and the cultural activities of the slaves in the late eighteenth century and the nineteenth (as described by Long, Edwards, Beckford, Stewart and Williams) is the way in which they mirrored topics and themes in English and European eighteenth century literature. While Abrahams points to British traditions as the source of performance English, there is no general recognition of the similarities between features of the slaves' activities and European literature. The eighteenth century is regarded as the age of satire in European literature. In English literature specifically, Swift, Fielding and Sheridan satirized social mores. Among the slaves, there was, as Edwards [1794, 2:85] said, "a talent for ridicule and derision, which is exercised not only against each other, but also, not unfrequently, at the expence of their owner or employer". In 1774, Long noted the slaves' "catching at any hard word that the Whites happen to let fall in their hearing; and they alter and misapply in a strange manner". In 1775, Sheridan's character in the play *The Rivals*, Mrs. Malaprop, became famous for her inappropriate use of words in her imitation of educated speech. During their 'entertainments', balls and parades at Christmas time, in their imitation of whites, the slaves proposed inappropriate toasts, exhibited 'genteeler behaviour' and behaved as if they were one with their masters. It should also be remembered that the slaves watched and participated in the English farces put on by the local whites and became familiar with their 'theatricals', their costumes, their toasts, their speech and their high society behaviour. Bearing this in mind, it is doubtful whether their imitation of white high social class behaviour can be discounted as incompetent imitation, or whether in fact it had a strong element of mockery and was a clever expression of the ridicule which they were said to have in great measure. In other words, the satire of European literature of the eighteenth century may have found a natural home in the cultural activities of the slaves.

Except during their festivities at Christmas, blacks generally had few contexts to display their 'formal' register of English. There are only odd references to blacks making speeches. For example, Dickson [1789: 75] refers to a black chaplain and his colleague:

I have heard the negro chaplain of a black corps preach to a large audience of whites and blacks. Though his dialect was, by no means, good; yet the weight of his arguments, and the native, untaught energy of his delivery were such as to command attention, and to repress ridicule. He had a colleague who gave out a hymn (I think from Watts) and prayed extempore. His dialect was even worse than that of the preacher; but his prayer was such as would have rendered laughter criminal, especially when he implored the Almighty Father of Mercies, with tears, to behold, with an eye of pity, the deplorable ignorance and debasement of his countrymen.

Even though Dickson regarded the speech of the two persons as nonstandard, it is clear that there was no lack of understanding among the audience, which would suggest either that the variety of English was not very different from standard English or that the audience was principally native born. In any case, it is very unlikely that such events, which might occasionally have involved free blacks speaking to an audience including whites, could ever have had slaves as main speakers.

The best and most cited example of superior behaviour among the slaves was the establishing of difference between creole slaves and African born slaves. The most apparent distinction between these two groups was proficiency in the English language. As a result of this, in encounters involving individuals from the two groups, each one would have tried to produce the best English possible – the one to establish superiority, the other to try to establish identity in order to avoid derogatory comments. It is this kind of pressure on the 'foreigner' to conform which probably had the greatest influence on the disappearance of African languages and the increase in the use of some form of English by new slaves. Intergroup conflict and communication among African and creole slaves, although constantly referred to, are not well documented linguistically because authors and their readers were not interested in such minor language differences between slaves.

In the various comments about refinement, scholarship and intellectual activity among the whites in the West Indies, specific islands were occasionally singled out for praise or criticism. For instance, Wentworth had a high opinion of Antigua and this is reflected in his view that this island

> ... appears to have enjoyed greater freedom from domestic dissension, and a more general diffusion of intelligence among the leading members of the community, promoting a greater degree of social order, and a stronger bond of union, than have generally existed among the inhabitants of the neighbouring British islands [1834, 2:178-79].

John Orderson, who was himself a Barbadian, was proud of the contribution of his native land. In the Preface to his 1842 historical novel he says: "Although the Author of the following pages feels himself incompetent to decide on the extent or general merits of *West Indian Literature*, he yet ventures to affirm, from his own observation, that Barbados has contributed her share, with no unlavish hand." Orderson obviously felt a sense of pride not only in the literary production of his own country but also saw West Indian literature as an already identifiable variety of literature in English. It is no accident that both these islands had had an almost untroubled association with British rule, in contrast to a number of others in which friction born of changing colonial rule did not leave the ruled well disposed towards the rulers.

Within the ruling class itself in Barbados, social divisions which were characteristic of social gatherings in England were preserved and strengthened. The Barbadian social scene was not only creole dominated by the beginning of the nineteenth century but was male dominated with women relegated to the background. This was so distinct by the time of Pinckard that he could describe the seating at dinner parties as follows:

> Instead of the different persons being, pleasantly, intermixed, it is too common to see the ladies grouped together in a crowd at the upper end of the table – the officers and strangers, just arrived from Europe, placed at one side – and the gentlemen of the island, who are mutual and familiar acquaintances, at the other side ... [1806, 2:103].

The separation of the sexes was so clear that, according to Pinckard, even before dinner the women did not join the men and after dinner they had to retire so that the men could "enjoy their bottle".

Interestingly enough, the drinking and the social separation of the sexes which was characteristic of Barbados contrasted with practice in Trinidad, if Carmichael [1833, 2: 322] is to be believed: "Drinking to excess is unknown in good society in Trinidad; the gentlemen join the ladies in the drawing-room, in a quarter of an hour after they have retired." Trinidad society, unlike Barbadian society, had not been overwhelmingly influenced by the British and their ways. In addition, the sharp division between the sexes in Barbados which was in evidence at dinner parties was of course a reflection of deeper seated beliefs about appropriate roles to be played by different groups. The distancing of foreigners, of course, was characteristic of a type of self-importance which was based on historical factors. The relegation of women to the background was a matter of self-interest – for as early as the 1730s they had been seen as being interested in foreigners, a fact that the Barbadian men could not accept. So, the men, who believed their women to be threatened on the one side by black slave men and on the other by white foreign men, sought to preserve their territory by keeping them secluded.

Bailyn's view of the frontier colony as a desolate outpost has to be modified in the case of the early West Indies, for the umbilical link between Britain and the West Indian colonies supported a symbiotic relationship and was a two-way conduit for models, philosophies and attitudes. In the same way that England provided models of behaviour for the West Indies, the West Indies provided models for England. In other words, social life in Britain was directly influenced by life in the West Indies. From the middle of the seventeenth century till about the beginning of the nineteenth many successful planters, colonial administrators and military persons returned to England with their black slaves and proceeded to maintain a lifestyle similar to that which they had in the West Indies. By the middle of the eighteenth century it became generally fashionable and necessary for society persons in England to have black domestics as show pieces. Glimpses of many of these persons have been preserved for posterity as they were featured in paintings by well-known painters like Hogarth, who used them to illustrate various themes (see Dabydeen [1992]).

In the area of music, the oft-mentioned prowess of the slaves led to their use in military bands. As Fryer [1984] points out:

Black drummers were first acquired by English regiments serving in the West Indies (p. 81).

The use of black musicians as military bandsmen in the British army, a tradition that reached its height towards the end of the eighteenth century, seems to have started in the second half of the seventeenth (p. 81).

The Coldstream Guards retained their black musicians until about 1840 (p. 85).

It is even claimed that the style and flair of these musicians influenced European composers of the period.

From the earliest years the West Indies provided stories and characters for English dramatists. Shakespeare's *Tempest* included Caliban and Ligon's [1657] story of Inkle and Yarico was transformed into an opera and a play, which had many versions. One of the most popular and long-lasting plays, one which also went through many editions, was *The West Indian* which featured the son of a West Indian planter arriving in England and his encounters thereafter. Added to these dramatic works were influential prose writings by persons with West Indian experience, for during the Emancipation debates in Britain there were two former slaves whose activities and writings made them famous and have given them a place in British intellectual history in the last quarter of the eighteenth century.

Ottobah Cugoana, a Fante, was taken to the West Indies in about 1770, spent almost two years in Grenada and other islands and then was taken to Britain in 1772, where he was set free. In 1787 he published *Thoughts and sentiments on the evil and wicked traffic of the slavery and commerce of the human species*, and in 1791 a shorter version of the same work appeared. Fryer [1984: 102] comments as follows on Cugoana: "Ottobah Cugoana was the first published African critic of the transatlantic slave trade and the first African to demand publicly the total abolition of the slave trade and the freeing of the slaves – a position which scarcely any white abolitionist had taken by 1787." The other former slave and better known personality was Olaudah Equiano, an Igbo, who was kidnapped and taken to Barbados in about 1756 but was almost immediately shipped off to Virginia. He was later taken to England and then back to Montserrat where he spent three years as a slave. After a very active life full of movement to and fro, both as a slave and as a seaman, he settled in England, became acquainted with the leading abolitionists and in 1789 published *The Interesting Narrative of the life of Olaudah Equiano, or Gustavus Vassa, the African*. Fryer [1984: 107] called this book "the most important single literary contribution to the campaign for abolition" and then went on to say: "For the first time the case for abolition, presented by a black writer in a popular form, reached a wide reading public ... And it was highly effective in raising public opinion." British public opinion and attitude toward slavery were therefore partly formed by the West Indian experience of these two Africans who became writers in English.

Through the umbilical cord, Equiano's influence worked its way back to the West Indies, for his book was supported by contributions to British newspapers, which were routinely circulated to the colonies. The direct link between the formation of philosophy and attitudes in Britain and those in the West Indies can be seen from the following comments by Fryer [1984]:

The name of 'Gustavus Vassa the African' was now a familiar one to readers of the *Public Advertiser*, one of London's most widely circulated newspapers, items in which were often copied by the provincial press. For the *Public Advertiser* Equiano wrote a review of two pro-slavery pamphlets by the racist James Tobin of Nevis (p. 108).

For the same newspaper, and equally trenchantly, Equiano reviewed Gordon Turnbull's 'Apology for Negro Slavery' [1786], a pamphlet which bore the sub-title: 'The West-India Planters Vindicated from the Charge of Inhumanity' (p. 109).

Philosophy and morals were therefore evolving simultaneously in Britain and the West Indies. The ruling class in the West Indies was acutely aware of the thinking and knowledge of persons in Britain. Their violent reactions to authors who wrote negatively about them is testimony to this, and their attempts to limit the literacy of the slaves and to control the written material available to them was to make sure not only that they were not exposed to the thoughts and recommendations of their former peers, but also that they have no such emancipated models to aspire towards or to try to emulate.

The umbilical cord and the symbiotic relationship it supported contrast with the notion of a one-way cultural transmission from mother country to colony and with the notion of development determined chiefly by economic necessity. Colonists going to the West Indies brought with them values and culture, and returned to England with money, experience, and a 'better' lifestyle. The creation and siphoning off of the economic profits was accompanied by social class trappings to accompany the use and display of these profits. Artistic and literary pursuits were part and parcel of the ostentatious living created by sugar wealth. Standards and distinctions were an integral part of middle and upper social class attempts to display achievement and wealth. On the other hand, the introduction into Britain of the West Indian planter lifestyle contributed to a heightening of public awareness of slavery, which in turn fostered debate and an increased output of printed material and printing. Printing for the general public led to the standardization of the English language, which itself fitted into the class system of standards and distinctions. The development of the English language in the West Indies was therefore not only contemporaneous with but integrally related to its development in Britain, which in turn was influenced by factors in the West Indies.

CONCLUSION

There is little doubt from the evidence available that over the years the most popular type of literary activity in the plantation slave society in the West Indies was drama. It appealed to all levels of people in the society and persons were even inspired to write plays or parts of plays. In this connection it is interesting to note that one of the first major literary works written by a West Indian was by William Walker, identified as a Barbadian, who wrote a play for the London stage in 1704. Plays were almost exclusively works to be performed and reflected the reality of the sociolinguistic variation of their time, for they often contained persons of different social classes whose contrasts in behaviour and speech were a deliberate feature of comedy or tragedy.

Poetry was also popular, but was generally a more sophisticated literary genre practised by a smaller number of persons who were familiar with written literature.

Poetry was inseparable from drama in that many plays were written entirely in verse or had prologues or epilogues in verse. Poetry was controlled by two traditions – the oral and the written – and budding poets in the West Indies had to know about the forms and structures of poems and try to fit their work within accepted traditions of British poetry. Poetry, which originally was aural in nature, became very much a written genre with one of its well-known characteristics being 'eye' rhymes (words matched visually even though they were no longer similar in pronunciation). In addition, because of its unbroken connections with Greek and Latin literature, sophisticated (European) poetry included many classical references and allusions which removed it from the ambit of the uneducated. However, unsophisticated poetry was easy enough to compose to make it popular for salacious and local topics.

Arguments and counter-arguments on various topics, scientific treatises, petitions in the form of letters, accounts of events and histories were presented in extended prose. Diaries also contained entries which were in extended prose. In some instances, arguments and counter-arguments were presented in the name of a group of persons rather than a single individual, in which cases, presumably, one person actually did the writing on behalf of the group. However, extended prose was of little influence within the West Indies before the emancipation debates heated up toward the end of the eighteenth century, for in most cases the exchange of information between persons in the West Indies and those in North America and Britain was not intense or sustained or threatening in nature. In any case, at that time, writing, as a form of agitation, was not used as the most direct and influential method of solving problems.

When drama, poetry and extended prose are related to the nature of the culture, it is easy to see that drama was very compatible with the group and social interaction which characterized the principally oral society that was the plantation slave society. Poetry, when it was mainly oral and unrelated to classical writing, fitted into the rhythmic and repetitive pattern of language identified by Ong as a characteristic of oral societies. On the other hand, extended prose did not fit into these societies very well because it is a characteristic of a literate society. It became a method of distance communication in the West Indies through necessity and not choice. It was used to respond to attacks and to argue for positions, *eg* the status quo. When attacks declined, the need to write extended prose declined. It was then reduced to a vehicle for carrying information, attitudes and values, especially from the mother country to the colonies.

The totality of literature, in whatever form, made West Indians more conscious of literate English. Drama, by its inclusion of verse, and poetry in itself made people more aware of the sounds of English. Thus, English was increasingly being appreciated from an artistic point of view, and the love of speechmaking no doubt heightened its artistic use. Performance English and other competitive cultural uses of language among the black population developed within this tradition in which word artistry was a dominant feature. Extended prose developed in a negative and unattractive climate of argument and intellectual discussion. The formality attached to it as well as the need to learn its rules and forms did not make it very appealing. In its history English prose had replaced Latin prose as the language of discussion and description. Latin used in this way had a long classical tradition and most of its baggage of grammar had been transferred to English. This type of English therefore required a background of general formal education before it could become a normal competence in a colonial society. Yet, overall, in spite of the attraction to drama and in spite of the greater consciousness of literate English, there was not a level of literary and other intellectual activity in the plantation slave society to promote and validate a literate variety of West Indian English, distinguishable in itself.

8

The Rise of Schools and their Effect on English

The level of literary and intellectual activity that there was in the plantation slave society, especially the production of English comedies and farces and the love of speechmaking, brought cultivated English more into focus and increased the need for competence in it among a small minority of the population. While proficiency in cultivated English was not a goal of the schools that arose in the West Indies, at least, as elsewhere, schooling came to be associated with the three R's, and two of them, reading and writing, became linked to 'grammar' because reading and writing had to be done in a specific language (in this case English). The English that was taught was thought to have a 'grammatical' or 'right' form and the literature that was used to illustrate it was the Bible and other church material, which transmitted some of the aura from the substance (matters relating to God) to the form of the language ('grammatical' English). In the growth of literacy through schooling, it is necessary, therefore, to understand first of all the functions which early schools in the West Indies arose to perform and secondly the nature of the schooling, especially as it related to the teaching of 'grammatical' English. It is these two areas that will be dealt with respectively in this and the next chapter. It has to be stressed, however, that inconsistency in the comments on schooling in the various islands (information which in most cases was only incidentally given by most writers) unavoidably results in an unequal representation of them in the illustrations.

The notion of a philosophy of education seems far too grand for plantation slave societies in the West Indies in their early years, no matter what segment of the population is identified. The sense of family and tradition took some time to develop among the colonists, whose immediate concerns were survival (from a medical point of view), safety (from hostile elements in the society), and financial gain (from crops and services). Moreover, the idea of sending children to school or of having them learn to read and write was not normal, as it is today, and in a growing colonial society with people from varied cultures, traditions and strata of society formal schooling for children was neither a strong nor a common factor.

In such conditions provision for local education of children was not a priority. In addition, the school, as a functioning institution in a society, required a common language of instruction and if there was one thing that the early colonial society did not have it was a language common to all of its inhabitants. Lack of a common language therefore was a determining factor in the selection of method and type of organization of teaching. In the situation in the West Indies where there was diversity of language and diversity in dialects of the same language, schooling had to start as private tuition for individuals and later for small groups before it could approximate the modern concept of a school. In other words, even if social and economic factors were not barriers to education, there could not have been mass schooling until a common language had evolved in the society.

Since language as well as social and economic factors ruled out formal teaching in large groups, the extent to which teaching did actually occur depended on the class and gender of the individual. From the start of the colonies and throughout the period of slavery formal education was clearly differentiated according to class and gender. Of the four broad classes in the slave society, the servants, the free coloured, the slaves and the masters, only the last mentioned had unfettered access to education and in this class only men were thought to be worthy of full education – the training of women was, by and large, restricted to knitting and sewing. Neither the servants nor the slaves had full control over their own children, which meant that they could not send them off to school even if such a facility existed.

THE SCHOOLING OF UPPER LEVEL WHITES

Among the white colonists in the early years formal education was a matter of private tutoring on an individual basis according to the resources and level of sophistication of households. Benjamin Franklin in his memoirs tells of a friend from his younger days (*ie* the 1720s) who went to one of the English islands as 'a tutor for the children of a gentleman'. This indicates that some families not only could afford private tutors from overseas but also that they thought such to be necessary or suitable. It also indicates that there was some similarity between New England and the islands of the eastern Caribbean in teaching philosophy and method. The use of private tutors in the West Indies actually started in the seventeenth century and such persons were not always distinct from those contracted within the indenture system. The practice of 'teaching' was extensive enough at the time to require general regulations. So, teachers who were contracted within the indenture system had to have their wages and terms of service set out within the laws dealing with indentured servants: "All Differences between Master and Servant, or Labourer, or Artificer, or School-Master or School-Mistress, in relation to Wages or Salaries, shall be heard and determined by the next Justice of Peace..." [Laws of Barbados (1676/1699/1704), Act 21 XVII, p. 263]. Some persons who worked as tutors were a part of a household while others, identified as 'school master' or 'school mistress', took in children from different households. Such a system of teaching was of course good only for those who could afford it.

According to Oldmixon [1708, 2:83], an attempt was made in Barbados in the late seventeenth century to start a free school: "Near this town [Speightstown] one Mr. Hancock built or gave a House for a Free-School. Whether it was endowed or not we cannot tell; but we are better informed of its present condition, which is going to decay, if not already a Heap of Ruins." Although this may have actually been one of a number of early attempts to provide schooling for the poorer whites and was not intended for the children of the masters, it is obvious that within the first fifty years of settlement the small number of children and the wide dispersal of them could not have created pressure for such schools. This factor alone may have resulted in the failure of early attempts to establish schools. Robertson [1730], writing from St Kitts, summed up the situation there in a way that applied to all the West Indian territories in the seventeenth century and early eighteenth: "... from their first settlement there has been little means of education for the masters themselves, but that expensive one of sending their children to Europe" (p. 13). Ironically, this sending away of children to Europe in itself delayed the need for schools.

Yet, in spite of this slow start to the provision of schools, Christopher Codrington in his will of 1703 envisaged a university level institution. In the will (as quoted in [Duke 1741]) he stated: "... and my desire is, to have the plantations continued entire... and a convenient number of Professors and scholars maintained there... who shall be obliged to practise Physics and Chirurgery as well as Divinity..." Such a desire could hardly have been made in a total academic wilderness and actually suggests some wider level of scholarship in the islands at the time. No doubt Codrington saw fundamental benefits to the West Indies in his vision, but the reasoning behind this kind of venture that is given by Oldmixon [1708, 2:135] is somewhat different:

For 'tis not every Planter who can be at the charge of sending his Sons to England to be educated; which the most wealthy of them have found inconvenient, by the Distance from their Parents and Guardians, and the Indulgence of their correspondents here: who, to flatter these young Gentlemen, in hopes of their Consignations, when they come to their estates, or to engage them to write kindly of them to their friends, give them what Money they ask for; and by this they often get a Habit of Extravagance, which ends in their Ruin: This wou'd be prevented, if there were fitting schools in Barbadoes; which they might easily have.

All these Expences and Inconveniences would, in a great measure, be prevented by erecting a College and Library at the Bridge, with learned and pious Professors in the Sciences, to breed up young Gentlemen, without exposing them to the Hazards of the Sea, and the more fatal Dangers of Temptation and ill Company in England; where, having Money at Will, when they are not of Years to know how to make use of it, they frequently continue in their Profusion and Prodigality, till they have none left to spend.

Oldmixon put the reason for the start of higher education in the West Indies in purely negative terms – to avoid the costs and risks of sending boys to England. There is no suggestion about its fundamental benefits, that is, the value of local education as opposed to foreign.

When the decision was made to execute the provision in Codrington's will to build a college on Codrington's estates, the Society for the Propagation of the Gospel in Foreign Parts intended it to serve all the West Indian islands, but Robertson [1730], writing from St Kitts, made comments which became familiar in discussions on regional education:

But in 1714, when that Society appointed deputies here to receive benefactions, the people of these islands [Leewards] would give nothing toward it, as believing that a college at Barbados could be of no benefit to them for these two reasons: 1. Because a hundred pounds will go further at Oxford than two hundred and fifty at Barbadoes, and 2. Because, after all that can be done, the education there will be less extensive than in England (p. 23).

These two reasons – local/regional cost vs. cost abroad, and breadth of education – were two of the major determining factors, from the earliest days of West Indian societies, in the development of education. The point about breadth of education is made again seventy years later by McKinnen [1804: 32]: "Indeed, from the superior advantages of European education, it [Codrington College] can only be an object of secondary concern." Individuals, institutions and governments in the West Indies used both of these arguments as reasons for sending students abroad to be educated instead of developing local and regional educational institutions. However, there were others who saw the benefits of a regional institution. For example, in 1825, more than a hundred years after Oldmixon made his comments and just twenty years after McKinnen, another Englishman, Henry Coleridge, repeated the call for a college:

A great desideratum in the West Indies is a place of study and retirement for young men. As it is, those, who cannot afford the heavy expense of going to Oxford or Cambridge, are obliged to break off the yet unfinished work of instruction, to set up at seventeen or eighteen for men, and undertake the charge of duties for which they are utterly unqualified. They come away from school half educated in heart and intellect, and are then for the most part placed in situations, where every temptation to licentiousness besets their path, and many dangerous privileges are of necessity committed to their discretionary exercise [Coleridge 1826: 54].

A college upon the plan of an university, that is to say, where a reasonable approach to universality of instruction is proposed, would supply this deficiency, remedy the consequent evils, and be a blessing and a source of blessings to the colonies [Coleridge 1826: 55].

At this time Coleridge foresaw no economic problems and in fact gave suggestions about the way in which 'surplus funds' should be used. Coleridge was of course a visitor who did not fully understand the dynamics operating in the West Indies which militated against the institution of a university. What he did realize, however, was that the colonists in the British West Indies were outward looking and that they regarded the colony "as a temporary lodging place" and "call England their home".

Over and above these last comments from Coleridge and the negative reasons given by Robertson [1730] above, the reason for the non-implementation of local university level education was that it was incompatible with and virtually unnecessary in a plantation slave society. Such an institution would have been disturbing in that it would have created pressures for the plantocracy to conform to standards of behaviour and enlightenment. The system that was in place protected the plantocracy and their offspring and since they were not particularly religious, university education was for them merely decorative. As a result, the following comment by Duke [1741] is not surprising: "Very large sums of money have been expended, to erect a college on one of the plantations, which is not yet finish'd; nor has much good arose from this well intended, and most noble donation" (Appendix, p. 3). However, four years after Duke's comment Codrington College opened as a grammar school.

Throughout the West Indies generally in the eighteenth century local grammar (secondary) schools for whites were started in an ad hoc manner, for there was no general plan for education in any of the West Indian territories based on either a state or church system. In addition, when the schools came into being, there was no major focus on the specific subjects which would be desirable in the local situation or the quality of teachers and teaching. It was simply a matter of trying to do what was done in England. The local grammar schools had, in some measure, to prepare pupils for higher education and from Robertson [1730] one gets the impression that at university level law and medicine were favoured areas of study, while Codrington's will mentions physics, surgery and theology. These subjects corresponded to the jobs for which it was thought persons needed specific training – doctors, lawyers and priests – and these were also the professions which were appropriate for the children of the ruling class.

The other job which became an automatic part of what schooling catered for in the West Indies was that of the teacher, meaning the pre-specialist or elementary level all-subject teacher. In fact, to a large extent schooling in the colonies was pre-specialist and was merely a self-perpetuating system – teachers teaching pupils to become teachers, who in turn would do the same thing. In this prespecialist (elementary and some secondary, in modern terms) education, the three R's were the main substance and in the three R's language (*ie* reading and writing) was dominant. This was the springboard from which language, specifically the English language, became a dominant force and a measure of level of education in West Indian colonial societies. The job of teacher, however, was not really appropriate for the ruling class whites.

In the eighteenth century West Indies there was actually a view of education which related to the sugar colony and which had the ruling class specifically in mind. This view came from Samuel Martin in Antigua and, for that day, it presented a lofty vision of the ideal master/planter. In 1750 Martin set out the qualifications for a good planter as follows:

A liberal education is undoubtedly the principal ingredient necessary to form a good planter, who ought at least to know the rudiments of all the sciences, if he attains not the mastery of them: but to be more precise, let us take a short view of the proper qualifications of a planter in his public and private capacity. If he is born to a large estate, or has acquired it by industry, he must expect to be a member of the legislature, and of the military order also. In the former character he must understand the whole science of good policy, founded upon the nature and ends of government in general; and in particular upon the constitution of Britain his mother country, and of the Island which he inhabits (p. viii).

In the capacity of a soldier the accomplished must be well read in the history of former wars; and become intimately acquainted with all the famous Generals of antiquity, as to their characters, genius, discipline, stratagems, and atchievements. Among the maxims of the best and wisest of them, he will find, that the meanest enemy is not to be despised, and the greatest may be subdued by superior Generalship.

As a magistrate he must be acquainted with the common forms of justice, and our statute-laws. In his private character he must be adept in figures, and in all the arts of oeconomy; something of an architect, and well skilled in mechanics; because there is in every plantation a variety of buildings and machinery, upon the right contrivance and use of which, much of the planter's success depends. He must also be an expert sugar-boiler, and distiller, if he expects to make the most of his estate. It is obvious of what benefit a little physical skill will be to his sick negroes; at least enough to cure such acute diseases as are incident to the country he inhabits; together with proper diet, and kitchen physic, which are generally more efficacious. But every planter should be more particularly a very skilful husbandman (p. xiii).

It is very true, that much time and close application must be allowed for the acquisition of all these accomplishments: and every planter can afford it, when the cares of the day are over. But there still remains a more arduous task, to become a real practical philosopher by the conquest, or government of all the human passions: for if these are not under absolute subjection to right reason; how can the planter exert all the social virtues upon so many and great occasions, as must every day call them forth? Or how can he govern some hundreds of his dependents with ease to himself, and happiness to them, without all the influences of a good example? (p. xiv).

It is quite unlikely that these ideals, as set out by Martin, were ever achieved by anyone, but the fact that this book was well known and republished several times suggests that persons of quality at the time saw them as realistic and ideally suited to the education of the planter class in the West Indies. However, Sheridan [1961: 353] points out that Martin's intended pupils were not really local: "Over the years a number of young planters came under Martin's tutelage. He wrote for Scots servants or English farm boys who were trained in the English system of husbandry." Even so, there could hardly have been a restriction to young British planters only.

Another book, Belgrove [1755], contained a set of instructions by Henry Drax, another successful planter, to his estate manager. This work, together with Martin's, clearly provided the educational requirements for a good planter and a good manager. They had a practical kind of philosophy but at the same time it was a cultured one – it spoke about informed management of people and institutions; it related literacy, accounts and accountability; it envisaged a noble planter and a respectable and competent manager to match obvious wealth and social duties; above all it had in view education fashioned for sugar colonies. However, such competence and sophistication could hardly have been the product of local education, considering the real hurdles that were in the way.

One such hurdle in achieving these goals locally in the West Indies in the middle of the eighteenth century was the lack of qualified teachers and the disposition of parents and pupils. If one can take the situation of Jamaica as comparable to that of the other colonies in the West Indies at that time, according to Leslie [1740], schooling did not have high priority or great esteem. It seems likely that the majority of teachers were of the status of servants and, as was said earlier, were governed by the indenture system. Many came out of the charity schools in England and saw the West Indies and North America as an opportunity to improve their fortune. These teachers had little control over their pupils, who were their social superiors. This kind of relationship explains the comment from Leslie [1740: 37] that ". . . young master must not be corrected; if he learns, 'tis well; if not, it can't be helped". From this comment one can see that there seemed to be no real necessity to learn well, since education could not substantially effect a change in status in that kind of society. There seemed to be a general satisfaction with little in the 'education' of young men, as suggested by Leslie [740: 37]: "After a little knowledge of reading, he goes to the dancing-school, and commences beau, learns the common topicks of discourse, and visits and rakes with his equals." In short, Leslie presents a picture of schooling in the mid eighteenth century in Jamaica as marginal and subordinate to the acquisition of social graces and skills. It is possible, however, that the situation in all the territories was not identical and that what obtained in Jamaica might have been worse than in the smaller islands.

Another hurdle in achieving the goals of Martin [1750] was overseas education. From the earliest days many of the English planters regarded the colonies as a 'temporary lodging place' and England as where there hearts were, for as Littleton [1689: 34] said: "Nothing but England can we relish or fancy; our hearts are here, wherever our bodies be. If we get a little money, we remit it to England. They that are able breed up their children in England . . ." The practice of sending children to England to be educated started not only because there were no schools in the colonies in the early years but also because the planters thought that their children should be educated at home (*ie* England). It is only those planters who could not afford it or did not care about education whose children remained in the West Indies. This, then, fostered the notion that education in England was the desirable thing and that that in the West Indies was, at best, only adequate.

It is not that education in England was clearly seen to be superior, for there was the constant complaint that many of the planters' children merely wasted their parents' money in England. Long [1774, 2:249] noted specifically in relation to Jamaica that: "Many I have noted, who arriving there after having (as it is called) *finished their education* in England, appeared unpardonably illiterate, and possessed of few attainments beyond what I have already enumerated." Even in the cases of the ones who succeeded in their education in England Long was not satisfied, because, as far as he was concerned, the education they received was inappropriate:

The education they usually receive in Great Britain does not qualify them for useful employment in Jamaica, unless they are bred to some of the learned professions; which nevertheless are not suitable to all, because those professions would soon be overstocked in the island, if every youth consigned from thence was to be trained to physic, divinity or law . . . [Long 1774, 2:248-49]

Besides the inappropriateness identified by Long, the other major problem was that a significant proportion of the children did not return to the West Indies. It was estimated that in the last half of the eighteenth century in Jamaica three-quarters of the planters' children were sent to England to be educated and less than two-thirds of these returned. Pitman [1917: 33] explains the reasons for this as follows: "Education in England, so frequently the reason for absence from the West Indies, often bred in young men a dislike for plantation affairs and weaned them from the land of their birth." Yet, in spite of these shortcomings, the grand vision of education in the mother country had from the earliest days of the colonies a very powerful effect on the mentality of West Indians. It was a vision that promoted the belief that excellence lay outside the West Indian community and West Indians. The logical reaction to the rosy vision of a British education, the assumptions on which it is based and its effects also has a long history. Pitman [1917: 33] quotes Governor Lawes of Jamaica as saying in 1719 to the legislature:

> I wish you would consider . . . of making some proper provisions to educate our youth at home; which will beget in them a natural and stronger affection for the place they are born and bred in, and a greater love for their native country than their fathers ever shewed; and, perhaps, become better benefactors to the island than any we can yet boast of.

The need to counteract the ill effects (psychological and financial) of children going abroad was in fact the most pervasive reason for the increase in secondary and attempts at tertiary education in the West Indies. West Indian education then found itself dominated by the need to compete with and match the model in England in order to convince the local population that local education was good enough. It did not, unlike that in North America, evolve to cater to its own peculiar needs and for a long time was not substantially influenced by its own experiences. For example, in spite of Samuel Martin's ideals, it in no way intended to produce better planters or managers or to develop any kind of expertise in agriculture.

The effect of education abroad on language in the colonies was not significant in the eighteenth century. Judging from Mathews' comment [1793: 21] that of the men in Barbados "few have had an European education", it would seem unlikely that the situation would have been different in the other islands. However, where once at the beginning of the eighteenth century the characteristics of London and England generally were not an overpowering influence, by the time of Emancipation they were clearly becoming so as a result of the standardization of the English language. This gradually led to prescriptive repression of local characteristics as West Indians imbibed and believed the invective that was being heaped on their customs and language by Englishmen in England and also by those travelling through the colonies. This was the start of a stultifying and self-demeaning experience which stifled the literary creativity of West Indians, which in turn merely confirmed what was already being believed about the apparent superiority of London and England.

What started out, therefore, as an excusable practice among the planters in the early years (*ie* sending children to Europe) gradually became a matter of preference among those who could afford it and was entrenched as an integral part of the values of the whole community. Unfortunately, a dilemma developed – education at home was not good enough and education abroad either created false values in those returning or discouraged persons from returning. This dilemma meant that Martin's ideals were unrealizable – neither European education nor West Indian, which copied it, was geared towards producing master/planters.

Martin's ideals were intended specifically for men; the role of the lady at the time was merely to supplement and be sociable. Leslie [1740: 37] gives some idea of the education of upper class women in Jamaica in the following: "Some of the ladies read, they all dance a great deal, coquet much, dress for admirers; and at last, for the most part, run away with the most insignificant of their humble servants. Their education consists intirely in acquiring these little arts." However, the education of women around the same time did not seem as negative as this. A partial assessment of the level of education of women in Barbados in the 1730s can be gleaned from letters and from comments in the early issues of the *Barbados Gazette*. In one instance, the editor of the newspaper, on receiving a poem "directed in a fine hand, on gilt paper and neatly done up", comments: "By these circumstances, and not from any faults in the spelling, I immediately guess'd it to come from a fair lady [Keimer 1741: 110]. Judging by this comment, the expectation was that women would make mistakes with language, but the reality in this specific case seemed to be that there were none, which suggests that some women were reasonably well schooled.

In fact, men's views of women's abilities at that time were not as backward as one would expect. Note the following piece of advice given to women by a correspondent to the *Gazette*: "Take well this essay, formed to wipe out these blemishes in your conduct; some of which are rather the fault of your situation in the world, and your education, than your natural disposition . . . [Keimer 1741: 56]. The letter further says: "But here we hold: For you'll say, Hey Day! We see bachelors and widowers wives are like to be sufficiently taught! [Keimer 1741: 57]. This last comment, however, is a recognition of reality in that it admits that for the 'future wives of bachelors and widowers' to achieve all the goals being suggested by the men who were writing the letters they would have to be formally instructed, a possibility which really was not likely at that time.

About twenty years later a brief and negative comment about women's education was made by Poole [1753]. Poole, unlike Leslie in Jamaica, did not see anything reprehensible about women's general conduct, but he believed that their speech reflected "want of proper care in their education" (p. 280). Thirty years after Poole, Ramsay [1784] dismissed creole women as being of low quality, but, in response to this, Tobin [1785: 71] claimed that

Thirty or forty years ago, the daughters of the West India planters were seldom sent to England for education . . . The case, at present, is widely different. The Creole young women are now indulged with an expensive education, at some capital boarding-school, in or near London where they acquire only the exterior and frivolous accomplishments now so much in vogue . . .

Commenting on the state of affairs in the West Indies about twenty years later, a resident in Dominica also gives a more favourable view of the number of women educated in England. He comments that: "The creole ladies are sent to England, with their brothers, at the early age of five or six, and return when their education is completed" [Resident 1828: 223]. This suggests that no distinction was made between boys and girls in this respect, even if the substance of their education was different. The only difference Resident [1828] points out is that the "West Indian manner" of the creole ladies, which they acquired from the female slaves, "in England, is deemed far from agreeable" (p. 223). Long's proposed solution for this 'problem', in the case of the white creole women who did not go to England, was "a boarding school for these girls... where they might be weaned from the Negroe dialect" [Long 1774, 2:250].

In spite of the hurdles identified as barriers to achievement in local schooling, the education of upper level whites expanded from the time of the first settlers, for whom it was marginal, up to the end of the eighteenth century. For example, in Antigua, according to Sheridan [1961: 346], during the period 1730-1775 "13 lawyers received some training at the Inns of Court, six individuals received university degrees, and 13 met Oxford matriculation standards". Although over a forty-five year period these numbers do not seem significant, the influence of these individuals in a small society over that period was considerable. In the case of Jamaica, although there was some progress, it was really only a beginning. In 1774 Long decried the fact that "Jamaica, an island more valuable and extensive than any other of the British sugar-colonies, should at this day remain unprovided with a proper seminary for the young inhabitants to whom it gives birth" [Long 1774, 2:246].

After going on to point out that Spanish Town School had 14 boys, Woolmers in Kingston had 15, Vere School had 6 and Mannings about 6, Long further commented:

Not therefore to speak of the rest, here are four schools, with as many different masters; all of whom have regular salaries, although their pupils, all together, not amounting to one half the number which one master in England is able to take charge of [Long 1774, 2:257].

While Long had reason to be distressed about the number of children being educated, at least the spread of the schools could be regarded as a positive development.

In the early years of the nineteenth century questions about education and language began to surface in the literature of the time. In a specific set of letters to the editors of newspapers in Barbados in the latter part of the year 1815,[1] there is an argument between the attorney-general and another gentleman in which are expressed views about university education and about grammar and style in the English language. The attorney-general, who admitted that he had not been to a university, had a low opinion of those who went, and repeated with specific persons in mind the old charge that had been levelled at those who went overseas to study that all they did was to waste their parents' money:

A young man may waste his own or his Father's fortune at a University, and leave it, a proud, pert and conceited coxcomb ... If those like me, who have never seen either of the Universities, were to judge of them, from the Specimen we have lately had of some young Fellows, who have returned from thence, they would naturally suppose that they were only veterinary Colleges, for all the knowledge they seem to have acquired, is that of the good or bad qualities of a horse [Ryan 1815: 9].

The other gentleman on the other hand pointed out that every university graduate in Barbados at the time "reflects the highest credit on his Alma Mater" [Ryan 1815: 14]. The argument between the two gentlemen arose as a result of a difference of opinion about which of two persons should have been given a job. From the exchanges one gets the impression that formal educational qualifications had not yet been accepted generally as a normal criterion in selection for posts. In other words, in the same way that judges were selected by the governor without consideration of legal qualifications (see Coleridge [1826: 288]), it seemed as if other areas were dealt with in the same way. However, the fact that one gentleman was putting forward an argument for the advantage of formal education, specifically a university degree, indicates that education was becoming a more influential force at that time.

The emerging focus on grammar and style in English in itself reflected the growth of general norms for the English language and concepts of grammaticality as well as preferences for certain literary traditions. For the colonial, removed from the source itself, these assumed greater importance as a badge of culture and sophistication. In the specific argument between the attorney-general and Mr Hamden, the latter made the point that "a critic should at least be conversant with the rules of grammar" [Ryan 1815: 29]. He then went on to pick holes in the attorney-general's writing, pointing to pronouns without proper antecedents, improper sentence structure, transitive verbs without the object expressed and lack of familiarity with the subjunctive. Mr Hamden was of course trying to humiliate a person that he did not like, but what is more important is that formal knowledge of the English language was beginning to be used as a social marker.

In contrast to this situation where education and standard English were gaining ground, Britain's newer colonies in the West Indies had a problem with schooling and language. Growth and development in all the New World colonies depended on a close alliance of language, religion, education and government. The following factors illustrate this – schooling depended on a common language of instruction; language went with specific European government; the principal intent of schooling was religious; religion went with European government; and there was a historical and administrative bond between church and state. Where there was compatibility, conscious or unconscious, between these elements, as in cases where there was no division of church and State and few changes in colonial masters, there was peace and development; where there was lack of compatibility, there was strife and sporadic growth.

In the older colonies among the white population the English language, a Protestant religion and British rule worked in concert. In the newer colonies, *ie* Trinidad, Grenada, St Lucia and Dominica, different possible combinations of these elements militated against a uniform system of education and in fact obstructed the development of schools. In these latter islands by the time the British finally took over, French, English (or Spanish in the case of Trinidad) could combine with Catholicism or Protestantism and with official British rule or with unofficial sympathies with France. Even though France declined in influence, the languages of Catholicism (Latin and French) were not easily or quickly replaced by English because there was not an abundance of trained British Catholic priests to service these colonies.

There was therefore a great deal of friction in the evolution of education in these islands. However, differences in the level of friction varied from island to island, as noted and highlighted by Coleridge [1826]:

At present it [St Lucia] is a British colony in little more than name. The religion is Romish, and the spirit of its ministers bigoted and intractable. The people are French in language, manners and feelings. No progress has been made in amalgamating the two nations; nay every attempt at it has been openly thwarted by the Romish clergy. They have no schools themselves, and they forbid any of their flocks to attend one in company with Protestants. Those who can afford it send their children to Martinique, the United States, or France; these return with French politics and French predilections; they submit sullenly to the English dominion, and look forward to a change (p. 125).

In Trinidad there is no religious animosity of any kind whatsoever; the Romish clergy are enlightened and liberal; the same school contains English, Spaniards, and French . . . The three languages are spoken almost interchangeably, although, as is most proper and necessary, the English is predominant and advancing (p. 126).

There is a school in Port of Spain very liberally maintained, in which English, Spaniards, and French are taught indifferently upon the plan of the national instruction in England . . . they all use the authorized version of the New Testament, and say the church catechism (p. 93).

In Trinidad a spirit of loyalty to the British crown has commenced and will increase; a permanency has been impressed on the society, and the aspect of the colony, if I may so express myself, is towards England. The reverse of all this is the case in St Lucia (p. 126) . . . there is [in Dominica] no public voice to call forth or public encouragement to support the exertion of individual virtue and talent; the community is first divided by language, then by religion, and the inconsiderable residue, which is supposed to represent the whole, is so torn to pieces by squabbles as bitter as contemptible, that the mere routine of government was at a dead stand, while I was in the island (p. 146).

Since it was not possible for the British to try to eradicate Catholicism from the colonies in the late eighteenth and nineteenth centuries as they had tried to do in

England itself in earlier centuries,[2] they had to depend on language as an instrument of control and schooling as a means of increasing the power of this instrument. This kind of policy is clearly enunciated by Coleridge [1826: 127]:

> The chief thing that I would aim at, If I were governor, would be the encouragement of the English tongue; for no society will ever be one and entire in its affections so long as nine tenths of the population speak a different language from the remaining handful of their masters. The changes either in religion or language which may be wrought in adults are trifling and imperceptible; the only effectual mode of operating on the mass of a society is by teaching the children.

This view shows that there was an awareness at the time of the power of language in schooling as a controlling force and as a means of forging uniformity to allow goals to be realized. There is little doubt then that the notion that English should be the sole language of instruction and that this would bring about progress in the society took root at this time among the colonial and religious administrators.

In conclusion, it can be said that the effects of private tutoring on the English of upper level whites were most likely very variable and effects of local schools for upper level whites were not much more significant because such schools were rare. The schooling of West Indians in England affected English in the West Indies in a symbolic way, in that British standards increasingly became the standards of the West Indies. Although university education was restricted to a few and although position in society generally did not reflect level of education, the English language had by the first half of the nineteenth century begun to be treated more critically in the older British colonies in the West Indies. Reading and writing, as skills, increased among the populations in the West Indies and those upper class whites who chose to exercise these skills in English by writing books, prayers, sermons and contributions to the newspaper adapted their language to suit the requirements of the emerging standards of the English language. In the newer colonies, however, it took some time before schooling made the English language functional among the upper class whites. These felt no particular kinship with persons in England and so were not inclined to send their children to a country with manners which were foreign to them. They themselves had been raised in a dominant French culture and were more inclined to send their children to France.

Differences in education between boys and girls had a significant negative effect on the development of the English language. The network of relationships between all the classes of women in the society had a major influence on language changes from generation to generation, and because upper level women did not receive a strong language education, in addition to the fact that they were only a small percentage of the total population, they could not impose standards of English on the society. It was therefore women of the lower classes in the society who superseded them in this respect.

THE SCHOOLING OF LOWER LEVEL WHITES

The plantation required a number of jobs, many of which at first were reserved for lower level whites e.g. overseers, bookkeepers, servants of all types, tailors, shoemakers, coopers, carpenters, masons, barbers, blacksmiths and skilled jobs in the factories. Outside the plantation there were also a number of jobs e.g. tradesmen, innkeepers, shipping people, seamen and fishermen. In the administrative services there were clerks and in the professional ranks there were priests, teachers and newspaper people. In addition to these there were small farmers, who in many cases were ex-servants who had completed the terms of their service. Not all of these were in a position to send off their children to England to be educated and so schooling in the West Indies was the only possibility for some of them. For others still, education of their children was a luxury which they could not afford – they could not dispense with the services of their children, who, as soon as they were able, were used to supplement the household income or to reduce payment for labour by doing odd jobs or by helping their parents in subsistence farming, fishing or whatever job or trade they were involved in. The parents themselves had no time to attend church, which was the main avenue for education, and therefore could attribute no particular value to formal schooling. These points are made by Dickson [1789: 58]:

> The extreme ignorance of many of the poor Barbadian whites, cannot justly be attributed to the want of opportunities of instruction; for there are schools, in every parish, which, I believe, are well attended to; at least, I knew two parochial schools where this was the case; but the poor creatures cannot always spare their children from home, after they become capable of giving them the least assistance in their field-labour. Nor are the clergy blameable for that ignorance . . . The poor whites very seldom enter a church, except at elections or funerals; and are then, generally, in a state of intoxication.

Dickson was referring specifically to Barbados, but his points were generally relevant.

As the plantation system and slavery became entrenched in the West Indies in the eighteenth century, people no longer came from Britain in numbers to fill the subordinate positions and the quotas which by law they were supposed to. Moreover, the condition of the lower level whites in the West Indies declined because there was no place for them in the plantation system based on slavery. They were generally displaced from the plantation jobs by slaves and had to survive on peripheral jobs outside the plantation. Eventually the number of whites in subordinate positions decreased so much so that it seemed apparent by the end of the eighteenth century that it was only in Barbados that there were significant numbers of lower level whites.

The creole whites who were in positions of authority continued the practice of their predecessors and sent their children to England to be educated. However, Resident [1828: 221] claimed that the lower level creole whites did not: "Creoles are generally sent to England early in life for education; except in Barbados, where the higher ranks only have this advantage . . ." The difference between lower and upper class whites was more pronounced in Barbados because of the existence in Barbados of a significant number of 'Redlegs' or poor whites, but the economic circumstances of lower level whites in all of the islands would have been similar and this would have prevented most of them from sending their children overseas to be educated.

With reference to Dominica, Atwood [1791: 214-15] noted that the whites were concerned about the education of their children and that "their whole endeavours are to accomplish it". However, some who were not wealthy took some time to accumulate the funds to send their children overseas and in the meantime, because there were no local schools, the children *"are usually put under the care of some old woman, or person of the other sex, equally as unqualified to teach them"*. Atwood goes on to point out that some children could spend several years under these tutors and even end up not going overseas if their parents suffered some financial misfortune.

The early schools in the West Indies came about through benefactions from well intentioned persons with money. The whites who could not afford to send their children to England were thus provided with schools. St Kitts, according to Cox [1984: 123], had a public school for whites in the eighteenth century and one of the earliest of these schools was one founded by Thomas Harrison in Barbados early in the century. William Duke in his 1741 history of Barbados thought the founding of the school and its early years important enough to deserve mention in his Appendix of contemporary events:

1730. Thomas Harrison Esq; caus'd to be erected, a convenient building near the church in Bridge-Town, which he conveyed to trustees, to be for ever used and employed as a Free school, under proper regulations. Many poor scholars are there taught and instructed, who probably, from the advantage they receive by this well designed benefaction, may prove useful member of society, and have the best reason, gratefully to remember their benefactor.

Although this comment on the effect of the school shows a growing appreciation for the education of the local white population, it did not mean that there was any structured attempt to provide this education. This specific school happened to survive, but others did not. In fact, it was not until the beginning of the nineteenth century that a more systematic approach to education was initiated.

The poor whites in the West Indies attracted the interest of groups like the Society for Promotion of Christian Knowledge (SPCK), which had been making provision for the children of the poor in Britain, to make similar provision in the

West Indies. The Appendix of the Eighth Annual Report of the Barbados SPCK therefore explains that "the Central-Schools at Barbados commenced in March, 1819, into which children of both sexes were admitted. The object of this Institution is to afford religious and suitable education to poor white children..." (p. 17). One of these schools was so successful that Coleridge could say with satisfaction in 1826:

At present about 160 white children are educated here, precisely upon the plan of the national schools in England; all of them are fed during the day, and the major part are well lodged. The beneficial effects of this charity are already confessed on all hands; principles of sobriety and devotion are instilled into their minds, and habits of regularity and peaceful subordination are enforced. From this class of boys, the master tradesmen, mechanics, overseers and even managers will hereafter be supplied; and when it is considered how much the comforts and improvement of the slaves must depend upon the characters of these persons, their education will be found to be, as it really is, a direct measure of general amelioration (p. 50).

Coleridge also went on to say, after visiting Antigua and other islands:

There is no reason why Antigua, according to its more limited population, should not furnish instruction to its native young on the same excellent plan which is so creditable to Barbados. I cannot but think it a reproach to the inhabitants of the other islands that the Central School in Bridge Town should remain an unique in this part of the West Indies (pp. 253-54).

Contrary to what Coleridge was suggesting, the schools in Barbados were not unique in 1825, because according to an 1826 document titled "Rules & Regulations for the government of the National Male & Female schools of Port of Spain" a national school for boys had been founded by *"the Illustrious Board of Cabildo in the Year 1823*... with the intention of affording to the male children of the poorer classes of the white and colored Inhabitants of the Island, the desirable advantage of Religious and useful Instruction, and with a view also to a more general use of the English language". In addition, a decision was made to establish a national school for girls in 1826. It was not only in Trinidad that there were national schools, for the 1826 Annual Report of the SPCK of the Grenada District Committee said:

In bestowing the benefits of Religious Instruction upon the lower classes of Society, the District Committee wish to mark their opinion, that one of the most important steps which can be taken, is the Establishment of Day Schools for the Children of the Poor White, Free Coloured, and Free Black Population. They feel a satisfaction in observing, that more than Eighteen Months ago, a School with this especial object in view, was established in the Town of St. George; In this School, 95 Boys and 43 Girls, making a total of 138 Poor children, are instructed under a Master and Mistress; the former of whom has been trained in the System pursued by the National Society [First Annual Report of the Grenada District Committee of the SPCK 1826].

The rules and regulations governing this institution stated that:

The Object of this institution is, to afford a plain Education to all poor free Children, teaching them Reading, Writing, and simple Arithmetic; and instructing them in Moral and Religious Duties on the principles of the Established Church of England... [Rules and Regulations, Second Report of the Society for the Education of the Poor – Grenada 1826, p. 6].

RULES & REGULATIONS

FOR THE GOVERNMENT OF THE

NATIONAL MALE & FEMALE SCHOOLS

OF

Port of Spain.

THE Illustrious Board of Cabildo having in the Year 1823, founded a School in Port of Spain, on the Madrass or National System, with the intention of affording to the male children of the poorer classes of the white and colored Inhabitants of the Island, the desirable advantage of Religious and useful Instruction, and with a view also to a more general use of the English language; and the Board having now the intention of extending the Establishment to Female Children, approve of the following Regulations for the direction of the Schools and government of the Scholars.

I. The two Establishments of a Male and a Female National School will be supported and maintained from the general funds of the Cabildo, under such Regulations as may be approved by the Board, with the sanction of the Governor and President.

II. The management will be delegated to a Committee of the Board.

III. The Board will request fit and proper persons to undertake the office of Visitors; and such persons shall be requested to visit the School weekly, and to make a written Report to the Managing Committee of any alterations that may appear to them necessary, and of any irregularities they may observe.

IV. An annual examination of each School shall take place, a Report of which shall be made by the Committee to the Board, and be published when their concurrence is signified.

V. All admissions to either School shall be gratuitous to persons unable to defray the expense. Such Parents or Guardians must produce a Certificate of one of the Members of the Cabildo, or of two respectable Proprietors, of their personal knowledge of the parties and of their general good conduct and behaviour, and a declaration, in writing, of their being without the means of paying the expense of the Education of their Children; which documents being presented to any Member of the Committee a Ticket shall be granted by such Member as will entitle the child to a free admission, provided the Parents or Friends sign an undertaking that they will cause the child to be punctual in its attendance, and that such child shall obey the Rules of the School. If the number thus recommended should exceed the accommodation, a preference will be given, in the first instance, to those children whose Parents may exhibit to the Committee a Certificate of Marriage.

VI. In order, however, to enable other than poor persons to send their children to either of these Establishments, it shall be in the option of Parents or Guardians either to pay the sum of £6 Sterling, annually, in advance; or should they prefer making a Donation amounting to £20 Sterling, the same shall be received, which, upon production of the Treasurer's Receipt, shall entitle them to recommend a Scholar, who shall be received by the Committee, provided he is furnished with the written undertaking described in the foregoing clause. Such Donations will be applied to the general expenses, but especially in furnishing articles of clothing to poor Scholars.

VII. No children to be admitted under 6 years of age, nor above 12 years, without the special permission of the Managing Committee; and none to remain at School after the completion of his or her 15th year.

VIII. The hours of Instruction will be from 8 to 12, and from 2 until 5. The Scholars must be cleanly and decently dressed, and they must account for any absence to the satisfaction of the Master; a repetition of it will be reported to the Committee, and if not satisfactorily explained, the child will be excluded. The School will open and close with Prayers.

IX. The children to assemble on Sundays at both Schools, and proceed to their respective Churches, under the care of the Master and Mistress. Such children as may be selected for the Psalmody of the Church, must attend as well on days to practice as on Sundays, and qualify themselves accordingly.

X. The Committee will keep a Book for the occasional inspection and approval of the Cabildo, in which will be recorded the Names, Ages, Residence, and Designation of the Children; their Parents or Guardians; the period of their Entry to the School, and under whose Certificate of Recommendation. The Master and Mistress will keep corresponding Books, in which they will note the progress of each Scholar; and of the exact number of days of attendance in the School; which Book will be open to the inspection of the Visitors and Committee.

JOSEPH GRAHAM.
JASPER LYON.

Issued by Cabildo Hall, 2d February 1826

FIGURE 8.1: Rules and Regulations for the government of the National Male and Female Schools of Port of Spain

Coleridge's view that the education of poor whites should fit them into a midlevel position in the social structure was certainly one which took hold in the West Indies. The nobility in England were not only the decision makers for the lower classes in England itself but also for the colonies. However, one major difference between England and the colonies was that the Nonconformists and the Catholics provided other dimensions to education in England to a degree that they could not in the West Indies. Variety in religious control also allowed the colonial United States to develop a more varied and responsive kind of education in contrast to the West Indies where the political structure was supported by a single established religion.

The desire to provide formal education for the poor whites was of course a very important development in that it caused to come into being schools which later became the premier local schools. In addition, the original intention of such schools to produce a disciplined middle class did not change very much over the years. With regard to language, formal education for the poor white was a means of achieving a badge of superiority to make up for obvious lack of wealth. In the case of Trinidad where French and French creole were dominant, one of the clearly stated purposes of the National schools was to expand the use of English. More generally, the reports on these schools do not indicate anything more than basic education, for the system of instruction was different from that in the grammar schools of the upper classes whose goals were much higher and whose language training was more classical. The beliefs about the standards of English which were inculcated in these central schools were most likely much stronger than the competence that was acquired in the language itself.

THE SCHOOLING OF THE COLOURED

The fate of coloured children was not always equivalent to that of poor whites: it was dependent on the circumstances and attitudes of their parents, especially their fathers. Those who were rich and so inclined gave their children the best possible education; those who were less well off left their children to fend for themselves. Most of the evidence about the education of coloured children comes from the nineteenth century because the coloured as an identifiable group and a social force came to the notice of white authors only toward the end of the eighteenth century. It is quite likely that pressure to educate coloured children varied according to how dark or light they were in colour – children of free coloured (concubine) women being given more advantages than children of black slave women.

The education of some coloured children differed little from that of upper level whites – they were provided with tutors in their early years and sent to Europe to finish their education. This practice, however, did not meet with general approval.

Resident [1828: 230] commented that "so long as the distinction of colour is thus strictly maintained, it must be bad policy to send coloured children to England for education"; and Carmichael [1833, 1:91] considered it "a very injudicious plan, unless they can be so provided for, or put in the way of providing for themselves, as to render them independent at home; for if they receive an European education, it totally unfits them for the scenes they must return to . . . ." The reality of this probably did deter some white fathers from sending their coloured children to Europe. In fact, the ill effects of a European education were a cause for concern to all West Indian parents, but these did not outweigh the advantages for most. They certainly would not have in the case where the parents themselves were free coloured of means. Apparently, the only distinction made in the education of the coloured was with females, for as Edwards [1794, 2:22] says in relation to Jamaica: ". . . for such are the unfortunate circumstances of their birth, that not one in fifty of them is taught to write or read. Profitable instruction therefore, from those who are capable of giving it, is withheld from them . . ." Resident [1828: 231], speaking about the same period but about Dominica and the neighbouring islands, said: "Few of the coloured women receive much education" (p. 231). Coloured women found themselves in the unenviable position of having to look to become the mistresses of white men or to remain useless and fruitless.

The coloured poor, together with the poor whites, were indirectly responsible for the rise of schools and general education in the West Indies, because they came to the notice of organizations in Britain which were specifically interested in the education of the poor. Schools for the poor therefore started in all the West Indian territories around the same time. A society called the Colonial Charity School was one of the first to provide religious education for the 'coloured poor' in Barbados. Its beginnings are described as follows:

In the latter part of the year 1818, a plan for the religious instruction of the Coloured Poor was set on foot by Lieut. Lugger (R.A.) . . . and patronized by Lord Viscount Combermere, the then Governor of this island. A convenient building of wood, calculated to contain 100 children, was immediately fitted up for the admission of such poor free and slave children, of both sexes, as applied; and on the 19th November, in the same year, the school was opened with 96 children, and their religious and moral instruction commenced [First Annual Report of the Society for the Education of the Coloured Poor . . . pp. 6-7].

The minutes of the meeting of 16 November 1818 on the 'Proposed Institution of a Colonial Charity School on the system of Dr. Bell' recorded that

This Institution is proposed for the Education in Reading, Writing, and Arithmetic, of such free and slave Children of the coloured and black Population of this Island, as, from pecuniary and other local impediments, have not the means of deriving these advantages from any other source than that of public charity . . .

By 1827 there were "under instruction 87 free boys, 60 free girls, 112 slave boys, 70 slave girls – making a total of 329 children of both sexes" [First Annual Report, p. 3]. In the previous year the ladies had formed a Ladies Branch, which succeeded at once in "providing a proper school-room for the sole use of the female children" (*ie* the 60 free and 70 slaves). This pattern of distribution of free and slave and the separation of male and female had parallels in other islands. In fact, except for the element of slavery the charity school in the West Indies was really an imitation of those in Britain where such schools for the poor had been in existence for some time.

The idea of religious education as a method of controlling the nonwhite population gradually became more attractive, so much so that a few years before Emancipation Coleridge [1826: 51] obviously thought of it as a way to save the West Indies:

> There is a large school of colored children, chiefly free, in the town, which was formerly supported by the Church Missionary Society, but has since been put by the colored managers of it entirely under the bishop's superintendence. The children are very well behaved, very docile, very sensible of the advantages which they acquire by a system of methodical instruction; and the actual difference between them and their untaught brethren of the same color and sometimes same condition would convince any unprejudiced witness, that it is not to emancipation but to education that the sincere philanthropist ought to direct his present labors.

These comments by Coleridge were on the system already in operation for a few years. The rudiments of this system had been successfully introduced in the decades preceding by priests of the Anglican Church in a situation where there were virtually no competing religious organizations or cultural groups.

Schomburgk [1848: 99] illustrated the differences between the territories in a comparative table showing the progress in the establishment of charity schools in the West Indies:

Name of Colony	Schools		
	1812	1825	1834
Barbados	2	8	155
Trinidad	...	2	4
Tobago	...	...	13
St Lucia	...	...	3
St Vincent	...	1	14
Bequia	...	...	2
Grenada	...	1	18
Carriacou	...	...	9
Guiana	...	2	37
Antigua	...	8	32
Montserrat	...	...	19

Barbuda	...	...	4
St Christopher	...	6	64
Nevis	...	6	19
Anguilla	...	...	2
Dominica	...	...	4
Total	2	34	399

Even allowing for size of population at the time, the difference between Barbados and the others, probably except for St Kitts, is considerable. What it really shows is that, among the smaller islands, Barbados had a headstart in formal education and more specifically in the learning of school English. However, over and above the differences between the territories, the dramatic jump from a total of 34 schools in 1825 to 399 in 1834 was remarkable, no matter how effective the schools actually were.

Information in the 1824 Report of the Jamaica District Committee of the SPCK for the years 1822 and 1823 also showed Jamaica, especially Kingston, in a fairly favourable light as far as the establishment of schools was concerned:

Kingston.

Here, according to the best information that could be obtained, are forty-six schools, at which upwards of one thousand eight hundred children are educated. Many of these schools have been largely supplied with books at reduced prices. The munificent institution of Wolmer's Free School, at which two hundred and eighty young persons are now under tuition, has been amply supplied ... (p. 6)

St Thomas in the East.

In this parish there are four schools, which have been established for the instruction of free persons of colour, in which one hundred children are at present enjoying the advantages of a useful education ... (p. 7)

St Thomas in the Vale.

There are three schools in the parish, the first the parochial school, for the education of ten poor children of free condition, and at which there were till within a few weeks back, when sickness diminished their number, ten private scholars (pp. 8-9).

Trelawny.

... at Falmouth, in this parish, there were six schools, attended by ninety-three scholars, and at Rio-Bueno one school with about thirty scholars (p. 10).

St James's.

... in this parish the free people of colour are increasing in number rapidly. Many of them, who are very poor, wish to have their children taught to read and write, &c. but cannot send them to school, on account of the expense (p. 10).

Westmoreland.

... Manning's free school ...

Vere.

In this parish there is a well endowed free school, which is now under the able management of the rector... The free people of colour are by no means numerous in this parish, and, as there is no school of any kind amongst them, I doubt if scarcely any of them can read.

From these extracts it may appear that, in most of the favourable situations throughout the island, the means of education of the free classes are by no means altogether wanting, and that there appears to prevail, at the present time, a very ardent desire to increase them (pp. 12-13).

This Report depended on people in the parishes contributing information on the number and functioning of schools, as a result of which the information in it is uneven across the parishes. Other parishes not mentioned either did not have adequate information submitted on them or were just about to set up schools or were planning to do so. In any case, the impression it creates is that schools were already spreading across Jamaica.

Although there are no consistent reports on the work in the charity schools in Grenada, St Lucia, Dominica and Trinidad, such schools were seen as especially important in these islands as instruments to increase competence in the English language and to replace French among the coloured population, which had had a major role in revolutions in Haiti and Grenada. In the case of Dominica, a general comment about the effect of schooling is made by Resident [1828: 230]: "When instructed in reading and writing, the young men of colour who have learnt trades generally do well."

However, the effect of schooling on the growth of the English language among coloured persons and others in these islands could not have been considerable before the middle of the nineteenth century because not only were the number of schools inadequate to service the whole population in each case but also English was not compulsory socially or legally.

THE SCHOOLING OF SLAVES

The type of education provided for the newly arriving African slave was a simple, informal apprenticeship system. Of course, there was no supervision of this system, but its effectiveness was tested in the most practical manner – the extent to which the slave understood instructions and carried them out. For the slave, education meant learning at least enough of the language of the territory to survive as well as learning to do some specific set of tasks on the plantation or wherever his/her owner was. The latter learning was of course dependent on the former. The new slaves had to learn the language of the territory with little explicit instruction in it and the extent to which they succeeded in doing this is attested by the variation in language competence pointed out in advertisements for slaves who had run away or were for sale. Advertisements made statements like the following:

"speaks very good English"

"can speak but very little English"

"speaks both English and French"

"speaks remarkable good English"

What is significant about these statements is that they were a normal part of the advertisements, which points to the importance of level and variety of language competence among the slaves in everyday plantation life.

The apprenticeship system was quite normal at the time, a system in common use with varying degrees of formality in the rural agricultural areas of England. So, its use by the slaveowners was not special in any positive or negative way; it was obviously the easiest and least costly way of training new additions to the workforce. In the West Indies therefore the method of instruction of the new slaves was part of a system of practical training for slavery.

Although this minimal language training was the normal practice, there is an indication that some slaves, as early as the seventeenth century, could read and write, according to Godwyn [1680: 13]:

> How should they otherwise be capable of trades, and other no less manly imployments; as also of reading and writing; or show so much discretion in management of business; eminent in divers of them; but wherein (we know) that many of our own people are deficient, were they not truly men?

Godwyn was a man on the spot, so that, even though his intention was to make the slaves seem as good as possible in order to be allowed to convert them to Christianity, it is quite likely that his report of some literate slaves is true. These slaves may have been taught to read and write by benevolent individuals and were certainly not as the result of a more general attempt to provide schooling.

In assessing the reasons for the resistance to the provision of schooling for slaves up until the last days of slavery, it would be easy to put the overwhelming emphasis on racist beliefs in the diminished capacity of blacks. This, however, would be misleading, for there was practical and everyday knowledge on the plantations about the capabilities of the different African slaves as well as creole ones. On a more general level, Porteus, writing in 1784, admits that there was at the time knowledge of intellectual and artistic achievements of blacks. To a great extent denial of education to Africans and their descendants was based on some very practical reasons with attempts made to justify it using religious and intellectual arguments.

One major stumbling block to the provision of education for slaves was language. In the early years in the older colonies and even in the later years in the newer ones, slaves, especially the constantly imported African ones, were unable to understand the English language or at least had great difficulty doing so. In early attempts in the 1730s to provide systematic religious instruction for slaves the problem was noted: "Free Negroes are baptized and some native-born slaves, but ignorance of the language prevents teaching new arrivals" [Manross 1965: 226]. In St Lucia, Dominica, Grenada and Trinidad, the Anglican Church, through its different agencies, could not put into operation the kind of plan it introduced in the older colonies in the second and third decades of the nineteenth century. There was no cohesion in culture and language in these territories and so no uniform philosophy of keeping the slaves and the coloured poor obedient and servile by using Christianity to produce "a reformation in mind and habits".[3] The problem is stated in the First Annual Report of the Grenada District Committee of the SPCK [1826] as follows: "... it is scarcely possible without an Interpreter, to communicate in their broken and corrupted French, the plain, wholesome, and pratical Truths of Christianity". The solution proposed by the Report echoed the opinion of Coleridge [1826: 127]: "Here again it appears to the District Committee, that the younger part of the Slave Population present the best and most promising objects of Instruction." What was interesting about this policy was that it was one not only that the English were keenly aware of historically but also one that had failed, as Brerewood [1614: 22-23] pointed out:

And indeede, how hard a matter it is, utterly to abolish a vulgar language, in a populous country, where the Conquerors are in number farre inferiour to the native inhabitants, whatsoever art bee practiced to bring it about, may well appeare by the vaine attempt of our *Norman* Conquerour: who although he compelled the *English*, to teach their young children in the Schooles nothing but *French*, and set downe all the Lawes of the Land in *French*, and inforced all pleadings at the Law to be performed in that language (which custome continued till King *Edward* the third his daies, who disanulled it) purposing thereby to have conquered the language together with the land, and to have made all *French*: yet, the number of *English* farre exceeding the *Normans*, all was but labour lost, and obtained no further effect, then the mingling of a few *French* words with the *English*.

Clearly, the English must have felt either that there was no other policy or that it would not fail in the case of Trinidad, Grenada, St Lucia and Dominica.

Perhaps the oldest reason for the denial of education to slaves was one that has always brought heartache to owners and employers – release for education means loss to the workforce. Robertson [1730: 20-21] explained this in detail as follows:

For, suppose the master of a hundred negroes was to have one fifth of them instructed in religion; if we consider that instruction is not to be forced on the quickest-witted of ourselves in a hurry, and that these slaves among other disadvantages are most of them intractable, it could not then but be found necessary to have them taught a little almost every day, and should that space of time amount in a fortnight (besides Sundays) to but one day, 'tis plain the planter, who seldom or never keeps more slaves than he has occasion for, but rather fewer, would lose one day in a fortnight of their work, and allowing their work, one with another to be worth to him six pence sterling per diem each (and a negroe's work is commonly valued here at above twice that sum) there is thirteen pounds per annum for him, or not much less, for ever; for the births upon the place, and the constant supplies from Africa, would make it very little short of a yearly charge.

The planter of that day would hardly have entertained the idea that money 'lost' through education would be 'recovered' many fold. The idea, however, was not new or unheard of then. Slaveowners were aware that there was a relationship between treatment, value and performance (*ie* of slaves). The choices that they made varied according to market forces, notions of self-preservation, and reason. However, slaveowners in many cases had no more formal education than their slaves and therefore could see no value in it.

Another reason for denial of education to slaves is again a familiar one – lack of teachers. As Robertson [1730] explained, the pious in England were only too ready to criticize the planters in the West Indies, but there was very little local expertise available to instruct the population even if the planters would have allowed this. Preaching and teaching were not favoured professions and those priests and teachers who came to the West Indies soon lost their zeal, if they had any, either because they were frustrated by the slaveowners or because the venal and other attractions were too strong to resist for very long. It was not until the central schools began to produce 'graduates' that this problem began to be resolved.

Another argument with a long history is that, in comparison with temperate climates, a tropical climate, such as that in the West Indies, militated against prolonged mental activity and was more suitable to frolic, dancing and singing, and licentious behaviour generally. One version of this argument is that it was a matter of a ceaseless summer, meaning that there could not be in such places the restricted, indoor, intellectual activity, which was fostered by the cold weather in temperate climates. Another version of the argument is expressed by Caldecott [1898: 39] in the following way:

> It would be a matter of astonishment if in such a state of society the higher interests of human life had won attention or attained much development. In literature, science, and art, the history of the British West Indies is almost a blank. Where external Nature is so profuse in scenes of beauty, the Fine Arts have scarcely any place even at this day, except the arts of Music and Dancing. The bareness of the walls of the drawing-rooms and dining-rooms of West Indian homes is at once explained when adjournment is made to the verandah in which so much of domestic life is passed. The balmy air of these balconies combined with the soft light of the moon makes evenings indoors out of the question. And thus it follows that reading is replaced by Conversation. For such a public no genius was impelled to exert itself in literature.

Of course, Caldecott was referring to the white population and was suggesting that they were drawn outdoors. With regard to the black population the general belief was that they knew nothing else but outdoor life and so were incapable of intellectual activity. Yet, in contrast to this view, almost a century earlier the Rev Dr Bell, who had developed the 'national system' in India, in an attempt to justify the proposal that the young slaves should be sent to school at the very earliest age (so that a few years later they would not have to stay away from the fields to go to school), used the argument that "children are more forward in warm than in cold climates" [Porteus 1808: 45], which was a repetition of the claim that Edwards [1794, 2:12] had made from his observations in Jamaica principally.

In the early years when unknown Africans were being imported in great numbers, the argument against schooling of slaves which was most real for whites in every plantation society was one which arose out of fear and insecurity. The importance of English as a factor in communication in early English colonial societies has already been pointed out and so has the belief on the part of the whites that widespread knowledge of English among the slave population would facilitate plots and rebellions. If mere knowledge of English was regarded as dangerous, ability to read and write was even more greatly feared then. Hunte [1975: 20] refers to correspondence in 1736 between William Johnson, Commissary and Rector of St Michael, Barbados and his superior in England, in which Johnson points out the fears of the local planters about instructing slaves to read and write:

He [Johnson] quoted planters as having expressed the view that such instruction was tantamount to arming the slaves, 'making them more Capable of Carrying on Plots & Contrivances against the Common safety'. Instances were cited of literate Negroes forging passes, 'giving Ticketts to runaways' and therefore using their newly acquired skills to defeat the slave system.

Schooling of slaves was therefore seen to be dangerous to the safety and security of the white masters in the early years. In addition, it was also regarded as a threat to the condition of the white servants, who were gradually displaced from semiskilled jobs by semiskilled blacks.[4]

However, as the creole slaves, speaking some form of English, grew in number, a negative policy was no longer a possible method of controlling them. They had then to be educated into accepting their lot in these societies. Religion, which was at first withheld from the Africans on philosophical grounds, now proved to be the most effective method of doing this. The English language, which was an integral part of the Anglican and other nonconformist religions, then assumed greater and greater importance.

Formal schooling of slaves came about through attempts to bring them nearer to Christianity. This was so in two ways. First in order for them to be taught the religious doctrines of the Anglican and other churches, they had to be able to understand the kind of English in which these were written; secondly, Protestant religious education in itself included in an integral way accomplishment in reading, for the confirmed or saved were expected to be able to read the scriptures on their own. However, the fact that all of the early literature pointed to language as a barrier to conversion suggests that it was only after a number of years had passed and a significant number of slaves were able to understand some English that realistic attempts could have been made to convert them and consequently to school them formally.

The inability of the English to conceive of any other language among their slaves except English was unlike cases of other ethnic groups in other parts of the Americas. No argument was put forward by English churches in the early years for the priests or teachers to learn the native languages of the slaves in the West Indian colonies or to have translations of religious material in those languages. In the case of the Anglican Church it is not that church doctrine or practice did not allow for this, for it certainly did. For example, Procter and Frere [1965: 203] point out:

> The missionary development of the Anglican Communion has in later years rendered necessary the translation of the Prayer Book into many languages. The Society for the Promotion of Christian knowledge has published alone all but one hundred versions in different languages, and has had a hand in a certain number of others, which have been printed in the Mission Field. The Prayer Book and Homily Society has also done something in this direction, and in America the Prayer Book has been printed in a number of Indian dialects by the American Board of Missions.

In fact, the catechism, which is the foundation for conversion to the Anglican Church, has at its end the following note: "So soon as Children are come to a competent age, *and can say, in their Mother Tongue,* the Creed, the Lord's Prayer, and the Ten Commandments; and also can answer to the other Questions of this short Catechism; they shall be brought to the bishop." There was therefore no formal regulation that prevented the use of the language of the intended converts in the case of the slaves in the West Indies; it was simply that the slaves were not thought to be speaking any real languages, other than the English which they were thought to be speaking badly. In addition, it could be argued that even if there was a will to use the languages of the Africans, it would not have been feasible because of the great number of languages spoken by the slaves and the small numbers of speakers of each language in each case.

Even after the slaves developed their own creole languages in the English colonies, there was still no deliberate attempt by the English to address them in these languages in the process of formal education. This contrasts with the practice of other Europeans, who from then regarded the languages of the creole slaves as a viable medium for religious conversion of them. For example, writing about the Danish Virgin Islands, Hall [1979: 3] says:

> The Moravians were nothing if not resourceful. Johann Dober and David Nitschman, potter and carpenter respectively, the first two missionaries who arrived at the end of 1732, took the trouble to learn the slaves' lingua franca, the Dutch based 'creolisk'. This simplified the task of instruction from the pulpit and at class meetings.

Hall goes on to point out that in the years between 1770 and 1798 Lutheran missionaries and others produced "a creole ABC book, translations of the New Testament and other religious works, a hymnal and a catechism". Again, it could also be argued that in the case of the creole slaves in the British colonies there was such a wide variety in their language competence that it would have been virtually impossible to produce translations to accommodate such variety. In fact, the only linguistic concession which seemed to have been made was one based on the presumed intellectual inferiority of the African. Yet, the proposal to teach the slaves "in language adapted to their capacities" [Associates 1786: 9] might not have been very different, as far as those teaching were concerned, from teaching them in their native language.

So, education in the English colonies was carried out in the English language from the earliest attempts to convert the slaves. These first attempts were made by the Quakers within twenty years after African slaves began to be introduced in numbers into the West Indies to cultivate sugar. At this time the Quakers were a young, zealous organization which was trying to spread its influence as widely and as quickly as possible. It had made major conquests in Philadelphia and it was trying the same in Barbados, Antigua and Jamaica. However, the colonists in the islands which were essentially controlled by Royalists were strongly opposed to them and introduced laws to try to curb their influence. One of these laws passed in April, 1676 was specifically designed to prevent the Quakers from teaching the slaves. The specific Act [An Abridgement of the Laws of Barbados (printed in 1699), Act 198 IV, p. 249] reads as follows: "None [Quakers] shall teach School unless such Persons first take the Oaths of Supremacy and Allegiance, before some Justice of Peace of the Parish where he lives, or have special Licence from the Governour."

This act was not new in itself because as far as education is concerned, the colonies were merely an extension of the intrigues and philosophies of the mother country. In the sixteenth century, Protestant England saw Catholic Europe as the enemy and in the seventeenth century to the Catholic enemy on one side was added the non-conformist Protestants (or Dissenters) on the other. This was a continuous struggle that went on not only in England itself but in all its colonies and the schools as builders of the future were a crucial part of it. Armytage [1965: 1] says: "To keep England Protestant, no instruments were more effective than its schools . . ." One of the most powerful acts passed to protect church and state was the Oath of Supremacy in 1563. This oath required every teacher, before being given a licence to teach, to swear to recognize the supremacy of the Queen (Elizabeth I at the time). In 1581 another law was passed which set a punishment of a year's imprisonment for any schoolmaster who did not attend the parish church on Sundays or holy days. (This law had its own version in the early years of the colonies in that every white man living within a certain radius of the parish church had to attend services every Sunday or face a stiff penalty.)

On their return to power in England in 1660, the Royalists tried to secure their position through the Anglican Church and in effect to bring all important activities in the society, including schooling, under the control of the state and the Anglican Church. In order to achieve this they had to unseat many nonconformists (dissenters) who had managed to gain positions and power. This they did by passing a set of laws which together are known as the Clarendon Code. Even when the dissenters fled to more rural areas in England and started private schools and what they called 'academies', a law was passed to prohibit them from teaching in any school. The bishop in each diocese had it as part of his duty to issue licences for teaching, licences which could be obtained only if the person swore loyalty to the Anglican Church. The bishop also had it as a part of his duty to seek out and have punished all those who contravened this requirement. It was therefore the same kinds of laws which were introduced into the West Indies a few years later to prevent the Quakers from teaching.[5] So, although the main intention was to consolidate the power of the Anglican Church, these laws in the sugar colonies also made sure that slaves were not educated.

In their attempts to discourage the Quakers, obviously the masters did not pay much attention to the following denial of wrongdoing by George Fox himself on his visit to the West Indies in 1671:

> This wicked slander (of our endeavouring to make the Negroes Rebell) our Adversaries took occasion to raise, from our having had some Meetings with and amongst the Negroes: For both I and other Friends had several meetings with them in several Plantations wherein we exhorted them to Justice, Sobriety, Temperance, Chastity and Piety, and to be subject to their masters and Governours: Which was altogether contrary, to what our envious Adversaries maliciously suggested against us [Fox 1694, 1:360].

Fox's denial, though it was disregarded, shows that from the earliest years the church's mission was in no way revolutionary. However, the policy of non-education of slaves was in the view of the masters necessary for the masters' own safety and protection, for in the last half of the seventeenth century the discovery of a number of slave plots made them extremely uncomfortable.

It was probably not until about forty years after the first attempts by the Quakers to educate the slaves that the Anglican Church made any effort to provide schools for them. Attempts at education of the slaves by the Anglican Church arose directly out of circumstances and developments in England. In England the argument that prevailed in the last half of the seventeenth century was that education should not disrupt the status quo and that supply should be related to demand. What was beginning to happen earlier in the century was that in the rural (agricultural) areas the grammar schools were increasingly taking in boys from the poorer classes and giving them a liberal arts education. Such boys were unwilling to return to the fields and crafts after they finished school, a fact that was seen as a dangerous threat by entrenched interests. The view of these entrenched interests was recorded by Christopher Wase (quoted in Armytage [1965: 39]): "There is an opinion commonly receiv'd that the scholars of England are overproportion'd to the preferments for letter'd persons . . .[those] whom nature or fortune had determin'd to the plough, the oar, or other handicrafts [were being diverted] to the study of liberal arts." In order to counter this 'miseducation' of the poorer classes and in order not to overproduce qualified persons in the preferred positions in the society (which would have made it harder for the privileged to walk straight into jobs), the SPCK was formed in 1699 with the specific purpose of establishing charity schools to produce better workers.

The SPCK, together with its companion organization, the Society for the Propagation of the Gospel (SPG), spread its work into the colonies with the same basic intentions. The SPG managed to become directly involved in the schooling of slaves because Christopher Codrington bequeathed his estates to this organization with specific instructions about the schooling of slaves. In the Proceedings of the Society for the Propagation of the Gospel in Foreign Parts for 1715 it is stated that: "Schools, in a competent Measure, are already established in many Places, and Care taken by Masters and Catechists to instruct the Negro Slaves, and the Children of Natives, in the principles of Christian Religion, and Duties of Morality". There is no substantial proof of these claims made about schools in many places and instruction of slaves by members of the Anglican Church in 1715, but these claims immediately precede mention of the proposed Codrington College which is well documented for this time. Whether or not there were Anglican schools in the West Indies in 1715, the SPG, because it was based in London and was not under the control of local planters, could afford to pursue Codrington's desire and to issue instructions in 1741 for

. . . two of the most promising Negro boys not under nor above sixteen years old to be put under the care of the Catechist to be thoroughly Instructed in the Principles of the Christian Religion & in Reading & Writing till they shall be fully Qualifyed for the instruction of their fellow Negroes (quoted in Hunte [1975: 21]).

Although the attempt to teach slaves at Codrington may have been of great interest at the time, it cannot be said to have had any great consequences for the general education of slaves, principally because it was an undertaking with no local support.

While the SPCK and the SPG had the same basic intentions in the West Indies as they did in England, there was one major difference among the slaves in the West Indies which had to be dealt with – West African supernatural beliefs. The reactions of all Europeans to these, however, were uniformly the same. From the earliest attempts of the Quakers right through to Emancipation, education in the case of the slaves meant religious and moral instruction, because it was believed that the African had neither religion nor morals. When the Africans came into contact with the Europeans in the West Indies, religious and cultural intolerance was the norm in practice among Europeans. Europeans had been for many centuries before persecuting and killing each other because of differences in religion and culture. There was no such concept as guaranteeing individuals freedom of religion and cultural practice. Church and state in most cases were integrated and subjects had to conform to the dictates of both. For instance, early laws in the English colonies specified that masters and servants had to go to church, but allegiance to church and state among the whites was probably more a matter of security and self-preservation than a matter of religious and civic zeal.

When the Europeans imported the Africans into the New World colonies, they were divided about the way they should treat them – whether to regard them as beings outside normal society or to integrate them into the society. There were, of course, those Europeans who were always opposed to the presence of Africans and whose solution was to get rid of them and replace them with white Europeans. The problem for the Europeans was made more difficult by the fact that the Africans were very different from 'foreigners' that they knew about – in language, dress, food, manners, physique and colour. These were differences which could not easily be eliminated, especially when the numbers were considerable. The easier solution for the most of the European colonists, then, was to leave the mass of Africans outside society. This situation was effected by treating the Africans as property, which meant automatically that they had no culture or religion, in the same way that one would not regard a horse or cow as having culture or religion. This solution and the consequential beliefs about Africans were cultivated and propagated as an integral part of the intolerant mind of the European of that day.

Armed with the view that the Africans were property and beings outside their society, the Europeans could not see among the slaves any organized religious practices which conformed to their concept of religion. Of course, then as now, it was normal for the European to believe that certain types of supernatural practices were civilized and so constituted religion whereas others were uncivilized and constituted superstition. This kind of reaction to the Africans influenced the following remark from Smith [1745: 229], which can be regarded as a typical, generalized and ignorant view: "Nay, the most intelligent of them, have no manner of religious worship, as far as I could ever discover; though I am told, that at Jamaica, the Negroes have, what they call, a hearing, in some Guinea tongue . . ." From this statement by Smith it is clear that his view of religion involved a gathering of people in one place with a priest of some type. Yet even though he had heard that something like this was happening in Jamaica, his own experience did not allow him to say that the slaves had a religion. In both his concept of religion and his experience of what the slaves did, then, ignorance was at the base of his comments.

The Catholic priest Labat, who had a more intimate knowledge of the slaves, recognized no other religion among some of them than that of Islam. He says [1724, 2:46]: "Presque tous les negres sont idolatres. Il n'y a que ceux du Cap-Verd, dont quelques uns sont Mahometans."[6] (More than a hundred years later Halliday [1837: 321], talking about Trinidad around the time of Emancipation, also refers to a separate group of Mandingo slaves being Muslims.) It is not that those whites who came into more consistent contact with the slaves were not knowledgeable of their habits and beliefs; it is rather that they treated their supernatural practices as superstitious and uncivilized. For example, Labat used the term 'idolatres' and William Duke spoke of "some pernicious principles and tenets in our slaves, that make them so much the dupes of superstition" [Associates 1786: 11].

The European view of the supernatural beliefs of the slaves never changed over the years. It provided a basis and rationale not only for formal schooling but for the broader concept of civilization. Paradoxically, though it was negatively fuelled by a history of religious intolerance, it was the very religious zeal that made the educational intent so forceful and long lasting.

Following the SPG's early attempt to implement the clauses of Codrington's will in 1715 and later in 1741, the next significant step in the development of a system of education for the slaves came about as a result of Rev. James Ramsay's return from St Kitts to England after spending nineteen years there. Ramsay proceeded to write a book on the treatment and conversion of slaves, but before it was published he gave it to Beilby Porteus, the Lord Bishop of Chester, who was to become the Bishop of London. Porteus, basing his ideas on the account of Ramsay, preached a sermon on Friday, 21 February 1783[7] before the Incorporated Society for the Propagation of the Gospel in Foreign Parts in which he made suggestions to the Society and more specifically for the treatment of slaves on the Codrington estates. One of the points Porteus made [1784: 18] was that natural increase among the slaves should be fostered because

Should this wise and humane practice become an established and universal custom, it would exceedingly facilitate the work both of instruction and conversion, by furnishing a succession of young Negroe catechumens, well acquainted with the English language, familiarized to the English customs, and uncorrupted by those heathenish principles and savage manners with which the constant importation of fresh slaves from Africa never failed to infect them.

This became the dominant philosophy in the attitude of the Anglican Church toward the slaves and from this point onward the movement for the conversion and instruction of the slaves gained momentum.

Local support in the West Indies for Porteus' ideas came indirectly through the SPCK in London. The work of this organization was spearheaded in its early years by Dr Bray, whose main intentions were to defeat Catholicism and to ameliorate, not change, the lot of lower class workers. After his death Bray's work and philosophy were continued by a group called 'the Associates of Dr Bray', among whose members was Benjamin Franklin. The work of the Associates of Dr Bray was extended to the West Indies and taken on by Rev Duke, rector of St Thomas parish church in Barbados in the 1780s. Rev Duke was a Barbadian, a landowner and slaveowner, so his attempt can therefore be regarded as marking a significant step in the history of education in the West Indies. Rev Duke's almost revolutionary[8] step is documented in the "Abstract of the Proceeding of the Associates of Doctor Bray for the Year 1785" as follows:

Negro Schools   Barbadoes

The following letter has been received from the Rev. Mr. Duke, Rector of the Parish of St Thomas in that Island.

Rev. Sir,

Your letter is just come to Hand; and as some Ships will in a Day or two sail for London, it may give you and the Associates some satisfaction to know, that it is my Intention to carry their scheme concerning a Charity-School for the Instruction of Slaves into immediate Execution. I have published among my Parishioners this benevolent Design, and have endeavoured to give them a proper Sense thereof; by informing them, that a religious Society in England for the Conversion of our Negroes, have requested me to institute a proper School in St Thomas's to teach Negro Children to read; that by such Instruction, and having good Books sent over to them, they may know the Doctrines and Principles of our holy Religion, and be trained up in the Faith and Fear of God [Associates 1786: 7].

It is clear from this quotation that the intention of the Associates and Rev Duke was a proselytizing one, that is, to make the slaves competent in reading so that they could be converted to the Anglican Church, thereby expanding and strengthening the church. There was no focus on the specific needs of the slaves and this is even further strengthened by the fact that Rev Duke left the selection of reading material in the hands of the Associates: "I shall once in the year send you particular Accounts of these Schools, and write for such Books as the Associates may think proper to send over" [Associates 1786: 8]. This provision of schooling was not intended to be for mass education, but to provide a sufficient number of black teachers to convert other blacks to the church. It therefore meant that those to be taught had to be specially selected, a system which involved subjectivity and favouritism. The way that Rev Duke presents it, however, in no way suggests this: "I shall select some of the best and most devout of the Negroes, whom I shall observe at my Lectures, and invite them to come to my House, on the Sundays I do not preach to the

Negroes, to be privately instructed, and prepared for Baptism" [Associates 1786: 9]. In any case, the idea of selecting a few and putting them to instruct lesser ones developed into a more formal system by the end of the eighteenth century.

While education is generally seen as a process beneficial to the individual, it is at the same time an institution of the society which tries to maintain the values and the structure of the society itself. The masters generally, especially in the early years, saw education of slaves as a threat to their safety and disruptive to the structure of the plantation society, but Rev Duke and the Anglican Church proposed religious education as a means of getting the slaves to accept their lot and so of preserving the society with less violence and coercion. This view is expressly enunciated in the following:

My reverent Brethren have often tried what could be done to their Slaves to civilize and amend them, and perhaps have found this Proverb too literally verified, that the Aethiopian can neither change his Skin, nor alter his Way of Life. But as the End of Preaching and Exhortation is to bring about a Reformation of Life, and not to be considered as a mere Adherence to the customary Forms prescribed to the Clergy by their Bubrick, or Ordinary, and expected by their Flock in the Way of Office, it may not be improper to try, whether some Instructions in the easy, familiar Way of Exhortation, may not succeed with our Slaves who have the least Ingenuity or Docility; and if not produce many, yet may make a few Converts to Christianity... My exhortations I shall digest into some Method, and deliver in as easy a Manner as I can, that I may avoid every Thing that has the Appearance of Cant and Rhapsody, and lead on my black Hearers by Degrees to the Knowledge of Christianity, and the Duties they ought to practise [Associates 1786: 10-11].

Rev Duke had set out the subject matter of his twelve proposed lectures to the slaves very carefully and again in some of them we see quite clearly the purpose of education of the slaves. Here are some of the subjects:

The Fourth. What Baptism means, the Benefit of this Sacrament. What is required of those who are baptized; ... Baptism shewn to be no Release from our outward Conditions, or temporal Connexions; but only an Admission to a new Covenant with God, and a release from a worse Bondage, the Bondage and Slavery of Sin [Associates 1786: 12].

In this lecture Duke was making sure to put the slaveowners' hearts at ease by making clear that he was not encouraging the slaves to think of freedom from their physical condition of slavery but from something spiritual and in the next world. This is exactly the same philosophy spelled out by George Fox, the Quaker, a hundred years earlier.

The Sixth. The ten Commandments shortly explained, in which the Sin of Murder will be shewn to be a heinous and grievous Crime, whether perpetrated by sudden Passion, or any secret Means shewn to be cruel and unlawful. A dissuasive from Self-Murder [Associates 1786: 12].

The intent of this lecture must be understood in the context of plantation slavery at that time. Killing and violence were in a sense much more normal in those days, but the masters had to make sure that whereas they could brutalize and kill slaves with impunity, the slaves on the other hand should be encouraged to accept their lot and not to be violent. They tried to make sure that slaves did not kill masters, other slaves or themselves. Such 'religious' instruction was therefore little more than part of a concerted policy of self-preservation and preservation of property. The same is true of attempts to destroy the culture of the slaves, an intention which is implicit in the eighth and ninth lectures:

The Eighth. The Negroes superstitious Notions concerning their Dead, their funeral Rites, and Commemoration of their dead Family examined and exploded [Associates 1786: 12].

The Ninth. All witchcraft, Obeah, Conjurors, Oaths or swearing upon Grave Dirt, shown to be foolish and absurd. The Scripture Account of the Dead, and Spirits examined in Contradiction to their Notions. The Art and Craft of their Obeah-people shewn to be absurd, and not worthy of credit. A caution against such Delusions, which may so far affect their Minds, as to occasion total neglect of their own Preservation, and thereby make them guilty of the Crime of Self-Murder [Associates 1786: 12-13].

Although the efforts of the Associates of Dr. Bray and Rev. Duke were not immediately copied all over the West Indies, they clearly began to prepare the climate for the philosophy of education in the early decades of the nineteenth century.

Porteus, as Bishop of London, in whose see the province of the West Indies fell and under whose care was the Codrington Trust, set out his thoughts and proposals for the education of slaves in the West Indies in documents ranging over the period 1784 to 1808. Porteus was of course aware of the proposals of the Associates of Dr Bray and also of those of the Rev Duke. Porteus apparently had also read the arguments made by Robertson [1730] in St Kitts, for his response to a specific argument about the time lost from work if slaves attended classes closely parallels the argument which Robertson had put forward. Another person whom Porteus had heard of was the Rev Dr Bell, who had developed a system of education in India in 1789 which involved putting pupils to teach pupils. Porteus contacted Bell and asked him to say how his system could be implemented in the West Indies. Bell responded in a letter to Porteus, which Porteus then included in a letter which he sent to "the Governors, Legislatures, and Proprietors of Plantations in the British West-India Islands" in 1808.

Even preceding the letter, the first action which Porteus took was, according to the same letter of 1808, to recommend the establishment of a special society. So, in the last years of the eighteenth century a society was formed with the specific purpose of converting and educating the slaves in the West Indies. This society, called The Society for the Conversion and Religious instruction and Education of the Negro Slaves in the British West India Islands, was founded in the year 1794 with Bishop Porteus as its president. At first, its membership was almost exclusively limited to priests of the Church of England in and around the area of London, but when bishoprics were established in the West Indies in 1824, control of the Society devolved into local hands and it began to flourish. The Society intended to achieve its goals by sending out chaplains and catechists from London to the West Indies, but in the early years of its existence, because of scarce resources, it was "unable to avail itself of the services of many pious and able young men" who offered themselves as chaplains. In addition, interference in local affairs in the West Indies involving slaves was bitterly resented. The Society therefore had little effect before the 1820s.

In 1823 in Barbados a body was formed called the Barbados Religious Association, but after the local bishopric came into being and the first bishop assumed office in 1825, this body was invited to become a Branch Association of the Society for the Conversion and Religious instruction and education of Negro Slaves in the British West India Islands. This it did and it immediately devised a plan for

the appointment of Lay Catechists, licensed by the Bishop, after previous examination and subscription, acting under and directed by the Minister of the parish, and paying every proper regard to the wishes of the Master as to the time and frequency of instruction [of the slaves] [First Annual Report of the Branch Association . . ., p. 6].

By 1826, when the Branch Association in Barbados produced its first report, a comprehensive system of education of slaves had gone into effect. The following, culled from the report, gives a picture of the extent of plantation schooling in all the parishes in Barbados as well as the extent of the instruction itself:

Parish	Number of plantations	Teachers	Frequency of instruction	Subject matter
St Michael	26 & 21 small	3 catechists	once a week	repetition of the Lord's Prayer, the Creed, the Commandments and a lecture
Christ Church	24	1 catechist	once a fortnight (weekdays)	the Catechism, Harte's Lectures. Prayers, a lecture read
	5	family members & the overseers	1 – on Sundays 2 – daily	
St James	27	1 catechist	24 – once a fortnight (weekdays) 3 – once a month	repeat Catechism, read Liturgy & New Testament, a lecture for adults, Crossman's exposition of the Church Catechism
St Lucy	11	1 catechist	some – once a fortnight	read the Liturgy & the Commandments,

Schools and their Effect on English / 229

Parish	Number of plantations	Teachers	Frequency of instruction	Subject matter
St Lucy (cont'd)			some – once a month	repeat the Catechism, a Lecture on St Matthew, learn by heart the Creed, the Lord's Prayer and the Commandments,
	3	subordinate white servants		repeat Crossman's Exposition, memorize the General Confession in the Liturgy
St Philip	41	1 catechist	once a fortnight	the Catechism, Harte's Lectures
St Thomas	22	1 catechist, overseers in his absence	15 – once a fortnight 6 – once a week 1 – once a month	Prayers, a Lecture, the Catechism; on 2 plantations – Crossman's Exposition
St John	22	1 catechist, Codrington – independent, 1 Moravian missionary	15 – once a week 5 – once a fortnight	the Catechism for the young, lectures for the adults, readings from the Liturgy and the New Testament.
	3			Young taught to read the Catechism.
St Peter	26	the chaplain	6 – daily 9 – once a week	the young taught to read and examined in the principles of Christian Knowledge and duty
St Joseph	18	1 catechist	once a fortnight	Lord's Prayer, Creed, Commandments, Catechism
St Andrew	24	1 catechist	16 – once a fortnight 8 – once every three weeks	Prayers, Catechism for the young slaves, Harte's Lectures for the older ones
St George	1	1 catechist	once a fortnight	Catechism, Prayers from the Liturgy read to all, Harte's Lectures

It should be borne in mind also that the education of the plantation slaves through Sunday schools and through the use of catechists was in addition to the education of some urban slaves, in the case of Barbados, in the Colonial Charity School, which opened in 1818 and was meant to include slaves among its pupils, although it was clearly specified that:

No slave Child to be admitted as a pupil without the particular permission of the owner, who, together with such permission, is required to state, in writing, to the Secretary, for the information of the General Committee, that he wishes the Child to learn [Proposed Institution of a Colonial Charity School, p. 5].

In the case of St Vincent, the First Annual Report of the St Vincent District Committee of the SPCK for the year 1826, published in 1828, said:

In the Sunday Schools, the Children are examined after Morning Service, in the broken or in the Crossman's Catechism, or are taught to read the new Testament and the tracts published by the parent Society; and the intelligence displayed by many of the children and young persons, both bond and free, and the general propriety of their conduct, is highly gratifying (pp. 5-6).

The number of Children	Free		Slaves	
	Boys	Girls	Boys	Girls
In the Central School is	48			36
In the School of the Benevolent Society, under the direction of the Diocesan	68	31	4	1
In Barrowallie School	14	4	5	7
In Chatteaubellair School	24			4

In the Bequia School About fifty Children

At Calliaqua (Master not yet appointed).

Nearly the whole of the Slave population, with the exception of the Calliaqua quarter, is visited by the Catechists (p. 7).

In addition, the First Annual Report of the St Vincent Branch Association of the Society for the Conversion and Religious instruction of the Negro Slaves of 1828 said:

On some of the Plantations, the younger people are perfect in the whole of the broken Catechism, on others they are only masters of half. On a considerable number, the adults also are permitted to attend, and benefit by the lecture, which is principally intended for their instruction.

There are many of the Negro Slaves who can read their Bible, in a creditable manner.

Similar data on St Kitts and Grenada are presented in Cox [1984: 123-131]. In the other islands, especially the older colonies, the pattern of development in education was different only to the extent that the Methodists and Moravians made a more significant contribution in the Leeward Islands. In general, therefore, the educational strategy and method of provision for schools used by British religious organizations were basically the same across all the islands.

The impression created by the Barbados Branch report was that the plantation owners were in favour of the system and actively helped to support it – the report specifically says: "... by the united exertions of the Clergy and their Catechists, with the personal cooperation of the proprietors, their family, and overseers, by far the greater number of the estates in this island are under religious instruction". Yet, in the first years of the Branch Association local subscription was not substantial enough and so the headquarters continued to provide support. The report of the Society dated 27 January 1825 states that the Society was at that time providing support for seventeen chaplains and catechists in the West Indies. As is the case with most such societies, part of the annual expenditure was for books and in the year 1824 the sum spent on "books, printing, advertising, &c. sundries" was £509. The success of the association led them to pass resolutions to start Sunday schools in every parish and to employ school masters to teach these Sunday schools.

The information above, taken mostly from Society reports, paints an encouraging picture of the education of slaves in the various islands. However, remarks by "a gentleman, who visited Barbadoes in the early part of the present year, 1830" (p. 2)[9] paint a different picture. This gentleman, who said that one of his first objects was to learn from the slaves themselves "how far they had benefited by the efforts to introduce education", visited the 'Colonial School' and interviewed the pupils and found that "... these children, with the exception of perhaps three or four, were *exclusively* the children of *free* people of colour" (p. 4). He then went on to say:

The children of slaves, on this island, receive instruction only in catechical form: in some instances they are taught to *repeat* hymns; but these opportunities for instruction are wholly confined to the morning of the Sabbath day, in all places which I saw and visited, except one instance in which the slaves were assembled *occasionally* under the parlour window and sung a hymn (p. 4).

This less than positive view of slave education was further reinforced by the gentleman when he said:

I inquired of all the slaves I could get an opportunity of conversing with, as to their having any knowledge of letters, and was certainly a good deal disappointed and mortified to find, that with a very small exception, I believe confined to two or three individuals, I met no slave who could read (pp. 4-5).

The gentleman explains that those slaves who could read were

slaves who held some places of more than common importance, in the establishment of persons of consequence in the island, and who bore a high character for great humanity and benevolence, and whose slaves showed that their masters were so distinguished, by their appearance and manners (p. 5).

In reference to St Vincent, Mrs. Carmichael, who spent a few years there in the 1820s, also makes the point that "some few slaves can read, but the number is very small who possess this advantage" and she also in identifying one of the slaves who could read said that he was a 'head-servant' [1833, 1: 220-21].

In all cases selection of slaves for preferential treatment (*ie* schooling) was determined in a subjective way. In general the children who, for one reason or another, were nearer to the house were preferred to those who were nearer to the fields. So, the lower down the social scale the person was, the lesser the chance of being taught to read and even lesser to write.

In most cases the schooling of slaves took place on the plantation because it was easier for the teacher to go to the pupils than the reverse. The teacher was either a catechist or some member of the plantation household. However, slaves also attended school away from the plantation, even from the days of Rev Duke. The difficulty involved in this, however, can be seen in the following comment by Duke:

In my Parish there are several deep gullies, to escape travelling through which there is a Circuitry of Paths, which occasions Distance to any central Place; so that as schools are interspersed through various Parts of this Parish, I must fix the young Slaves among those best suited for their Attendance [Associates 1786: 8].

An attendant problem in this was that social distinctions were being threatened when slave children went to schools attended by free children. This would hardly have suited the plantation system which was based on strict demarcations.

When schooling began to be made more general through the agency of institutions attached to the Church of England, the slave market, which had long been seen as an abomination of the Sabbath by people of the Church, came under more direct attack and was specifically identified as an obstacle to progress in education:

There can be no doubt that, when the Law, for the early termination of the Sunday Market, is *fully put in force*, and the benefits of the Sunday Schools are more duly appreciated, great numbers of the younger domestics about the towns will be sent for instruction on the Sabbath [First Annual Report of the St Vincent District Committee of the SPCK for 1826 (printed 1828), p. 6].

This was a clear case where the culture of the mother country and its main institution was in direct conflict with the culture and economics of the colonies. It was a case where the culture transmitted from England came to prevail eventually in the colonies.

THE EFFECT OF SCHOOLING ON ENGLISH IN THE WEST INDIES
UP TO THE TIME OF EMANCIPATION

The schooling of West Indian children was a combination of foreign education, imported education, education for local purposes, and no formal education. For each class, education was meant to be functional, that is, to allow its members to perform and perpetuate their role in society; it was not primarily intended to be and it was not a class changing activity. 'Success' was achieved by determining for each class the range and level of the subject matter permissible in the schooling process. For those children who went to England to be educated, there was no direct parental or church control over what they did, as a result of which the pursuit of social graces and social indulgence, rather than scholarship, became normal for the majority of them. For those children whose schooling took place in the West Indies, direct parental and social control together with Church control put the emphasis on discipline, practical application, and, to some extent, scholarly achievement. The agencies of the Church of England devised a colonial system of schooling that bolstered the church itself, maintained the class structure, and provided some enlightenment for the individual. In this way, schooling made sure that literacy was socially appropriate, but it could not limit it absolutely. Ironically, it was the very philosophy of the church, that education should be of benefit to the poor, and the institutionalizing of schooling which together gave literacy the impetus to move beyond the social levels of appropriateness in the West Indies.

The rise of schools in the West Indies up to the time of Emancipation was to become a major factor in the movement in these islands from oral societies to literate ones. From societies dependent on drums, bells, flags, guns and other visual and aural methods of communication, these societies began to have available more written material, which though less immediate as a medium of communication was more long lasting. As the volume of written and printed information in English increased and as the language differences between the social classes decreased, knowledge acquired through literacy began to make a difference and to cause the lower classes to be more aware of the doings of the upper classes and of persons and groups in Britain and Europe. It was not only the content of the language which increased in influence but also the language itself. Language norms automatically evolved in these societies while at the same time standard English established itself in Britain as the language of society and education.

Paradoxically, as West Indian societies developed their own varieties of language, they started to clutch more tightly on to the norm of the mother country and tried to establish this as their very own. This was to some extent the reverse of the spirit of independence and self-sufficiency which fuelled the USA. British norms were introduced into what was practically an educational vacuum in the West Indies and started on their way to becoming absolute standards. For the literate person generally, the printed word inadvertently becomes the standard against which the spoken language is judged and as a consequence the printed word comes to exert a controlling power over the society as literacy increases. In the West Indies the printed word, which came directly and indirectly out of Britain, increasingly caused the local varieties to be disregarded and written British English to become monolithic in the minds of literate people.

However, English was not the same for all West Indians and it did not affect them equally. For some upper class whites English was, without much difficulty, the language of instruction as well as the language of literature. This was also so for some lower level whites and coloureds whose parents could afford full education for their children. To other coloureds and slaves English was the language of literacy and religion. To the majority of the population, including persons at all levels especially in the eighteenth century, standard English was for practical purposes nonexistent. The effect of written English on the various groups in the society was different because it was intended to be so. The rich had books on literature; those in the middle had accounts books and registers, and those at the bottom, if they had any books, they were the Bible and prayer books. These books not only contained different types of English, but because of their subject matter they also had different effects on their users.

While education for upper class whites and rich coloureds offered a range of possibilities in the professions and the newspaper business, for lower class whites it was tailored towards mid level bureaucratic and skilled jobs. For those in the lowest levels in the society it was the language of religion. For the whites and some coloureds education was geared for the young. In the case of the slaves, education (*ie* religion) was not restricted to any specific age group, although when schools for the poor started only children attended because adults (those over six years old) were not allowed to miss work.

The effect of schooling on the language of the slaves was negligible up to the middle of the nineteenth century. If the total slave population is considered, little was done in the way of education and it was only done in a constructive way a decade or two before Emancipation. Even if one considers only those slaves who received some amount of instruction, it is difficult to see how this instruction could have translated into actual language use. There was little opportunity for them to read English other than in the Bible and prayer books, and even these were not a commonplace in their homes at that time. Only a few had access to newspapers and these also were not common and consistently available in some islands. There were even fewer occasions to write English – love letters and family letters are mentioned in the historical literature, but these are rare. Invitations to dances were also another opportunity for writing, but these were written in a set format which was copied with little modification. In any case, dances requiring invitations were not everyday events. On the occasional plantation a slave may have kept the account book or register, but generally this kind of job was reserved for whites.

The effect of schooling on spoken English was probably greater because much of the religious content had to be memorized, which meant that slaves committed to memory the pronunciations, words and structures of their teachers and priests, and learnt to intersperse them in their normal speech to impress their masters and mistresses in some way. Yet, only a small percentage of the slaves, and very likely few of the field slaves, would have had this advantage. Since proficiency in English would have been of little benefit, unless it went with lightness in colour, few slaves would have immediately sought to improve their speech through education. It is probably only in the case of young slave children that schooling could have affected their language significantly, but even for these there were few contexts for use of learned English in their everyday lives as they grew up.

NOTES

1   These were collected and reprinted in Ryan [1815].
2   According to Caldecott [1898: 121] "The Articles of Capitulation of Trinidad, agreed upon between the Government of Spain in surrendering the island, and the British Government in taking it over, were quite explicit in providing for the toleration of religious views . . ."
3   First Annual Report of the Branch Association of the island of Barbados in aid of the Incorporated Society for the Conversion and religious instruction and education of the Negro Slaves in the British West India Islands, p.17.
4   Note, for example, that Drax in his instructions to his plantation manager [Belgrove 1755: 62] specified that the bookkeeping should be done by a white servant.
5   Even up to the time of Emancipation the British tried to curb the influence of Catholic priests in Grenada by requiring them to obtain licences before they could carry out their duties.
6   "Almost all the negroes are idolaters. It is only those from the Cape Verde, some of whom are Mahometans."
7   This sermon was printed in 1784.
8   Especially when compared with the reaction in St Kitts – See *Some Gentlemen of St. Christopher* [1784].
9   *The Negro's Friend: Notes on Slavery, made during a recent visit to Barbados 1830.*

9

English Language and Literacy in the Early Schools

The rise of schools and schooling in the West Indies represented an alteration in social values and an attempt to use literacy as a controlling force in the future development of the society. An examination of what took place in the schools during the same period up to the time of Emancipation will give a more precise understanding of the effect of schooling and the possible extent of development and competence in English. Some of the elements in the teaching-learning process, *eg* socioeconomic conditions, constraints and attitudes, have been partially examined in the preceding section. Discussion in this chapter will focus on the differences between the schools, the quality of the teachers, the age of the pupils, the curriculum, teaching materials, and the methods of teaching employed. The different reasons for educating the various groups in the society meant that there was of course variation in these elements.

The system of education which began to be implemented in the West Indies carried with it certain assumptions about language teaching and literacy for persons in the West Indies. The colony, its schools and its pupils were believed to be below the level of the mother country, and so the standards of achievement set out by the mother country were in a sense unreachable targets. Adaptation of the language of instruction according to local circumstances was unavoidable, and restriction of academic goals to suit the social structure was seen as necessary to maintain stability in a plantation colony. There therefore developed in the West Indies double and triple standards of achievement – rating of performance according to the context within the territory; rating of performance by comparison with other territories; rating of performance according to perceptions of the absolute performance in the mother country. These ratings were directly related to the status and realistic aspirations of the different pupils in the West Indies. In addition, bearing in mind that English in the West Indies was both a subject and the medium of instruction, English teaching became a confused task of slavishly following British teaching practice, of inculcating British standards and values, and of introducing non-native biblical and religious forms of English to West Indians.

TEACHERS: THEIR LANGUAGE AND COMPETENCE

In the early years teachers were imported, whether they were young indentured servants from England or tutors from the North American colonies, and the model of English that was presented to the children of whites born or being raised in the West Indies was foreign and not sophisticated in any sense. A little later when more of the instruction was taken over by religious persons, there was no significant change in the foreignness of those teaching and in their lack of sophistication. Caldecott [1898: 58-59] says, for example:

Few of the clergy were Creole, born in the Colonies . . . in the main each clergyman was a fresh comer; without colonial traditions or family ties . . . Of the inferior quality of those who came out the evidence is crushing . . . 'Some labourers of the Lord's vineyard have at times been sent who were much better qualified to be retailers of salt-fish, or boatswains to privateers, than ministers of the Gospel'. . .

In Jamaica, the low status of teachers in the middle of the eighteenth century is highlighted in the comments of Leslie [1740: 35]: "The Office of a Teacher is looked upon as contemptible, and no Gentleman keeps Company with one of that Character . . . A Man of any Parts or Learning, that would employ himself in that Business, would be despised and starve." Less than seventy years later, at the beginning of the nineteenth century, the low opinion of teachers in Jamaica was restated and amplified by Stewart [1808: 165]: "But the misfortune is, the teachers in general here are little better than half-educated adventurers, caught fortuitously up in the country, who are little solicitous about the improvement of their pupils, and still less about morals . . ." However, in contrast to the comments by Leslie and Stewart, an advertisement of services by a teacher in *The Antigua Gazette* of 11 November 1767 does not convey the same view of a teacher as a person to be despised, although the fact that he had to advertise his services indicates that people were not flocking to make use of them. After enumerating his offerings, education and talent, the teacher said that he hoped they would "plead in his behalf, and gain him the affection of every lover of sound education, as well as introduce him to the countenance of every well inclin'd man". There are few other significant remarks about teachers at the time to permit a realistic assessment. One notable one, however, is by Dickson [1789: 75]:

A black teacher, who is employed by several white families in Bridge-town, writes a variety of hands very elegantly. I do not say that this implies any great strength of reason; but it implies a taste for the beauty arising from the combination of flowing lines and accurate proportions, a faculty very nearly allied to reason. yet more: he teaches English and arithmetic; and, I believe, assists a certain able geometrician and worthy man in instructing the pretended superior race, in mathematics.

Even though black teachers would have been rare and even rarer black teachers of white children, the very fact that blacks were allowed to do such work suggests that it was not very highly regarded. In any case, there is little doubt that in the mid eighteenth century the influence of teachers on language and culture in the West Indies was minimal.

Yet, almost in contradiction of the low status and morals, qualifications for schoolmasters set out by the Society for the Propagation of the Gospel in Foreign Parts were very noble. Among the listed specifications was the following:

That no Person be sent as a School-master by the Society, till he has been tried and approved by Three Members, appointed by the Society or Committee, who shall testify, by Word or Writing, his Ability to teach Reading, Writing, and the Catechism of the Church of *England*, and such Exposition thereof, as the Society shall order [A Collection of Papers of the SPG, p. 39].

This was just one of a number of stipulations which aimed for high ideals and proven experience in teachers. The obvious unavailability of such persons in sufficient numbers led to a situation where guidelines had to be disregarded and then a system of self-sufficiency pursued. It was in the late eighteenth century and the beginning of the nineteenth that local voices began to be heard in the schools for local whites, as a result of the adoption in the 1820s of the mutual or monitorial teaching structure and the National[1] system of education. The system, when it was first adopted, was one which looked to self-sufficiency on three levels – the Central schools, as the schools of the National Society were called, were designed to produce teachers for themselves, schoolmasters for parochial schools and, in the case of Barbados, schoolmasters for other islands. This system was really the start of the influence of Barbadian(-trained) teachers on neighbouring islands. Early evidence of the achievements of the school in Barbados is given in the Ninth Annual Report of the Barbados Society for the Education of the Poor in the Principles of the Established Church [1828]:

The same system, which has hitherto been pursued, of receiving Training Masters and Mistresses, has been carried on during the last year; and the Committee have the satisfaction to state, that one Master has been trained at the Boys'-school for the island of Tobago, and another for that of Montserrat – while, from the Girls'-school, one Mistress has proceeded to take charge of the School lately formed in Bridge-town . . .; a second has gone to the island of Montserrat, and a third to that of Antigua, thus contributing to make the Central-Schools in this island the means of diffusing the benefits of religious and suitable education among the poor, not only in this, but also in the Sister Colonies (p. 13).

Further evidence of the influence of Barbados is found in the Second Report of the Society for the Education of the Poor in Grenada [1826] which, in its account of activities, said:

> Mr. Rapier, the Master, as announced in the last Report, proceeded to Barbados for the purpose of being himself instructed in the National System of Education by the Reverend Mr. Packer, Master of the Central School in that Island. He returned bringing with him satisfactory Testimonials of his attention, zeal, and ability; and the schools have since been conducted on these Principles, which it will be observed it is now determined are to be rigidly adhered to (p. 14).

The importance of this outward radiating system for the diffusion of British education, the tenets of the Anglican Church and formal knowledge of English is very clear.

The system of supplying other parishes and islands with teachers, as a way to self-sufficiency, was a fairly obvious policy; the method of making a school self-sufficient in teachers without significant cost was an innovation. It was achieved by the mutual or monitorial structure, which meant that the school was like a pyramid in structure. There was a hierarchy of teachers, with the teacher at each level having a specific name. The head of the school was the *Schoolmaster*, who was the only teacher that received a salary; all the other teachers were actually pupils. Under the *Schoolmaster* was the *Teacher*, who was in charge of the class and guided the *Assistant Teacher*, who in turn was in charge of the *Tutor*. The *Tutor* it was who taught the lowest level, the *pupils*.

The workings of this pupil-teacher system are explained by Porteus [1808: 39] as follows:

> Each class is paired off into tutors and pupils. The Tutor sits by the side of his Pupil, and assists him in getting their common lesson.

> To each class is attached an Assistant Teacher, whose sole business it is to attend his class, to prevent idleness, to instruct and help the Tutors in learning their lesson, and teaching their Pupils, and to hear the class, as soon as prepared, say their lesson under

> The Teacher, who has charge of the class, directs and guides his Assistant, intends him in hearing the class, or himself hears both the Assistant and the Scholars say their lesson; and is responsible for the order, behaviour, diligence, and improvement of the class.

One of the benefits of this pupil-teacher system, as stated by Porteus [1808: 42], was that it "cultivates the best dispositions of the heart, by teaching the children to take an early and well directed interest in the welfare of one another". In essence, this was a system of streaming which was continually modified according to the progress of all persons involved. Porteus [1808: 39] explains this as follows: "The scholar ever finds his own level not only in his class, but also in the ranks of the school, being promoted or degraded from place to place, or class to class, according to his proficiency." The streaming of pupils was actually the same as the streaming of teachers and it meant that the most knowledgeable were at the top and the most ignorant at the bottom.

The schools for children of the slaves and the coloured poor were not meant to be supply-schools in the same way, for the slaves were not mobile and independent persons. What was outlined for these schools was a pupil-teacher system which harmonized with the plantation system. The schoolmaster was to be selected, according to Porteus [1808: 44], "from among the Book-Keepers, or other Europeans or Natives in the employment of the Planters", but, in actual fact, some of these *schoolmasters* were products of the Central schools. In the early stages of the implementation of this system of education the teachers were generally no better than they had been previously, when they were "*half-educated adventurers*". Among the black population in the years after Emancipation the competence of some teachers was questionable, so much so that Thome and Kimball [1838: 32] were moved to comment that "many children in the schools of six years old read better than their teachers". In fact, at all times in such a system it would have been common for some of those teaching not to know a great amount of the subject which they were supposed to be teaching, as was actually the case in England where the scheme was fully implemented.

Although the monitorial structure was associated with the Rev Dr Andrew Bell,[2] an Anglican clergyman, who developed it in India, ideas of this kind, intended specifically for the slaves, had been voiced much earlier in St Kitts by Rev Robertson [1730], and even Bishop Porteus himself, in an article first published in 1784 which was adapted and republished in 1807, had broached the idea:

... it would be of the utmost use to select six or seven of the quickest and most docile of their children; to train them up with peculiar care and diligence to a complete knowledge of the English language, and the most essential doctrines and duties of christianity and then employ them as assistants in teaching the other Negroes (pp. 184-85).

It was in fact a system of religious proselytizing which was converted into a teaching system for schools. It was a system that was perfect for the church to introduce into the West Indies because it was inexpensive and not in conflict with the business of the plantation, it facilitated the widespread development of schools and actually resulted in the start of schools in several parishes of most islands. The major consequence for language was that since the pupils were also the teachers, local varieties of English or creole English became the norm as the medium of instruction.

Teaching in the West Indies did not start as a noble profession and neither did it involve persons in the early years who saw it as a path to glory or wealth. Teaching evolved as a practical necessity and as part of a self-perpetuating system. Formal education could not be sustained by imported labour and was regarded as a system which had to produce for its own consumption. The young, imported, barely literate servants, who were the earliest teachers, were gradually replaced by young, local, barely literate whites coming out of fledgling schools, whose task it was, in part, to prepare the next generation of teachers. From the early years of formal education in the West Indies the foreign teacher posed a problem in that there was not always accurate communication between teacher and pupil, since the two did not speak the same language. This was even more so in the case of slaves. Carmichael [1833] prefaces her comments on the instruction of her slaves by saying: "As soon as I perfectly understood the negro dialect, I commenced a regular system of instruction ..." From this one can see that Mrs Carmichael, like most dedicated teachers, realized that it was necessary to understand what the pupils were saying. Few teachers, as can be seen from Mrs Carmichael's "perfectly understood", thought that there was any difficulty involved in doing this. On the other side of the coin, there was little thought given to the idea that the pupils had serious difficulties with the teacher's version of the English language or with the literate form of English when they managed to articulate English words in an intelligible manner and to ape the teacher's pronunciation. In the case of the schools for slaves, teacher/pupil communication was not a problem, seeing that there was no distinction between the two. What was really remote was the possibility of either teacher or pupil ever acquiring "a complete knowledge of the English language", as was the stated intention.

PUPILS: SCHOOL AGE AND LENGTH OF SCHOOL DAY

Because literacy and schooling were merely paths to religious and moral education especially for the black population in the plantation West Indies, and because religious and moral education was meant for young and old alike, age was not really critical to the intent of education of the black population. Education for them at that time was not very distinct from preparation for confirmation or baptism or whatever the specific religious organization called the initial formal rite prescribed by their doctrine. This was especially so in the case of Sunday schools, which began to proliferate around the time of Emancipation. The lack of distinction in age is seen, for example, in the case of St Paul's Sabbath School examination in Barbados in 1837, which Thome and Kimball [1838: 71] comment on as follows: "There were about three hundred pupils present, of all ages, from fifty down to three years." Age was therefore not a deterrent in the Sunday schools. In fact, religious instruction seemed to be viewed as lifelong, for Porteus [1807: 177] proposed that the Negro children be instructed by the catechist till they were fifteen years of age and then they would join the adults to be instructed further by someone else.

However, day schools for the black and coloured population were of necessity restricted by age, not because there was an essential difference in philosophy, but because persons over a certain age had to work, and the starting age for working at that time was very early. In the case of slaves, in the years leading up to Emancipation, when some masters did not overtly oppose attempts at schooling, the only available time for such was between the time the children were babies in the estate nursery and the time when they had to start work in the third gang.

The matter of school age was specifically addressed by Dr Bell in his proposals for an educational system for slaves in the West Indies. Being aware that no normal work time should be lost in pursuit of schooling, Bell, in response to the question of school age, said:

... no age is too early. As soon as children can articulate, they may be taught to pronounce the letters, the printed characters of which they are afterwards to distinguish by the eye and form with the finger. But into the proposed schools, if within due distance, they may enter at four ...

So, the starting age had little to do with readiness for school, but with the amount of time allowed for education and the age at which it had to finish. This was quite clearly pointed out by Thome and Kimball [1838: 32]: "... children were not allowed to attend day school after they were six years old". Therefore, between the ages of four years and six years the slave children had to complete their formal education. The syllabus, if it could be so called, had to be completed within two years, but, according to an example given by Bell, it could be completed in a much quicker time:

John Friskin, a Teacher of twelve years and eight months old, with his Assistants of seven, nine, and eleven years of age, has taught boys of four, five and six years, to read distinctly, and spell every word accurately as they go along, who were only initiated into the mysteries of their ABC eight months before.

A period of two years was not seen as short because there was no model for slave education: it was regarded as a concession and a privilege.

The matter of the number of hours per day which should be allotted to schooling was also addressed by Bell. He suggested that "... if it be only a Sunday school, I should think two hours early in the morning before divine service, and one after evening Service ... If it be a week-day school, one hour every day in the school will be sufficient [Porteus 1808: 46]. Without doubt, therefore, the intention was to put into operation a school system which would cause no loss of slave hours to the planters.

Although concentration on the very young was overtly a plan to appease local planters, it was also a policy which was seen as having important linguistic and religious consequences nationally. This policy is outlined by Porteus [1807: 177]:

This instruction of the Negroe children from their earliest years is one of the most important and essential parts of the whole plan; for it is to the education of the young Negroes that we are principally to look for the success of our spiritual labours. These may be easily taught to understand and speak the English language with fluency.

This would be the same policy later proposed by Coleridge [1826: 127] for the acculturation of St Lucia, Dominica, Grenada and Trinidad, all of which had at the time a strong French influence. This concentration on the very young, whether laudable or insidious, recognized the power of the school and the language of instruction as instruments of colonization and change.

Even after the decision about when children should start to work was removed from the masters (by Emancipation) and put into the hands of parents, there was no substantial change because parents had little choice but to use children to supplement the household income. Therefore, because of the restricted number of years available for the schooling, there was no choice but to start as early as possible. In addition, within a short period of time they had to be given enough to serve as a foundation for the rest of their lives. It is not surprising, then, that Thome and Kimball [1838: 33] could report that in Antigua

Such cases as the following were common in every school: children of four and five years old reading the Bible; children beginning in their A,B,C's, and learning to read in four months; children of five and six, answering a variety of questions on the historical parts of the Old Testament; children but a little older, displaying fine specimens of penmanship . . .

The need to get as much done as quickly as possible meant that what was done was an appearance of learning rather than genuine learning.

In the case of the poor whites and coloureds, school was in a sense a preparation for work in mid level jobs. The school actively sought to place the pupils, especially the poor whites, at the end of their schooling as apprentices in various businesses and trades. The time they actually left school was therefore determined partly by their progress in school, partly by availability of jobs and partly by the resources available for them to stay in school. The Rules and Regulations of the Free-School of Tobago related school leaving to academic achievement: ". . . none to remain after they have learnt and are proficient in Arithmetic as far as Simple Interest" [Fourth Annual Report of the Free-School of Tobago 1832: 6]. On the other hand, schools in Barbados related school leaving to age, and there were instances where pupils were being sent out of school simply because of their age, according to Orderson [1827: 12], who complained that

With scarce more than a smattering of reading and the first rudiments of arithmetic, and with all the predominant indiscretions of vulgar juvenility, it has been the practice as soon as these children arrive at a certain age to dismiss them from school, leaving in general to the parents the entire guidance and direction of their future pursuits.

In other cases attempts were made to try to prevent "the premature departure of the boys from school to trades and other employments, before they are sufficiently qualified" [Ninth Annual Report 1828: 9]. In other words, pupils were leaving when jobs became available, because working was obviously more important than completion of schooling. Despite these and other slight variations, there was a general notion of an age at which children ought to leave school, which was in their mid teens and the stipulations of the National Male and Female schools set up by the Cabildo in Trinidad in the 1820s can be taken as roughly applicable to all Central Schools: "No children to be admitted under 6 years of age, nor above 12 years, without the special permission of the Managing Committee; and none to remain at School after the completion of his or her 15th year" [Rules and Regulations 1826]. Age was therefore a strong controlling factor in a social philosophy which saw childhood as the time for school and adulthood as the time for work. Economic factors gave a sharper definition to this philosophy by determining for each class or group when childhood finished and adulthood began – for the slave the period of childhood was extremely short, for the children of the masters childhood could stretch up to the late teens.

As to the length of the school day, in the case of the National Male and Female schools in Trinidad it was specified as follows: "The hours of instruction will be from 8 to 12, and from 2 until 5" [Rules and Regulations 1826]. In the case of the schools in Barbados it was from 9 to 12 and 2 to 4 [11th Annual Report 1830: 4]. The variation here again was minimal because all the Central Schools across the islands tended to follow similar daily routines.

TEACHING MATERIALS

Monaghan [1989] gives a detailed analysis of literacy instruction in the North American colonies in which it is pointed out that the seventeenth century reading curriculum was the hornbook (a text made of durable material containing the alphabet, the Lord's Prayer and Roman numerals), the primer (a prayer book used to teach children to read), the Psalter (the Book of Psalms), the New Testament and the Bible. Monaghan [1989: 54] says specifically:

The hornbook formed the novice's introduction to reading.

Primers [were] the next step in the reading curriculum.

The next text in both the religious and reading curriculum was the Psalter (the Book of Psalms).

The final two stages in the reading curriculum consisted of mastering the New Testament and then the entire Bible (both Old and New Testaments).

There was not a great deal of difference between the elementary reading materials and reading stages which Monaghan described for seventeenth century America and those used in the West Indies at the end of the eighteenth century. Dickson [1789: 76] gives some information on the reading stages and materials in the West

Indies in the following: "Of nine negro ship-carpenters, now in his Majesty's yard at Antigua, three can read very well, four read in the bible, and two in the spelling-book." It does not seem as if the hornbook was commonly used in the West Indies. It is mentioned by Zouch in his catalogue of 1715 but an advertisement in the *Antigua Gazette* of 11 November 1767 mentions only "testaments, psalters, spelling books, slates and pencils", thereby suggesting that hornbooks were not in common use.

Although most of the teaching materials came directly from England in the eighteenth century especially, there were actually a few books which were either written by West Indians or printed in the West Indies in the eighteenth century and the early nineteenth. In spite of the fact that the 1820s SPCK reports referred to English grammar as a new subject in the schools in the West Indies, an English grammar book had been published much earlier in Antigua; it was written and published in St Johns some time between 1752 and 1756, according to McMurtrie [1943a: 5], and described as follows: "An English Grammar, wrote in a plain familiar manner, adapted to the youth of both sexes. To which are added, some general rules in orthography, – stops or points, – emphasis, – and composition . . ." Presumably there was a great enough demand for this grammar book to justify a local printing of it. Besides this grammar book there was a collection of lectures used as content material. In 1808, Porteus, the Bishop of London, proposed the following for the West Indies:

The schoolmaster also may be directed to read to them a plain, useful discourse, selected from some of our English printed sermons, or from the abridgement of Bishop Wilson's Instructions for the Indians, or from Mr. Duke's Lectures to the Negroes, and other publications of the same nature . . . [Porteus 1808: 15-16]

From this it is evident that Rev Duke's lectures, which had been proposed to the Associates of Dr Bray in 1785, had been written, published and were now being suggested as a text for schools throughout the West Indies. Yet another text which came out of Barbados and, according to Caldecott [1898], was "to be found even to-day among the cottage books of English parishes" was *Lectures on the Gospel of St Matthew*. This book was printed in London in 1824 for the Society for the Conversion and Religious Instruction of Negro Slaves in the British West India Islands and was used extensively among the slaves. It was written by the Rev William Harte, who, like Rev William Duke in the 1780s, was a Barbadian and an Anglican priest.

The publications of Duke and Harte were no doubt influential, but the two major books which had a long and sustained effect on English in the West Indies were the Bible and the Book of Common Prayer. They were used in both school and church. In those islands where Methodists and Moravians were influential, the

Book of Common Prayer gave way to the relevant hymn and prayer books of the denomination. In Barbados where the Anglican Church was all-powerful, from as early as the end of the seventeenth century the Laws of Barbados (p. 251) stated: "The Book of Common-Prayer and Administration of the Sacraments, &c. according to the Use of the Church of England, shall be solemnly read by the Minister or Reader in every Church in this Province." When Sunday schools and other religious schools started, they used the Book of Common Prayer to start and end the school day. Both the Bible and the Book of Common Prayer provided West Indians with a constant seventeenth century model of English for over three hundred years. The close relationship between literacy and the model of written English in the Book of Common Prayer can be seen in the following:

> Some of the adults throughout the parish [St. Lucy] have found means, through their own resources, of having themselves taught to read; and the attendance of those persons at Church, with their Common Prayer books in their hands, reading and joining in the service, is truly pleasing [First Annual Report of the Branch Association of the Island of Barbados in aid of the Incorporated Society for the Conversion and religious instruction and Education of the Negro Slaves in the British West India Islands 1826: 11].

The fact is that for all except the ruling class in the plantation slave society there was very little else to read other than church material. For those who belonged to the Anglican Church the Book of Common Prayer was like a textbook in the sense that it was constantly and repeatedly read by the minister and followed by the congregation until it was known by heart. The Bible was not used in the same way, but its advantage was that it was not restricted to the Anglican religion.

By 1837 when Thome and Kimball visited Antigua, by their account the Bible had become the only textbook in use in schools: "We learned that the Bible was the principal book taught in all schools throughout the island. As soon as the children have learned to read, the Bible is put into their hands. They not only read it, but commit to memory portions of it every day..." [1838: 32]. The former slaves were therefore still being retained within the bounds of religious education, and literacy was still being seen simply as a medium for the retention, acceptance and propagation of Christian doctrine and literature.

Beyond the elementary level of religious instruction and literacy, education was intensely practical. The best known school books of the time comprehended a wide range of subjects. For example, *The American Instructor; or Young Man's Best Companion* (the ninth edition of which was published in Philadelphia in 1748) was based on an English 'textbook' (*Fisher's Young Man's Companion*) and gave instruction on almost every conceivable job at the time. It was a small, but dense and thick book, which covered topics such as reading, writing, arithmetic, higher levels of mathematics, prose and verse writing, legal contracts and bonds, diseases and cures, other trades and professions, history, geography and meteorology. It was like a small encyclopedia and was intended as a reference book to be consulted for guidance whenever required. Since there was constant communication between Philadelphia and the West Indies, the American version was available and used in the West Indies.[3] The English version, however, appears in a list of schoolbooks advertised for sale in the Saturday, 8 November 1800 issue of *The Charibbean Courier; or, St. Christopher Chronicle*:

Fisher's Young Man's Companion
Ditto's Arithmetic
The Schoolmaster's Assistant
School Bibles
Testaments of different sizes
Watt's Divine Songs and Hymns.

These books were intended for the teacher, who used them as the absolute authorities on the subjects that they dealt with.

Within the schools themselves, especially those set up by agencies of the Church of England, there was a certain rigidity in the daily procedure and in the texts used. For example, in the schools for poor whites and coloureds there was a similarity in the texts used in the various islands. The 11th Annual Report of the Barbados Society for the Education of the Poor [1830: 5] said that: "The books used are, in the upper classes, the Bible, and Trimmer's *Abridgement of Scripture*: and in the lower, the Elementary books recommended by the National Society. The rudiments of English Grammar are taught, from Murray's Abridgement, to the head class, twice in the week."

The similarity in school texts resulted from a rigid policy in the National system of 'Central Schools', which was transmitted from England to the various islands as well as from Barbados to those islands which were dependent on Barbados.

METHODS OF INSTRUCTION

The method of instruction was substantially determined by the fact that education was primarily training in the texts of a specific denomination. It was a matter of learning by heart prayers (especially the Lord's Prayer), the Apostles' Creed, the Commandments and even the Liturgy. Memorization was therefore the first and main method of learning. The significance of this is that West Indians, especially those of the lower classes, were adding the literature of a new religious culture on to the residual traditional beliefs which they inherited from their parents and grandparents, as well as committing to memory and so adding to their repertoire a variety of English which was foreign as well as old. In addition, since the texts were presented to the pupils orally, it is quite obvious that what the pupils heard, *ie* their interpretation of the actual forms, was in many cases different from what was said. The variety of English heard had to be mediated through the pupils' own variety of English. For example, parts of words in weakly articulated positions would not have been heard, and in fact many of the noun and verb endings of English would not have been perceived by pupils whose language had no such distinctive markers.

However, pupils were able to memorize substantial portions of texts while understanding very little of them. This kind of performing without understanding is ridiculed by Coleridge [1826: 228] who, on witnessing church activity in Anguilla, said:

The serenity of the neighbourhood was disturbed in the evening when I was there, by the worse than Popish mummery of class meetings; the young women and children were screaming out by rote some hymns and songs with an asperity and discordance of tone which seemed to make Nature angry, and exhibiting a scene of such mechanical superstition and senseless perversion of Christian worship as might well have caused a wiser man than me to weep for the possible absurdities of mankind.

This was not simply memorization but choral repetition and singing. Although this was a normal part of religious practice, what made it seem absurd to Coleridge was that there seemed to be little understanding.

Singing, as a technique of persuasion, had been specifically commented on by Bishop Porteus in his policy statements on education for the West Indian slaves. In his collected *Tracts on Various Subjects*, which were republished in 1807, he recommends "composing short hymns... set to plain, easy, solemn psalm tunes, as nearly resembling their own simple melody as possible... This would make them see christianity in a much more pleasing light than they generally do..." (p. 183). The importance of singing as a technique of persuasion and as a feature of rote learning is shown by its being maintained later in the more famous "mico schools",[4] a practice pointed out, and again ridiculed, by Day [1852, 2:274-75]:

Singing seems to be the grand feature, and I hear the children singing in chorus half the day. Pious ejaculations are accompanied by the drollest tunes. As a specimen, I may mention one of the St Vincent melodies:

'Holy Bible, book divine, tural-ural, tural-ural,
Precious, precious, thou art mine, tural-ural, tural-ural.'

The tune was 'Bonnie laddie, sodger laddie'.
'A boat, a boat unto the ferry', is another infantile chorus, whilst the children promenade round the school-room.

When the children were dismissed, the seminary was attended by adult teachers from seven P.M. until nine o'clock, and then I had the benefit of the full choir. 'Here's a health to all good lasses', was a favourite glee. Coloured ladies as teachers joined the class, and gave the 'Canadian Boat Song'.

As can be seen from the songs identified by Day, by that time the material had moved outside the strictly religious, but singing as feature of learning continued to play a significant role in school activity.

From the more secular songs identified above by Day one can see quite clearly that the references and contexts would have been outside the experience and understanding of the West Indians who were forced to memorize them. The same was also true about the Christian material which was 'taught' to West Indian slaves from much earlier. This point is made by Mrs Carmichael, also writing about St Vincent:

> Our own people always attended, and invariably asserted that they 'understood all that the parson told them'; but when I came to examine them upon what they had heard, it was evident that they had not one rational or distinct idea upon the subject, although many of them had attended regularly for years [vol. 1:237].

In further comments on the teaching/learning process among the black population in St Vincent Carmichael [1833, vol. 1] says: "... that led me to the conviction that religious instruction had not hitherto been conveyed to the negro in a sufficiently plain form ... (p. 221) ... I feel convinced ... that the slave population comprehended almost nothing of it ..." (p. 237). Although much of Mrs Carmichael's prejudice was caused by the presence of Methodists in St Vincent at the same time, the comments about the comprehension of religious material were quite valid. From these and other comments made by Mrs Carmichael it is clear that the form of the language itself came to have greater significance as a 'sign of Christianity' more so than the understanding of what it represented.

This was a system in which form of language and meaning were not in synchrony, but where execution of form was often the criterion used to measure achievement. Note, for example, the points made by Coleridge [1826], firstly about a school in Trinidad:

> The boys read and repeat English so well that it is difficult to detect the foreign accent ... (p. 93)
>
> In the school in Port of Spain boys of various nations read the authorized version of the New Testament, and repeat the catechism of the Church of England, and none but a practised ear can detect the vernacular tongue of the speaker (p. 127).

and secondly about a school in Antigua: "There is one small school for the education of white children of both sexes, which, as far as it went, was in good order, and the scholars taught to read and speak with a pure accent" (p. 253). The absence of comment about the learners' understanding of the material and the repetition of emphasis on the 'accent' leaves no doubt about the assumptions of educators at the time. No doubt teachers believed that understanding automatically accompanied or followed good execution of form. This kind of language learning theory must not be seen to be deliberately perverse, for it has existed for a long time outside of colonial situations and up until recently was boldly propounded within behaviourist approaches to learning.

There were some important consequences for the West Indies of this method of rote learning which had been adopted from Europe. First, rote learning was in keeping with a social system which required the mass of the population to carry out orders without question. It was not a method that encouraged the learner to think, challenge or create, but one which facilitated the perpetuation of the status quo. Secondly, the emphasis on aping the pronunciation of the English in the school system partially explains how social values attached to language form came to dominate West Indian society at large, to separate persons into classes, and to be an indicator of level of achievement. For example, the statements in an issue of *The Barbados Gazette* of 1732, in Poole [1753: 288], in Thompson [1770: 126] as well as in Carmichael [1833, 1:77] which point out that white women and children showed the influence of the slaves' language more than the men testify to the social significance of different registers. Poole specifically claims that in the case of women the reason for it was *the want of proper care in their education*. If this is true, it means that language education was already being seen, from as early as the first half of the eighteenth century, as a way for the whites to distance themselves from the black population. It means also that the practice of an acquired 'accent' or the schooling away of the native 'accent' was one of the earliest goals of education in the West Indies.

In fact, rote learning fitted perfectly into the general process of acculturation and deculturation in which imitation of British culture and the English language was as much the target on the one hand as was the removal of all traces of Africa on the other. This was so for everyone. So, while imitation was being diligently pursued on the one hand, the whites had to be kept from the influence of the blacks and the creole blacks had to be kept from the influence of the Africans. In this connection, note the comment of Porteus [1807: 189]: "Another great means of promoting and facilitating the conversion of our [Codrington Estate] Negroes would be to prevent as much as possible their communication with the Negroes of the other plantations, and the importation of fresh slaves from Africa." This was an early expression of the belief that acquisition of one culture and language could be disrupted by exposure to another.

As to the methods used to teach writing, Day [1852, 2:315] identified one which he witnessed in Antigua and which one must assume had been used from earlier, because it was apparently a simple, practical, oral method:

Another class was learning to write, on a most extraordinary principle, and one which I cannot think good. It will be best understood, by supposing a monitor to call out 'pot-hook', 'hangar', or 'curve with a tail', and 'curve without a tail', though these were not the actual words used. The consequence is, that the formation of the letters, though quite correct, is quite mechanical, and is done without reference to their character as letters.

Here it seems as if the letters were not being referred to (solely) by their normal names, but were being described according to their shape in simple and appealing terms so that the young learners could better remember them. Although there is no evidence to show how widespread this kind of method was, there is no doubt that the lack of an adequate supply of writing materials and the absence of a long normative history of the teaching of writing would have caused teachers to be creative in various sorts of ways.

Day was, no doubt, driven by his characteristic prejudice when he suggested a negative consequence of the method used, which focused on the shape or formation of the letters almost exclusively rather than on the sound-symbol relationship, that is, on what today is the substance of the phonic method. Day situated this within a general context of 'parrot-like' learning by children in the West Indies, which by the way he describes it indicates that this was not so in England and was obviously devised for the 'simpler' minds in the West Indies. This notion of developing techniques for the simpler mind was quite pervasive in the literature of the time so that even William Harte, who was a Barbadian, was very concerned in his lectures on the Gospel of St Matthew to reduce his material to simplicity. Even if in the case of the teaching of writing it cannot be proven that a method which concentrates on shape is worse than one which establishes sound-symbol relationships, because the method identified by Day was a part of a general approach which assumed simple-mindedness on the part of the learner, it would have been in that sense not good for the learner since it was forming and propagating a dangerous attitude.

LANGUAGE AND THE CURRICULUM

The curriculum that was intended for the education of upper-level whites in the few grammar schools available to them or by private tuition in the West Indies was exactly the same as that in England. Curtis [1968: 110] referring to the situation in England at the end of the sixteenth century says:

In their curriculum and methods of instruction the schools had settled down to a narrow, formal, and academic outlook which was out of contact with the growing demands of the age. The discovery and settlement of new lands resulting in a great expansion of commerce, the new outlook which was developing as a consequence of the growth of mathematical and scientific knowledge, the freshly awakened spirit of philosophy, and the rich contributions to life and thought made by perhaps the greatest period in the history of our literature, had little impact upon the schools, which concentrated upon the learning of Latin grammar and the rather pedantic study of a few classical authors. More and more, the grammar schools occupied themselves with the task of preparing their pupils for entrance to the universities, from which they emerged to become clergymen, lawyers, doctors, or even schoolmasters, and thus help to perpetuate the system.

It is clear from this that the grammar school was the hub of a self-perpetuating system which favoured a small select number of jobs in society – jobs which in time came to be thought of as requiring special education, were distinguished by the designation 'professions', and also conferred on those persons who practised them a high level of social esteem. Those West Indians who wanted to go to a university in England followed the same classical grammar education.

English grammar as a subject for study became increasingly popular in the second half of the eighteenth century. After Samuel Johnson's dictionary was published in 1755 and became an arbiter for words and meanings in English, *The Rudiments of English Grammar* by Joseph Priestly appeared in 1761. In 1762 *Short Introduction to English Grammar* by Lowth and *The British Grammar* by Buchanan both appeared. In 1794 *English Grammar* by Lindley Murray was published to add to the increasing number of authorities on the English language. All these works and others of prescriptive intent projected the image of English as formal, standard and uniform and as an area of knowledge to be mastered through rigorous schooling. The school teacher rules emerging out of these books moved far beyond techniques for mastering written English and were seen to be part of a course of logic, culture and discipline necessary for the proper upbringing of all children.

If one is to judge from an advertisement in *The Antigua Gazette* of 11 November 1767, language teaching in the West Indies was not restricted to the classical languages and English grammar, for one of the offerings advertised by the schoolmaster at a boarding-school was ". . . that most useful and necessary branch of education, the French language, universally spoke throughout all the courts of Europe". Another advertisement in the *Barbados Mercury* of 18 August 1787 identifed not only French but also Spanish:

John LeBlanc
Lately from Europe

Respectfully informs the public that he has had the honour of His Excellency's permission to open a school in the island, which he proposes to do for the instruction of young ladies and gentlemen, in the French and Spanish Languages, grammatically, upon the most approved plan practised in England, where he has had the honor of residing some time in the capacity of tutor . . .

Whether French was regarded with the same attitude in the other older British colonies at the time and whether there were teachers qualified to teach it cannot be easily determined.

The school curricula for lower social levels which were gradually introduced into the West Indies were also patterned on those in England. However, economic factors and social structure delayed the introduction of these in a comprehensive way for a number of years. Educational needs for the (lower-level) whites in the mid eighteenth century West Indies were not thought to be extensive, as can be seen from the remark of Leslie [1740: 35], which refers specifically to Jamaica: "... to read, write and cast accounts, is all the education they desire..." The number of lower-level whites was small and the range of jobs which they did was limited. The schools for poor whites could therefore follow a fairly narrow curriculum without any disruption to them or the society. While the words of Leslie suggest a fairly secular education, the very opposite was the main intention of schools set up at the beginning of the nineteenth century. When the Colonial Charity School began in Barbados in 1818, its stated aim was "the Education in Reading, Writing, and Arithmetic", but this was within a specific and quite clearly stated framework:

The most prominent feature in this Institution, shall be a well-digested system of religious education, *in strict and undeviating conformity with the principles of the Established Episcopal Church*, and subject, in this respect, to the regulations and restrictions of the Colonial Clergy, under future arrangements [Proposed Institution of a Colonial Charity School, p. 3].

When the National Society school system was a little later introduced into all the islands, the concerns of the school did not widen significantly, as is clear from the following:

The course of instruction pursued is strictly according to that of the National Schools in England, with the addition of English Grammar and the higher rules of Arithmetic to the upper classes... Religious instruction, reading, writing, and cyphering[5] (alternately) occupy the morning and afternoon in the Boys' School. The Girls are occupied in needlework in the afternoon; and even the Boys, who are boarders, make and mend all their own clothes; and it is in contemplation to have them farther instructed in book-binding [8th Annual Report BSPCK 1827: 17].

A more detailed account of what went on during the school day appears in the 11th Annual Report of the Barbados Society for the Education of the Poor [1830: 4-5]:

At nine o'clock the School is opened with prayers, which are read by the Reverend Mr. Redwar, the Master, after the Morning Hymn has been sung. The prayers used are the Collect for the Sunday previous, the Collects for Peace and Grace, and the Lord's Prayer, concluding by the Apostolic Benediction. Each class is then catechised till ten o'clock in the Church Catechism, in the Catechism broken into short questions, and in that by Crossman, according to the respective attainments and rank of each. Two hours are then devoted to reading, to writing (on paper and slate), and to arithmetic, which subjects occupy the remainder of the day from ten till twelve; between this hour and one, the children are again employed in making or mending their clothes, and in preparing their table neatly for dinner, which is served to them at one o'clock. At two, School is re-opened, and the boys are exclusively engaged in reading, writing, and arithmetic. At four, the School is closed with prayers and a hymn. The boarders are called in at six, from their play-ground, to supper; and in the course of the evening, for about an hour, one of the elder-boys reads aloud in turn, from some work of amusement and general instruction out of the School Library. At eight, they retire to their dormitory, where the short prayer for a young person from Crossman's Catechism is read aloud by the head-boy.

The subjects covered in these schools prepared the school leaver mainly for bookkeeping jobs on the plantation or in businesses. In addition, he/she was supposed to be practical and self-sufficient.

The extent of the curriculum was even narrower for the slaves. All that the slave was thought to need in the eighteenth century and the early nineteenth century West Indies was religious education. What this meant in actual subjects was reading, English and religious knowledge, and in actual practice these three were collapsed into one since the material used to teach reading was religious and written in English. The Instructions for Schoolmasters employed by the SPG specified that the main purpose of the teachers was "the instructing and disposing Children to believe and live as Christians" [A Collection of Papers 1715: 35], and that to achieve this they were to

... teach them to read truly and distinctly, that they may be capable of reading the Holy Scriptures, and other pious and useful books, for informing their Understandings, and regulating their Manners.

... instruct them thoroughly in the Church-Catechism; teach them first to read it distinctly and exactly, then to learn it perfectly by Heart; endeavouring to make them understand the Sense and Meaning of it, by the Help of such Expositions as the Society shall send over.

... teach them to write a plain and legible Hand, in order to the fitting them for useful Employments; with as much Arithmetick as shall be necessary to the same purpose [A Collection of Papers 1715: 35-36].

Even this seemed too much for some, for an argument was put forward that religious education could be given orally and without use of written material. To counter this, Porteus [1808: 21] put forward the following argument: "It has been said that *oral* instruction will be sufficient to make the Negro Slaves good Christians. It may possibly succeed with some of good memories and a better sort of understanding. But with the bulk of dull African Negroes it will not." Ironically, then, access to literacy was justified, not because it was a useful additional skill, but on the grounds that it was a support for poor memory and low intellect. The same argument was not made for writing, which at the time was distinct from reading.

At all social levels some form of literacy was taught, but as is evident in citations above, reading and writing were treated as different subjects. Reading was a matter of deciphering written material and was done by an oral method. In this method the pupils imitated and repeated the teacher's spoken version of the written symbols until they were known. Practice continued as pupils moved from symbols to words to sentences. No writing was involved. The distinction between reading and writing was quite clear in the early days of education in contrast to today when the two skills are referred to as if they are synonymous and simultaneous. The difference had to do with the purpose for which the skill was intended. In those days reading

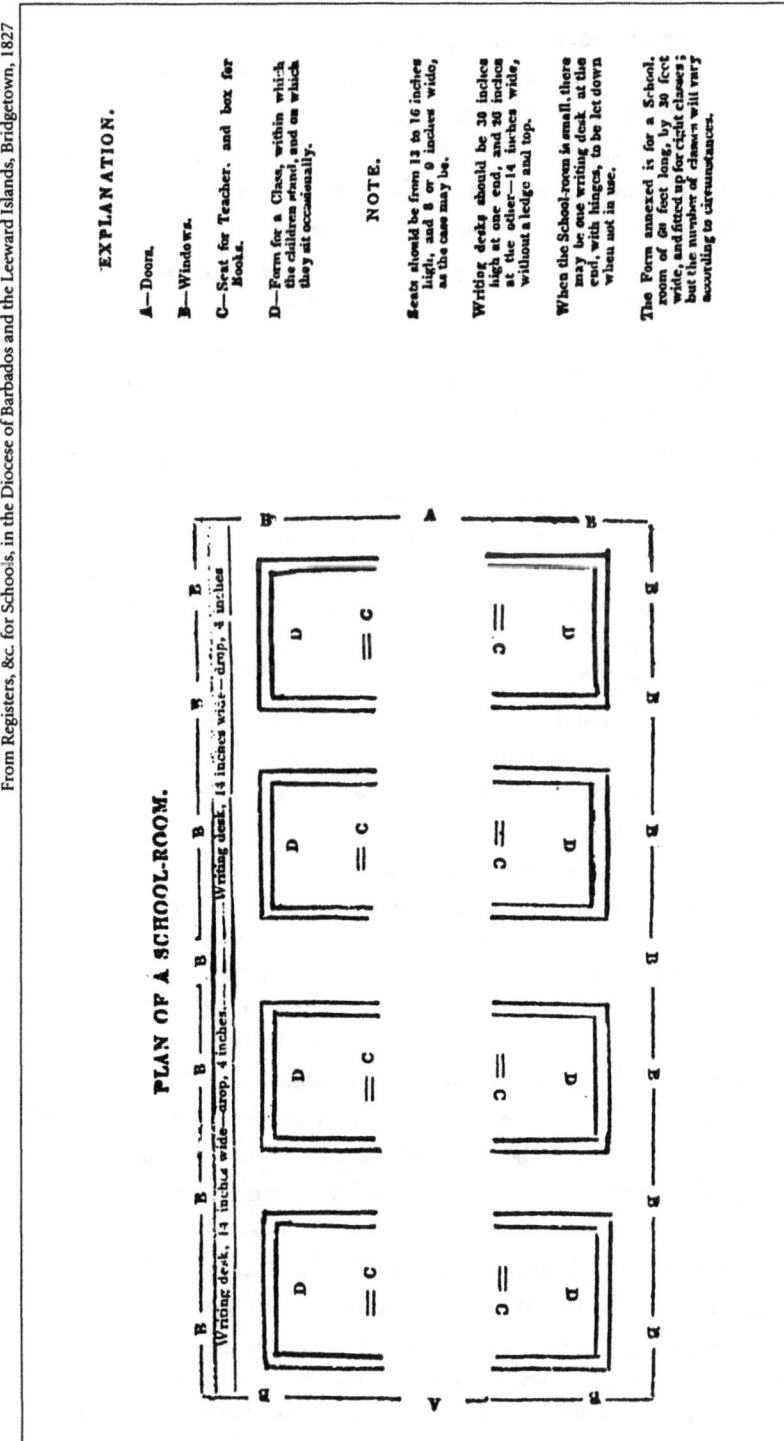

FIGURE 9.1: Plan of a School-Room

was meant to be a receptive and passive process – children, especially of the working classes, were being converted into becoming members of a church and conditioned into being well behaved and docile members of society. Reading was therefore a way of opening a door for them to enter the church and to participate as individuals by being able to read the Scriptures and to follow the service on their own.

The concept of writing today is one of manual dexterity as well as creativity in reflective language. Before the nineteenth and twentieth centuries writing was more the former than the latter; it conformed more with the idea of a scribe, a person who could copy and transcribe language. In society of that time writing was required in a general way for book and record keeping purposes, and in a more specific way the intelligentsia needed it to disseminate and discuss ideas, philosophies and research, although for this latter purpose the number of people who needed to write was relatively small and restricted. Teaching of writing was therefore a matter of coaching in different scripts, as explained in an advertisement in *The Antigua Gazette* of 11 November 1767: ". . . the strong bold text, the German text, the secretary, the round and Italian hands, in a neat penmanlike manner . . ." It was certainly not meant to be a medium for creative works, especially in a plantation slave society.

Teaching the children of the coloured poor and slaves to write was therefore to give them a competence to do jobs from which they were normally barred. This was clearly unacceptable to entrenched interests whose views were that certain jobs had to be protected and social stability had to be maintained. In commenting on the curriculum for the slaves, Porteus [1808: 22n] says:

> It should be recollected also, that in the plan here proposed, there is no mention of teaching the Negro children to write but only to read; which will always be a strong mark of discrimination, a wall of partition, between them and the white inhabitants; will always preserve a proper distinction and subordination between them and their superiors, and present an insurmountable barrier against their approaching to anything like an equality with their masters.

These words of the Bishop of the Anglican Church who had direct responsibility for the West Indian islands show how the curriculum was to be deliberately restricted and used openly with the church's blessing to maintain racial separation.

This restriction remained in force up to the time of Emancipation and so the teaching of writing to the children of the free coloured and slaves was prohibited. The following extract from Coleridge [1826: 51-52] points this out, while conceding at the same time that such a restriction would eventually disappear:

> . . . These children [in schools opened by Bishop Coleridge] are chiefly of the lowest order of the free colored and the domestic and mechanic slaves in Bridge Town and the immediate vicinity. They are not at present taught to write, a point certainly not of any vital importance, and wisely conceded to prejudices which will in due time melt away under a conviction of the propriety of the knowledge and the futility of the prohibition.

Part of the reason for the disappearance of the restriction was the decline of the white population and the greater need for writing as West Indian societies at large moved nearer to the practices of more literate societies. The Industrial Revolution, which influenced European and North American countries and made general education and the ability to read and write become a part of the life of all classes of individuals, gradually affected the West Indies in the same way.

ASSESSMENT OF PROGRESS

Schooling was controlled by reports, which were written. The reports were intended to make sure that set policy (written rules and regulations) was followed without deviation. The dominance of report books in the school system can be seen in the following stipulation:

The Committee will keep a Book for the occasional inspection and approval of the Cabildo, in which will be recorded the Names, Ages, Residence, and Designation of the Children; their Parents or Guardians; the period of their Entry to the School, and under whose Certificate of Recommendation. The Master and Mistress will keep corresponding Books, in which they will note the progress of each scholar; and of the exact number of days of attendance in the School; which Book will be open to the inspection of the Visitors and Committee [Rules and Regulations 1826].

Record keeping was seen as an essential element in decision making in the assessment procedure, that is, in determining promotion as well as in determining whether children should be retained in school. The register of attendance and the register of progress became the crucial instruments for the teacher. The rigid system together with the two registers, while understandable from an administrative point of view, therefore tended to consume the energies of the school masters.

Both the school and the pupils were constantly assessed in a scheduled as well as an ad hoc manner. The assessment of the school could done by persons identified as 'visitors' in the following way: "Two Visitors from the General Committee to be appointed every week, who will make it their business, individually and collectively, in the morning and at noon, to visit the School, see that the proper system is kept up, and to correct irregularities . . ." [Proposed Institution of a Colonial Charity School, p. 7]. As far as the pupils at the Central schools were concerned, progress was assessed and rewarded in various ways. For example, at the level of the teacher, in those classes which were privileged to be taught writing, slates were used generally but a writing book was given as a reward for good writing. Prizes and compliments were also given for good attendance and behaviour, based on the reports. In addition, prizes were awarded for reading and writing based on examination results. The first Annual Report of the St Vincent District Committee of the SPCK [1828] recorded with pride "the extraordinary proficiency of the following pupils, to whom prizes were awarded" for:

Boys first class	best reader
	next best reader
	best writer
Boys second class	best reader
Girls first class	best reader
	next best reader
Girls second class	best reader

These were identified as prizes given for performance in the examination which took place before the Christmas vacation.

There were also examinations given to the pupils by visiting dignitaries. For example, when the governor, his wife and daughter visited the Central school in St Vincent, it is recorded in the minutes that: "At the desire of these exalted visitors, the first class of both sexes were examined, with whose improvement his Excellency expressed himself much pleased, and desired that a holiday should be given the children" [St Vincent District Committee of the SPCK 1828: 11]. There was also a scheduled Public Annual Examination of the children which took place at the end of the school year in August, described in the minutes of the Twelfth Annual Report of the Barbados Society [1831]:

The Bishop very condescendingly undertook to conduct the examination; and at the conclusion of it, his Lordship was pleased to express a very favourable opinion of the manner in which the children of both schools had acquitted themselves. Their proficiency in reading, writing, and arithmetic, and their correct answers to the questions proposed to them, were creditable to themselves, and afforded very general satisfaction (p. 11-12).

There seemed to be much in common between the public examination for the school and the 'examination' during the confirmation ceremony in the church.

What these procedures for assessment indicate, above all, is that these early schools must have been very authoritarian and tense places with a strict hierarchy of control. They must have been frightening at times for both teacher and pupils. It seemed as if they had always to be ready to be assessed at any moment and that there had always to be an appearance of order and activity in conformity with a set programme.

THE EFFECTS OF FORMAL EDUCATION

Literacy is said to have many consequences, but the question which is not easily answered is whether literacy automatically and independently has any direct consequences. In many studies of development, it has been shown, for example, that as literacy increases in a society the birthrate decreases. In such a correlation, it is obvious that there is no direct connection between the brain and the organs of

Language and Literacy in Schools / 259

Present State and Proficiency of the Boys' School, March 29, 1831.

CLASS.	No. in Class.	Daily Attendance.	READING.	WRITING.	CYPHERING.	RELIGIOUS INSTRUCTION.	REMARKS.
First..	25	21	The Bible and Nat. School Reader.	OnPaper.	Practice, Rule of Three, Reduction, &c. &c. &c.	Crosman's Catech.daily; and Collect, Epistle, and Gospel for Sunday previous repeated on Monday morning—Ch Catech. once a week.	This class reads Trimmer's Selections from O. and N. Test., with the Script.Catech., as well as the Bible, and the N. S. Reader is read twice a week.
Second	10	10	Trimmer's Selections from Old and New Testament.	Ditto.	Rule of Three.	Crosman's Catech., and Collect, Epistle, and Gospel—Ch. Catech. once a week.	
Third	22	19	New Testament.	Ditto.	Weights and Measures.	Ch. Catch. broken into short questions—Collect and Gospel.	Only some of this class write on paper—a writing-book is given as a reward for good writing.
Fourth	22	19	Miracles.	OnSlates.	Short Division.	Church Catech. and Collect.	
Fifth	25	18	Parables.	Ditto.	Addition and Subtraction.	Ditto.	
Sixth	25	20	N. S. S. Book No. 2, Spelling Cards and Alphabet.		Addition and the Digits.	Ditto and Collect, with the Lord's Prayer, Belief, Ten Comdts., and Grace before and after Meat.	This class is divided into two parts—one of boys, reading N. S. S. Book No. 2, another of boys in spelling cards & alphabet.
Total	129	107					

Of this number 42 are boarders, and 87 day-scholars.

N.B.—All the boarders who are clothed by the Society, make their own clothes at intervals between the hours of School. The hours of School are from 9 to 12, and from 2 to 5 o'clock every day, Saturday excepted. On Sunday they attend Church twice a-day, and a few attend for the purpose of singing at the third or Evening Service.

Present State and Proficiency of the Girl's School, March 29, 1831.

CLASS.	No. in Class.	Daily Attendance.	READING.	WRITING.	CYPHERING.	RELIGIOUS INSTRUCTION.	REMARKS.
First..	19	15	Psalms and Mrs. Trimmers Abridgments.	Collects and parts of Scrip. on slates.	Three qrts. of an hour daily, Long Division.	Crosman's and Church Catechism, three quarters of an hour daily.	Can make fine Shirts.
Second	16	14	Ostervald's abridgment of the Bible.	Writing from Script Cards on Slates.	Multiplication Simple.	Church Catechism broken into short questions.	Can make coarse Shirts.
Third	15	13	Our blessed Saviour's Sermon on the mount.	From Script Cards on Slates.	Addition.	Church Catechism.	Can Hem and Sew.
Fourth	17	14	N. S. C. S. Book. First Part.	From Script Cards on Slates.	Digits.	Church Catechism.	Learning to Hem and Sew.
Fifth	3	3	Learning the Alphabet.	Making Letters on Slates.		Learning the Lord's Prayer. Belief, Graces, &c.	Ditto.
Total	70	59					

Of this number 24 are boarders, and 46 day-scholars.

From the Twelfth Annual Report of the Barbados Society for the Education of the Poor in the principles of the Established Church

FIGURE 9.2: Present State and Proficiency of the Boys' School, 29 March 1831 and Present State and Proficiency of the Girl's School, 29 March 1831

reproduction – the change can be said to be the result of knowledge and reasoning. Much of recent debate on literacy has concentrated on making a distinction between factors which can be verified to be exclusively a result of the acquisition of literacy and factors which simply follow the acquisition of literacy. Works such as Graff [1979], Street [1984], Scribner and Cole [1981] do not support generally held beliefs about either the intellectual, social or economic benefits afforded the individual simply by learning to read and write. Their claim is, and justifiably so, that unless literacy is accompanied by other freedoms and facilities, it will not unlock doors that are deliberately shut. This is especially so in cases of racial and other types of segregation. In the West Indies, for example, where whites set up barriers to protect themselves physically, to protect their women and to protect their jobs, the removal of these barriers was not achieved and could not have been simply by black literacy.

However, rather than pursue the current arguments about the verifiable consequences of literacy exclusively, it is more useful to treat literacy as having a cultural ecology from which in reality it is not separated and which in its context has certain consequences. So, although one can distinguish between competence and actual practice, it is the reality of the situation that is important. For example, an individual may be able to read and write, but that individual may not be in the habit of doing either because his everyday life does not require either. Or it may be that the immediate context of the individual has no materials of literacy (*eg* an isolated rural community). In neither case can the competence of the individual be said to be of any immediate benefit. This was exactly the situation of the majority of people, black and white, in the plantation slave society.

Since literacy can never be separated from its cultural ecology, even a positive answer to the question whether literacy has cognitive consequences is insignificant unless there is a context which gives it advantage. This fact is especially relevant to slave societies, which contained rigid stratification and racial segregation deliberately set up to restrict mobility. Note, for example, that on Codrington's estates provision was made, according to Codrington's will, for slaves to be taught to read, but this had little practical effect, as is pointed out by Thome and Kimball [1838: 60]: "The negroes belonging to the estate have for upwards of a hundred years been under this kind of instruction. They have all been taught to read, though in many instances they have forgotten all they learned, having no opportunity to improve after they left school." Even when slavery was formally discontinued, most of the social structures which maintained it were not removed.

The lack of effect of illiteracy in such contexts is pointed out by Graff [1979: 81]: "To a racial minority, faced with racial discrimination, education brought no discernible benefits and illiteracy no detriments, race carried an independent influence." Graff is here talking about Blacks in Canada in the nineteenth century, but in the West Indies in the slavery period the same was true. Blacks, because of their colour, were excluded from participation in 'intellectual' and literacy activities. For a long time this did not matter, for there was little advantage to be gained from being black and literate, especially in an agricultural society. However, as methods of management in these societies changed increasingly from oral to written, the need for literacy grew and so did the belief in the powers of literacy.

Yet, in spite of the absence of materials of literacy and in spite of the barriers set up, there was a belief and fear on the part of the whites that literacy and education would be liberating forces. The idea of access to knowledge as a liberating force is summed up in the following by Coleridge [1826: 322]:

For it will be impossible to circumscribe the educated slave within his present bounds; those limits will not contain his dilated form. It will be impossible to march the negros on the road of knowledge and compel them to stand at ease within the old entrenchments of ignorance. There is a natural connection between moral refinement and political amelioration; they can be divorced by violence alone and they bear in their essences a mutual and indestructible tendency to an equilibrium.

The same kind of thinking is implicit in the following taken from Shephard [1831: 210] in relation to St Vincent:

The Legislature has removed the disabilities attendant on colour, but these concessions will be of no actual benefit to that race, unless they become qualified by education and morals, to assume their advanced station in society, and to perform the duties required of them, and this will depend on their exertions, to obtain property by their industry, and respect by their integrity; the road to fame and eminence is open to all.

Even more recently, Salvino [1989: 150] makes a claim for the transcendent power of literacy by saying that: "It is possible that the acquisition of literacy – supported by the belief that literacy is a means to freedom – led to an increased awareness of the possibilities of escape or resistance to slavery, and provided an effective weapon in implementing escape plans. However, even if literacy could be said to have provided the possibility to go outside the prescribed and the status quo, social pressures against independent thought were strong and those putting forward such thoughts were branded as socially disruptive. From George Fox in 1671 to William Harte in 1825 the reaction of the ruling class to the teaching of literacy to the slaves was vehemently negative and threatening. In such conditions and with such conditioning, it was hardly possible for literacy to be a liberating force to the slaves or the poor whites.

This idea of an inherent power in literacy and knowledge clearly relegates other social and economic forces to subordinate positions. The obvious argument behind this idea is that knowledge will create a powerful, irresistible and relentless demand for more knowledge which will culminate in mental and physical freedom. There is no thought given either to the volume of information that will become available or, more importantly, the prejudices and slant of the information and what effect this will have on the receiver. It is as if knowledge is pure and this pure knowledge will lead all to the same destination.

Abbott Ferris in Wilson and Ferris [1989: 252] makes the point that in the southern states of the USA ". . . word of mouth, song, and story were prominent means of cultural transmission". The same was true for the West Indies. Word of mouth was virtually the only means of transmitting knowledge among West Indian slaves, but still they were part of a society in which the printed word was becoming increasingly important. For the slaves, the printed word had to be relayed through those few who could read and then disseminated by word of mouth to the many across the country. This method of transmitting information was in fact typical of the plantation society as a whole, which was at the initial stage of the movement from an oral culture to a more literate one. For example, laws had to be read out in church; a single notice had to be taken from plantation to plantation, which the manager in each case had to acknowledge in some way and then, where appropriate, announce to his people by word of mouth.

The disadvantage that is always pointed out about word of mouth transmission is distortion. This is especially so when the information in question is of direct relevance to the individual or is emotional in nature. Carmichael [1833, vol. 2], in reference to news emanating from England about the impending changes in status of slaves, highlights the idea of distortion in the movement from the printed word through the word of mouth process:

The negroes whose business it is to go to town, hear all that is going on in England; and though they cannot read, they have the substance of all that is printed from those who can (pp. 192-93).

. . . those negroes who go to town, though generally chosen for the situation in consequence of intelligence and ability, are nevertheless exposed to the contact of bad advice. They return heated with liquor, and of course with exaggerated stories in their heads; these they retail to all their comrades at night, as they sit eating their suppers, outside their doors (p. 194).

Even though in general, in discussions of the strengths and weaknesses of oral and literate cultures, the printed word is said to result in just as much distortion as the oral and probably, in some cases, is more dangerous in that it has permanence and by its very nature assumes an aura of fact, yet in this case there is no question that oral transmission resulted in distortion and lack of uniform coverage across the plantations. The slaves' access to knowledge was therefore limited and because of the way information was diffused, it militated against concerted action and the realization of power through numbers.

The achievement of literacy, which is believed to be a path to intellectual improvement and freedom, is vested in a specific language. If that language, as presented in the attainment of literacy, embodies and inculcates values which are inimical to the freedom of the individual, then literacy can be regarded as a web which traps the individual. It is the more harmful to the individual when the method of 'learning' is one of memorizing and regurgitating, when the individual accepts without question what is presented and cheerfully believes it to be the best. This was the reality of the English language in formal education for the native population of the West Indies during the eighteenth and early nineteenth centuries.

From the beginning of the West Indian colonies the link between church and state meant that formal education was intended to preserve and strengthen the establishment. It also meant that formal schooling had a large measure of religious doctrine and philosophy. The moral values and aspirations of the young were shaped by the church, which, it must be remembered, was not just a local establishment, but an integral part of the colonial structure with its head in England or Europe. This control of the education of the young was achieved in a practical way by the fact that not only did priests and other church officials have a daily dual role in the church and in the school, but also the children who were to succeed had to perform in both church and school.

In this method and philosophy of education there was no distinction between 'proper' behaviour and a 'good' education, and it succeeded so well in the West Indian colonies that Sir Andrew Halliday in his book on the West Indies [1837: 82] was moved to make the following claim:

> More crowded or more devout congregations I never witnessed in any country than in Barbados, and in others of the colonies; and it is gratifying to observe the progress which many grown-up people have made in the knowledge of the great truths of religion. As to the rising generation, they will be as well, if not better educated than the children of the lower classes in England. The ministers of all denominations of Christians are not less improved in their manners and conduct, than are the members of the Establishment . . .

Such comments, which seem flattering on face value, must also be interpreted to mean that the masses of the population in the colonies were being tightly controlled and acculturated into acceptance of values and aspirations which were not of their own making and were not necessarily in their best interests. Yet, on the other hand, uniformity in policy and zeal in execution meant that it was easier to rule, to set goals, to pursue them and to assess progress, especially in situations where there was a diversity of ethnic groups. Education was therefore also meant to make these societies cohesive and homogeneous.

As to whether formal education raised the level of competence in English itself in West Indian societies generally during the period, there were too many negative factors for this to have been achieved to any appreciable extent. Language learning involves both the acquisition of literacy skills and the acquisition of competence in a specific language. The acquisition of literacy skills relates to the written form of a specific language initially, although these skills can be later transferred with minor alterations to other languages. The acquisition of competence in a specific language in formal education involves acquisition of knowledge of both the written and spoken forms of the language. In the slavery period in the West Indies language learning was substantially different from what it is today. Not only was there a clear distinction in the literacy skills between reading and writing but there were also substantive differences in language and culture between the persons involved *eg* between English and French, between the slaves of the French and those of the English, between the English and the Scottish, between African and Creole slaves, between Mande and Kwa slaves, between the free coloured, the house slaves and the field slaves. In such a situation the notion of norms and uniformity as well as standard language which a formal education system conjures up was clearly absent. In effect, this meant that the learning of English within a context of formal instruction was largely ad hoc and variable, and increases in competence were negligible and restricted to a small number of persons.

The promotion of literacy today is based on a philosophy that the individual needs some measure of intellectual independence. It also presumes that there is material to read and time to read it. Such presumptions were reality only for a restricted number of persons in slave societies and certainly were not so generally for the servants and the slaves. Literacy was thrust upon them, as many other things were, to suit the desires of the ruling class. Language education at the elementary level from the early years right up to the mid nineteenth century was inseparable from religious education both in intent and substance. Language education therefore put English, the English and England in a position of prominence and power while it kept the West Indies, West Indians and their varieties of language in a subordinate, subservient and dependent relationship.

The British model of education, presenting language and social values through religion, was specifically geared to maintain a predictable and well structured society. Much of this literacy, especially in the earlier years, was functional rather than autonomous in that generally it was a part of the mechanism of Protestant education and as such maintenance of church power. In the business of the plantation and colonial administration it was a part of record keeping and book keeping, and as such was factor in the maintenance of control of people and property. The values being instilled, which were an integral part of all this, automatically preserved the status quo. The peculiar status of the slaves as property was a more powerful force than the role of literacy in Protestantism, for though the Protestant religion viewed literacy as the bulwark of evangelization and the strengthening of the church, in the case of the slaves it was for a long time withheld from most of them as not being necessary or useful.

On the eve of Emancipation the whip was being replaced by literacy as a method of control – a method of overt, physical control replaced by a method of intellectual manipulation. It is clear from the expressed purpose of Rev Duke and others that the intent of education was to remove African cultural values from the black population and to replace them with English values. Insidiously, however, the deculturation/acculturation process was linked to perceived changes in intellect. This link, which was generally accepted, was expressly stated by Wentworth [1834, 2:219]: "The greater the number of those who have become creolized, or removed from the physical characteristics of the African, the greater advancement has been made in intellectual improvement." The general acceptance within the population, black and white, of such a view meant that there was increasing rejection and ignorance not only of African cultural values but also of African languages since language was the medium for transmission of these values. Standard English, which embodied the history and values of the ruling class in Britain, eventually came to be adopted as the beacon of achievement by the white population as well as the black population. English, especially as presented in formal education, had a well promoted literature to back it up, knowledge of which fostered the notion of 'intellectual improvement'.

The image of the white European giving the Bible to the native on the one hand and taking the native's land on the other is a strong image illustrating the power of literacy and is relevant to colonial situations in Africa. In the case of the West Indies, it is labour rather than land which the Europeans took. The Bible was not immediately and readily given because it contained ideas which did not sit well with enslavement. One of the fundamental ideas in the Bible is freedom – in the early part of the Old Testament it is symbolized by the Jews' delivery from bondage and in the prophecies there is repetition of the idea of freedom to come; in the New Testament freedom is symbolized by Christ.

Conscious of the strong idea of freedom which pervades the Bible, the European was at first reluctant to expose the slaves to the Bible, thinking that from a practical point of view such a powerful idea would cause the slave to rise up and destroy the whole system of enslavement. Thinking Europeans wrestled throughout the period of slavery with the philosophical question whether a slave could be a Christian or whether this was a contradiction in terms. The matter was resolved by introducing the Bible to the slave and stressing the New Testament after-life (Christ) version of freedom as opposed to the Old Testament (Jews) deliverance from bondage. Note, for example, that in Barbados, when the Rev William Harte lectured to the slaves he used the Gospel of St Matthew. In addition, it was Harte's lectures which the SPG agreed to publish in book form and use as a model text for the instruction of the slaves. In fact, the Bible was specifically tailored to suit the situation of the slaves with the intention of holding them to their actual status and promising them everything good after death. Since many of the slaves already had as part of their religious ethic the notion of transmigration of souls, the Christian theology easily changed their concept of the ultimate resting place from the ancestral home (*ie* Africa) to heaven.

With the conflict resolved by a tailored Bible, nothing could have been more important then to the European than this tailored version of the Bible. The Bible was made the corner-stone document of literacy in the colonial West Indies – it was through this document that West Indians were introduced at one and the same time to the vaunted power of the written word and to a philosophy of freedom as a 'civilized' person. The oral tradition began to give way to the literate and freedom became a matter of adjustment and accommodation to the status quo – a matter of rendering to Caesar what is Caesar's and to God what is God's. The power of literacy, therefore, was itself modulated by the very material through which it was introduced.

In addition to the negative features which were an integral part of the type of religious education introduced into the West Indies, there were also some psychological problems which could have affected persons who actually did manage to achieve some level of competence in the subjects taught. The situation of a bright child who is discriminated against because he/she sticks out from the peer group is a problem which individuals resolve in different ways. However, when the attitude of the peer group develops into a more entrenched and widespread position and requires dissociation from 'foreign' things, it is clear in these cases that literacy and education could become serious liabilities socially. In fact, it is not only socially that literacy and education may bring one into conflict with one's peers. The initial difficulty in the kind of situation just mentioned stems from intellectual differences – the educated person may have ideas which differ from those which are traditional and those of the peer group. There is then a conflict between the presumed benefits of literacy and education on the one hand and the benefits of the peer group. The extreme effect of this conflict for the individual concerned is isolation, introversion and despondency.

In the case of slaves in the West Indies who learned to read and acquired some measure of education, this feeling is captured in the statement: "education was a disagreeable companion for a slave" [Thome and Kimball 1838: 20].

What this is pointing out is that education and slavery were virtually incompatible bedfellows. In fact, Thome and Kimball explained the dilemma of the educated slave as one in which "his sense of degradation grew more intense in proportion as his mind became more cultivated" [1838: 20]. Literacy and education did not confer power in such situations; what they did do was to make the educated feel powerless. In fact, the consequences were even more serious in that such persons often redirected their frustrations onto themselves and their own, indulging in self-hatred and trying to get as far away from their own image as possible.

NOTES

1. 'National' because it was supported and promoted by The National Society for promoting the Education of the Poor in the Principles of the Established Church.
2. In England a rival but similar system was associated with Joseph Lancaster, a Quaker.
3. Wentworth [1834, 1:250] mentions the American version.
4. About these famous schools, which started functioning after Emancipation, Day [1852, 2:274] said: "...amongst the drollest establishments of the West Indies, are the 'mico schools', founded by some old lady with more money than wit".
5. cyphering = arithmetic.

10

The Legacy of Colonial Literacy in the West Indies

MOVEMENT AND NETWORKING IN PLANTATION-BASED AND SMALL ISLAND SOCIETIES

In preliterate West Indian society, communication was achieved through movement of people. So, the extent to which individuals in the early colonies moved about and the number of people they came into contact with at different social levels determined the range of their linguistic competence. Some individuals found themselves moving or being moved from one place to another, whereas others spent their entire lives in rural isolation. Slaves were sold and resold, moved from one plantation to another, and from one territory to another according to the fortunes of their masters. Servants served their time, remained where they were or set out for new shores to make their fortune. Overcrowding or visions of wealth caused white colonists to move from one territory to another. As a result of all this movement, there was over time a generalization of features in the medium of communication.

What was constant movement, looking at the society as a whole, was for the individual, at most, periodic movement. In contrast to the movement from one home to another, daily life was characterized by a routine which limited social interaction to a small area filled with known persons. Legal restriction on the movement of slaves and absence of regular social events among the masters and servants reduced the early plantation to a self-contained unit. The network of communication for each individual therefore involved the same persons, and, except for occasional interaction with persons outside the plantation, there was little reason to adapt speech to make it comprehensible to others and there was little opportunity to adopt new features of language from others. For such a dense network of familiar persons, a much more limited and in some ways particular form of communication was sufficient. So, for the society as a whole, the constant contact of different language varieties over time added peculiarities to West Indian English and kept it in its most divergent forms distinct from British English; for the individual, limited, everyday movement and constant contact with the same persons made for a high degree of linguistic conservatism.

The use of indentured servants to mind babies and teach young children did not prove to be long lasting and widespread in the face of free slave labour. Soon the rearing of all children by slaves – the whites by young women and the blacks by old women – established the slaves' language as the foundation language of creoles in West Indian society. On the other hand, compulsory attendance at church in the early years made religious language and standardized English familiar only to the white population and very few of the black. For most whites, however, church experience was their only brush with literate English and they only developed a passive recognition of it.

The differences between one island and another were determined by external forces, that is, the varying fortunes of the English in their struggles internally with the Irish and Scottish and externally with the French. These struggles resulted in different concentrations of these ethnic groups throughout the islands. Consequently, peculiarities of language varied from island to island. In contrast, parallels in the contact situations across the different territories and constant migration resulted in linguistic similarities.

LITERACY AND COLONIZATION

Literacy is a later and nonautomatic stage in language learning which is celebrated to be the channel through which cognitive limits and cultural viewpoints are expanded. However, this was not what literacy did in the West Indies in the eighteenth and early nineteenth centuries. By adding a symbolic dimension and by giving permanence to the English language, literacy made the culture which the language embodied more dominant, and, being selective, it made the culture seem more glorious than the actual reality from which it sprang. This was made even more so by printing, which represented the mechanization, the mass production and standardizing of the values, directions and limits of the English language and British culture. It is true that the status quo at times found printing (i.e. newspapers, pamphlets and books) to be mischievous and a challenge to authority, but in such cases it implemented measures to control the effects. On the other hand, printing allowed the intellectual and artistic to be self-indulgent, which had little or no effect on the wider community.

British culture distinguished sharply between the functions of literacy for the intelligentsia (literary and scientific) and the functions for the rest of the society. Literacy for all but the intelligentsia was closely bound up with the identification of property, accounting and discipline; it was a literacy for management and control. It was supposed to allow people to follow orders better, to reject the illogical and foreign, and to follow religious doctrine through the approved texts. So, in order to make sure that these functions of literacy prevailed, a formal educational system was developed to structure and reinforce them, as well as to distinguish between the practical and the intellectual.

Among the whites in the West Indies there was little need for literacy in the business and daily life of the plantation. The need for literacy which arose was because the plantation had to keep books and make returns to local authorities and to absentee landlords. There was also an occasional need to use a note in communicating between plantations and there was also an occasional need to communicate by letter with persons in other colonies and in England. By the middle of the eighteenth century when written forms of legal documents took precedence over verbal ones, this did not require a daily and widespread need for literacy except by those who had to note down what contracting parties dictated to them.

On the other hand, from the early part of the eighteenth century newspapers began to appear and even proliferated. People wrote plays, prologues to plays and epilogues. Some wrote poems, had books, and were familiar with current as well as famous authors. Authors living in the West Indies, not necessarily natives, documented, with the help of natives, the flora and fauna of the islands. Others documented diseases and other illnesses together with their cures. The ideal planter, as outlined by Samuel Martin in the middle of the eighteenth century, clearly was a literate person. The idea of 'making paper talk' was seen even by the slaves as advantageous. Literacy, therefore, even without a practical purpose, was recognized as a mark of sophistication or at least a level beyond the common and ignorant. In addition, it had in itself an element of curiosity and fascination, like a key to open a door.

In the West Indies the spread of literacy was by association, since it was not a practical necessity. Prosperity caused some to aspire to grandeur and by associating with literate people it encouraged them to educate their children to assume the mantle of master. Whether or not the level of literacy increased as ostentatious living did, the fact that literacy was seen to be part of sophistication meant that it was a positive asset. This, however, did not lessen the suspicion and fear of those who saw it as dangerous when extended to the enslaved lower orders of West Indian society. For them slavery involved considerations of religion, safety and money; literacy gave access to notions of freedom and equality in the religious texts. The spectre of literacy as a liberating force frightened them until they found out how to turn it to advantage. The differences between the British social system and the plantation system were discussed and resolved over a period of time. Literacy may have seemed to be a threat to the plantation system, but in fact the British system of literacy was a logical development for the plantation society and did not prove in the main to be a disruptive force.

Yet, though the liberating aspect of literacy and printing was controlled to some extent, it did affect the isolation in plantation society and the practice of slavery. For instance, the newspaper centralized advertising and made it more effective: every plantation which received a newspaper knew of runaway slaves, slaves for sale, goods for sale, materials recently arrived, the arrival and departure of ships, services available and proposed social events. The link between literacy and commerce, rather than that between literacy and the arts, sustained the need for printing and literacy even among those whose sole interest was money. From the point of view of language, this was the beginning of the development of the condensed advertising format and the effective use of language to give adequate information. Consequently, those sending advertisements or making any other contribution to the newspaper had to think carefully about what they wanted to say, which meant that they had to pay attention to the language itself.

The isolated plantation became a thing of the past. The newspaper among the whites and the market among the blacks effected communication through a central place, usually the main town. In the newspaper the medium of communication was the written language and so the newspaper displayed the standard form of the written language for the community. In the marketplace the medium of communication was oral and so the market stabilized the vernacular and was a major source of generalization of features across the society. These two, the newspaper and the marketplace, were separate: the market had little direct effect on the language of the whites and the newspaper had little effect on the language of the blacks. However, the increased flow of information in both of them could not be kept separate because the plantation slaves who came to town, the urban slaves, the free coloureds and blacks, and the house slaves, all helped consciously or unconsciously to circulate information from the newspapers to the slaves on every plantation.

In fact, the increased flow of information went beyond the exchange between town and plantation, for availability of printing services in the West Indies provided an additional and alternative outlet for views in disputes. The rhetoric about slavery started in England from the earliest days of the implementation of the sugar plantation system, but it was only effective after the introduction and consolidation of printing in the West Indies. For instance, when Rev Robertson wrote his letter from St Kitts to the Bishop of London in 1730, there was little visible reaction to it.

This was before printing had come to St Kitts and neighbouring islands. In 1740, less than a decade after printing was introduced into Barbados, the dispute between Governor Byng and Speaker Peers in Barbados provoked a little more discussion in print: there were some comments locally in *The Barbados Gazette* while a pamphlet was written by Thomas Baxter, a Barbadian who supported Byng, and this was published in London. Forty years later, the amount of discussion in print increased significantly in the dispute initiated by Rev James Ramsay. When Ramsay returned to England from St Kitts and showed the draft of his book on slavery to Bishop Porteus, Porteus preached a sermon in 1783 using Ramsay's views and material. Both Ramsay's book and Porteus' sermon were printed and published in England the following year. 'Some Gentlemen of St Christopher responded in print, locally published, the same year. James Tobin also responded in like fashion the following year, but this response was published in London. Four years later William Dickson joined the argument by supporting some of the claims made by Ramsay; this support was in the form of collected letters and these were published in London. A year later, in 1790, Moreton wrote from London about Jamaica in the same vein as Ramsay about St Kitts. This provoked a sharp response from Mathews in 1793, a response which was published locally.

There were several significant consequences of these exchanges in print. First, there was an increase in the presentation of primary evidence, which no doubt enlightened all readers. Secondly, besides the personal attacks, there developed a format of argument and refutation which involved close and detailed study of claims. Thirdly, the use of earlier, printed material increased – authors used the notions and views of previous writers, as well as reproduced or copied previously appearing material. All this facilitated the development of general notions in the West Indies and Britain about slaves, about Creoles and about West Indian society generally, not least of which were the kind of English spoken by the slaves and by creole whites. Fourthly, the increase in hostility in print between the local whites and those in England eventually led the slaves, who were getting their information indirectly, to believe that the local whites were not acting in their interest. So, the increase in literacy and printing facilitated and in fact fomented heated discussion, which in time helped to bring about change.

Hostile exchanges in print between white factions were not restricted in subject matter to slavery. Local newspapers and pamphlets were used over the years to complain about the behaviour of office holders and to air views about those preferred for jobs. When it was known that such complaints and views could reach beyond the local society, even though the immediate reaction on the part of the offended was to seek stern repression and redress, the eventual consequence was modification of unbridled power and abuse. This incipient globalization of information occasioned by literacy and printing changed attitudes and behaviour in the plantation societies of the West Indies, no matter how slightly, even in the seventeenth, eighteenth and nineteenth centuries. In fact, it can be said that the dismantling of slavery was one of the early, classic examples of the power of the printed medium and the power of the foreign, metropolitan press over small dependent states.

COLONIAL EDUCATION

In Britain and America there was a direct relationship between educational institutions and educational materials on the one hand and the printing press on the other. Within the West Indies there was no such direct relationship. Even though a grammar book was produced by an early printer in Antigua, printing presses in the West Indies were in no way associated with educational institutions and the production of educational material. In addition, they were not run by the church or state. Educational materials for the West Indies came through English presses from principally English authors who reflected the doctrines of the Anglican Church and notions of British empire. British concepts, views, values and prejudices were thus transmitted to the West Indies through printed material. However, competence in the English language itself could not be transmitted in that way; it depended on the teachers and the methods used locally or the actual experiences of those who went abroad. Since these factors varied substantially, competence in English also did. Economic and social class factors relegated formal education in the West Indies to a very low position. Education was not allowed to interfere with the routine and production of the plantation or family business and could only be done at times outside normal working hours or by those who were not yet capable of working. So, cultural transmission from England through printed material was initially of little influence because local economic and social factors combined to reduce the education of West Indians to the minimal and irrelevant.

The differences between the social classes did not always result in a corresponding scale of educational achievement. In relation to the education of white children who went to Europe there were complaints about the useless and impractical things they learned. In relation to the education of the coloureds who were sent to Europe there were complaints that what they learnt made them ill suited to return to their social position in the West Indies. In neither of these cases were there comments about achievement in the English language specifically, other than the remark that the placing of white infants and young children under the care of black nurses made it almost impossible for their language to be standardized thereafter. In fact, it seemed as if those white children who went to England and returned generally did not achieve very much and did not put what they learned to good effect. In the case of the coloureds, their focus on self-improvement led them in the direction of trying to achieve the advantages of whiteness.

Those few at the lower end of the social scale who were exposed to schooling in the West Indies benefitted little from it, especially in the area of language. The monitorial system ensured that there was little difference between teacher and pupil, which resulted in a low level of achievement. In addition, there were few areas for application of what was learned, so it was soon forgotten in the bareness of life. The poorer whites passed time in school until a suitable job opening was available. The blacks, free and slave, could, at best, only read the Prayer Book or Bible or the odd newspaper if it came their way.

Yet, formal education was not a complete failure. As a system for improving knowledge, skills and procedures, it was a beginning, one which provided a foundation for growth. As a system of control, it was very successful. It subjected all to the language and philosophy of Christianity, and the pyramid structure of the school meshed admirably with the pyramid structure of the plantation. The monitorial system was a specifically colonially bred system, not meant for the intellectual, the artistic or the creative. Those who aspired to these heights had to go to the mother country. The monitorial system was one which aimed at reproduction and transmission of elementary knowledge and discipline. In effect, only those who aspired to go to the mother country needed a good knowledge of English; for those who remained at home the vernacular was good enough.

POWERLESSNESS IN THE UMBILICAL RELATIONSHIP

The language situation in the first half of the nineteenth century in the West Indies was the beginning of the tussle between local and global tendencies. Externally, English had become standardized and was on the path toward globalization through the British Empire. Internally, local forces had produced a creolization of English through the interaction of different ethnic groups searching for social equilibrium in communication in a polarized society. This was a tussle between the outward looking and the inward looking, between centralization and uniformity on the one hand and self-determination and individuality on the other, between the awe and aura of the metropolitan and the immediate reality of the local, between the transcendent power and global influence of the standard as opposed to the solidarity and psychological comfort occasioned by the use of a dialect.

The standardization of English in England was essentially a result of increase of wealth and an attempt to sustain class and ethnic differentiation by the wealthy. This was evident not only within England in the distinction between courtly London and the rest of Britain but also in the distinction between England and its overseas possessions. London became the economic centre and then imposed itself as the cultural centre – the Irish and the Scottish were consistently maligned and the impression was created either expressly or by default that the English were normal and therefore the norm which should be copied. The characteristics of overseas possessions were dismissed either as provincial or because they were 'tainted' by lower races, even when they were originally characteristics of the English themselves. In the literary and intellectual areas, it was very necessary for the English to establish and maintain hegemony, because by creating an aura of intellectual superiority, they legitimized dependence and masked economic exploitation in a framework of legality, cultural sophistication and Christian values. This was successfully achieved through literacy and printing, the agents of standardization of the English language.

In effect, therefore, the colonies indirectly caused the English to standardize their language in an attempt to remain aloof and in control. This was a case of language evolution spurred on by the tendency towards social differentiation and exercise of power. In the West Indian colonies it was aggravated in its assignment of stigma by the presence of racially different people, and standard English appeared to move away from the West Indian varieties as the economy, culture and racist beliefs of the British grew stronger. Although words originating in the West Indies found their way into the English language, these were mostly native American words. Words, meanings and concepts emerging out of the creolization process had little chance of becoming a part of standard English, since these did not represent the preoccupations of the intellectual and powerful in England. Even if they could have, because the tradition of standardization started with Latin and Greek as the models of excellence and moved grudgingly toward English itself, any concept or word coming out of the West Indies would have been subject to this hierarchy and would have had little chance of survival. The reinterpretation of the word *carabi* as *Charib* exemplified this tendency to look toward the classical languages.

Standardization was directly linked to writing, and writing, in contrast to speech, is a delayed form of communication in which the writer and reader are most often not in the same immediate context. The body language and voice modulation of face-to-face communication are absent and cannot be used by either writer or reader. The actual words used in writing assume a heavier responsibility in conveying meaning and the reader depends more on personal knowledge to interpret the meaning of written words. In face-to-face communication there is instantaneous interpretation and subsequent modification of interpretation through the use of memory. In contrast, writing allows or causes the reader to reexamine the words of the message and reflect on them, thus permitting variation in interpretation according to the 'intelligence' and culture of the individual. In face-to-face communication there may be more actual variation in language forms used, but the context of communication normally clarifies or restricts the number of probable interpretations. By reducing contextual clues, body language, meaning through intonation, by requiring additional skill in deciphering written symbols, and by allowing more time for reflection and thus for more meanings, writing made language more difficult.

Standard English was therefore more difficult because it was less tied to the immediate context, it was less communication centred and more logic and grammar centred, less holistic and more analytical. It was essentially a tool for maintaining control; its artistic and creative function was secondary, in nature less rule governed, and especially in the West Indian colonies was restricted to a few in the ruling classes. As a classroom subject, it was controlled by the details of prescriptive grammar which gradually became an intellectual exercise in logic and projection. The introduction into West Indian schools of English grammar, with its monolithic uniformity prescribed by educated but narrowmindedly British teachers and editors influenced by the grammars of dead classical languages, put West Indian varieties into sharp contrast and gradually relegated them to the dung-heap. Flexible systems of communication which had emerged through interaction of people to service all actual domains of life were belittled and stigmatized. The rich interplay and fusion of different languages and cultures, which were the very backbone of English itself, was in the case of the West Indies branded as a corruption of English.

Standard English in London had as its constant lifeline and supply line all the British regional dialects and to a lesser extent the neighbouring languages of Europe. Standard English in the West Indies was imported through written materials and not fed by West Indian varieties. In effect, literacy and printing locked West Indians into a standard language over which they had no control, little power to influence and from which the majority of the population was excluded. What the rise of literacy had done in the case of European cultures was to validate Greek and Roman works of art and European literary figures (*eg* Shakespeare) to give Europeans a belief in their culture and superiority as well as a belief in their right to govern and 'civilize' other people. Colonial literacy, in a sense, had to maintain this purpose and image, rather than to promote local culture which would of course have resulted in a challenge to hegemony. Those features of local culture which clashed with European culture could not be validated and those which could be validated had to be within beaten paths and genres.

GALATEA AND CALIBAN

While the link between mother country and colony can be regarded as a female relationship if it is seen as metaphorically deriving from the umbilical cord linking mother to child, one can conceive of the male version of the relationship between the West Indies and Britain in two different ways, using European literary sources – as either the Pygmalion to Galatea relationship or the Prospero to Caliban relationship. In the former Galatea is a beautiful woman loved by Pygmalion; in the latter Caliban is an ugly man and provokes aversion in Prospero. In Bernard Shaw's dramatic reprise of the Pygmalion myth (made into the film *My Fair Lady*), Higgins (Pygmalion) changes Eliza (Galatea) into a beautiful lady and falls in love with his creation. He 'civilizes' her by changing her speech from common, everyday London speech to sophisticated upper class speech. He does this because he is an expert in phonetics. In Shakespeare's play *The Tempest*, Prospero's first step in 'civilizing' Caliban was to give him language (meaning a European language), but Prospero does not succeed with Caliban in the same way that Higgins does with Eliza. One may surmise that Prospero failed in his purpose because his books were magic books and not books on phonetics. However, the more likely reason for Prospero's failure to recreate Caliban in his own image was that Caliban was presented as different. Another reason was that Galatea was female and conceived of as a creation by and for her creator, whereas Caliban was male and presented as a threat who wanted to have his master's daughter.

To the British the slave, both African and creole, was a 'Caliban' and male, for the female slaves did not occupy the minds of the British or other Europeans. Yet, it was thought possible, after early views to the contrary, that by giving him language and by making him imitate the master's words perfectly (as was done in the schools) the slave could be brought nearer to the image of his master. Caliban would never become Galatea, an object of love and beauty, but at least he would become docile and should be grateful to his master-creator. It is quite obvious that whatever stage in the acculturation process between Caliban (the son of an African) and Galatea (the creation of a European) the slave reached, he/she would remain to some extent the subject of Prospero or the work of Pygmalion. The descendants of the slaves as well as other West Indians found themselves dominated by this dilemma and the cultural images which sustained it, and almost unable to break free, for the literary material which promoted these images grew in volume and conviction as literacy grew.

Bibliography

PRE-TWENTIETH CENTURY

A brief, but most true relation of the late barbarous and bloody plot of the Negro's in the island of Barbados on Friday the 21 of October, 1692 . . . In a letter to a friend. 1693. London.

A collection of papers printed by the order of the Society for the Propagation of the Gospel in Foreign Parts. 1715. London.

An Ode on the King of Prussia. 1760. Antigua.

Associates of Dr. Bray. 1766. *An Account of the Designs of the Associates of the late Dr. Bray; with an Abstract of their proceedings.* London.

Associates of Dr. Thomas Bray. 1786. *Abstract of the Proceedings of the Associates of Doctor Bray for the year 1785.* London.

Atwood, Thomas. 1791. *The history of the island of Dominica.* London.

Barrell, Theodore. 1843. Sketches of Demerary incidents. Typescript.

Bates, William C. 1896. Creole folk-lore from Jamaica. *Journal of American Folk-Lore* 9-10: 38-42, 121-28.

Baxter, Thomas. 1740. *A Letter from a gentleman at Barbados to his Friend now in London concerning the Administration of the late Governor B....g.* London.

Bayley, F.W.N. 1829. *The Island Bagatelle Containing Poetical Enigmas on the Estates in Each Parish in the Island of Grenada in Six Parts Interspersed with Tales and Other Miscellaneous Poems.* Grenada.

———. 1833. *Four Years' Residence in the West Indies During the years 1826,7,8 and 9.* 3rd edition enlarged. London: William Kidd.

Beckford, William. 1788. *Remarks upon the Situation of Negroes in Jamaica, impartially made from a local Experience of nearly thirteen years in that Island.* London.

———. 1790. *A descriptive Account of the Island of Jamaica.* London.

Belgrove, William. 1755. *A treatise upon husbandry or planting.* Boston.

Blome, Richard. 1672. *A description of the island of Jamaica with the other isles and territories in America, to which the English are related.* London.

Borde, Pierre Gustave Louis. 1876, 1882, 1883. *Histoire de l'ile de la Trinidad sous le gouvernement espagnol.* Paris.

Brerewood, Edward. 1614. *Enquiries touching the Diversity of Languages, and Religions through the cheife parts of the world.* London.

Bridgens, R. 1837. *West India Scenery, with Illustrations of Negro character, The process of making sugar, &, from Sketches taken during a voyage to, and residence of seven years in the Island of Trinidad.* London.

Briggs, Sam. 1885. A list of the names of the inhabitants of Barbadoes in the year 1638, who then possessed more than ten acres of land. *Narragansett Historical Register,* III, nos. 3 & 4: 230-36, 282-88.

Browne, Patrick. 1756. *The Civil and Natural History of Jamaica.* London.

Butel-Dumont, Georges Marie. 1758. *Histoire et commerce des Antilles angloises.* Paris.

Campbell, Douglas. 1891. The origin of American institutions as illustrated in the history of the written ballot. *American Historical Association Papers* 5: 163-86.

Chalkley, Thomas. 1766. *A collection of the works of that ancient faithful servant of Jesus Christ.* London.

Coke, Thomas. 1808. *A history of the West Indies.* Liverpool.

Colman, George. 1788. *Inkle and Yarico: an Opera in three Acts as performed at the Theatre-Royal in the Hay-Market on Saturday, August 11th, 1787.* Dublin.

Croese, Gerard. 1696. *The general history of the Quakers.* London.

Croker, Temple. 1790. *Where am I? How came I here?* . . . Basseterre, St. Christopher's: Edward Low.

Crouch, Nathaniel. 1739. *The English Empire in America.* London.

Cuffy The Negro's Doggrel Description of the Progress of Sugar [1823?]. London.

Cumberland, Richard. 1771. *The West Indian: a comedy.* London.

Dallas, R.C. 1803. *The history of the Maroons, from their origin to the establishment of their chief tribe at Sierra Leone: including the Expedition to Cuba, for the purpose of procuring chasseurs; and the state of the island of Jamaica for the last ten years; with a succint history of the island previous to that period.* London: Longman and Rees.

Daniel, Evan. 1897. *The Prayer-Book: its History, Language, and Contents.* London.

Dasent, Sir George. 1858. *Popular tales from the Norse.* New York.

Day, Charles. 1852. *Five years' residence in the West Indies.* London.

De Rochefort, C. 1658, 1665. *Histoire naturelle et morale des iles antilles de l'Amerique.* Rotterdam.

Debret, Jean Baptiste. 1834. *Voyage pittoresque et historique au Brésil.* Paris.

Declarations, &c. of Catechists, in the diocese of Barbados and the Leeward Islands. 1827. Bridgetown, Barbados.

Dickson, W. 1789. *Letters on Slavery . . . To which are added, Addresses to the whites and to the Free Negroes of Barbadoes, and accounts of some Negroes eminent for their virtues and abilities.* London.

Du Tertre, Père J.B. 1661-1667. *Histoire générale des Antilles habitées par les Français.* 2 vols. Paris.

Duke, William. 1741. *Some memoirs of the first settlement of Barbados and other CARRIBBEE Islands with the Succession of the Governors and Commanders in Chief of Barbados to Year 1741 . . .* Barbados.

Easel, Theodore. 1840. *Desultory sketches and tales of Barbados.* London.

Edwards, Bryan. 1793, 1794. *The history, civil and commercial, of the British colonies in the West Indies.* London.

Equiano, Olaudah. 1789. *The interesting narrative of Olaudah Equiano, or Gustavus Vassa the African, written by himself.* London.

Fermin, Phillippe. 1769. *Description générale, historique, géographique et physique de la colonie de Surinam.* Amsterdam.

Fielding, Sir John. 1768. *Extracts from the Penal Laws, as particularly relate to the Peace and Good Order of this Metropolis.* London.

Fisher, George. 1748. *The American Instructor; or Young Man's Best Companion, Containing, Spelling, Reading, Writing, and Arithmetick, in an easier way than any yet published . . .* Philadelphia.

Ford, John. 1799. Two narratives by female slaves at Barbados, written down there by John Ford, 1799. Manuscript held in Oxford University's Bodleian Library.

Fowler, John. 1774. *Summary account of the present flourishing state of the respectable colony of Tobago in the British West Indies.* London.

Fox, George. 1671, 1694. *A journal or historical account of the life, travels, sufferings, Christian experiences and labour of love in the work of the ministry of that ancient and faithful servant of Jesus Christ, George Fox, who departed this life in great peace with the Lord, the 13th of the 11th month, 1690.* London.

———. 1743. *Instructions for Right Spelling and Plain Directions for Reading and Writing True English.* Boston.

Franklin, Benjamin. 1793. *Works of the late Benjamin Franklin.* London.

Frere, George. 1768. *A short history of Barbados, from its first discovery and settlement to the present time.* London.

Godwyn, Morgan. 1680. *The Negro's and Indians Advocate.* London.

Gray, George. 1687. Letter sent to James Harrison. Held in Boston Public Library.

Great Newes from the Barbados, or a true and faithful account of the Grand Conspiracy of the Negroes against the English and the happy discovery of the same with the number of those that were burned alive, beheaded, and otherwise executed for their horrid crimes with a short description of that plantation with allowance. 1676. London.

Hakluyt, Richard. 1589 (1903-5). *The Principall Navigations, Voiages, and Discoveries of the English Nation.* Glasgow.

Halliday, Sir Andrew. 1837. *The West Indies: the natural and physical history of the Windward and Leeward colonies.* London.

Harte, William Marshall. 1824 and 1826. *Lectures on the Gospel of St. Matthew* (vol. 1, 1824; vol. 2, 1826). London.

Hay, John. 1823. *A narrative of the insurrection in the island of Grenada.* London.

Higginson, Thomas. 1886. English sources of American dialect. In *Proceedings of the American Antiquarian Society.* Worcester, Mass.

Hillary, William. 1759. *Observations on the changes of the air.* London.

Hofland, Mrs. [1818] 1871. *The Barbadoes Girl. A Tale.* London.

[Hulton, Henry]. 1757. *A Poem, Addressed to a Young Lady.* Antigua.

Isert, Paul Erdmann. 1793. *Voyages en Guinée et dans les iles Caraibes en Amerique avec ses amis.* Tr. de l'allemand. Paris.

Johnson, J. 1830. *An Historical and descriptive account of Antigua.* London.

Labat, Père. 1724. *Nouveau voyage du Père Labat aux isles de l'Amerique.* La Haye.
[Langford, Jonas]. 1706. *A brief account of the sufferings of the servants of the Lord called Quakers.* London.
Lanigan, Mrs. 1844. *Antigua and the Antiguans.* London.
[Laws of Barbados] *An Abridgement of the Laws in Force and Use in Her Majesty's Plantations of Virginia, New England, Jamaica, New York, Barbadoes, Carolina, Maryland.* 1704. London.
Leslie, Charles. 1739. *A new and exact account of Jamaica.* Edinburgh.
_____. 1740. *A new history of Jamaica from the earliest accounts, to the taking of Porto Bello by Vice-Admiral Vernon. In thirteen letters from a gentleman to his friend.* London.
Lewis, Matthew G. 1834. *Journal of a West Indian planter in Jamaica.* London.
Ligon, R. 1657. *A true and exact history of the island of Barbados.* London.
Littleton, E. 1689. *The Groans of the Plantations.* London.
Lloyd, William. 1837. *Letters from the West Indies during a visit in the autumn of MDCCCXXXVII.* London.
Long, Edward. 1774. *The History of Jamaica, or General Survey of the Antient and Modern state of that island: with reflections on its Situations, Settlements, Inhabitants, Climate, Products, Commerce, Laws and Government.* (New edition with a new Introduction by George Metcalf of King's College, 1970. London: Frank Cass & Co. Ltd.)
Lovell, Langford. 1818. *A letter to a friend, relative to the present state of the island of Dominica.* Winchester.
Luffman, John. 1789. *A brief account of the Island of Antigua . . . written in the years 1786, 7, 8.* London.
Martin, Samuel. [1750] 1765. *An Essay on Plantership.* London.
Mathews, Samuel. 1793. *The Lying Hero or an Answer to J.B. Moreton's Manners and Customs in the West Indies.* St. Eustatius.
_____. 1822. *The Willshire Squeeze, to which are added specimens of the Negro familiar dialect and proverbial sayings with songs.* Demerara.
Mathison, Gilbert. 1811. *Notices respecting Jamaica, in 1808 – 1809 – 1810.* London.
M'Callum, Pierre F. 1805. *Travels in Trinidad.* Liverpool.
McKinnen, Daniel. 1804. *A tour through the British West Indies in the years 1802 and 1803.* London.
M'Neill, Hector. 1788/89. *Observations on the Treatment of the Negroes, in the Island of Jamaica, including some account of their temper and character, with remarks on the importation of slaves from the coast of Africa.* London.
Moister, Rev. William. 1883. *The West Indies, Enslaved and Free: A concise account of the islands and colonies: their history, geography, climates, productions, resources, populations, manners, customs, colonisation, slavery, emancipation, and Christian missions.* London.
Montlezun, Baron de. 1818. *Souvenirs des Antilles: voyage en 1815 et 1816, aux Etats-Unis, et dans l'archipel Caraibe.* 2 vols. Paris.
Montserrat code of laws: from 1668 to 1788. 1790. London.
Moore, John. 1713. *A sermon preach'd before the Society by John, Lord Bishop of Ely.* In *Proceedings 1712-1721 of the Society for the Propagation of the Gospel in Foreign Parts.* London.
Moreton, J.B. 1790. *Manners and Customs in the West Indies.* London.

Ogilby, John. 1671. *America, being the latest, and most accurate description of the New World.* London.

Oldmixon, John. 1708. *The British Empire in America.* London.

Orderson, J.W. 1827. *Leisure hours at the Pier; or, a treatise on the education of the poor of Barbados.* Liverpool.

_____. 1835. *The fair Barbadian and faithful black; or, a cure for the gout. A comedy in three acts.* Liverpool.

_____. 1842. *Creoleana: or, Social and domestic scenes and incidents in Barbados in days of yore.* London.

Paton, William Anew. 1896. *Down the Islands: a voyage to the Caribbees.* New York.

Pinckard, G. 1806. *Notes on the West Indies.* 3 vols. London.

Poole, Robert. 1753. *The beneficent bee: or, traveller's companion.* London.

Porteus, Beilby. 1784. *A Sermon preached before the Incorporated Society for the Propagation of the Gospel in Foreign Parts; at their Anniversary Meeting in the Parish Church of St. Mary-Le-Bow, on Friday, 21 February 1783.* London.

_____. 1807. *Tracts on various subjects, all of which have been published before.* London.

_____. 1808. *A letter to the Governors, Legislatures, and Proprietors of Plantations in the British West India islands.* London.

Poyer, John. 1808. *History of Barbadoes from the first discovery of the island, in the year 1605, till the accession of Lord Seaforth, 1801.* London.

Proceedings 1712-1721 of the Society for the Propagation of the Gospel in Foreign Parts.

Ramsay, Rev. J. 1784. *Essay on the treatment and conversion of African slaves in the British sugar colonies.* London.

_____. 1788. *Objections to the abolition of the slave trade.* London.

Renny, Robert. 1807. *An History of Jamaica with Observations on the Climate, Scenery, Trade, Productions, Negroes, Slave Trade, Diseases of Europeans, Customs, Manners, and Dispositions of the Inhabitants. To which is added, an illustration of the advantages, which are likely to result, from the Abolition of the Slave Trade.* London.

Resident. 1828. *Sketches and Recollections of the West Indies.* London.

Ridpath, George. 1703. *The case of Scots-men residing in England and in the English plantations.* Edinburgh.

Robertson, Rev. R. 1730. *A letter to the Right Reverend the Lord Bishop of London, from an inhabitant of His Majesty's Leeward-Caribbee-Islands. Containing some considerations on His Lordship's two letters of May 19, 1727, the first to the masters and mistresses of families in the English plantations abroad; the second to the missionaries there. In which is inserted, A short essay concerning the conversion of the negro-slaves in our sugar-colonies: written in the month of June, 1727, by the same inhabitant.* London.

Ryan, Michael. 1816. *A Series of Letters published in the Barbados News-papers, commencing from the 11th September, 1815; Collected and printed in succession as they appeared by Michael Ryan, Editor of the Times.* Bridgetown, Barbados.

Schomburgk, Robert. 1848. *The History of Barbados.* London.

Shephard, Charles. 1831. *An historical account of the island of Saint Vincent.* London.

Sheridan, Thomas. 1783. *A rhetorical grammar of the English Language.* Philadelphia.

Shervington, William. 1748. *The Ladies Advocate: a Poem.* St John's, Antigua,

_____. 1763. *Miscellanies.* Antigua.

Simmonds, Peter. 1841. Statistics of newspapers in various countries. *Journal of the Statistical Society* 4, Part 2: 111-36.

Singleton, John. 1767. *A general description of the West-Indian islands, As far as relates to the British, Dutch, and Danish Governments, from Barbados to Saint Croix. Attempted in Blank Verse.* Barbados.

———. 1777. *Description of the West Indies: A poem in four books.* The second edition. London.

———. 1777a. *A description of the West Indies.* London.

Sloane, Hans. 1707. *A voyage to the islands Madera, Barbadoes, Nieves, S. Christophers and Jamaica.* 2 vols. London.

Smith, John. 1630. *The true travels, adventures, and observations of Captaine John Smith. In Europe, Asia, Africa, and America, from Anno Domini 1593 to 1629.* London.

Smith, William. 1745. *A Natural History of Nevis.* London.

Snelgrave, Captain William. 1754. *A New Account of Guinea and the Slave Trade.* London.

Some Gentlemen of St Christopher. 1784. *An Answer to the Reverend James Ramsay's Essay on the Treatment and Conversion of Slaves, In the British Sugar Colonies.* Basseterre, St. Christopher.

St. Clair, Thomas Staunton. 1834. *A soldier's recollections of the West Indies and America With a narrative of the expedition to the island of Walcheren.* London.

Stanhope, George. 1714. The early conversion of islanders. In *Proceedings 1712-1721 of the Society for the Propagation of the Gospel in Foreign Parts.* London.

Stedman, John Gabriel. 1806. *Narrative of a five years' expedition against the revolted negroes of Surinam, in Guiana, on the wild coast of South America.* London.

Stewart, John. 1808. *An Account of Jamaica and its Inhabitants. By a Gentleman Long resident in the West Indies.* London.

The Negro's Friend Notes on Slavery, made during a recent visit to Barbadoes. 1830. London.

The young clerks assistant; or Penmanship made easy. 1733. London.

Thomas, Isaiah. 1810. *The History of Printing.* Worcester, Mass.

Thome, J., and J. Kimball. 1838. *Emancipation in the West Indies; The Anti-Slavery Examiner no. 7.* New York.

Thompson, Edward. 1770. *Sailor's letter's.* Dublin.

Tobin, James. 1785. *Cursory Remarks upon the Reverend Mr. Ramsay's Essay on the Treatment and Conversion of African Slaves in the Sugar Colonies.* London.

Towne, Richard. 1726. *A treatise of the diseases most frequent in the West Indies, and herein more particularly of those which occur in Barbadoes.* London.

Trollope, Anthony. 1860. *The West Indies and the Spanish Main.* New York.

[Turnbull, G.] Eyewitness. 1795. *A Narrative of the Revolt and Insurrection of the French Inhabitants in the Island of Grenada.* London.

Ulloa, Don Antonio de. 1772, 1792. *Noticias Americanas: Entretenimientos físico-históricos sobre la América meridional, y la septentrional Oriental.* Madrid.

Uring, Nathaniel. 1725. *A relation of the late intended settlement of the islands of St Lucia and St Vincent . . . 1722.* London.

Walker, William. 1704. *Marry or Do Worse. A Comedy.* London.

Warren, George. 1667. *An impartial description of Surinam upon the continent of Guiana in America.* London.

Waterton, Charles. 1825. *Wanderings in the Antilles.* London.
Wentworth, Trelawney. 1834. *The West India Sketch Book.* 2 vols. London.
West India Merchant, Being a Series of Papers Originally printed under that signature in the London Evening Post. 1778. London.
Williams, Cynric. 1827. *A Tour through the island of Jamaica, from the western to the eastern end in the year 1823.* Second edition. London.
Wright, Joseph. 1898-1905. *The English Dialect Dictionary.* London: Oxford Univ. Press.
Young, Sir William. 1764. *Considerations which may tend to promote the settlement of our West Indian colonies.* London.
_____. 1795. *An account of the black charaibs in the island of St. Vincent's.* London.
Zouch, [Arthur]. 1715. *Barbadoes A catalogue of books to be sold by Mr. Zouch in the town of St. Michael Alias the Bridge-town.* London.

REPORTS (listed by year)

First Annual Report of the Barbados Society for promoting Christian Knowledge. 1821. [Handwritten].
Report of the Barbados Society for Promoting Christian Knowledge. 1823. Printed at the Barbadian Office.
Fifth Annual Report of the Barbados Society for promoting Christian Knowledge. 1824. [Handwritten].
Report of the Jamaica District Committee of the Society for Promoting Christian Knowledge, with an Account of the Receipt and Expenditure, from its Commencement to the 31st December, 1823. And the Sermon preached at the Annual Meeting of the Clergy on the third day of December last. 1824. St. Jago de la Vega, Jamaica.
[Statement of] The Society for the Conversion and Religious Instruction and Education of the Negro Slaves in the British West India Islands. 1825.
Sixth Annual Report of the Barbados Society for the Promotion of Christian Knowledge. 1825. Printed at the Barbadian Office.
Report of the Barbados Society for Promoting Christian Knowledge. 1826. Printed at the Barbadian Office.
First Annual Report of the Branch Association of the Island of Barbados in Aid of the Incorporated Society for the Conversion and Religious Instruction and Education of the Negro Slaves in the British West India Islands. 1826. Bridge-town.
First Annual Report of the Grenada District Committee of the Society for Promoting Christian Knowledge. 1826. St. George's.
Second Report of the Society for the Education of the Poor. 1826. Grenada.
Eighth Annual Report of the Barbados society for Promoting Christian Knowledge With an Appendix. 1827. Printed at the Barbadian Office.
First Annual Report of the Society for the Education of the Coloured Poor in the Principles of the Established Church and for Other Charitable Relief. 1827.
First Annual Report of the Ladies' Branch Association for the Education of Female Children of the Coloured Poor on the Principles of the Established Church of England. 1827. Bridge-town, Barbados.

Third Report of the Society for the Education of the Poor. 1827. Grenada.
The Sixth Annual Report of the Society for the Education of the Coloured Poor, in the Principles of the Established Church. 1827. St. Vincent.
Second Annual Report of the Ladies' Association for the Relief of the Indigent Sick and Infirm of Bridge-town, and its Environs. 1827. Bridge-town.
Report of the Barbados Diocesan Committee of the Society for Promoting Christian Knowledge 1827. Bridge-town.
Ninth Annual Report of the Barbados Society for the Education of the Poor in the Principles of the Established Church. 1828. Printed at the Barbadian Office.
Report of the Committee appointed to examine the State and Progress of the School for the Education of the Poor White Children of the Parish of Saint Peter. 1828. Bridge-town.
First Annual Report of the St. Vincent Branch Association of the Society for the Conversion and Religious Instruction of the Negro Slaves. 1828. St. Vincent.
First Annual Report of the St. Vincent District Committee of the Society for Promoting Christian Knowledge. 1828. St. Vincent.
The Seventh Annual Report of the "Society for the Education of the Coloured Poor, In the Principles of the Established Church, &c." 1828. St. Vincent.
Fourth Annual Report of the Ladies' Branch Association for the Education of Female children of the Coloured Poor on the Principles of the Established Church of England. 1831. Bridge-town.
Twelfth Annual Report of the Barbados Society for the Education of the Poor in the Principles of the Established Church. 1831. Bridge-town.
The Sixth Report of the Wesleyan Methodist Missionary Auxiliary Society for the Saint Vincent District. 1831. The Barbadian Office.
Fourth Annual Report of the Free-School of Tobago. 1832. Scarborough.

NEWSPAPERS

The Weekly Jamaica Courant,	Wednesday, 30 July 1718
	Wednesday, 5 Aug 1718
	Wednesday, 15 April 1719
The Barbados Gazette,	2 Aug 1755
The Antigua Gazette,	12 April 1755
The St. Christopher's Gazette,	Wednesday, 4 Sept 1765
The Royal Grenada Gazette,	vol. 11, no. 54, Saturday, 25 Jan 1766
The Barbados Mercury,	vol. iv, no. 35, Saturday, 1 Feb 1766
The Freeport Gazette; or the Dominica Advertiser,	vol. 11, Numb. 110, Saturday, 18 July 1767
The Antigua Gazette,	no. 653, Wednesday, 11 Nov 1767
The Barbados Mercury,	vol. ix, no. 15, Saturday, 22 Sept 1770
	vol. ix, no. 17, Saturday, 6 Oct 1770,
	vol. ix, no. 18, Saturday, 13 Oct 1770
Gazette des Petites Antilles,	no. 2 du mardi 12^e juillet 1774
The Freeport Gazette; or, The Dominica Chronicle,	vol. v, Saturday, 6 May 1775

The Barbados Mercury, vol. iii, Saturday, 2 Sept 1775
The Charribbean and General Gazette; or,
The St. Christopher Chronicle, vol. vii, Wednesday, 13 Dec 1775
The Antigua Chronicle, or *Post-Office Intelligencer*, vol. 1, no. 2, Saturday, 13 Jan 1781
Antigua Gazette, Wednesday, 8 June 1785
The Antigua Chronicle, vol. vi, Friday, 8 Dec 1786
Barbados Mercury, 18 August 1787
Antigua Gazette, Thursday, 21 Feb 1799,
18 April 1799
25 April 1799
27 June 1799
17 Oct 1799
31 Oct 1799
The Charibbean Courier; or, *St. Christopher Chronicle*, vol. 1, no. 42, Saturday, 8 Nov 1800
vol. 1, no. 44, Saturday, 22 Nov 1800
Antigua Gazette, 18 Oct 1810
Antigua Gazette, 15 June 1815

MINUTES OF MEETINGS

Meeting of the Board of Council, Barbados, 1 November 1803. Microfilm 14, Lucas Papers, Barbados Public Library.
Proposed Institution of a Colonial Charity School, on the system of Dr Bell. Under the patronage of His Excellency the Governor. Barbados, 16 November 1818.
Rules and Regulations for the Government of the National Male & Female Schools of Port of Spain. 1826. Trinidad, Cabildo Hall.

TWENTIETH CENTURY

Abrahams, R., and J. Szwed. 1983. *After Africa*. New Haven: Yale Univ. Press.
Alleyne, M.C. 1961. Language and society in St Lucia. *Caribbean Studies* 1:1-11.
_____. 1971. Acculturation and the cultural matrix of creolization. In *Pidginization and Creolization of Languages*, edited by D. Hymes, 169-86. Cambridge: Cambridge Univ. Press.
_____. 1980. *Comparative Afro-American*. Ann Arbor: Karoma.
Armytage, W.H.G. 1965. *Four hundred years of English Education*. Cambridge: Cambridge Univ. Press.
Bailyn, Bernard. 1992. The boundaries of history: the Old World and the New. Address on the occasion of the Dedication of the Caspersen Building of the John Carter Brown Library, Providence, R.I.
Barber, Charles. 1993. *The English Language: a Historical Introduction*. Cambridge: Cambridge Univ. Press.

Baugh, Albert C., and Cable Thomas. 1978. *A History of the English language*. Englewoods Cliffs, N.J.: Prentice-Hall.

Beckles, Hilary. 1992. White women and slavery in the Caribbean. Mimeo.

Bennett, Louise. 1966. *Jamaica Labrish*. Kingston, Jamaica: Sangsters.

Bethell, Leslie (ed). 1984. *Colonial Latin America*. Vol. 2, *The Cambridge History of Latin America*. Cambridge: Cambridge Univ. Press.

Bickerton, Derek. 1984. Language bioprogram hypothesis. *Behavioral and Brain Sciences* 7 (2):173-188.

Birdwhistell, Ray L. 1970. *Kinesics and Context: Essays on Body Motion Communication*. Philadelphia: Univ. of Pennsylvania Press.

Bolster, William Jeffrey. 1991. African-American seamen: race, seafaring work, and Atlantic maritime culture. PhD diss., Johns Hopkins Univ.

Bourcier, Georges. 1981. *An Introduction to the History of the English Language*. Cheltenham: Stanley Thornes.

Boyer, Paul, and Stephen Nissenbaum (eds). 1977. *The Salem Witchcraft Papers: Verbatim Transcripts of Legal Documents of the Witchcraft Outbreak of 1692*. New York: De Capo.

Bracey, Robert, O.P. 1925. *Eighteenth Century Studies and Other Papers, 1925*. Oxford.

Brathwaite, Edward. 1971. *The Folk Culture of the Slaves in Jamaica*. London: New Beacon Books.

Breen, Henry H. [1844] 1970. *St. Lucia: Historical, Statistical and Descriptive*. Reprint, London: Frank Cass & Co. Ltd.

Brook, Stella. 1965. *The Language of the Book of Common Prayer*. London: Deutsch.

Burnett, P. 1986. *The Penguin Book of Caribbean Verse in English*. Middlesex, England: Penguin Books.

Burns, A. 1954. *A History of the British West Indies*. London: Allen & Unwin.

Caldecott, A. [1898] 1970. *The Church in the West Indies*. Reprint, London: Frank Cass & Co. Ltd.

Campbell, P.F. 1982. *The Church in Barbados in the Seventeenth Century*. Bridgetown, Barbados: Barbados Museum and Historical Society.

Carmichael, Mrs. C. [1833] 1969. *Domestic Manners and Social Condition of the White, Coloured, and Negro Population of the West Indies*. 2 vols. Reprint, New York: Negro Universities Press.

Carrington, L.D(ed). 1983. *Studies in Caribbean Language*. Port of Spain, Trinidad: Society for Caribbean Linguistics.

Cassidy, F. 1980. The place of Gullah. *American Speech* 55: 1-17.

_____. 1986. Barbadian creole – possibility and probability. *American Speech* 6, no. 3: 195-205. (3):195-205.

Cassidy, F., and R. LePage. 1967. *Dictionary of Jamaican English*. Cambridge: Cambridge Univ. Press.

Cave, Roderick (ed). 1974-76. Working papers on West Indian printing. Mona, Jamaica: Dept. of Library Studies, Univ. of the West Indies.

_____. 1982. West Indian printing. *Encyclopedia of Library and Information Science* 33: 25-38.

_____. 1987. *Printing and the Book Trade in the West Indies*. London: The Pindar Press.

Christie, Pauline. 1982. Language maintenance and language shift in Dominica. *Caribbean Quarterly* 28, no. 4: 41-51.

_____. 1983. In search of the boundaries of Caribbean Creoles. In *Studies in Caribbean Language*, edited by L. Carrington et al., 13-22. St Augustine, Trinidad: Society for Caribbean Linguistics.

Coleridge, Henry Nelson. [1826] 1970. *Six Months in the West Indies in 1825*. Reprint, New York: New York Universities Press.

Collymore, Frank A. 1970. *Barbadian Dialect*. Bridgetown, Barbados: Barbados National Trust.

Cooper, Vincent. 1984. The St Kitts Angolares: a closer look at current theories on language development in the Caribbean. Paper presented at the 5th biennial conference of the Society for Caribbean Linguistics, Mona, Jamaica.

Cox, Edward L. 1984. *Free Coloreds in the Slave Societies of St Kitts and Grenada, 1763-1833*. Knoxville: The Univ. of Tennessee Press.

Crahan, M., and F. Knight (eds). 1979. *Africa and the Caribbean: the Legacies of a Link*. Baltimore: Johns Hopkins Univ. Press.

Cressy, David. 1983. The environment of literacy: accomplishment and context in seventeenth century England and New England. In *Literacy in Historical Perspective*, edited by D. Resnick, 23-42. Washington, D.C.: Library of Congress.

Cruickshank, J. 1911. Negro English, with reference particularly to Barbados. *Timehri*, 3d ser., 1:102-106.

Cruickshank, J. 1916. *Black Talk*. Demerara: Argosy.

Cugoana, Ottobah. [1787] 1791. *Thoughts and sentiments on the evil and wicked traffic of the slavery and commerce of the human species*. Reprint, London.

Cundall, Frank. 1909. *Bibliography of the West Indies*. Kingston, Jamaica: The Institute of Jamaica.

_____. 1911. Some notes on the history of secondary education in Jamaica. Kingston, Jamaica: Institute of Jamaica.

Curtis, S.J. 1968. *History of Education in Great Britain*. London: Univ. Tutorial Press.

Dabydeen, David. 1992. The role of black people in William Hogarth's criticism of eighteenth-century English culture and society. In *Essays on the History of Blacks in Britain*, edited by Jagdish Gundara and Ian Duffield, 30-57. Hampshire: Avebury.

Davidson, Cathy N. (ed). 1989. *Reading in America: Literature and Social History*. Baltimore: Johns Hopkins Univ. Press.

Day, Richard R. (ed). 1980. *Issues in English Creoles: Papers from the 1975 Hawaii Conference*. Heidelberg: Groos.

Devas, Raymund. 1965. *The History of the Island of Grenada*. Bridgetown, Barbados: Advocate Printery.

Dillard, J.L. 1972. *Black English: its History and Usage in the United States*. New York: Random House.

Dulay, Heidi, Marina Burt, and Stephen Krashen. 1982. *Language Two*. New York: Oxford Univ. Press.

Dunn, R. 1969. The Barbados Census of 1680: profile of the richest colony in English America.*The William and Mary Quarterly*, 3d series, vol. xxvi, no.1: 3-30.

Durham, Harriet. 1972. *Caribbean Quakers*. Florida: Dukane Press.

Eames, Wilberforce. 1928. The Antigua press and Benjamin Mecom, 1748-1765. *American Antiquarian Society* 38: 303-47.

Edwards, Paul, and James Walvin. 1983. *Black Personalities in the Era of the Slave Trade.* Baton Rouge: Louisiana State Univ.

Eibl-Eibesfeldt, I. 1972. Similarities and differences between cultures in expressive movements. In *Non-Verbal Communication*, edited by R.A. Hinde, 297-312. Cambridge: Cambridge Univ. Press.

Eisenstein, Elizabeth. 1985. On the printing press as agent of change. In *Literacy, Language, and Learning: the Nature and Consequences of Reading and Writing*, edited by David Olson, Nancy Torrance and Angela Hildyard, 19-33. Cambridge: Cambridge Univ. Press.

Ferguson, C. 1971. Absence of copula and the notion of simplicity: a study of normal speech, baby talk, foreigner talk, and pidgins. In *Pidginization and Creolization of Languages*, edited by D. Hymes, 141-50. Cambridge: Cambridge Univ. Press.

Ferriss, Abbott L. 1989. Illiteracy. In *Encyclopedia of Southern Culture*, edited by C.R. Wilson and William Ferris, pp. 251-53. Chapel Hill: Univ. of North Carolina Press.

Fields, Linda. 1992. Early Bajan: creole or non-creole. Paper presented at the ninth biennial conference of the Society for Caribbean Linguistics, Univ. of the West Indies, Barbados.

Figueroa, Peter, and Ganga Persaud (eds). 1976. *Sociology of Education: a Caribbean Reader.* Oxford: Oxford Univ. Press.

Foster, Philip. 1971. Problems of literacy in Sub-Saharan Africa. In *Current Trends in Linguistics 7: Linguistics in Sub-Saharan Africa*, edited by T. Sebeok, 587-617. The Hague: Mouton.

Fryer, Peter. 1984. *Staying Power: the History of Black People in Britain.* London: Pluto Press.

Gilmore, J.T. 1979. The Rev. William Harte and attitudes to slavery in early nineteenth-century Barbados. *Journal of Ecclesiastical History* 30, no. 4: 461-74.

Goodridge, Sehon. 1981. *Facing the Challenge of Emancipation: a Study of the Ministry of William Hart Coleridge, First Bishop of Barbados, 1824-1842.* Bridgetown, Barbados: Cedar Press.

Gordon, S. 1963. *A Century of West Indian Education.* London: Longmans Green & Co.

Graff, Harvey. 1979. *The Literacy Myth: Literacy and Social Structure in the 19th Century City.* New York: Academic Press.

Grant, William (ed). 1931. *The Scottish National Dictionary.* Edinburgh.

Greenfield, S. 1966. *English Rustics in Black Skin.* New Haven: College and Univ. Press.

Hall, N.A.T. 1979. Establishing a public elementary school system for slaves in the Danish Virgin Islands, 1732-1846. *Caribbean Journal of Education* 6, no. 1: 1-45.

Hallewell, Laurence. 1982. *Books in Brazil: a History of the Publishing Trade.* N.J. and London: Scarecrow Press.

Hancock, I. 1980. Gullah and Barbadian – origin and relationships. *American Speech* 55: 17-35.

Handler, J. 1971. *A Guide to Source Materials for the Study of Barbados History 1627-1834.* Carbondale: SIU Press.

———. 1974. *The Unappropriated People: Freedmen in the Slave Society of Barbados.* Baltimore: Johns Hopkins Univ. Press.

_____. 1991. *Supplement to A Guide to Source Materials for the Study of Barbados History 1627-1834*. The John Carter Brown Library, Providence, R.I. and The Barbados Museum and Historical Society, Bridgetown, Barbados.

Handler, J., and F. Lange. 1978. *Plantation Slavery in Barbados: an Archaeological and Historical Investigation*. Cambridge, Mass.: Harvard Univ. Press.

Harlow, V.T. [1926] 1969. *A History of Barbados, 1625-1685*. Reprint, New York: New York Univ. Press.

Herskovits, Melville J. 1941 [1958]. *The Myth of the Negro Past*. Reprint, Boston: Beacon Press.

Herzog, George. 1945. Drum signaling in a West African tribe. *Word* 1: 217-38. (Reprinted 1964. In *Language in Culture and Society*, edited by D. Hymes, 312-29. New York: Harper & Row.)

Higman, B.W. 1988. *Ecological Determinism in Caribbean History*. Sixth Elsa Goveia Memorial Lecture. Cave Hill, Barbados: Univ. of the West Indies.

Hinde, R.A. (ed). 1972. *Non-Verbal Communication*. Cambridge: Cambridge Univ. Press.

Holder, J. 1988. *Codrington College*. Bridgetown, Barbados.

Holm, J. 1981. Sociolinguistic history and the creolist. In *Historicity and Variation in Creole Studies*, edited by A. Highfield and A. Valdman, 40-51. Ann Arbor: Karoma.

_____. 1986. The spread of English in the Caribbean area. In *Varieties of English Around the World: Focus on the Caribbean*, edited by M. Gorlach and J. Holm, 1-22. Amsterdam: John Benjamins.

_____. 1988, 1989. *Pidgins and Creoles*. 2 vols. Cambridge: Cambridge Univ. Press.

Hopper, Paul J., and Elizabeth Closs Traugott. 1993. *Grammaticalization*. Cambridge: Cambridge Univ. Press.

Hunte, Keith. 1975. Church and society in Barbados in the eighteenth century. *Proceedings of the VI Annual Conference of the Association of Caribbean Historians*. Association of Caribbean Historians.

Hymes, Dell (ed). 1964. *Language in Culture and Society*. New York: Harper & Row.

_____(ed). 1971. *Pidginization and Creolization of Languages*. Cambridge: Cambridge Univ. Press.

Izard, Carroll E. 1979. Facial expression, emotion, and motivation. In *Non-verbal Behavior: Applications and Cultural Implications*, edited by Aaron Wolfgang, 31-49. New York: Academic Press.

Johnson, Julie Greer. 1988. *The Book in the Americas*. Providence, R.I.: John Carter Brown Library.

Joyner, Charles. 1989. Creolization. In *Encyclopedia of Southern Culture*, edited by C.R. Wilson and William Ferris, 147-49. Chapel Hill: Univ. of North Carolina Press.

[Keimer, Samuel (ed)]. [1741] 1978. *Caribbeana*. London. Reprint, Millwood, N.Y.: Kraus.

Key, Mary Ritchie. 1975. *Paralanguage and Kinesics (Nonverbal Communication)*. New Jersey: Scarecrow Press.

Kokeritz, H. 1953. *Shakespeare's Pronunciation*. New Haven: Yale Univ. Press.

La Faye. 1984. Literature and intellectual life in colonial Spanish America. In *Colonial Latin America*, edited by L. Bethell, 663-704. Cambridge: Cambridge Univ. Press.

Lamming, G. [1953] 1970. *In the Castle of my Skin*. Port of Spain, Trinidad and Kingston, Jamaica: Longman Caribbean.

Laqueur, T. 1983. Toward a cultural ecology of literacy in England, 1600-1850. In *Literacy in Historical Perspective*, edited by D. Resnick, 43-57. Washington, D.C.:

Lederer, Richard. 1985. *Colonial American English*. Essex, Conn.

Lehiste, Ilse. 1988. *Lectures on Language Contact*. Cambridge: MIT Press.

Leontiev, Alexei A. 1981. *Psychology and the Language Learning Process*. Oxford: Pergamon Press.

LePage, R. 1957-8. General outlines of creole English dialects in the British Caribbean. *Orbis* 6: 373-91; 7: 54-64.

_____.1984. The need for a multidimensional model. Paper presented at the 5th biennial conference of the Society for Caribbean Linguistics, Mona, Jamaica. (Reprinted 1987. In *Pidgin and Creole languages*, edited by G. Gilbert. Honolulu: University of Hawaii Press.)

LePage, R.B., and Andrée Tabouret-Keller. 1985. *Acts of Identity: Creole-based Approaches to Language and Ethnicity*. Cambridge: Cambridge Univ. Press.

Lewis, Gordon K. 1983. *Main Currents in Caribbean Thought: the Historical Evolution of Caribbean Society in its Ideological Aspects, 1492-1900*. Baltimore: Johns Hopkins Univ. Press.

Little, Kenneth. [1948] 1972. *Negroes in Britain: a Study of Racial Relations in English society*. Reprint, London: Routledge & Kegan Paul.

Makouta-Mboukou, J-P. 1973. *Le français en Afrique noire*. Paris: Bordas.

Manross, William Wilson (comp). 1965. *The Fulham Papers in the Lambeth Palace Library*. London: Oxford Univ. Press.

Matthews, John. [1788] 1966. *A voyage to the River Sierra-Leone, containing an account of the trade and productions of the country and of the civil and religious customs and manners of the people, by John Matthews during his residence in that country in the yeaars 1785, 1786, and 1787, with an additional letter on the African slave trade*. Reprint, London: Cass.

McMurtrie, Douglas. 1932. *The First Printing in Dominica*. London.

_____. 1933. *Early Printing in Barbados*. London.

_____. 1934. *The First Printing on the Island of Jamaica*. Metuchen, New Jersey.

_____. 1942. *The First Printing in Jamaica*. Evanston.

_____. 1943a. *Early Printing on the Island of Antigua*. Evanston.

_____. 1943b. *The First Printing on the Island of Tobago*. Fort Worth. Reprinted from *National Printing Education Journal*, April 1943.

_____. 1943c. *Notes on the Beginning of Printing in the Island of Trinidad*. Fort Worth. Reprinted from *National Printing Education Journal*, May 1943.

Monaghan, E. Jennifer. 1989. Literacy instruction and gender in colonial New England. In *Reading in America: Literature & Social History*, edited by C.N. Davidson. Baltimore: Johns Hopkins Univ. Press.

Mühlhäusler, Peter. 1986. *Pidgin and Creole Linguistics*. Oxford: Basil Blackwell.

Nettleton, George H. 1906 (ed). *The Major Dramas of Richard Brinsley Sheridan: The Rivals, The School for Scandal, The Critic*. Boston, New York, Chicago, London: Ginn & Co.

Niles, Norma. 1980. Provincial English dialects and Barbadian English. PhD diss., Univ. of Michigan.

Nketia, J.H. 1971. Surrogate languages of Africa. In *Current Trends in Linguistics: Linguistics in Sub-Saharan Africa*, edited by T. Sebeok, 699-732. The Hague Mouton.

Odlin, Terence. 1989. *Language Transfer: Cross-linguistic Influence in Language Learning.* Cambridge: Cambridge Univ. Press.

Oldendorp, C.G.A. [1770, 1777] 1987. *History of the evangelical Brethren on the Caribbean islands of St. Thomas, St. Croix, and St. John*, edited by Johann Jakob Bossard and translated by Arnold Highfield and Vladimir Barac. Ann Arbor: Karoma Publishers.

Olson, D.R. 1977. From utterance to text: the bias of language in speech and writing. *Harvard Educational Review* 47: 257-81.

———. 1986. The cognitive consequences of literacy. *Canadian Psychology* 27: 109-21.

Olson, D.R., N. Torrance, and A. Hildyard (eds). 1985. *Literacy, Language and Learning: the Nature and Consequences of Reading and Writing.* Cambridge: Cambridge Univ. Press.

Ong, Walter J. 1982. *Orality and Literacy: the Technologizing of the Word.* London: Routledge.

Patterson, Orlando. 1967. *The Sociology of Slavery.* Jamaica: Sangsters.

Payne, Cyrlyn. 1976. Official printing in Barbados. In *Working Papers on West Indian Printing* no. 23, edited by R. Cave. Jamaica: Dept of Library Studies, U.W.I.

Philippe, J.B. [1824] 1987. *Free Mulatto.* Reprint, Port of Spain, Trinidad: Paria.

Pitman, Frank Wesley. 1917. *The Development of the West Indies 1700-1763.* New Haven: Yale Univ. Press; Oxford: Oxford Univ. Press.

Proctor, F., and W. Frere. 1965. *A New History of the Book of Common Prayer.* London: Macmillan.

Puckrein, Gary. 1984. *Little England: Plantation Society and Anglo Barbadian Politics, 1627-1700.* New York: New York Universities Press.

Pyles, Thomas, and John Algeo. 1982. *The Origins and Development of the English Language.* New York: Harcourt Brace Jovanovich.

Reinecke, J. 1938. Trade jargons and creole dialects as marginal languages. In *Social Forces* 17: 107-118. (Reprinted 1964. In *Language in Culture and Society*, edited by D. Hymes, 534-42.)

Reisman, Karl. 1970. Cultural and linguistic ambiguity in a West Indian village. In *Afro-American Anthropology: Contemporary Perspectives*, edited by Norman E. Whitten, Jr. and John F. Szwed, 129-44. New York: The Free Press.

Resnick, Daniel (ed). 1983. *Literacy in Historical Perspective.* Washington, D.C.: Library of Congress.

Retamar, Roberto. 1989. *Caliban and Other Essays.* Translated by Edward Baker. Minnesota: Univ. of Minnesota Press.

Rickford, John R. 1987. *Dimensions of a Creole Continuum: History, Texts and Linguistic Analysis of Guyanese Creole.* Stanford: Stanford Univ. Press.

Rickford, John R., and Jerome S. Handler. 1992. Textual evidence on the nature of early Barbadian speech (1676-1887). Paper presented at the ninth biennial conference of the Society for Caribbean Linguistics, Univ. of the West Indies, Barbados.

Roberts, Peter A. 1988. *West Indians and Their Language.* Cambridge: Cambridge Univ. Press.

———. 1988a. The misinterpretations of Brer Anancy. *Folklore* 99, no. 1: 98-101.

Rodway, James. 1919. The press in British Guiana. *Proceedings of the American Antiquarian Society*, October 1918, vol. 28, pt. 2, 274-90. Worcester, Mass.

Roy, J. 1986. The structure of tense and aspect in Barbadian English Creole. In *Varieties of English around the World: Focus on the Caribbean*, edited by M. Gorlach and J. Holm, 141-56. Amsterdam: John Benjamins.

Salvino, Dana. 1989. The word in black and white. In *Reading in America: Literature and Social History*, edited by C.N. Davidson, 140-56. Baltimore: Johns Hopkins Univ. Press.

Schaw, Janet. [1921] 1934. *Journal of a lady of quality; being the narrative of a Journey from Scotland to the West Indies, North Carolina, and Portugal, in the years 1774 to 1776*. Edited by Evangeline Walker Andrews, in collaboration with Charles McLean Andrews. Reprint, New Haven: Yale Univ. Press.

Schumann, John H. 1978. *The Pidginization Process: a Model for Second Language Acquisition*. Rowley, Mass.: Newbury House.

Scribner, S., and M. Cole. 1981. *The Psychology of Literacy*. Cambridge: Harvard Univ. Press.

Sharp, Sharon A. 1989. Black dance. In *Encyclopedia of Southern Culture*, edited by C.R. Wilson and W. Ferris, 149-51. Chapel Hill: Univ. of North Carolina Press.

Sheppard, Jill. 1977. *The "Redlegs" of Barbados: their Origins and History*. Millwood, New York: KTO Press.

Sheridan, Richard. 1961. The rise of a colonial gentry: a case study of Antigua, 1730-1775. *The Economic History Review*, 2nd series 13, no. 3: 342-57.

Shilstone, Eustace. 1958. Some notes on early printing presses and newspapers in Barbados. *Journal of the Barbados Museum and Historical Society* 26, no. 1: 19-33.

Shyllon, Folarin. 1977. *Black People in Britain 1555-1833*. Oxford: Oxford Univ. Press.

⸺. 1992. The Black presence and experience in Britain: an analytical overview. In *Essays on the History of Blacks in Britain*, edited by Jagdish Gundara and Ian Duffield. Hampshire: Avebury.

Simmonds, Peter. [1841] 1975. Notes on West Indian newspapers. In *Working Papers on West Indian Printing*, no. 9, edited by R. Cave. Reprint, Jamaica: Dept. of Library Studies, UWI.

Simpson, George Eaton. 1980. *Religious Cults of the Caribbean: Trinidad, Jamaica and Haiti*. 3d ed. Rio Piedras, Puerto Rico: Institute of Caribbean Studies, Univ. of Puerto Rico.

Spencer, John. 1971. Colonial language policies and their legacies. In *Current Trends in Linguistics: Linguistics in Sub-Saharan Africa*, edited by T. Sebeok, 537-47. The Hague: Mouton.

St Luce, Naula. 1976. Early Dominican newspapers. In *Working Papers on West Indian Printing*, no. 25, edited by R. Cave. Jamaica: Dept. of Library Studies, U.W.I.

Street, Brian. 1984. *Literacy in Theory and Practice*. Cambridge: Cambridge Univ. Press.

Stryker-Rodda, Harriet. 1986. *Understanding Colonial Handwriting*. Baltimore: Genealogical Publishing Co.

Swan, Bradford. *circa* 1956. A checklist of early printing on the island of Antigua (1748-1800). *Bibliographical Society of America* 50, 3rd quarter: 285-92.

⸺. 1970. *The Spread of Printing – Western Hemisphere: the Caribbean Area*. Amsterdam: Vangendt & Co; London: Routledge and Kegan Paul.

Taylor, Douglas. 1977. *Languages of the West Indies*. Baltimore: Johns Hopkins Univ. Press.

Telesford, Mona. 1976. Notes on Guyanese newspapers. In *Working Papers on West Indian Printing*, no. 24, edited by R. Cave. Jamaica: Dept. of Library Studies, UWI.

Turner, Lorenzo Dow. 1949. *Africanisms in the Gullah Dialect*. Chicago: Univ. of Chicago Press.

Warner-Lewis, Maureen. 1971. Trinidad Yoruba – notes on survivals. *Caribbean Quarterly* 17, no. 2: 40-49.

_____. 1979. The African impact on language and literature in the English-speaking Caribbean. In *Africa and the Caribbean: the Legacies of a Link*, edited by M. Crahan and F. Knight, 101-23. Baltimore: Johns Hopkins Univ. Press.

Whitten, Norman E. Jr., and John F. Szwed (eds). 1970. *Afro-American Anthropology: Contemporary Perspectives.* New York: The Free Press.

Wierzbicka, Anna. 1992. *Semantics, Culture, and Cognition: Universal Human Concepts in Culture-Specific Configurations.* Oxford: Oxford Univ. Press.

Willyams, Cooper [1796] 1990. *An account of the campaign in the West Indies in the year 1794.* Bibliothèque d'histoire Antillaise (Collection publiée par la Société d'histoire de la Guadeloupe, 12. Reproduction of the 1796 edition. Basseterre).

Wilson, Charles Reagan, and William Ferris (eds). 1989. *Encyclopedia of Southern Culture.* Chapel Hill: Univ. of North Carolina Press.

Winer, Lise. 1984. Early Trinidadian creole: the Spectator texts. *English World-Wide* 5, no. 2: 181-210.

Wolfgang, Aaron (ed). 1979. *Nonverbal Behavior: Applications and Cultural Implications.* New York: Academic Press.

Wood, Donald. 1968. *Trinidad in Transition: the Years after Slavery.* London: Oxford Univ. Press

Wood, P. 1974. *Black Majority: Negroes in Colonial South Carolina from 1670 through the Stono Rebellion.* New York.

Wright, Louis B. 1939. The classical tradition in colonial Virginia. *The Papers of the Bibliographical Society of America* 33: 85-97.

Wyld, H. 1937. *A History of Modern Colloquial English.* 3d ed. London: T. Fisher Unwin Ltd.

Index

Abrahams & Szwed 50, 184
addressing the dead 59-60, 61
Africans
  ethnic differences 30, 82-84
  hostility between 35-37
  language diversity 72-73, 78, 84-85
  language acquisition 80-81, 68
  orientation 37
  saltwater negroes 29, 83, 84
  wisdom 44
  ancestor veneration 68
Anglican (Church) 112-114, 132, 151, 19, 22l, 222, 225, 226, 227, 232, 233, 239, 240, 246, 256, 273
Anguilla 73, 74, 248
Antigua 12, 13, 52, 56, 73, 74, 88, 89, 136, 137, 138, 139, 140, 142, 143, 147, 148, 152, 153, 154, 174, 178, 180, 182, 186, 197, 202, 238, 243, 245, 246, 249, 250, 252, 256, 273
Antilles 1
apprenticeship 37, 77, 214, 215, 243
Armytage 142, 151, 220, 222
Atwood 40, 55, 60-61, 93, 94, 207

Bailyn 160, 187
Barbados 9, 11, 12, 19, 22, 28, 31, 47, 48, 49, 54, 62, 71, 72, 73, 74, 77, 78, 79, 80, 81, 82, 83, 84, 85, 86, 87, 88, 89, 90, 93, 95, 96, 99, 100, 101, 102, 103, 109n9, 113, 115, 117, 118, 119, 121, 126, 133, 134, 135, 136, 137, 138, 140, 141, 142, 145, 147, 148, 149, 150, 152, 153, 154, 163, 165, 166, 168, 170, 171, 173, 177, 178, 179, 180, 181, 186, 187, 194, 195, 201, 202, 203, 206, 207, 208, 211, 212, 213, 218, 220, 225, 228, 229, 230, 231, 235n3, 238, 239, 241, 243, 244, 245, 246, 247, 252, 253, 258, 263, 265, 272

Barrell 21, 116-117
barter 118
Baxter 122, 147, 272
Bayley 109n8, 178, 180, 181
Beckford 46, 48, 50, 117, 184
Belgrove 78, 115, 116, 198, 235n4
Bell, Dr. 211, 218, 227, 240, 242
bells 19, 20-21, 25, 33, 33n2, 39
Bennett, Louise 6
Bickerton 10
Birdwhistell 32-33
Black Caribs 94, 108
black seamen 98-9
Blome 33n2, 74, 79, 92, 168
boatmen 55
Bolster 98
Book of Common Prayer 114, 130, 219, 245-246, 274
bookkeepers 117
books lll, 112, 113, 114, 115, 116, 117, 118, 120, 123, 125, 126, 129, 164, 166, 167, 168, 169, 171, 173, 174, 175, 177, 178, 179, 205, 213, 225, 231, 234, 270, 277
branding 30-31
Bray 225, 227, 245
Breen 47
Brerewood 216
Bridgens 29, 95
burials (slave) 35, 60-65, 67
Burnett 50

Caldecott 181-182, 217, 235n2, 237, 245
Caliban 187, 277
calypso 4, 5, 7
Campbell 121

Carmichael, Mrs. 20, 21, 28, 29, 31, 40, 41, 53, 89, 90, 94, 102, 103, 127, 153, 155, 186, 211, 231, 241, 249, 250, 262
carnival 4, 11, 47
Cassidy 86
Catholicism 92, 204-205, 210, 220, 225
Central schools 208, 217, 230, 239, 240, 244, 247, 257
Chalkley 116,
character/personality of the slave 41-42, 56-57, 105-106
Christie 93
Christmas 34, 46-48, 50, 127, 185
climate (influence of) 166, 176, 181-182, 218
Coleridge, H. 57, 96, 105, 153, 177, 178, 179, 195, 196, 203, 204, 205, 208, 210, 212, 216, 243, 248, 249, 256, 261
colonial propaganda 75-76
coloured (people) 91, 92, 96, 101, 102, 103, 104, 180, 193, 208, 210-214, 234, 271, 273
communication 16-20
 by bells 19, 20-1, 25, 33n2, 39, 233
 conch shell 20, 25
 drum 19, 26, 27, 33, 48, 110, 233
 fire 25, 28
 flags 22-23, 32, 33, 110, 233
 guns 18, 19, 20, 21, 22, 23, 32, 33, 65, 110, 114, 233
continuum 13
cordon sanitaire 77, 92
Cox 91, 92, 207, 230
Creoles 74, 82, 83, 84, 89, 99, 207
creole language 10, 11-12, 35, 44, 66, 81, 86, 87, 98, 101, 161, 219
Cressy 162, 163
Cuffy 20
cullunjee 48-50
cultural transmission thesis 19, 162, 165, 166, 168, 176, 189
Curtis 251

Dabydeen 187
Dallas 176
Day 50, 57, 90, 95, 96, 102, 148, 153, 155, 157, 248-249, 250-251, 267n4
De Rochefort 75, 164
death (celebration of) 59-60, 63, 65, 67
Devas 91
dialect 33
 African 84

Barbados 79-84
 British 79-80, 87
 Creole 84
 Dominica 12
 Jamaica 86
 Kittitian 70, 79
 negro 50
 sailor 86-87
 Scottish 87-90
 social 81-82
 St Lucia 12
 Trinidad 12, 84, 90, 92
 Vincentian 89-90
Dickson 20, 21, 31, 38, 72-3, 102, 103, 146, 147, 151, 173, 185, 206, 237, 244, 272
Dillard 10, 109n7
Dominica 11, 12, 52, 72, 73, 89, 90, 92-94, 113, 137, 140, 141, 142, 143, 201, 204, 207, 211, 213, 214, 216
drama 168, 175, 178, 180, 181, 189, 190
dress 31
drums 19, 26, 27, 33, 48, 110, 233
Duke, W. 119, 141, 194, 196, 207
Duke, Rev. 224, 225, 227, 232, 245, 265

Easel 28
education
 European 194, 195, 200, 207, 210-211, 232
 philosophy of 192-193
Edwards, B. 27, 29, 30, 36, 37, 39, 40, 42, 45, 50, 55, 59, 60, 63, 65, 66, 68, 87, 124, 125, 176, 184, 211, 218
Eisenstein 148, 158, 169
English
 African 81
 British 79-80, 87, 95
 Dominica 12
 growth 73-75, 92-94
 immigrant 95-96
 Trinidad 12, 96
 varieties of 33, 85, 87
 West Indian 5, 6, 7, 8, 9-15, 106, 191, 269
Equiano, Olaudah 156, 188
estate nursery 37-38, 39, 68, 242
ethnic differences 70-71, 88-89

fashions 56-57
Fermin 42
Ferris 262
festivals 4, 34, 35, 36, 60

Fielding 97
fields (life in the) 39-40, 82
fire 25, 28
flags 122-123, 32, 33, 110, 233
Fox 113, 221, 226, 261
Franklin, B. 136, 149, 150, 174, 193, 225
French Creole 11, 12, 90, 91, 92, 93, 210, 216
Fryer 109n6, 159n4, 187, 188
Fula 123, 125
funerals 62, 63, 64, 206

gangs 38-39
Gazette (Barbados) 116, 121, 139, 142, 150, 151, 152, 153, 154, 165, 169, 170, 171, 172, 173, 201, 250, 272
gens de couleur 91, 92, 95, 96, 101, 102
Godwyn 82, 215
Graff 260, 261
grammar 192, 208, 245, 247, 251, 252, 253, 276
grave dirt 61, 65, 66
Gray 119, 133, 134, 135
greetings 40-41
Grenada 73, 90-92, 113, 126, 137, 141, 143, 177, 178, 204, 208, 212, 214, 216, 230, 235n5, 239, 243
guns 18, 19, 20, 21, 22, 23, 32, 33, 65, 110, 114

Hall 219-220
Hallewell 133
Halliday 125, 224, 263
Hancock 86
Handler 166, 181
Handler and Lange 80, 81
Harlow 72, 85, 112
Harte 228, 229, 245, 251, 261, 265
Herzog 26, 27
Hillary 171
Holm 73
Hunte 218, 222

illiteracy 6, 117, 119, 121, 129, 163, 183
Industrial Revolution 14
invitations (printed) 127, 130

Jamaica 6, 11, 12, 13, 29, 30, 37, 46, 47, 48, 52, 55, 65, 72, 73, 86, 87, 93, 101, 113, 117, 119, 124, 125, 136, 137, 138, 139, 142, 143, 144, 150, 154, 156, 166, 167, 168, 169, 171, 173, 177, 178, 198, 199, 200, 201, 202, 213, 218, 220, 223, 237, 253, 272
Jews 79

Johnson, Julie 136, 159n1
journal (plantation) 116-117
Joyner 31

Keimer 137, 145-146, 148, 149, 150, 201

Labat 125, 126, 138, 164, 224
language bioprogram 10, 15
language policy 76-78
Lanigan 43, 109n8
Laqueur 112, 162
LePage and Tabouret-Keller 95
Leslie, C. 48, 49, 101, 171, 173, 177, 198, 200, 201, 237, 253
Lewis, G. 120, 161-162
Lewis, Monk 52-53
Ligon 18, 20, 33n2, 48, 49, 78, 81, 88, 114, 141, 163, 187
Littleton 199
Lloyd 124, 125, 180
Long, E. 45, 184, 199, 202
Luffman, J. 147, 174-175, 180, 182

Mandingoes 124, 125, 224
Manross 148, 216
market 34, 35, 54-58, 66, 68, 232, 271
Martin, Samuel 140, 174, 176, 197-198, 199, 200, 270
Mathews, Samuel 3, 50, 51, 52, 121, 155, 156, 157, 200, 272
Mathison 57
Matthews, J. 49, 65
Mavrile de S. Michel 164
M'Callum 27, 74, 96
McKinnen 22, 195
McMurtrie, D. 136, 138, 139, 147, 174, 245
message carrying 18
Methodists 230, 245, 249
M'Neill 125
Moister 64
Monaghan 244
monitor (mutual) system 239, 240, 274
Montlezun 95
Montserrat 18, 19, 26, 34, 89, 90, 119, 120, 137, 188, 238
Moravians 219, 245, 249
Moreton 272
M'Queen 30
Muslims 39, 40, 123, 124, 125, 129, 224

National Society (schools) 204, 208, 209, 210, 218, 244, 247, 253, 267n1
native American (Carib, Arawak) 72, 80, 93, 94, 108n2
nautical language 86-87
Nettleton 182-183
Nevis 73, 78, 119, 137, 174, 188, 213
New Year's day 46-48, 127
newspapers 22, 30, 112, 121, 128, 133, 139, 154, 157, 162, 168, 169, 170, 172, 173, 174, 175, 180, 188, 201, 202, 205, 271, 272, 274
Niger-Congo languages 13, 15
Nketia 24
notes (money) 118

obeah 27, 31, 32, 42
Oldendorp 123, 125
Oldmixon, J. 74, 75, 78, 82, 83, 88, 165, 166, 168, 194-195
Ong 107, 183-184
Orderson, J. 178, 181, 186, 243

parties 46, 47, 127
Paton 119
Patterson, O. 163-164, 172
peer group 38
Philippe 180
Pinckard 23, 41, 49, 61, 63, 96, 100, 101, 186
Pitman 199, 200
plantation journal 116-117
plays 43, 50, 175, 181, 270
poets/poetry 6, 45, 107, 166, 168, 169, 170, 172, 190, 270
Poole, R. 19, 22, 48, 57, 62-63, 65, 119, 171, 201, 250
poor whites 102, 206, 207, 208, 210
Porteus 118, 128, 215, 218, 224, 227, 239, 240, 241, 242, 245, 250, 254, 256, 272
Poyer 33n1, 121, 141, 145, 148, 152
printing 271, 272
  for government 138-139
  growth in English colonies 122-123, 136-138
  newspapers 142-155
  scholarly 139-141
private theatricals 49, 130
Procter and Frere 219
Protestantism 112-113, 204, 218, 220, 264
proverbs 43-44, 131, 184

Quakers 113, 119, 133, 138, 141, 220, 221, 223, 226, 267n2

Ramsay 38, 105, 121, 155, 156, 174, 201, 224, 272
Raynal 91
'reds' and 'blues' 47, 49
reggae 4, 5, 7, 12
religious practices 58-66, 67-68
Renny 50
Resident 23, 37, 49, 55, 89, 94, 99, 100, 201-202, 207, 211, 227
Ridpath 87-88
Robertson, Rev. 25, 35, 56, 78, 126, 171, 174, 194, 195, 196, 216-217, 240, 271
Rodway 139, 152
Roman Catholic (Church) 91, 92, 112, 113, 137, 151, 204, 2210, 220, 224, 235n5
rote learning 246, 248, 250
Ryan 202-203, 235n1

sailors
  black 98-99
  language 86-87
saltwater negroes 29, 83, 84
Salvino 261
satire 184-185
Schomburgk 113, 118, 177, 178, 212
Schumann 10
Scottish 71, 74, 79, 80, 87-90, 93, 95, 96, 173, 264, 274
Scribner & Cole 260
secret methods of communication 24, 25
servants (black/domestic) 83, 97, 101, 102, 124, 129, 231
servants (white/indentured) 79, 80, 81, 85, 86, 88, 100, 112, 115, 117, 121, 166, 193, 194, 198, 201, 206, 218, 223, 229, 235n4, 269
Sharp 26
Shephard 261
Sheridan R. (1961) 88, 89, 202
Sheridan, R.B. 173, 182, 184, 198
Shyllon 97, 98
Simmonds 152
singing 48, 50
Singleton 183
slave boatmen 55
slave personality/character 105
slaves' imitation of whites 46, 130
Sloane 29, 86-87, 93, 164
Smith, J. 71
Smith, W. 34, 39, 60, 223-224
Snelgrave 123

Some Gentlemen of St. Christopher 155, 156, 235n8, 272
songs 39, 50-54, 68
speeches
　slaves 44-46, 85, 185, 191, 192
　whites 181-184, 191, 192
Spencer 76
St Clair 54
St Kitts 3, 56, 70, 73, 78, 79, 121, 126, 137, 140, 164, 173, 174, 194, 195, 207, 213, 224, 227, 230, 235n8, 240, 271, 272
St Lucia 12, 13, 70, 73, 137, 175, 204, 212, 214, 216
St Vincent 29, 36, 73, 89, 90, 94, 127, 137, 152, 153, 155, 212, 230, 231, 232, 248, 249, 257, 258
Stedman 40, 49, 61, 67, 77, 104
Stewart, J. 34, 44, 46, 47, 48, 50, 61-62, 124, 125, 177, 178, 184, 237
story-telling 43, 68
Street 260
Stryker-Rodda 133
sugar 14, 81
suicide 63
Suriname 13, 40, 42, 49, 61, 74, 77, 86
Swan 139, 145, 164

talking drums 26-27
tattoos 29-30, 31
Taylor, D. 72, 108n2
teachers 194, 196, 197, 198, 206, 217, 220, 225, 228, 229, 232, 234, 236, 237 241, 242, 247, 248, 249, 252, 254, 257
teaching materials 244-247
terms of address 40-41, 104
terms (descriptive) 103-104
theatre 174, 175, 178, 180-181, 185
Thome and Kimball 28, 58, 154, 240, 241, 242, 243, 246, 266
Thompson 3, 74, 89, 90, 250
ticket (pass) system 114, 218
Tobago 73, 136, 137, 138, 212, 238, 243
Tobin 38-39, 188, 201, 272
transmigration of souls 60, 67

tribal markings 29, 30, 31
Trinidad 3, 11, 12, 29, 74, 84, 90, 91, 92, 95-96, 109n4, 113, 125, 136, 137, 177, 196, 204, 208, 210, 212, 214, 216, 224, 235n2, 243, 244, 249
Trollope 165,
tuk 49
Turnbull [Eyewitness] 91-92, 188
tutors 193, 205, 207, 210

Ulloa 45
umbilical link 179, 189

verbal duelling 57

Walker 189
Warner-Lewis 84
Weekly Jamaica Courant 142, 143, 144, 168, 169
Wentworth, T. 37, 40, 44, 50, 56, 58, 68n1, 101, 103, 127, 128, 157, 180, 181, 186, 265, 267n3
West Indian (definition) 1-4
West Indian English 5, 6, 7, 8, 9, 10, 11, 12, 13, 14, 15, 106, 191, 269
West Indian literature 8-9, 186
whites
　speech 80, 100-101, 108
Williams, C. 46, 47, 48, 50, 52, 124, 125, 184
Willyams, Cooper 77
Winer 109n3
women 170, 172-173, 186, 193, 200-202, 207, 211, 269
Wood 96
Wright, L. 175-176, 182
writing 111, 117, 118, 123, 124, 126, 127, 128, 129, 130, 131n2, 192, 197, 203, 205, 208, 211, 215, 222, 234, 238, 246, 251, 253, 254, 256, 257, 258, 259, 264

Yoruba 84
Young 94

Zouch 166, 168, 174, 245

www.ingramcontent.com/pod-product-compliance
Lightning Source LLC
Chambersburg PA
CBHW061429300426
44114CB00014B/1606